OXFORD WORLD

THE OXFORD SH

General Editor · Stanley Wells

The Oxford Shakespeare offers new and authoritative editions of Shakespeare's plays in which the early printings have been scrupulously re-examined and interpreted. An introductory essay provides all relevant background information together with an appraisal of critical views and of the play's effects in performance. The detailed commentaries pay particular attention to language and staging. Reprints of sources, music for songs, genealogical tables, maps, etc. are included where necessary; many of the volumes are illustrated, and all contain an index.

R. B. PARKER, the editor of *Coriolanus* in the Oxford Shakespeare, is Professor of English, Trinity College, University of Toronto.

m. Carey - op
L. a. 2011

Currently available in paperback

The rest of the plays are forthcoming.

OXFORD WORLD'S CLASSICS

WILLIAM SHAKESPEARE

The Tragedy of Coriolanus

Edited by
R. B. PARKER

OXFORD
UNIVERSITY PRESS

OXFORD
UNIVERSITY PRESS

Great Clarendon Street, Oxford OX2 6DP

Oxford University Press is a department of the University of Oxford.
It furthers the University's objective of excellence in research, scholarship,
and education by publishing worldwide in

Oxford New York

Athens Auckland Bangkok Bogotá Buenos Aires Cape Town
Chennai Dar es Salaam Delhi Florence Hong Kong Istanbul Karachi
Kolkata Kuala Lumpur Madrid Melbourne Mexico City Mumbai Nairobi
Paris São Paulo Shanghai Singapore Taipei Tokyo Toronto Warsaw

with associated companies in Berlin Ibadan

Oxford is a registered trade mark of Oxford University Press
in the UK and in certain other countries

Published in the United States
by Oxford University Press Inc., New York

First published by the Clarendon Press 1994
First published as a World's Classics paperback 1994
Reissued as an Oxford World's Classics paperback 1998

British Library Cataloguing in Publication Data

Data available

Library of Congress Cataloging in Publication Data

Shakespeare, William, 1564–1616.
Coriolanus / edited by R. B. Parker
(Oxford world's classics)
1. Coriolanus. Cnaeus Marcius—Drama. 2. Heroes—Rome—Drama.
I. Parker, R. B. II. Title. III. Series. IV. Series: Shakespeare,
William, 1564–1616. Works. 1982.
PR2805.A2P35 1994b 822.3′3—dc20 94–9778

ISBN–13: 978–0–19–283605–2
ISBN–10: 0–19–283605–6

8

Printed in Great Britain by
Clays Ltd, St Ives plc

PREFACE

THIS edition aims to present an accurate modernized text of *Coriolanus* based on the 1623 Folio, with appropriate textual notes, commentary, introduction, illustrations, and appendices. A special effort has been made to provide information which may be of value to actors and directors of the play.

I am grateful to the Social Sciences and Humanities Research Council of Canada, the Folger Shakespeare Library, Balliol College, Oxford, and the Humanities Research Council of the Australian National University for fellowships during the academic session 1988–9, when most of the basic research for the edition was completed, and to Trinity College and the University of Toronto for several small grants-in-aid to defray the costs of xeroxing, word-processing, and travel.

I should like to thank my typists Herma Joel, Maria Giordano, and especially Kartini Rivers for coping with difficult handwriting; Luigi Agostino, Iska Alter, Sam Barron, Ronald Bryden, William Long, and Philippa Sheppard for help with details about productions of *Coriolanus*; Annabel Patterson, Fred Langman, Kristina Bedford, David George, Thomas Clayton, and my fellow graduates of the Shakespeare Institute, Alexander Leggatt and John Ripley, for sharing with me their research-in-progress on the play; Frances Whistler of OUP and Christine Buckley for their efficient and courteous assistance; and especially Stanley Wells, director of the Institute and general editor of this series, for many kindnesses and sound advice, for providing me with a cassette of Olivier's 1959 performance, and for much patient checking. Whatever errors may have slipped through are my responsibility, not his. And, as always, my greatest debt of gratitude is to my wife for her encouragement and unfailing support.

BRIAN PARKER

Toronto, 1992

CONTENTS

Contents

LIST OF ILLUSTRATIONS

INTRODUCTION

At the end of Act 4 the Volscian leader, Tullus Aufidius, comments on the self-deluding nature of Coriolanus' character and the impermanence of political judgements and human values in general:

> So our virtues
> Lie in th'interpretation of the time . . .
> One fire drives out one fire, one nail one nail;
> Rights by rights falter, strengths by strengths do fail.
>
> (4.7.49–50, 54–5)

This is one of Shakespeare's bleakest comments on human history. Aufidius accepts that only might is right and that right itself is therefore relative and temporary; and the play then shows him acting on this cynicism successfully. Plutarch's reminder, in the play's major historical source, that Rome eventually vanquished the Volscians and Aufidius himself was killed is omitted by Shakespeare.

The dramatic power of *Coriolanus* depends in large part on the steadiness with which it confronts the bitter element of truth in Aufidius' analysis without succumbing to it. The contradictory values held by patricians and plebeians, by Martius, Volumnia, Menenius, Aufidius, and the Tribunes, are so evenly balanced that they seem to cancel each other out. No party is wholly true to its principles, moreover: each is opportunistic; and the evasions and antitheses that characterize the language of the play exist not only between the rival power groups but also, more tellingly, within each faction and indeed within each character's own rhetoric. The result is brilliantly complex, and *Coriolanus* has accordingly been interpreted in widely different ways: as tragedy, as debate, as satire, and even as comedy; as a vindication of traditional hierarchy, or as an assertion of the common people's rights; as a deeply pessimistic play which sees no value on either side of the class struggle; as a play whose vision transcends both extremes with serenely stoic or Christian (or ironic) impartiality; and, more recently, as an anticipation of post-modernist

I

deconstruction. Every generation, in short, has felt itself free to interpret *Coriolanus* according to its own intellectual and political bias, and the great variety of effect that has ensued is legitimized by the sophisticated balance and irony of what is increasingly recognized as 'Shakespeare's most complex play'.[1] As H. J. Oliver remarked in 1959, '*Coriolanus* is perhaps the least dated of Shakespeare's plays';[2] yet at the same time it reflects most accurately of all the canon the time when it was written. Its universals are firmly rooted in the specific.

Date of Composition

There is no entry for *Coriolanus* in the Stationers' Register before 1623 and no record of any contemporary performance, but consensus is that it was probably written and first produced in the period between mid-1608 and late 1609, when Shakespeare was forty-four and the King's Men first began to use the Blackfriars Theatre. Evidence is scanty, however, and mostly inferential; the most one can be confident of is that the play appeared between 1605 and 1610.

Though such evidence is unreliable,[3] stylistically *Coriolanus* fits in well with *Timon of Athens, Antony and Cleopatra,* and *Pericles* in its flexibility of verse form, fondness for short lines, and concentrated, rapidly shifting imagery. Its adaptation of North's translation of Plutarch's 'Life of Caius Martius Coriolanus' is skilful and controlled, and is sophisticatedly related to contemporary social and political events. Geoffrey Bullough (pp. 454–5) suggests that Shakespeare may have taken up *Coriolanus* when he decided to abandon *Timon*, using the parallel 'Life of Alcibiades' as a bridge between them, and that he may then have seen *Coriolanus* and *Antony and Cleopatra* as explorations of the contrary evils of irascibility and concupiscence.

More objective evidence for dating was provided by Edmond Malone, who as early as 1790 noted two literary influences.

---

[1] Brian Vickers, *Shakespeare: Coriolanus* (1976), p. 7.

[2] H. J. Oliver, 'Coriolanus as Tragic Hero', *SQ*, 10 (1959), p. 57.

[3] See J. Leeds Barroll, *Politics, Plague, and Shakespeare's Theatre* (1991), pp. 233–9, '*Appendix 4*: The Difficulty of Dating Shakespeare's Plays through Internal Evidence', and 240–2, '*Appendix 5*: The Date of *Coriolanus*'.

For the earliest date he pointed out that the phrasing used by Menenius in his fable of the belly-and-members (1.1.93–152, particularly the use of 'gulf' at 95) is closer to a version of the story attributed to Pope Adrian IV in William Camden's *Remains of a Greater Work concerning Britain* published in 1605 than to the account in North's Plutarch or to any other contemporary version. For a final date Malone noted the mockery of Shakespeare's odd phrase 'lurched all swords of the garland' (2.2.99) at 5.4.227 in Jonson's comedy *Epicoene*, first produced in late 1609 or early 1610. A boy's ability to masquerade as a woman, to which the phrase refers in *Epicoene*, comically inverts the idea of Martius' manliness aged sixteen despite an 'Amazonian chin', and Jonson's close phrasal echo—'You have lurched all your friends of the better half of the garland'—presupposes that *Coriolanus* was well enough known at the time of Jonson's play for the joke to be intelligible.[1] Another close literary parallel occurs in Robert Armin's *Phantasma the Italian Tailor and his Boy*, published in 1609, in which the phrasing of 1.1.209–10 of *Coriolanus* is echoed by Armin's reference in his preface to

A strange time of taxation, wherein every pen and ink-horn boy, will throw up his cap at the horns of the moon in censure although his wit hang there, not returning unless monthly on the wane. (Sig. A4)

Armin, the main 'fool' for the King's Men from 1599 to 1610, was probably a member of the original cast of *Coriolanus*. However, T. W. Baldwin's suggestion that he played First Citizen[2] rests on nothing more substantial than the bad theatrical tradition of presenting First Citizen as a clown; a more likely role for Armin is the humorous Menenius, who is present when Coriolanus uses this trope in the play and unexpectedly throws up his own cap at 2.1.102. On the other hand, the gesture is said to signify 'censure' in Armin, whereas in *Coriolanus* it represents joy; and both may derive independently from a common proverbial phrase (see Tilley C60).

---

[1] See p. 88 n. 2 below.
[2] *The Organization and Personnel of the Shakespearean Company* (1927), p. 241. For Armin, see Martin Holmes, *Shakespeare and Burbage* (1978), p. 194.

1. Title-page of Thomas Dekker's *The Great Frost: Cold Doings in London* (1608)

A date of late 1608 or early 1609 is also supported by two possible echoes of George Chapman's translation of the first twelve books of the *Iliad* (entered in the Stationers' Register 14 November 1608). Martius' prayer for his son (5.3.70–5), which is not in Plutarch, may have been influenced by the prayer of his reputed ancestor Hector for the baby Astynax in Book VI of the *Iliad* (though there are no close parallels of thought or phrase); and Third Citizen's comment that the plebeians 'willingly consented to his banishment, yet it was against our will' (4.6.153–4) is interestingly anticipated by Zeus' 'I grant thee willingly, although against my will' to Hera in Book IV, 43,[1] which ensured Hector's death and the burning of Troy. This last point may also have suggested Martius' intention of burning Rome, which is not in Plutarch either, though it does not help with dating because Troy's

[1] See John A. Scott, 'An Unnoticed Homeric Phrase in Shakespeare', *Classical Philology*, 33 (1938), p. 414.

4

burning was a commonplace that Shakespeare had used before.[1]

Two non-literary clues are helpful for narrowing the date further. Martius' comparison of the plebeians' untrustworthiness to 'the coal of fire upon the ice' (1.1.170) probably refers to the 'Great Frost' in the winter of 1607–8, when, according to Edmund Howes,

The eighth of December began the hard frost which continued seven days ... And the two and twentieth the same month the Frost began again very violently so as within four days many persons did walk half-way over the Thames upon the ice, and ... passed over the Thames in divers places. And ... many set up booths and stands of sundry things to sell upon the ice ...

In a letter of 8 January 1607/8 John Chamberlain says 'certain youths burned [i.e. heated] a gallon of wine upon the ice and made all the passengers partakers',[2] while Thomas Dekker wrote a pamphlet, *The Great Frost*, 1608, which describes how 'pans of coals' were placed on the ice at which pedestrians might warm their hands.[3]

Secondly, Martius' warning to the Roman patricians that the overweening tribune Sicinius will 'turn your current in a ditch | And make your channel his' (3.1.98–9) probably refers to the goldsmith Hugh Middleton's scheme to bring clean water into London by channels from streams in Hertfordshire, on which work was begun 20 February 1608/9, and which, again according to Howes, subjected Middleton to 'many causeless hindrances and complaints of sundry persons through whose ground he was to cut his water passage'.[4] This project was probably discussed well before the work began, however, and again suggests a date between late in

[1] Less likely as an influence is Herostratus, who in 356 BC set fire to the temple of Artemis in Ephesos in order to immortalize his name. He is mentioned in Montaigne's essay 'Of Glory' (Everyman edn., ii. 350) and in Valerius Maximus.

[2] John Stow, *Annales: or, a General Chronicle of England, Begun by John Stow; continued by Edmund Howes ... unto ... 1631* (1631); *Letters written by John Chamberlain*, ed. M. E. McClure, 2 vols. (1936), i. 253.

[3] See Bullough, pp. 560–3.

[4] Quoted in G. B. Harrison, 'A Note on *Coriolanus*', in *J. Q. Adams Memorial Studies*, ed. J. G. McManaway *et al.* (1948), 239–52; p. 240.

1608 or early 1609.[1] Malone's conjecture that Volumnia's advice to emulate 'the ripest mulberry' (3.2.81) showed influence from a royal grant of 19 January 1608/9 encouraging the cultivation of mulberries is undercut by two much earlier references in *Venus and Adonis* (1103) and *A Midsummer Night's Dream* (3.1.159), but a composition date late in 1608 is also supported by the play's relation to contemporary social and political events.

The most important of these was serious rioting among the peasantry of Northamptonshire, Warwickshire, and Leicestershire, which effectively lasted from May Day to the end of July 1607 but had political repercussions right into 1609, and became entangled with the House of Commons's struggle against King James's absolutism in such matters as the royal court's rights of 'purveyance' and contention about the proper authority to decide disputed elections. The trope of the 'body politic' and abuse of parliamentarians as 'tribunes of the people' characterized the rhetoric of this very stormy period, and Shakespeare as both court servant and a Stratford landowner was certainly in the thick of it. The 'levellers'' initial protest was against enclosure of the common lands and the wholesale conversion of arable land to pasture, but by the middle of 1608 this had focused into protests about the shortage of grain—partly the result of the severe winter of 1607–8, already mentioned—and its attendant evils of hoarding and price-rigging; and one of Shakespeare's main changes from Plutarch is to focus particularly on famine as the chief cause of the plebeians' revolt, and to develop this thematically as one of the key image clusters of the play (see Introduction, p. 77). Shakespeare seems to have been in Stratford for an extended period in the autumn of 1608,[2] handling business

---

[1] David George, '*Coriolanus* at the Blackfriars?', *NQ*, NS 38 (Dec. 1991), 489–92, cites a similar scheme proposed by a man named Sturtevant, which is mentioned in a letter by Thomas Chaloner as early as March 1607/8. I am not persuaded that *Coriolanus* can be dated this early, however, nor that it was performed at the Blackfriars in June 1608 before that 'winter house's' lease had been transferred to the Burbages.

[2] In August 1608 Shakespeare sued John Addenbrooke at Stratford; his mother died there on 2nd September and was buried there on the 9th; two weeks later his nephew, Michael Hart, was christened there; and on 16th October he stood godfather there to the son of his old friend Henry Walker; during this time, moreover, the London theatres were closed by plague.

complications and various family matters, including—significantly—his mother's death and funeral early in September, and this must have brought him into personal contact with the grim circumstances of the Midland Uprising, whose centre had been very close to Stratford.

Almost equally important as the Uprising were the struggles and debates about democratic representation which were being waged in 1608 at all levels of government: not only vehement discussions in the House of Commons itself for the whole period between 1604–10, but also debate about the appointment of churchwardens at St Saviour's, in whose parish the Globe Theatre stood, which had to be resolved by Parliamentary fiat in 1607–8; and a struggle by the City of London against the Crown which resulted in a new charter for the City in 1608.[1] This charter extended the City's traditional prerogatives to such previous royal 'liberties' as West Smithfield, Whitefriars (where there was a theatre), and Blackfriars, where in August the King's Men had resumed the lease of the indoor, 'private' theatre to use as their 'winter house'; so it is certainly something Shakespeare would have been aware of, especially if, as will be argued under 'First Production', it is likely that *Coriolanus* was composed and later marked up with production at the Blackfriars specifically in mind.

From stylistics and intertextual and contextual data, therefore, the most likely date for the composition of *Coriolanus* is late 1608, with the reference to Hugh Middleton's irrigation scheme possibly, but by no means necessarily, pushing it forward to early 1609.

Place in the Canon

If 1608 is correct as the date of composition, *Coriolanus* was the last of Shakespeare's tragedies. *Antony and Cleopatra* and probably *Timon of Athens* immediately preceded it, and *Pericles*, following so closely it may even have overlapped, is the first

See Mark Eccles, *Shakespeare in Warwickshire* (1961), p. 110; S. Schoenbaum, pp. 240–1.

[1] See p. 38 and p. 40 n. 2, p. 41 nn. 1 and 2 below.

of those final 'romances' which conclude with unambiguous reconciliations between parents and children. *Coriolanus* is thus the culmination of a long series of history plays and political tragedies; and it is in the context of these political predecessors as a whole and, more narrowly, of Shakespeare's specifically Roman plays that its achievement can best be recognized.

Shakespeare's Political Development. To grasp the deeper co-herence of the play and understand what Shakespeare finds to oppose to the savage relativism of Aufidius, it is necessary to consider more deeply the term 'political' itself. And to get at this, the play must first be placed within the context of Shakespeare's developing, and darkening, concept of polit-ical life. Though only ten of his plays are officially classed as 'Histories' in the 1623 Folio, in fact well over half of the canon has politics as its central or strong secondary con-cern. And following these plays through chronologically as they were written, one can discern a distinct pattern of de-velopment whose key seems to be a progressive questioning of political orthodoxy, as Shakespeare tests it by application to actual persons in particular circumstances. Yet this pro-gressive disillusion is accompanied by an unfalteringly tough-minded recognition that there can be no shirking of politics, no evasion of social responsibility. Mankind is necessarily and inevitably a political animal, as Aristotle pointed out in Book I of the *Politics*, because he must learn to live in communities, in the *polis*.

The development of Shakespeare's political thought goes something like this. The early history plays—the three parts of *Henry VI* and *Richard III*—are ideologically orthodox. They cover a period of national breakdown, but interpret it against the secure medieval doctrine that, because of the Fall of Man, the state must limit Original Sin by imposing a fixed, hier-archical order under the King's unquestioned authority, rebel-lion against which is heinous sin. This doctrine assumes that psychological, ethical, and political values all run neatly in parallel—though already, even this early, there is a discon-certing ability in Shakespeare to empathize with the human vulnerability of his titular villains, Joan la Pucelle and Richard of Gloucester. And it is to this view of society that the analogy

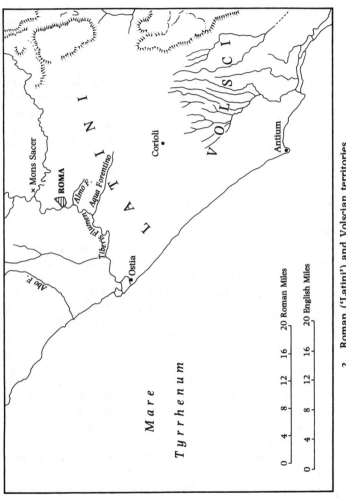

2. Roman ('Latini') and Volscian territories

of the body politic to the physical body, which Menenius misuses at the beginning of *Coriolanus*, belongs.

A crucial change occurs with the writing of *King John* probably around 1594, between the two tetralogies on the struggle between the houses of Lancaster and York. In *King John* Shakespeare was confronted with opposed traditions: a protestant tradition which saw John as England's champion against interference by the Catholic powers of Europe; and an older, no less powerful tradition which saw him as a usurper who had his nephew murdered to secure his throne. Shakespeare does not really manage to combine these polarities, and the exercise they afforded him in exploring contradictory motives seems to have deepened his awareness of the complexity of political decision, of the possible antagonism between politics and ethics as rival systems of value, and of what Ernst Kantorowicz has documented as the 'king's two bodies'—the split between the central office of power and the fallible man who holds it.

Thus, as we continue further into 'York and Lancaster's long jars', from the first tetralogy into the second, though we move from the weakest king, Henry VI, to the strongest, Henry V, two realizations progressively darken the political assurance of the earlier plays. There is, first, an increasing scepticism about the value of war honour and kingship itself, and recognition of the price even a good king must pay for political efficiency. The early plays about unsuitable kings are followed by plays in which suitable—i.e. successful—kings are seen with an irony which dips close to tragedy in Henry V's speech before Harfleur and his discussion of responsibility with Bates and Williams on the eve of Agincourt. There is a growing sense that power isolates, dehumanizes, and eventually brutalizes. Moreover, this is accompanied by a dismal feeling that the process may be historically unending; after Henry V, as the epilogue reminds us, we get back to Henry VI once more. So Jan Kott and others have argued that Shakespeare came to see politics as an absurd 'Grand Mechanism', an endless conveyor belt which raises new rulers to power only to destroy each of them in turn.

However, this is not the end either. Shakespeare digs further in *Julius Caesar, Troilus and Cressida* and the great tragedies.

The classical plays remove the issues from the religiously loaded (and politically dangerous) question of kingship. There can be few more scathing indictments of egotistic war honour and false patriotism than *Troilus and Cressida*; and, as Granville-Barker has shown,[1] in *Julius Caesar* the ethical–political dilemma of the high-minded assassin Brutus leads straight into the problems of the tragedies, where political issues are seen as subordinate to tragic flaws of character. This culminates in the huge excavation of *King Lear*, where Shakespeare seems to arrive at a dialectical concept of values, in which psychology, ethics, and politics interact rather than merely run parallel, and where all are shown to stem from personal relationships, particularly the bond between parent and child which is the basic unit of society.

By the time he reaches *Coriolanus*, then, Shakespeare seems to understand politics in a much wider sense than he did in his early plays—or than we normally use the term today. He includes the narrower meaning, of course: the struggle for power and the question this raises of which are the best institutions for authority; but he sees these as interacting with what we may call more broadly 'culture' (in the anthropological sense). That is, he shows a triple interaction between three forces: individual character; that individual's institutions, including the family which is the basic institution; and society as a whole, which is at the same time the product and the cause of the other two. Hence the cultural knot between mother and country which Coriolanus cannot untie, and of which Volumnia is as much the victim as the agent.

Shakespeare's Rome. Interestingly, the seeds of this development can be traced very early in the works Shakespeare wrote about Rome. Although since Pope it has been customary to praise Shakespeare for differentiating between the Rome of the Republic and Imperial Rome, in fact from the early *Rape of Lucrece* and *Titus Andronicus* (where Coriolanus is mentioned at 4.4.68), through *Julius Caesar* at the turning point of his career, to the last tragedies, *Antony and Cleopatra* and *Coriolanus*—and beyond,

---

[1] 'From *Henry V* to *Hamlet*', *Proceedings of the British Academy*, 11 (1926), 283–309.

more obliquely, in the romance of *Cymbeline*—his attitude to Rome is remarkably consistent. He revels in its military glamour, civic pomp, and eloquence, but sees a moral weakness at its core.

For Shakespeare Rome is always intensely patriarchal, with a strict, military code of personal 'honour' and duty to the state to which all other values must be subordinated. It is torn by constant struggles for power,[1] in which aggression is more often between friends, fellow countrymen, and relatives than against external enemies. Valour is Rome's 'chiefest virtue' (2.2.82), wounds and blood its currency for popular acclaim and public office; and in a universe where the gods remain ironically aloof, posthumous fame becomes man's highest aspiration. Except for vestal virgins, women only have status through their relationships to men; and the private loyalties of marriage, parenthood, and friendship are invariably sacrificed for public good—as Titus Andronicus offers up his sons, Brutus his friend Julius Caesar (and indirectly his wife Portia), and Volumnia her 'boy, Martius'. Psychologically, this entails a ruthless subordination of instinctive and emotional needs: appetite is repudiated, tears scorned as childish or womanish, and sexuality either idealized to negative chastity—as Coriolanus approvingly compares Valeria to an icicle (5.3.65–6)—or perverted to an aggression that ultimately turns against itself. Thus suicide in what Cleopatra calls 'the high Roman fashion' is singled out by Maurice Charney as one of three distinguishing characteristics of all Shakespeare's Roman plays,[2] performed less as an escape from shame than wilfully as a final act of self-assertion. Shakespeare's Rome is thus a place of ironically tinged tragedy, where double endings give an effect of 'deliberate anticlimax';[3] and its ultimate repudiation is quite clear in *Antony and Cleopatra*, at a time when Rome had just reached its apogee under Octavius Caesar.

---

[1] 'Power' is used 28 times in *Coriolanus*, 20 times more than in any other Shakespeare play.

[2] Charney, pp. 209–14 (Titus Andronicus and Coriolanus allow themselves to be killed).

[3] Jacqueline Pearson, 'Romans and Barbarians: The Structure of Irony in Shakespeare's Roman Tragedies', in M. Bradbury and D. J. Palmer, eds., *Shakespearian Tragedy* (1984), pp. 180–1.

Whereas *Antony and Cleopatra* criticizes Rome from without, however, by contrasting it to Cleopatra's Egypt, *Coriolanus* criticizes it from within. It analyses the obsessively repetitive effect of the Roman belief that the *polis* and individual character must both be human 'constructs', willed against the flux of nature, and the consequent reduction of the ideal of human community to individual competitiveness with its dangers of solipsism and inability to sympathize with others.[1] The resulting tragedy is arguably one of the most profound political analyses in the language, because Rome's weakness is traced not to later degeneration and vice (as in Jonson's *Catiline* and *Sejanus*) but to the very characteristics that made Rome great, and the connection between public ethos and private tragedy is for the first time located clearly in the middle ground of family neurosis.

'*Deep Sources*'. Besides its relation to these major strands of Shakespeare's development, *Coriolanus* also draws on detail from individual earlier plays, which it will be useful to consider briefly before looking at its more substantial debt to Plutarch. Coriolanus is the last of Shakespeare's increasingly sceptical characterizations of war heroes, beginning with Talbot in *1 Henry VI* and Titus Andronicus, and progressing through Hotspur, Henry V, Hector, Achilles, Othello, and Macbeth, to Alcibiades in *Timon of Athens* and the 'Roman' side of Mark Antony. Of these the most important analogues are *1 Henry IV* and *Troilus and Cressida*.

An obvious parallel to the former is the likeness of Menenius' relation with Coriolanus to that of Falstaff with Prince Hal. Both father-figures are ageing *bons vivants*, vulgarly at ease with commoners they intend to exploit, with an attractive verbal wit that can become bitterly destructive, as Menenius' does in 5.4. Without being cowards, each tries to avoid direct involvement in fighting, and there is a striking resemblance between the curt rebuffs they both receive at the end of each play after too possessive demands in public—to which

---

[1] David Kranz, 'Shakespeare's New Idea of Rome', in P. A. Ramsay, ed., *Rome in the Renaissance* (1982), p. 375; cf. Michael Long: 'All the cruces of [Martius'] character are crises of Rome and Romanness', *The Unnatural Scene: A Study in Shakespearean Tragedy* (1976), p. 59.

the audience responds ambivalently in either case. Similarly, the rivalry and personal combat of Martius and Aufidius are anticipated by Hal and Hotspur, though characterization is interestingly reversed, with Coriolanus resembling Hotspur and Hal's streak of calculating policy relating him rather to Aufidius. Hotspur, like Martius, recklessly attacks without sufficient support and fatalistically courts death after a parent has betrayed him; and like Martius (and Othello) he is contemptuous of symbolic language, habitually speaking 'thick' and comically hard to silence once he begins to rail, yet dangerously unaware of his own sensitivity to words—which emerges in unexpected gleams of poetry in his own speech and renders him an easy prey for verbal manipulation by his politic uncle and father, as Martius too is manipulated by Volumnia, the Tribunes, and Aufidius.

Even closer to the Martius and Aufidius relationship is that between Hector and Achilles in *Troilus and Cressida*. Hector, who was referred to as the ideal warrior in *1* and *3 Henry VI* and *Titus Andronicus*, is spoken of as Martius' ancestor at 1.9.11–12, and Volumnia says she prefers Hector's forehead spitting blood to his mother's milky breasts (1.3.41–4). Coriolanus' departure into exile and the scene where the women plead with him to spare Rome parallel Hector's impatience when his womenfolk try to persuade him not to return to battle; while Coriolanus' prayer for young Martius has often been compared to Hector's for his infant son, Astynax. Though there is considerable overlap with Achilles, most of Coriolanus' heroic traits can also be traced to Hector, who sees 'honour' as a wholly subjective absolute, overriding consistency and loyalty; insists on fighting the enemy champion as his only chivalric equal; and equates war with a hunt for fame and honour, which in pursuit of symbolic golden armour betrays him to his death.[1] Achilles, on the other hand, though he is described as totally self-sufficient (2.3.161–4) in a way that Coriolanus would only like to be, is actually more like Aufidius in his murderous sense of injured reputation and the homosexual tinge of his friendship for Patroclus; and this foreshadowing is particularly striking in the way his

---

[1] See p. 98.

Myrmidons (the equivalent of Aufidius' Antiates) rescue him from defeat in single combat with Hector, then ignobly help him to murder the latter when he is caught unarmed. Like Aufidius, Achilles vaunts this murder as a personal victory, and vindictively dishonours his enemy's corpse: none of which occurs in Plutarch's Life of Coriolanus.

The tragedies take this analysis of flawed heroism further by exploring its relation to various forms of sexual dependency and the consequent perversions of eros into aggression. Othello anticipates that aspect of Coriolanus which, unable to move from 'th' casque to th' cushion' (4.7.43), cannot accommodate martial simplicity to the ambiguities and compromise required by political manœuvre and personal relationships.[1] His farewell to the military profession when he believes himself betrayed (3.3.352 ff.) has interesting resemblances of phrase and structure to Martius' similar speech at 3.2.113 ff.; he too is vulnerable to the suggestiveness of language, about which he boasts himself immune; and it is Othello who provides the closest analogue to Coriolanus' death, as he passionately affirms the simplicities of his earlier heroism before killing himself—or, in Coriolanus' case, letting himself be killed.

Similar contaminations of heroism by sexual dependency are explored in *Macbeth* and *Antony and Cleopatra*,[2] but surprisingly, considering their manifest differences, the psychologically most suggestive 'deep source' for Coriolanus is Hamlet. Like Martius, Hamlet is cripplingly dependent on love–hate for his mother, and though Hamlet is self-consciously verbal to a fault whereas Coriolanus seems to have no skill at introspection, both men go through a similar pattern of development. Youthful idealism is corrupted by society (reflected in imagery of disease and surgery), with a consequent swing to nihilistic revenge, and this is followed by death-accepting fatalism when that revenge seems thwarted—

[1] See Richard Marienstras, 'La dégradation des vertus héroiques dans *Othello* et dans *Coriolan*', *Études Anglaises*, 17 (1964), 372–89; Marion B. Smith, *Casque to Cushion: A Study of Othello and Coriolanus* (1979), pp. 1–5, 95–173.

[2] See G. K. Hunter, 'The Last Tragic Heroes', in J. R. Brown and B. Harris, eds., *Later Shakespeare* (1966), 11–28; D. W. Harding, 'Women's Fantasy of Manhood: A Shakespearian Theme', *SQ*, 20 (1969), 245–53.

Coriolanus' 'But let it come' (5.3.190) echoing Hamlet's 'let be' (5.2.170; omitted in the Folio text) as he accepts the final duel and 'But let it be' (5.2.290) as he gives up trying to justify himself while dying. The irony of the soldier's funeral that Fortinbras gives Hamlet is pushed further in *Coriolanus*, because Aufidius is so blatantly exploiting the inevitable swing of public sympathy to the loser—as Bolingbroke had done in *Richard II* and Octavius in both *Julius Caesar* and *Antony and Cleopatra*. Most intriguing of all, however, is the two protagonists' awareness of a lack of correspondence between 'seems' and 'is', and their focusing of this gap on the hypocrisy of acting. There were touches of this earlier, of course: Volumnia's advice to Coriolanus in 3.2 on how to please the voters is very like the description of Bolingbroke's cynical wooing of the crowd in 5.2 of *Richard II* (while Martius' reaction corresponds to Richard's own confusions of role and identity): Caesar, Brutus, and Antony are all guilty of deliberate role-playing in *Julius Caesar*; and Cleopatra is expert at such theatrical manipulation; but in no play is the acting–deception trope developed so thoroughly as in *Hamlet* and *Coriolanus*.

Finally, the most fruitful 'deep source' of all is *King Lear*. The plebeians' complaints at 1.1.15–21 combine the phrasing of Lear's acknowledged need to share society's 'superflux' (3.4.35) and Gloucester's lesson that 'distribution should undo excess' (4.1.64). *King Lear* also relates political ethos to the quality of relationships between parents and children, and like *Coriolanus* exploits the stage effects of kneeling and silence to convey fluctuations in this relationship. Imagery of flies, wanton boys, and gilded butterflies carries similar significances in both plays, as do cannibalism, hunting, animal, and monster metaphors: rebels against authority are envisaged eating one another; and like Coriolanus, Lear ambiguously calls himself a 'dragon'. Physical violation expresses political breakdown and emotional pain in both plays; and revenge is recognized as a psychic defence against the danger of degenerating to 'a kind of nothing' (5.1.13). Most important of all, *King Lear* uses a similar anticlimactic structure (as *Othello* and *Troilus and Cressida* also do, less grandly), in which disaster occurs even after *anagnorisis* and reconciliation have apparently been achieved, with a remorselessness that Samuel

3. 'Women of the Gracchi' from Jan van der Straet, *Celebrated Roman Women* (1573)

Johnson, for one, found unendurable. Thus, the cortège to a 'Dead March' that concludes *King Lear* has the same ambivalence as the funerals of *Hamlet* and *Coriolanus*.

North's Plutarch and Other Sources

The main source of the play is undisputedly 'The Life of Caius Martius Coriolanus' in Plutarch's *Parallel Lives*, written in Greek about AD 2. This reached Shakespeare via a 1560 French version by Jacques Amyot, which was translated into English by Sir Thomas North with the title of *The Lives of the Noble Grecians and Romans*: first published in 1579 and reprinted in 1595, 1603, and 1616. Shakespeare had used North's translation previously for *The Rape of Lucrece* and *Julius Caesar* and, more recently, for *Antony and Cleopatra* and *Timon of Athens*. The edition he consulted for *Coriolanus* seems to have been that of 1595,[1] and besides the Coriolanus story proper

[1] See Brockbank, pp. 21–2, 29; and E. A. J. Honigmann, *The Stability of Shakespeare's Text* (1965), pp. 146–7, and 'Shakespeare's Plutarch', *SQ*, 10 (1959), 25–33.

he also made use of Plutarch's comparison of Coriolanus with Alcibiades, especially for the characterization of Aufidius.

Further sources that have been suggested are Book II of Livy's *Ab urbe condita*, translated by Philemon Holland as *The Roman History Written by Titus Livius*,[1] and a digest of Livy in Book I of Lucius Annaeus Florus' *Epitome bellorum omnium annorum*[2]—both of which were familiar Elizabethan school texts —as well as Plutarch's own source, the *Roman Antiquities* of Dionysius of Halicarnassus, and Machiavelli's commentary, *Discourses Upon the First Decade of T. Livius*, which was not published in translation until 1636 but which Shakespeare could have read in Italian or in several manuscript translations that were circulating in the early seventeenth century.[3] The only sure instances of extra borrowing, however, are for Menenius' fable of the belly-and-members in the first scene and for the naming of one of Aufidius' servants at 4.5.3 and the two spies in 4.3.

From particular word choices and other small details it is evident that Shakespeare went beyond Plutarch to consult versions of the belly fable in William Camden's *Remains . . .* (1605)—itself derived from John of Salisbury's *Policraticus* (*circa* 1159) v. 2, where the story is attributed to Pope Adrian IV—and also in Holland's translation of Livy (1601), William Averill's *A Marvellous Combat of Contrarieties* (1588), and possibly Sir Philip Sidney's *The Defence of Poesy* (1595).[4] This raises the question of why he took such unusual pains with this particular aspect of the play. One possible reason is that by 1608 the belly fable was an over-familiar commonplace,[5] as Menenius admits (1.1.87–9) and the sing-song readiness of First Citizen's embellishment supports (112–16). Presum-

---

[1] See Bullough, pp. 460–2, and the articles by Velz and Barton below.

[2] John Velz, 'Cracking Strong Curbs Asunder: Roman Destiny and the Roman Hero in *Coriolanus*', *ELR*, 13 (1983), 58–69.

[3] See Anne Barton, 'Livy, Machiavelli, and Shakespeare's *Coriolanus*', *ShS*, 38 (1985), 115–29.

[4] See K. Muir, *Shakespeare's Sources I: Comedies and Tragedies* (1957), p. 224; Brockbank, pp. 29–30.

[5] See P. Archambault, 'The Analogy of the "Body" in Renaissance Political Literature', *Bibliothèque d'Humanisme et Renaissance*, 29 (1967), 21–53; David G. Hale, *The Body Politic: A Political Metaphor in Renaissance English Literature* (1971), pp. 96–107; Leonard Barkan, *Nature's Work of Art: the Human Body as Image of the World* (1975), pp. 95–108; and Zvi Jagendorf, '*Coriolanus*: Body Politic and Private Parts', *SQ*, 41 (1990), 455–69.

ably, therefore, Shakespeare would want as comprehensive a version as possible, particularly since the fable suggests an ideal that the rest of the action shows Rome failing to achieve and also establishes one of the play's main threads of imagery. More intriguingly, it is also possible that Shakespeare may have intended to exploit two significantly different emphases with which the trope had been interpreted. One tradition, stemming from Plato and to be found in such influential Tudor theorists as Sir John Fortescue, *De laudibus legum Angliae* (*c.*1470) or Erasmus' *Institutio principis christiani* (1515), stressed the good of the whole community and used the fable to illustrate social harmony; the other, stemming from Aristotle, through Aquinas, to Sir Thomas Elyot's *The Book Named the Governor* (1531) amongst others, emphasized rather the supremacy of the head of state and used the trope to support the legitimacy of hierarchy and the duty of those governed to obey. Thus the belly fable could either be an argument for social co-operation—which is how First Citizen seems to understand it, with his emphasis on each member's particular service—or an argument for class subordination and what is now called the 'trickle down' theory of economics—which is Menenius' interpretation (though his more immediate purpose is merely to delay the rebels until help can arrive). His leisurely exposition of this trope—including the jocular vulgarity of designating First Citizen 'the great toe' and what A. P. Rossiter has called 'the only belch in English blank verse'[1] (see 1.1.105 n.)—is intended to co-opt the citizens' appeal to physical realities more basic than abstractions of state; but his bias is betrayed not only by patrician 'architectural' references that begin to contaminate his body imagery (l. 130 ff.) but also by Shakespeare's focusing of plebeian discontent on famine instead of usury, in which new context the fable is obviously insensitive and specious. The whole point of the uprising in the play is that the belly is *not* nourishing its members.[2]

---

[1] *Angel with Horns* (1961), p. 247.

[2] See David G. Hale, '*Coriolanus*: the Death of a Political Metaphor', *SQ*, 22 (1971), 197–202; Andrew Gurr, '*Coriolanus* and the Body Politic', *ShS*, 28 (1975), 63–9; Thomas Sorge, 'The Failure of Orthodoxy in *Coriolanus*', in Jean E. Howard and Marion F. O'Connor, eds., *Shakespeare Reproduced: the Text in History and Ideology* (1987), 225–41.

Besides the belly fable, it has been suggested that Shakespeare also incorporated details from elsewhere in Plutarch's *Lives*, specifically from the stories of Theseus, Pelopides, Lycurgus, Numa, and Cato.[1] Evidence for this is very thin, however, except in matters of naming. Cotus, the name given to one of Aufidius' servants, is most likely a variant of Cotys, the King of Paphlagonia who switched allegiance from Egypt to Sparta in Plutarch's 'Life of Agesilaus', a source Shakespeare had already used for *King Lear*. Adrian, the Volscian spy in 4.3, is probably borrowed from the 'Life of Lucullus', where he is involved in a quarrel over spoils; while the Roman traitor, Nicanor, may also come from the same source but, even more appropriately, may derive from a Nicanor in the 'Life of Phocion' who, betrayed by the Athenians, plotted revenge against their city.[2] Thus all three names seem to have been chosen to foreshadow Coriolanus' career among the Volscians.

Apart from these two areas the play relies solely on the 'Life of Coriolanus', which it often follows very closely, particularly in such rhetorical set speeches as Coriolanus' denunciation of tribunes and free corn doles in 3.1, his appeal to Aufidius in 4.5, or Volumnia's plea for Rome in 5.3. Even here there are often significant small improvements. In 5.3, for instance, Volumnia's comment in North, 'No man living is more bound to show himself thankful in all parts and respects, than thyself' becomes the far more ambiguous and aggressively impersonal, 'There's no man in the world | More bound to's mother' (ll. 159–60). And the play often departs quite markedly from North in ways that many scholars have analysed in detail.[3] Besides changes made in order to focus on the issues

[1] Brockbank, p. 30 n. 3.

[2] See Bernard Kytzler, 'Classical Names in Shakespeare's *Coriolanus*', *Archiv für das Studium der Neueren Sprachen und Literaturen*, 204 (1967), 133–7; Brockbank, pp. 30–1. The latter notes that all three names also occur in Holland's translation of Livy (1600) and of Plutarch's *Moralia* (1603), so the precise source remains uncertain.

[3] Besides Brockbank, Bullough, Honigmann (p. 17 n. 1) and Muir (p. 18 n. 4), see also David C. Green, *Plutarch 'Revisited': A Study of Shakespeare's Last Roman Tragedies and their Source* (1979), pp. 130–242, M. W. MacCallum, *Shakespeare's Roman Plays and Their Background* (1910), pp. 454–627, and Hermann Heuer, 'From Plutarch to Shakespeare: A Study of *Coriolanus*', *ShS*, 10 (1957), 50–9.

of famine and representative government, which will be dis-cussed more fully under 'Contemporary Background', these alterations serve two main purposes: elaboration of character and irony in structure.

Characterization. The key relationship in the play is that be-tween Coriolanus and Volumnia, and the latter is charac-terized quite differently from in the source. Instead of the passive, overindulgent parent recorded by Plutarch, Shake-speare transforms her into what Swinburne called 'Volumnia victrix', an archetype of those ambitious, strong-minded Roman matrons who were exemplified for the Renaissance by Cornelia, mother of the Gracchi.[1] Far from being indulgent, Volumnia is severe and proud, emphasizing her son's double duty to obey herself and serve the state. She uses him to fulfil her own ambition, since women were not allowed to hold office in Rome; and, as Tacitus accuses Agrippina (*Annales*, xii. 64), reacts impatiently to any show he makes of inde-pendence from her. Thus, in the play it is Volumnia's ambi-tion that Coriolanus become consul, not Coriolanus' own (2.1.199–200) as it was in Plutarch; whereas in Plutarch she is moved to joyful tears at his victorious return, Shakespeare gives this reaction to Virgilia and has Volumnia gloat instead over the number of his wounds; and in the play she is given skills (indeed, delight) in politic dissimulation of which there is no inkling in the source. Except for 5.3, the scenes in which Volumnia appears are entirely Shakespeare's invention: 1.3 shows the family milieu that has formed Martius; 2.1 estab-lishes Volumnia's ambition for him, whether he will or no; and 3.2 reveals her political cynicism and illustrates exactly how she controls her son emotionally. This anticipates the tactics of her plea for Rome in 5.3, to which Shakespeare adds a final twist of personal bullying (5.3.179–83) of which Plutarch's Volumnia is wholly innocent. Moreover, in Shakespeare it is

[1] See Beryl Rawson, ed., *The Family in Ancient Rome: New Perspectives* (1986), esp. pp. 1–57, 170–200; Suzanne Dixon, *The Roman Matron* (1988); and Valida Dragovitch, *Roma Materna: Rome et le personnage de la mère dans les tragédies romaines de Shakespeare* (1989), esp. pp. 213–98. Other famous exemplars were Aurelia, mother of Julius Caesar; Julia, mother of Mark Antony; and Apia, mother of Octavius. Cornelia and Julia even had famous pleading scenes like Volumnia's.

Volumnia who organizes this plea, not Valeria as in the source; and Plutarch's idea that it was supernaturally inspired (and rewarded) is abandoned completely. On the other hand, there are elements in 4.1, 4.2, and the enigmatic 5.5 which hint at possible complexities in Volumnia that go beyond stereotyping (see 'Interpretation').

Three details are worth mentioning that show how closely Volumnia has been recreated to conform to the pattern of the traditional Roman matron. 'Fond of no second brood' (5.3.163), she represents herself as the ideal '*univira*' who has rejected second marriage; though, significantly, Volumnia thinks of this only in terms of further sons (cf. 1.3.22–5), never in terms of another husband. Indeed, her husband is not once mentioned.[1] Secondly, it was traditionally part of a Roman matron's duty to participate in the household chore of 'wool-work',[2] as Volumnia is shown doing in 1.3—though, unlike Virgilia, she is quite ready to drop it at Valeria's instigation. And, according to Cicero, Roman mothers were particularly concerned to teach their sons eloquence, so that they were 'reared not so much in their mother's laps as in their speech' (*Brutus*, 210–11): a characteristic reflected not only in Martius' frequent echoings of his mother's vocabulary (e.g. 3.2.8–13) but also in the actual lesson Volumnia gives him, both verbally and gesturally (3.2.75 ff.), in the rhetoric of flattering voters.

This transformation of Volumnia affects the characterization of Virgilia, Valeria, Young Martius, and Menenius, and, at a deeper level, also of Aufidius. Roman matrons like Volumnia habitually chose wives for their sons, and, according to Plutarch, Volumnia went beyond this and untraditionally kept the couple living in her own house. Certainly, on first acquaintance Virgilia seems exactly the sort of timid, uncompetitive wife Volumnia would choose. Before the end of 1.3, however, she has revealed a quiet will of her own, which subsequent scenes confirm;[3] and there is a growing realiza-

[1] Typically, she would have been married very young to a much older husband: see Dixon, pp. 6, 20–2, 31, 36 n. 4.
[2] Cf. Dixon, p. 3: 'We know some distinguished mothers who did wool-work with their own hands.' See Fig. 3 of Cornelia, mother of the Gracchi.
[3] Cf. J. Middleton Murry, 'A Neglected Heroine of Shakespeare', *Countries of the Mind: Essays in Literary Criticism*, First Series (1922), pp. 29–50; Una Ellis-Fermor, *Shakespeare the Dramatist* (1961), pp. 60–77. In the 1977 RSC

tion that in her 'gracious silence' (2.1.171) she represents for Martius a physically based tenderness that is strong enough to resist Volumnia's interference. This is strikingly demonstrated in 5.3 when Shakespeare reverses the earlier order of greetings in 2.1 to have Coriolanus give Virgilia a kiss 'Long as my exile' (5.3.45) before turning to kneel before—but not embrace—his mother: both alterations of the source. At the other extreme, Valeria is transformed from Plutarch's inspired vestal virgin, who organizes the women's appeal for Rome, into the brittle social gossip of 1.3, a female equivalent of Menenius; and in 5.3 itself she is reduced virtually to a supernumerary, though her continued presence in that scene maintains, at least vestigially, Plutarch's idea that the deputation represents all the women of Rome—virgin, wife, and mother—not just Martius' own family.[1] The two toddlers who are Martius' children in Plutarch are transformed to the wilful Young Martius, who replicates both his father's education and the element of 'boy' that Coriolanus himself has been unable to outgrow. More sinisterly, he is also an assurance that Coriolanus' mistakes are likely to continue. Nineteenth-century producers sentimentalized this relationship in order to emphasize Martius' affection for his family, but there is little evidence of strong feeling on either side. At 5.3.23–4 Coriolanus talks of Young Martius not as his son but as Volumnia's 'grandchild'; and his 'sea-mark' prayer (5.3.70 ff.) reveals more about how he sees himself than genuine parental love. Like the unexpectedly poetic 'moon of Rome' welcome to Valeria (and possibly also his nervous assurances of chastity to Virgilia), it reflects his own strained grasping for traditional proprieties in a grotesquely embarrassing situation. They are the kind of speeches that Martius thinks he ought to make to 'play | The man I am' (3.2.15–16). Significantly, none comes from Plutarch.

production, Jill Baker gave 'the statuesque silences of Virgilia a strong erotic, private appeal' and her reunion kiss with Martius in 5.3 'spoke of a full erotic history': Daniell, pp. 25, 39.

[1] The fact that all three names begin with 'V' adds to our sense of them as a group. In the 1989–90 RSC production Valeria's change from rapturous admiration of Coriolanus in 2.1 to icy disdain in 5.3 showed how his reputation had suffered in Rome.

When a Roman boy was left fatherless in his minority, it was customary for the widow to choose a family friend as 'tutor' for him, not to be teacher but to oversee his inheritance and act as male advisor.[1] This is the role Shakespeare has created for Menenius, adapting the relation between Falstaff and Prince Hal. In Plutarch, Menenius is merely a 'pleasant old [man] ... acceptable to the people' who disappears from the story before the famine riots, after he has told the belly fable to pacify an earlier rising against usury; he has no connection whatsoever with Martius.[2] Similarly, the consul Cominius is transformed into Martius' very conventional army patron, individualized by making him nervously aware of his own inadequacies as a leader, which he covers by bluff military cliché and extravagantly generous praise of Coriolanus' success—into which a note of puzzled criticism, perhaps even revulsion, sometimes creeps. These characterizations help to personalize the Act 5 embassies that plead with Coriolanus to spare Rome (which Shakespeare has reduced to three from Plutarch's four), so as to present them in increasing order of intimacy—Cominius, Menenius, Volumnia—to emphasize how Martius can resist all loyalties except the crippling tie to his mother.

Martius' enemies are also individualized by Shakespeare. The way the Tribunes are made directly responsible for his downfall, their characterization in terms of the radical right of London magistrates and the House of Commons, and Shakespeare's ambivalence towards what they represent, will be discussed under 'Contemporary Background'. Their new complexity is more political than psychological, but such added touches as Brutus' reference to his wealth (4.6.168–9) and his eventual mobbing by the crowd, and Sicinius' increasing—if edgy—comradeship with Menenius and final exit with him to join Volumnia's triumph are also worth noting, because they provide small clues for differentiating between the two. Aufidius, on the other hand, is developed psychologically. One brief remark in Plutarch about rivalry between Martius and

---

[1] See Dixon, pp. 31–2.
[2] According to Livy he died in the same year Corioles was captured and before the Roman famine: there may possibly be a glance at this in Martius' humorous greeting, 'And live you yet?' (2.1.176).

the Volscian leader is elaborated into a complex relationship of love-hatred with distinctly homoerotic overtones, the psychology of which will be discussed under 'Interpretation'. While Martius is made less politically ambitious and acute than Plutarch represents him, Aufidius is endowed with elements of treachery and a politic concern for public appearance that seem to derive equally from Plutarch's comparison of Alcibiades with Coriolanus and such previous Shakespeare characters as Bolingbroke, Achilles, and Octavius. An ironic dimension is added to this rivalry, moreover, by introducing it as early as 1.2 and having Aufidius vow his treachery before the end of the first act. The contrast between his foot on Martius' body yet final repentant epitaph (both added by Shakespeare) provides the major discord on which the play concludes; and, typically, his last word is the hypermetrical 'Assist'. For good and ill, Aufidius can never act alone (cf. 2.1.33).

Coriolanus, on the other hand, is compulsively a 'loner', and many of Shakespeare's key changes from Plutarch emphasize this. Though Plutarch says Volumnia had 'children', the play emphasizes that Martius is an only son. The small band of followers, who in Plutarch accompany him in both the capture of Corioles and at his departure into exile, are eliminated. He is made to forget the name of his Corioles host and merely drop the topic. Contrary to Plutarch, he objects to seeking plebeian votes; no second consul is named for Rome; an added scene shows him musing alone before Aufidius' house; to Young Martius he represents himself as a solitary 'great sea-mark'; and at the end, instead of being drowned out by his Volscian murderers as Plutarch records, he is allowed a final speech about capturing Corioles that culminates in the boast 'Alone I did it' (5.6.117). Shakespeare also makes him more formidable as a fighter but reduces his astuteness as a general. Thus, while Plutarch says he killed one soldier in his maiden battle, Cominius tells the Senate he killed three and also beat King Tarquin to his knees. The defeat of Aufidius in single combat is added by Shakespeare, as is the scene in which the blood-soaked hero is lifted up by cheering soldiers as he exults 'O, me alone!'[1] Yet his later

[1] See p. 64.

capture of Antium is omitted, though this obscures the reason for Brutus' accusation that he has not shared out his booty (3.3.4–5), which consequently sounds like a malicious lie. His tricking of the Volscians to renew the attack on Rome is also cut; as is his plan to split the Roman opposition by sparing patrician estates during the Volscian advance, thereby creating an alliance between the aristocrats of both nations. And Aufidius' dark assurance that Martius has 'left undone | That which shall break his neck' (4.7.24–5) remains obscure until we read in Plutarch that, instead of taking Rome when it lay at his mercy, Coriolanus declared a thirty-day truce and withdrew the Volscian forces to allow the Romans time to consider his surrender terms. These omissions, together with other key places where Coriolanus' motives are left deliberately unclear, give the impression that he makes decisions impulsively, from emotion not from policy, an impression that is confirmed by his threat to burn Rome and slaughter all its inhabitants.

His reiterated distrust of language helps support this also, though Plutarch reports that actually Coriolanus was both witty and eloquent. Certainly, in the play Martius is amusing in a rough, soldierly way—inventively cursing rioters, cowardly or looting soldiers, and Aufidius' insolent servants; teasing his mother; or joking with his fellow commanders—and some actors have turned this to account (most notably, in quite different ways, Laurence Olivier and Tommaso Salvini). And, on occasion, he can also argue eloquently, as he does most inopportunely against corn doles and the tribunate, or in offering his services to Aufidius. More characteristically, however, his solitariness is reflected in terse, reluctant speech or tense passages of silence—before cheering troops, the Senate, the Roman voters, his mother's persuasions in 3.2, his accusers in the market-place before he draws his sword, the embassies of Cominius and Menenius, and climactically during Volumnia's long plea that he spare Rome. This stubborn refusal to speak is one of Shakespeare's most significant changes to Plutarch, and together with the other alterations, it creates the characterization of a man who in large measure is responsible for his own destruction. The irony of this is also driven home by major changes in structure.

Structure. Plutarch's discursive narrative is converted into a five-act structure in which juxtapositions and, particularly, repetitions are as important as logical sequence. The several years covered by the historical events are telescoped to a period that seems no longer than a few weeks,[1] with exposition of Martius' earlier career skilfully folded into Volumnia's boasting in 1.3 and Cominius' subsequent eulogy to the Senate (2.2.85 ff.). Plutarch's recital of the Martian lineage is cleverly converted into a sneer by Brutus, though this produces some anachronisms (see notes to 2.3.234–5, 236, 238) as does Titus Lartius' earlier comparison of Martius to Cato's ideal warrior (1.5.30).

Attention is secured immediately by beginning with the bread riots, which do not occur until a third of the way into Plutarch's account; and the early introduction of Aufidius in 1.2 and Volumnia in 1.3 allows Martius' three main conflicts—with the plebeians, the Volscians, and his mother—to be 'plaited'[2] together from the start. This makes clear their interrelationship in terms of Martius' psychology and also establishes immediately the multiple perspectives through which we continue to view him throughout the play, as plebeians, patricians, Menenius, the Tribunes, Aufidius, Volumnia, and Virgilia—and later many others—comment on his behaviour, producing a much more complex, contradictory characterization than Plutarch's univocal analysis. In effect, 'By the middle of the first act all of the important psychological, political, and military aspects of the play have been revealed and put into action',[3] and its main imagery has also been established.

The action then falls into three main movements, curiously (and perhaps deliberately) straddling the act divisions. The rest of Act 1 is occupied by Martius' defeat of the Volscians, culminating—across the act division—in his triumphant return to Rome in 2.1. The rest of Acts 2 and 3 cover his

---

[1] The time scheme can be compressed into as little as eleven days: see Furness, p. 738.

[2] 'Plait' comes from Madeleine Doran, ' "All's in Anger": The Language of Contention in *Coriolanus*', *Shakespeare's Dramatic Language* (1976), pp. 182–217, 200; *Romeo*'s first three scenes have an almost identical structure.

[3] W. S. E. Coleman, 'The Peculiar Artistic Quality of Shakespeare's *Coriolanus*', *On-Stage Studies*, 7 (1983), 73–84; p. 75.

struggle against the plebeians for the consulship, with an initial reversal made worse by his mother's interference in 3.2, prompting a second attempt that leads finally to his exile. The natural end of this second movement is not when Coriolanus is banished, however, but after he has left Rome and his wife and mother have cursed the Tribunes in 4.2—a scene which Shakespeare added. If an intermission came here (which is where most modern productions put it), then the interval and adventitious scene of the spies that follows (4.3—another Shakespeare invention) could together create an adequate sense of time-lapse between Coriolanus' departure from Rome and his arrival at Antium to begin the play's third movement. (Alternatively, if one wished to end Act 3 strongly with the banishment, one might cut all intervening scenes and begin Act 4 with the arrival at Antium, as was the usual practice throughout the eighteenth and nineteenth centuries.) The act division here seems a mistake, and indeed may not have been by Shakespeare himself; on the other hand, there was a similar overlap earlier with 2.1, and 5.6 later functions like a separate coda; so the asymmetry may be intentional. Apart perhaps from one intermission, such act divisions would have no effect on production at the Globe Theatre, but they would be significant if the play was also designed for the Blackfriars, as is argued under 'First Production'.

A fresh beginning in Act 4 is common in Jacobean drama because 'the imaginative system is dissolved and another must replace it when the play is resumed after the interval'.[1] In *Coriolanus* this takes the form of Martius' volte-face to attack Rome, which is only stopped by his mother's embassy in 5.3, with the consequent jubilation of Rome in 5.4 and 5.5. The last scene then acts as both coda and reprise, with a downbeat second climax which undermines the affirmations of the pleading scene to produce an extremely ambivalent conclusion. Although one element of the triple 'braid' dominates each of these movements, the other two are always present; and careful positioning of the scenes also allows constant ironic anticipation, especially towards the end. For example, Cominius' eulogy in 2.2 does not square with the rashness and

---

[1] Emrys Jones, *Scenic Form in Shakespeare* (1971), p. 71.

near defeat of Coriolanus that we have observed in Act 1's battle sequence; the Tribunes' happy interlude at the beginning of 4.6 is hollow because we already know the Volscians are renewing their attack on Rome; Aufidius' self-proclaimed treachery in 4.7 gives a sinister edge to his presence during Volumnia's plea in 5.3 (in Plutarch he is away at Antium raising reserves); and any reliance we may have in Menenius' good sense is undermined by his confidence at 4.6.75–6 that Martius and Aufidius can never 'atone' together and assurance in 5.4 that Coriolanus will not heed his mother, both of which we have just watched taking place. These structural ironies combine with other ironies introduced by Shakespeare, such as Aufidius' repeated failures to recognize Coriolanus at Antium in 4.5 or the deliberate 'bad timing'[1] of Titus Lartius' premature obituary in 1.5, to give the play a pervasively sardonic tone, which is increased by the element of comedy Shakespeare has also injected—among the plebeians, Menenius with the Tribunes, the women in 1.3, the spies, and Aufidius' servants, as well as in Coriolanus' own rough humour, already remarked on—and especially by excision of the source's pieties about the inspiration for the women's plea and the reward of a temple to them afterwards (which is reduced to a passing compliment by Martius, 5.3.207–8).

Ironic effect is intensified further by three devices: by 'mirror scenes', by *aporia* (or omissions) that leave motivation unexplained, and especially by repetition. The most obvious 'mirror scene' is 4.3, the spies scene. This is cut in most modern productions, though it not only helps to bridge the time gap between Coriolanus' exile and his appearance at Antium, but also has thematic[2] and tonal value. It ironizes Martius' treachery to Rome in 4.5, anticipating his encounter with Aufidius by the initial non-recognition, then slightly effusive cordiality of the spies and their final exit together to a feast. Even more obviously the vignette of Young Martius mammocking a butterfly in 'one on's father's moods' (1.3.69) reflects Coriolanus' immature choler and the education that has fostered it. And Menenius' belly fable too functions as a

---

[1] Poole, p. 24; cf. Christopher Givan, 'Shakespeare's *Coriolanus*: The Premature Epitaph and the Butterfly', *Shakespeare Studies*, 12 (1979), 143–58.

[2] Cf. other 'spying' references at 1.1.222, 1.2.2, 1.7.18–19, 3.2.43–7, etc.

sort of distorting 'mirror scene', like Ulysses' order speech in *Troilus and Cressida* or the Archbishop's beehive trope at the beginning of *Henry V*, by setting up an ideal that is not matched by subsequent behaviour.

A very special characteristic of this play is its use of 'over-determined' choices:[1] decisions, that is, for which no motives are given, not because there are none but because too many, conflicting emotional subtexts are possible. This is particularly the case with Coriolanus himself, but is not confined to him. Though it provokes him to his closest equivalent to a soliloquy, his decision to join forces with Aufidius is never really explained. In Plutarch he and his companions plan revenge immediately he goes into exile; but there is no hint of this in the parting scene, 4.1. In fact, the behaviour of the patricians in that scene completely contradicts his condemnation of them (4.5.76–9)—though Menenius confirms this (4.6.129–31)—and modern directors have had to resort to noises-off to supply the hooting of him from Rome.[2] Climactically, in 5.6 he gives no explanation at all of his decision to return to Antium instead of accompanying Volumnia and Virgilia back to Rome (this will be discussed under 'Interpretation'); but the most striking example of the technique occurs at the moment in 5.3 when Martius finally crumbles under his mother's pressure, and we get one of the most famous stage directions in the canon: '*Holds her by the hand, silent*' (5.3.183.1), where Shakespeare has added 'silent' to Plutarch's 'holding her hard by the right hand'. Actors prolong this moment for as long as they can manage, gauging its length each night by audience response. The longest seems to have been Nicol Williamson (RSC, 1973), who paused for sixty seconds before he stretched out his hand, then was able to hold the silence for an incredible ninety seconds more before he finally sobbed out, 'O mother, *mother*! . . . What . . . have . . . you . . . DONE?', giving each word 'like a pint of blood', according to Alan Brien.[3] What this long silence conveys, of course, is the

[1] For Shakespeare's use of *aporia*, see Philip Maguire, *Speechless Dialect: Shakespeare's Open Silences* (1985), *passim*.

[2] See p. 100; cf. Frances Ann Shirley, *Shakespeare's Use of Off-Stage Sounds* (1963), p. 90.

[3] *Plays and Players*, XXI, no. 3 (Dec. 1973), p. 33.

struggle of contradictory emotions within him, a silent battle while he listened with averted face to Volumnia's long plea, whose incongruities he had foretold immediately the embassy appeared (5.3.24–37).

There is a similar obscurity about the Tribunes' unexpected reduction of Martius' death sentence to banishment, in spite of Sicinius' earlier realization that 'To eject him hence | Were but our danger' (3.1.289–90) and the repeated insistence of both on execution from the Tarpeian rock. The respect for Martius' past services, which they offer as their reason for the clemency, presumably masks their actual fear of armed resistance or reprisals, but this is suggested only very obliquely in the scene itself by a request they make after Martius has left for a guard to attend them through the city. Terry Hands solved this problem in the 1977 RSC production by making Brutus a sentimentalist; so it was to Brutus that Menenius pleaded to give Coriolanus another chance to meet the voters, and Brutus (not the Folio's Sicinius) who agreed; and it was Brutus alone (without Sicinius' collaboration) who impulsively commuted the death sentence. Thus, it seemed logical that in 5.4 it is Brutus whom we are told the citizens have turned against because of Martius' march on Rome. (Other productions have had the Tribunes whisper agitatedly together before commuting the sentence, to provide some sense of motive.) Their fear of reprisal has been prepared for by Menenius' warnings of possible civil war at the end of 3.1, and appears openly later when in 4.2 they agree to seem humble now their plan has worked; but in the banishment itself their change of sentence comes as a surprise of whose cause we cannot be sure.

A similar moment, which is left for the actors and directors to interpret, is Volumnia's triumphant return to Rome in 5.5, which must contrast ironically with Martius' subsequent entry into Antium however it is played. An anomaly of this scene is the curious absence of an entry for the citizens (nor is there one for Menenius and Sicinius, though ostensibly they exit from the previous scene in order to join the celebration), but even more strikingly enigmatic is the lack of any indication of how the women themselves behave in it. The normally voluble Volumnia is completely silent. At one extreme, she may see this moment as her first personal triumph, no longer having to rely on Martius as her surrogate. Bridges-Adams certainly directed it this way in 1933 and, in fact, made this tiny scene (which is only six and a half lines long) the most elaborate and crowded of his production. The small-cast RSC production of 1977 also interpreted it this way, but introduced a final ironic twist, which was also incorporated into the RSC production of 1989. At the climax of the civic welcome, Volumnia flung back her cloak to reveal Young Martius, dressed and armed as a replica of his father in the battle scenes. Clearly, nothing had been learned; the psychological warping and political struggles would go on. At the other extreme, both productions at Stratford, Ontario (1961, 1981) emphasized the ironies of the situation by reducing the triumph to a torch-lit procession under cover of night, with the black-garbed women hurrying home grim-faced and weeping among huge flickering shadows.[1] Each of these interpretations simplifies to a single response, however, and the dramaturgy's ambivalence was captured more accurately by the National Theatre's production of 1984 in which Irene Worth combined exultation with grief, acknowledging the crowd's applause with outstretched arms while tears streamed down her face: 'Small, twitching smiles acknowledge the plaudits, but the eyes express a terrible desolation, since she already realizes he must die.'[2]

Finally, irony is conveyed even more powerfully by repetition, which is Shakespeare's main structural innovation in *Coriolanus*. The triumph in 2.1 (a Shakespeare addition) finds ironic parallels in both 5.5 and 5.6, which may well have been emphasized in the original staging; and another added scene, Volumnia's persuasion of her son to return to the voters in 3.2, not only inverts scenes where Coriolanus himself is the petitioner (2.3 and 4.5), but, more importantly, anticipates exactly the wheedling–sophistry–threats–withdrawal pattern of Volumnia's crucial pleading in 5.3. Coriolanus' capitulations to Volumnia twice drive him into intolerable situations from which his only release is a retreat into self-

---

[1] It was also played this way at the Old Vic in 1954 and in the 1972 RSC production.

[2] Francis King, *Sunday Telegraph*, 23 Dec. 1984.

destructive rage (added by Shakespeare in 5.6), and in each case the accusation of 'traitor' helps to trigger this. Similarly, his 'mean apparel' at Aufidius' house in Antium reflects his appearance in a 'gown of humility' in 2.3 (and, in turn, is reflected by the shabbiness of the women remarked on at 5.3.95–7), while *exile* from Rome is escalated to *assassination* in Antium. Thus, 'what happens to Coriolanus happens twice'.[1] And the last scene, in effect, offers an ironic reprise of the whole action, undermining Martius' fragile moral victory of 5.3 by delving, like the final act of *Lear*, to confront the ultimate defeat of death.

Combined with repetitions of imagery and phrasing, these many instances of 'anticipated echo'[2] give the play an extraordinary sense of control, and produce a feeling of inevitability in which social and psychological conditioning have replaced Plutarch's transcendental piety and the play is made to end in distressing ambivalence instead of with Plutarch's reassurance that the Volscians were soon to be defeated and Aufidius himself to die.

Contemporary Background

One of Shakespeare's main changes to Plutarch's 'Life of Coriolanus' is in the focus of plebeian rebellion in Rome. He alters Plutarch's account in two respects. He makes the main plebeian grievances the dearth of corn, the Senate's lack of action to redress this situation, and Martius' personal opposition to corn doles. In Plutarch the main grievances were unrewarded war service and usury (touched on only briefly in the play at 1.1.78–9), and the corn issue was only raised after the Volscian campaign (which helped to create it) and after Coriolanus had been refused the consulship. Secondly, there is the question of the tribunate—the principle of popular representation and its possible misuse. In Plutarch the right to tribunes had been granted before the corn riots, and these tribunes played no part in Martius' failure to become

---

[1] See F. E. Langman, ' "Atmosphere" and Repeated Action in *Coriolanus*', *Southern Review*, 3 (Adelaide, 1969), 324–33.

[2] Ibid., p. 30. Bullough (p. 477) considers *Coriolanus* to be Shakespeare's 'most unified play'.

consul—though they did play a part in his later banishment, to the extent of insisting on a vote by tribes instead of voting by 'centuries' (see 3.3.9–11 n.) which unduly favoured the patricians. Both of these changes—the emphasis on corn riots and the focus on Coriolanus' struggle with the Tribunes (and their manipulation of voting procedures to ensure his banishment)—reflect events in England during the first years of James I's reign which must have been evident to the play's original audience and may well have attracted Shakespeare to the story in the first place.

The Midland Uprising, 1607–8. The beginning of James's reign was a time of exceptionally bad harvests and soaring food prices, a cycle that had begun in the last years of Elizabeth and which the Poor Law Statutes of 1598–1601 only exacerbated—as is reflected in First Citizen's complaint about 'piercing statutes [that] chain up and restrain the poor' (1.1.80–1). In 1607–8 this resulted in an outbreak of rioting in several Northern and Midland counties, including Warwickshire—where Shakespeare's family, of course, still lived in Stratford-upon-Avon, only a few miles from Ladbroke and Hillmorton, two of the major centres of insurrection, and where he had recently bought property and may already have begun to live in semi-retirement. It was William Combe the elder—the man from whom Shakespeare had bought his Stratford property three years earlier—who, in his capacity as High Sheriff of the County, reported to Lord Salisbury from Warwick on 2 June 1608:

I am overbold to acquaint your lordship with such grievances as the common people of this country [i.e. county] . . . are troubled with: *videlicet*, with dearth of corn, the prices rising to some height, caused partly by some that are well stored, by refraining to bring the same to the market out of covetous conceit that corn will be dearer, and by engrossing of barley by maltsters, of the chief townsmen in every corporation, amongst whom the Justices of the country have no intermeddling. The matters make the people arrogantly and seditiously to speak of the not reforming of conversion of arable land into pasture by enclosing.[1]

---

[1] *State Papers Domestic: James I*, xxxiv. 4.

Unlike previous revolts, these were purely peasant uprisings, not led by disaffected gentry;[1] they were ill organized and pathetically ill equipped, and were put down savagely by the local gentry themselves, because, beyond the engrossing of corn, their ultimate target was the enclosure system, the amassing of large estates by driving peasants off their small-holdings in order to convert arable land to sheep pasture. The Crown at first encouraged this suppression of the uprising and, though it restricted the use of grain for starch and brewing, denied that serious famine existed. By mid-1608, however, the Privy Council had come to recognize the severity of the situation and had effectively admitted the justice of the rebels' cause by declaring an amnesty for the 'levellers'—those not already killed or executed—and reaffirming existing laws against enclosures and hoarding that had been allowed to lapse.[2] In several places phrasing in the play is very close to that of a petition from 'The Diggers of Warwickshire to all Other Diggers' (c.1607),[3] and the plebeians' arguments throughout, with their imagery of cannibalism (1.1.81–2), idle bellies (1.1.95–6), cormorants (1.1.118), and First Citizen's comment that 'the leanness that afflicts us ... is as an inventory to particularize their abundance; our sufferance is a gain to them' (1.1.18–21) draw on a vocabulary of 'moral economy'[4] complaint against enclosure and grain hoarding

[1] The Venetian ambassador emphasized this: see *Catalogue of State Papers Venetian*, ed. H. F. Brown (1904), ii. 146.

[2] For documentation see James F. Larkin and P. L. Hughes, eds., *Stuart Royal Proclamations* (1973), I, pp. 136–41, 152–4, 154–8, 161–2, 186–7, 188–92, 200–2, 202. The chief authorities on the 1607 uprising are E. F. Gay, 'The Midland Revolt and the Inquisition of Depopulation of 1607', *Transactions of the Royal Historical Society*, NS 18 (1909), 196–238; and John E. Martin, *Feudalism to Capitalism: Peasant and Landlord in English Agrarian Development* (1983), Part III, 'Case Study: The Midlands Revolt of 1607', pp. 159–215. See also E. C. Pettet, '*Coriolanus* and the Midlands Insurrection of 1607', *ShS*, 3 (1950), 34–42; Gordon Zeeveld, '*Coriolanus* and Jacobean Politics', *MLR*, 57 (1962), 321–34; F. E. Langman, 'Tell Me of Corn: Politics in *Coriolanus*', in Dennis Bartholomeusz, ed., *Studies in Shakespeare*, 1 (Monash UP, 1990), 1–19; Richard Wilson, 'Against the Grain: Representing the Market in *Coriolanus*', *The Seventeenth Century*, 6, no. 2 (1991), 111–48.

[3] Printed in J. Halliwell-Phillipps, ed., *The Marriage of Wit and Wisdom*, Shakespeare Society, vol. 22 (1846) pp. 140 ff.; cf. 1.1.4–5 n., 19–20 n. See Appendix B.

[4] The term was coined by E. P. Thompson, 'The Moral Economy of the English Crowd in the 18th Century', *Past and Present*, 50 (1971), 76–136.

that goes back to such early Tudor social critics as Hugh
Latimer, Robert Crowley, Thomas Becon, and—pre-eminently
for a collaborator in *The Book of Sir Thomas More*—to Thomas
More's scathing indictment in Book 2 of his *Utopia* (1514),
in which Raphael Hythloday complains that to equate nobility
with birth or wealth produces a 'pride' which 'measures
prosperity not by her own advantage but by the disadvantage
suffered by others [and tries to live] in circumstances where
her happiness can shine more brightly by comparison with
their miseries'.[1]

Because Shakespeare was a land-speculator, had recently
acquired a coat of arms, and was listed in 1598 as a storer
of malt in Stratford, it has been argued[2] that he *must* have
sided with the gentry in this struggle; but this seems questionable. External evidence for Shakespeare's attitude is ambiguous but, if anything, suggests opposition to enclosure rather
than support of it;[3] and his basic sympathies are more
safely gauged from Lear and Gloucester's hard lesson that it
is necessary to share 'the superflux' so 'each man have
enough' (*Lear*, 3.4.35, 4.1.65)—the phrasing of which is
closely echoed in 1.1.15–17 of *Coriolanus*, written very soon
after—and from his more sympathetic presentation of the
Roman populace in *Coriolanus* than of such earlier rebels as
the crowds of *2 Henry VI, Julius Caesar*, or even *Sir Thomas
More*, or—come to that—of the Volscian servingmen in *Coriolanus* itself. London would have given him ample experience
of mob violence by the 'masterless men' who were casualties
of enclosure and Elizabeth's ruinous wars; but if Shakespeare
was at Stratford for any length of time in the autumn of 1608,

[1] *Works of Sir Thomas More*, ed. E. J. Surtz and J. H. Hexter (1965), v. 242.
[2] e.g. by Pettet and Zeeveld; also by C. C. Huffman, *Coriolanus in Context*
(1971) and Green, *Plutarch Revisited*. That Shakespeare was more probably
pro-plebeian in this play is argued by *inter alia* John Palmer, *Political Characters
of Shakespeare* (1945), pp. 250 ff.; Brents Stirling, *The Populace in Shakespeare*
(1949), pp. 35–49; Kenneth Muir, 'In Defence of the Tribunes', *Essays in
Criticism*, 4 (1954), 331–3; Jonathan Dollimore, *Radical Tragedy* (1984),
pp. 218–30; Annabel Patterson, *Shakespeare and the Popular Voice* (1989),
pp. 120–43; and Shannon Miller, 'Topicality and Subversion in William Shakespeare's *Coriolanus*', *SEL*, 32 (1992), 287–310.
[3] See Chambers, ii. 99, 104–11, 125–6, 141–52; Eccles, pp. 92 ff.; Schoenbaum, pp. 178–80, 230 ff.; Edgar I. Fripp, *Master Richard Quyny* (1924),
pp. 126 ff., 167 ff., and *Shakespeare, Man and Artist* (1964), ii. 577–8.

he must also have encountered the miseries of famine at first hand among his neighbours; and I find no suggestion in the play that he did not sympathize with First Citizen's cry that 'the gods know, I speak this in hunger for bread, not in thirst for revenge' (1.1.22–3) nor the desperation of the choice he offers his fellows: 'You are all resolved rather to die than to famish?'—which echoes a paradox of the Diggers' Manifesto (see 1.1.4–5 n.). The balance of attitudes in the play seems rather to match that of the Reverend Robert Wilkinson, whose June 1607 sermon on the insurrection, delivered at Northampton before the Lord Lieutenant and members of a parliamentary commission to investigate the crisis, weighs compassion for the poor and indignation at hoarding and enclosures against condemnation of extremists who wish to level social hierarchy completely.[1]

Seventeenth-century Gentry. In the early seventeenth century the myth of the epic warrior to which *Coriolanus* belongs was also under pressure. Disaffection with Elizabeth's Irish wars a few years earlier had resulted in widespread resistance to enlistment, frequent desertions, and even mutiny; military machismo was already being questioned as an anachronism;[2] and the arrogance of the gentry, so obvious in the 1607 troubles and in the characterization of Martius, was a matter of growing concern. As Lawrence Stone and Anthony Esler have documented exhaustively,[3] the social mobility of the late Elizabethan and early Stuart period threw the whole definition of class into question; and the aristocracy, many of them 'new men', reacted with fierce self-assertion. There were plenty of young noblemen in the courts of Elizabeth and James who resembled Coriolanus, but two in particular stand out. Robert Devereux, second Earl of Essex and Queen Elizabeth's favourite, who was a close friend of Shakespeare's patron the Earl of Southampton and had been hailed by Shakespeare as

[1] See Appendix B; Wilkinson makes much use of the belly–members trope.
[2] See C. G. Cruikshank, *Elizabeth's Army* (rev. edn., 1966), pp. 30–2; Cyril Falls, *Elizabeth's Irish Wars* (1950), pp. 226–8; Paul A. Jorgensen, *Shakespeare's Military World* (1956), pp. 208–314; David Quinn, *The Elizabethans and the Irish* (1966), pp. 131–4.
[3] Lawrence Stone, *The Crisis of the Aristocracy, 1558–1641* (1965); Anthony Esler, *The Aspiring Mind of the Elizabethan Younger Generation* (1966).

'the general of our gracious empress' in the Chorus of *Henry V*, was executed in 1601 for trying to take London by force after a disastrous campaign in Ireland, and was specifically compared by Bishop Barlow in a sermon at Paul's Cross 'to Coriolanus, a gallant young, but a discontented Roman, who might make a fit parallel for the late Earl, if you read his life'.[1] And in some ways an even closer model was Sir Walter Ralegh, another favourite of the old queen and Essex's successful rival, who was notorious for his anti-Spanish warmongering, for his choleric pride, and for holding monopolies on several basic commodities, including cloth and wine, which kept their prices high. When he was put in charge of mobilizing the Cornish miners at the time of the Armada, Lord Treasurer Burleigh was warned they would not follow such a leader; the London mob attacked him when King James had him arrested in 1604; and, while Shakespeare was writing his play, Ralegh was actually in the Tower on trumped-up charges of treason, after a trial that, like Coriolanus', was a travesty.

The Question of Popular Franchise. Yet ironically, though the Londoners could not be expected to have known this, Ralegh's concept of government was much more democratic than the King's. James had set forth his absolutist doctrine of monarchy-above-the-law in a book called *The Trew Law of Free Monarchs* in 1598; and when he came to the throne of England five years later this brought him into immediate confrontation with the English House of Commons. One particularly relevant area of conflict was the King's right of 'purveyance'—the commandeering of supplies for the royal households—expenses for which rose astronomically in 1603 because Queen Anne and Prince Henry kept separate households and James himself was ridiculously extravagant. The Commons refused to ratify these expenses in 1604 and renewed their attack in 1606, raising the same questions of

[1] See Millar McLure, ed., *The Paul's Cross Sermons* (1958), pp. 80–6, 220. Essex may have been the model for Achilles in *Troilus and Cressida*, which was published in a revised text in 1609 with a cancel preface claiming it had never been 'clapper-claw'd with the palms of the vulgar', possibly after the same sort of 'private practice' as is suggested for *Coriolanus* below.

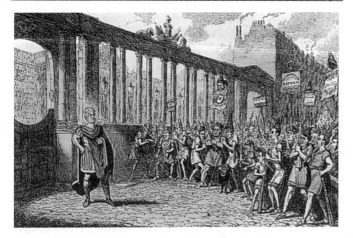

4. George Cruickshank, *Coriolanus addressing the Plebeians* (1820).
George IV (as Kemble) confronts radicals outside Carlton House

responsible stewardship as the plebeians raise about corn supplies in Rome.

Several details of this struggle are particularly relevant to the play. While the moderates repeatedly urged that the debate be conducted 'mildly'—the same word that is urged on Martius when in 3.2 he is forced back to face voters who have repudiated him—James reacted with characteristic vehemence and, in keeping with his attempt to identify his regime with Imperial Rome, disparaged his parliamentary critics as 'Tribunes of the people, whose mouths could not be stopped', warning that 'if any such plebeian tribunes should incur any offense . . . Parliament would correct them for it'.[1] The Commons counter-attacked immediately with an *Apology of the House of Commons, made to the King, touching their Privileges* (1604), in which they insisted on the people's

---

[1] Quoted in Zeeveld, p. 327. James was using '*Tribuni plebis*' to attack 'imagined Democracie' as early as his *Basilikon Doron* (1599), ed. James Craigie (1944), p. 77; cf. Jonathan Goldberg, *James I and the Politics of Literature* (1983), *passim*, for James's self-identification with Augustus. There was a climactic disagreement about absolutism and common law in 1608 when James offered to strike Chief Justice Coke and the latter was forced to kneel to express submission to the king: see Roland Usher, 'James I and Sir Edward Coke', *English Historical Review*, 18 (1903), p. 72; D. H. Willson, *King James VI and I* (1956), p. 259.

prerogative to approve laws which affected them, citing the traditional *vox populi, vox dei,* 'the voice of the people, in the things of their knowledge, is said to be the voice of God'— which is reflected in the play's emphasis on 'voices'.

The spokesmen of this parliamentary oppostion were puritanically inclined lawyers, who consistently bolstered their arguments by appeals to Common Law and established precedent, even when, in fact, they were extending Parliamentary authority; so that 'The winning of the initiative by the House of Commons was a radical step achieved under the smokescreen of the conservative ideology of a return to the past'.[1] This same appeal to tradition appeared simultaneously at lower levels. In 1607 a dispute arose about whether the Churchwardens of St Saviours in Southwark should be elected by all the parishioners—as an act of 32 Henry VIII (1541) had established—or be appointed by the rich families of the parish as had become the custom over the last fifty years, and in 1608 this was appealed to Parliament, which ruled firmly in favour of the traditional franchise. This could hardly have escaped Shakespeare's notice, since St Saviours was the parish in which the Globe was situated, and several details of the dispute parallel details of his play. It was alleged, for instance, that parish income had been used for 'private feasting' instead of for relief of the poor, and the Parliamentary ruling reiterated strongly the right of the 'common people' to their 'voices': 'In all Ages and Countries where Civil Offices are elective, the common People and Handicraftmen (tho' they were never admitted to exercise any Publick Offices) yet they were never denied Voices in Elections of Civil Officers.'[2] Similarly, the City of London appealed to tradition to defend itself against the Crown's encroachment on the right to tax and distribute foodstuffs landed from the Thames and against interventions by the royal marshals—in riots reminiscent of 3.1—when city magistrates attempted to arrest lawbreakers

[1] Lawrence Stone, *The Causes of the English Revolution* (1972), p. 93. There was no such tradition of constitutional freedom to appeal to in Coriolanus' Rome.

[2] John Stow, *A Survey of the Cities of London and Westminster ... Corrected, Improved, and very much Enlarged ... to the present Time; by John Strype* (1720), vol. ii, Book 4, p. 10.

in the purlieus of the Tower. So successful were such arguments that James granted London a new charter in 1608, the year when *Coriolanus* was probably written, not only guaranteeing its traditional prerogatives but even extending them to such previous royal 'liberties' as Blackfriars, Whitefriars, and West Smithfield.[1] As Blackfriars sheltered the King's Men's new theatre, this is certainly something that would have attracted Shakespeare's notice, and a comparable exploitation of 'legal antiquarianism' (to borrow a phrase from Christopher Hill) lies behind the play's pervasive legal terminology and the Tribunes' constant appeals to custom and traditional right—neither of which can be found in Plutarch.[2]

Electoral Procedures. A final area of conflict between James and Parliament, in fact, which is again reflected in the play's divergencies from Plutarch, is the problematics of Coriolanus' election to consul. As Mark Kishlansky has pointed out, Shakespeare's procedure here contaminates Roman with English custom. Coriolanus in this play is the only nominee for a single position, rather than one of three candidates for two consulships, and instead of canvassing the citizens' votes before appearing before them *en masse* for election, as in Plutarch, Shakespeare's Coriolanus is first selected by the Senate, then sent to seek what is presumed to be merely formal *acclamation* by the people's 'voices', which he sees no reason, except custom, to solicit. This reflects current English practice, where

[1] See W. H. Overall, ed., *Analytical Index to . . . the Remembrancia of London . . . 1579–1664* (1878), pp. 426–38, and Chambers, *Elizabethan Stage*, ii. 480, 511. The struggle between the King and City is discussed at length in Chap. 4 of Leah Marcus, *Puzzling Shakespeare: Local Reading and Its Discontents* (1988).

[2] Even closer to home, in 1601 Sir Edward Greville tried to enclose the common lands at Stratford-upon-Avon and opposed the re-election as town bailiff of Shakespeare's friend and close neighbour Richard Quiny, on the grounds that it was his own prerogative to appoint to that office. Quiny and the town clerk, Thomas Greene (Shakespeare's cousin by marriage and lengthy house-guest at New Place), went to London to plead Stratford's *traditional rights*, basing their appeal on a document drawn up after consultation with four of the oldest inhabitants, including the playwright's father, John Shakespeare. Thanks to intervention by the Attorney General, Sir Edward Coke, the case was ruled in Stratford's favour, though a few months later Quiny was killed in a scuffle with Greville's followers. In 1616 Quiny's son Thomas was to marry Shakespeare's younger daughter, Judith.

a predetermined candidate was confirmed by collective shouted assent 'grounded on participation rather than choice, and on unanimity rather than majority',[1] and where individual canvassing was rejected as undignified and, in fact, had specifically been forbidden by the Privy Council in 1604.

The period saw the beginning of changes in this pattern of election, however. Inflation enabled more people to reach the income of forty pounds a year that determined eligibility to vote; local voters began to demand more say in whom they chose and more influence over their representative's choice of policy; and there was a growing number of disputed elections, with the crown and Parliament bickering from 1604 onwards as to which should have jurisdiction over them.[2] Shakespeare may even have had personal experience of such a disputed election in 1601, when the senior MP for Warwickshire, Fulke Greville, was not returned, apparently because the voters changed their minds like the plebeians in the play, and Sir Thomas Lucy, the County Sheriff, tried to postpone a return until he could consult the county as a whole. The Privy Council, however, accusing Lucy of a plot to supplant Greville, ordered him not only to rehold the election immediately but also to make sure that the person 'chosen' was Fulke Greville—whose services as Secretary to the Navy were urgently needed because of a Spanish invasion in Ireland; and it was only with the acknowledged help of Shakespeare's friend Richard Quiny and the voters of Stratford-upon-Avon that Lucy finally accomplished this.[3]

The exact extent of Parliamentary opposition to James and of changes in attitudes to election as early as 1608 are currently matters of hot debate among historians, and it would be rash to speculate about Shakespeare's own opinion by deductions from *Coriolanus*. It is significant, however, that his treatment of the election principle should be so current, and, as Kishlansky points out, *Coriolanus* goes beyond contemporary practice by having one citizen assume that what is needed is

[1] Mark Kishlansky, *Parliamentary Selection: Social and Political Choice in Early Modern England* (1986), pp. 4–5, 7–8.

[2] See Derek Hirst, *The Representatives of the People: Voters and Voting in England under the Early Stuarts* (1975), *passim*.

[3] See *Acts of the Privy Council, New Series*, ed. John Roche Dasent (1907), vol. 32, pp. 247–9; Edgar I. Fripp, *Master Richard Quiny* (1924), p. 190; and Wilson, 'Against the Grain', pp. 126 ff.

a majority vote, not acclamation: 'But that's no matter, the greater part carries it' (2.3.35); by having another emphasize the importance of individual choice: 'He's to make his requests by particulars; wherein everyone of us has a single honour in giving him our own voices with our own tongues' (2.3.41–3); and by having Sicinius interpret Plutarch's tactic of counting votes by 'tribes' apparently as a head-count: 'Have you a catalogue | Of all the voices that we have procured, | Set down by th' poll?' (3.3.8–10). Some reformers were already urging this practice in England, but it was not actually instituted till after 1625. This does not prove that Shakespeare advocated such a reform, of course. What is important is that his play is politically sophisticated enough to open up such issues and to expect his audience to appreciate them.

Interpretation

The special brilliance of *Coriolanus* is its insight into the mutual influence of psychology and politics. There are two distinct political levels in the play. The obvious one is the class conflict between patricians and plebeians, which is complicated by external war against the Volsces and raises the problems of right government. But there is also the more basic question of 'patriotism'. What is it shapes the link between an individual and his society before class-conflict even appears? This involves the way that family relationships shape individual identity, and the dependence of those relationships in their turn on the wider values and expectations of society as encoded in its institutions and its language. And this then, inevitably, raises the tragic question of whether there can ever be such things as human freedom or 'individuality'. Thus, *Coriolanus* operates on at least three levels simultaneously: political, psychological, and philosophical—or, more precisely, 'existential'. And these levels no longer parallel each other neatly, as they did earlier in the Shakespeare canon; they interact in a complex, open dialectic which requires the utmost flexibility of response.

Political. We have seen that, besides being in the line of Shakespeare's developing concept of politics, *Coriolanus* also

5. Volumnia (Wanda Capodaglia) and Virgilia (Relda Ridoni) in Giorgio Strehler's 1957–8 production at the Piccolo Teatro, Milan

touched certain sensitive issues of the early 1600s which eventually resulted in the Civil War of 1642. What was basically in question was the concept of the state as a fixed hierarchy, with authority as unquestionable—a form of government that historically had been found the most efficient in protecting a society's food supply from external attack. This tradition of hierarchy is presented in the equally traditional parable of the belly-and-members with which Menenius 'diverts' the rioters in the first scene. One of the recurrent conservative errors in interpreting *Coriolanus* is to take this parable, and Menenius himself, too seriously and then to assume that they represent Shakespeare's own opinion. The allegory is clearly shown to be at variance with the facts of Roman life; but, even beyond this, I think it is meant to be questionable as an ideal. For a seventeenth-century audience, accustomed to hearing the image used as justification for kingship (it was a favourite with King James), it would seem odd in the first place to apply it to a non-monarchical state;

and this is pointed by the fact that, though the Second Citizen brings up the 'kingly, crownèd head' (1.1.112), Menenius' parable has no head; just members, and the smiling sovereign belching belly. Moreover, the abstract, inflexible power structure behind Menenius' advocacy has already been exposed in his earlier warning to the rioters:

> you may as well
> Strike at the heaven with your staves as lift them
> Against the Roman state, whose course will on
> The way it takes, cracking ten thousand curbs
> Of more strong link asunder than can ever
> Appear in your impediment.
>
> (1.1.64–9)

Later, the same juggernaut image of a resistless, impersonal machine will be applied several times to Coriolanus, the creature of this dehumanizing process.

Besides these limitations of the body politic ideal itself, there is also the fact that anyway it is clearly lip-service, ignored in practice by the patricians as much as by the plebeians. Menenius himself uses it as a way of quietening and delaying the rioters. As soon as Martius shows up, his tune changes to 'Rome and her rats are at the point of battle' (1.1.159). Menenius is a dangerous character dramaturgically because, in addition to his conciliatory pragmatism, he is a surrogate father-figure whose wit and *joie de vivre* are a welcome relief from the strain of Roman *gravitas*, and there is no doubt that he has genuine affection for 'my son Coriolanus'. It must be recognized, however, that Menenius is a voluptuary and drunkard, revelling in feasts while he sympathizes with the starving poor; a wily clown who uses humour for selfish ends; with a touch of the scurrilous railer too whenever his personal interests are crossed (e.g. 3.1.257–62, 298–9; 5.4.12–29). Politically he is pure opportunist, not conservative at all: a sail-trimmer, who backs up Volumnia when she tells Martius that there is no need to be sincere in wooing plebeian votes, yet grows 'most kind' to the Tribunes when they in turn are in power; who separates Rome from her 'rats' when all is well, but wriggles from responsibility by calling it 'your doing' (as Cominius calls it 'your Rome') when news comes of

Aufidius' renewed attack. His confidence that Martius will spare the city if only he has dined well shows grotesque misunderstanding of the man he persists in calling 'son', though it tells us as much about Menenius as the belly fable earlier; dramatic irony is used twice in the final scenes to undermine whatever confidence we may have left in his sagacity (see 'Structure'); and in 5.2 his boasts about lying on Coriolanus' behalf, rancorous suggestion that the Volscian guard be tortured to death, and artificial address to Martius, with its purely rhetorical claim to tears (l. 71), combine to show him in the worst possible light. We feel sorry at his rebuff, but scarcely surprised; and, appropriately, he disappears from the play as Sicinius' companion in 5.4, replacing the unfortunate Brutus. It is impossible to imagine this Menenius dying penniless as he does in Plutarch! And the rest of the patricians are no better. They do not defend Coriolanus and even let him be hooted out of Rome by the mob—a Shakespeare addition which helps explain his un-Plutarchian anger against patricians and plebeians alike and provides him with a rationalization for his deeper urge to join Aufidius.

Yet the citizens on their side are also seen to be unreliable, and recent historicist critics who have argued for a subversive, left-wing intention in the play overstate their case. The plebeians are certainly presented more favourably than rebellious crowds in previous Shakespeare plays, and it is clear that Shakespeare sympathizes with their desperation (see p. 36). He shows them individually as humorous and shrewd, touchingly self-critical, and requiring only that their votes be asked for 'kindly' (2.3.71), meaning 'also human', naturally 'kin'. *En masse*, however, they are the usual Shakespeare mob: irrational, unstable, savage, and at the mercy of every whim and demagogue; and the Folio text itself includes such unflattering directions as '*Citizens steal away*', '*Enter a rabble of Plebeians*', '*this mutiny*', '*Enter . . . the rabble again*' (1.1.248; 3.1.181.1, 229.1, 265). They are also, for the most part, bad soldiers, reluctant to fight, ready to run, and eager to loot: all Shakespeare additions. Their own Tribunes describe them scathingly and manipulate them as cynically as the patricians. Yet the Tribunes are not villains either. Their cause is basically just; historically, their triumph ushered in the centuries of Roman greatness; and Shakespeare contradicts Plutarch's picture of a Rome left dangerously divided by Martius' exile to give us an attractive, if slightly ludicrous, vignette of their satisfaction with a conciliatory Menenius and the grateful Roman populace before news comes of the Volscians' renewed attack. However, as John Palmer suggests, the cynical explanation they find in scene one for Martius' willingness to serve under Cominius—that this will let him take credit for a victory but leave Cominius to bear responsibility for defeat—gives us their measure immediately. The Tribunes are clever but mean-minded men, chiefly concerned to maintain their own authority, skilful at internal politics but unimaginative about foreign affairs. On the other hand, they learn quickly. They help Cominius persuade Volumnia to plead with Coriolanus, and at the end Sicinius politically (in both senses) hurries off to join Menenius in Volumnia's victory parade.

Thus, the facts of Roman life on both sides, including his own character, give Menenius' parable the lie. What we see is no organic body politic but a Rome torn by factional strife, Machiavelli's politics of the power struggle, reflected in the play's imagery of bodily fragmentation. Characteristically, however, the only person who states openly what all confess to privately is Coriolanus himself. His grasp that

> when two authorities are up,
> Neither supreme, how soon confusion
> May enter 'twixt the gap of both and take
> The one by th'other

$$(3.1.111-14)$$

is essentially correct; but his way of dealing with it is all wrong. Like Volumnia he is willing to see politics as no different from war; but, unlike her, he sees war romantically, not in terms of clever tactics but as defiant solo heroism: a very different vision from the realities of drying blood upon the face, aching wounds, the tears of widows and orphans, hostages, rape, pillage, espionage, and the arbitrary decrees of an army of occupation, of which Shakespeare carefully reminds us.

But if Coriolanus has no personal ideal of the body politic— merely of the realities of power or, at best, a sense of patrician solidarity—what then is his link to the state? It is, of course, the link of personal loyalty, working mainly through his mother. Besides testing the tradition of a body politic—the trope of Menenius' famous speech—Shakespeare's play also tests the commonplace of mother country, 'our dear nurse' (5.3.111) as Volumnia puts it, identifying Rome as usual with herself. And the crucial phrase, on which the whole play hinges, is Aufidius' taunt of 'boy of tears'—the image of a damaged adolescent, agonizingly dependent on his mother, with which Martius' self-control is broken down in Antium to betray him to his death. This term 'boy' is both the psychological and political heart of *Coriolanus*, because clearly Martius is Volumnia's creation, as Volumnia is Rome's; and the invented account of Young Martius, ripping apart a butterfly to his grandmother's delight, shows just how Coriolanus has been raised.

Psychological. Whereas Romantic and Victorian critics idealized Volumnia as 'a Roman matron, conceived in the antique spirit',[1] late twentieth-century commentators have been just as extreme in condemning her as an emasculating virago;[2] and, paradoxically, none more vehemently so than recent feminist critics.[3] This view too is oversimple, but it reveals much more than idealization did.

It is obvious from the start that Martius is both Volumnia's husband surrogate—'If my son were my husband' (1.3.2) are almost her first words[4]—and her means to vicarious power in a society where women's status depends wholly on their men. She shows almost no feeling for him as a separate person. She exults grotesquely with Menenius over the number of wounds he is bringing back—their glee deliberately contrasted

[1] Anna Jameson, *Characteristics of Women, Moral, Poetical, and Historical* (1837), p. 282.

[2] e.g. Coppélia Kahn, *Man's Estate: Masculine Identity in Shakespeare* (1981); Marjorie Garber, *Coming of Age in Shakespeare* (1981); Peter Erickson, *Patriarchal Structures in Shakespeare's Drama* (1985).

[3] Cf. Lisa Lowe, ' "Say I play the man I am": Gender and Politics in *Coriolanus*', *Kenyon Review*, NS 8 (1986), 86–95, and Madelon Sprengnether, 'Annihilating Intimacy in *Coriolanus*', in Mary Beth Rose, ed., *Women in the Middle Ages and the Renaissance: Literary and Historical Perspectives* (1986), 89–111, both of whom emphasize the way that Volumnia has internalized the patriarchal culture of Rome (cf. 4.2.18–20 n.)

[4] In Livy 'Volumnia' is actually the name of Coriolanus' wife.

to Virgilia's distress—and is almost beside herself with triumph in 2.1 as she realizes the way is now open for him to be elected consul, the 'one thing wanting' to complete 'the buildings of [her] fancy' (ll. 196–7), despite his own demurral. The narcissism which leads her later to identify with Rome (5.3.123–6) and with Rome's tutelary goddess, Juno (4.2.56)—who incidentally bore Mars, the war god to whom Martius is so often compared, without male impregnation[1]— makes her regard her son as a mere extension of herself. Husband, father, and military commander, he is still 'my *boy* Martius' (2.1.97), 'my gentle Martius' (2.1.168); 'Thy valiantness was mine' (3.2.131), she tells him, 'Thou art my warrior, | I holp to frame thee' (5.3.62–3). And Martius' oddly impersonal identification of her as 'the honoured mould | Wherein this trunk was framed' (5.3.22–3) shows just how basically he has accepted her appropriation.

Whereas Plutarch says Volumnia's fault was overleniency, Shakespeare with brilliant insight makes her rather oversevere —one of the 'taboo-on-tenderness' school of childrearing.[2] According to Object Relations psychology, overdependency can result if a mother disturbs the balance of an infant's autonomy-attachment by being either too lenient or too strict, and the play suggests that Volumnia has been both. She can be indiscriminately indulgent to Young Martius because at that age upper-class Roman (and Jacobean) infants were looked after by the servants; later, however, when the mother herself took over a son's education, there was apt to be what Suttie calls an abrupt 'psychic weening'. We hear that when Martius was still 'tender-bodied', Volumnia sent him to 'a cruel war' to earn 'renown' or die, though she boasts that even other Roman mothers would not have parted with him.[3] She, however, has always demanded that her love be earned.

---

[1] See Ovid, *Fasti* (v. 229–60), trans. J. Frazer (Loeb edn., 1959), pp. 277–9; cf. Peggy M. Simonds, 'Coriolanus and the Myth of Juno and Mars', *Mosaic*, 18 (1985), 33–50.

[2] Ian D. Suttie, *The Origins of Love and Hate* (1935, repr. 1963), pp. 86–100, esp. p. 91.

[3] She sent Martius to war when he was sixteen (2.2.85) and still 'impubes' (without facial hair), which was a year before an adolescent was supposed to begin his military service: Michael J. G. Gray-Fow, *The Nomenclature and Stages of Roman Childhood* (1985), p. 157.

The citizens immediately tell us that Martius' 'services for his country' were done partly 'to please his mother' (1.1.35–6); and when Volumnia forces him back to face voters who have broken their word to him, she combines the authoritarianism of 'Go, and be ruled . . . He must, and will' (3.2.92, 99) with seductiveness:

> I prithee now, sweet son, as thou hast said
> My praises made thee first a soldier, so,
> To have my praise for this, perform a part
> Thou hast not done before.
>
> (3.2.109–12)

This scene, in fact, exposes the methods by which Volumnia habitually manipulates her son. She wheedles, flatters, teases, browbeats, seduces, and uses emotional blackmail; and her final trick, which always works, is icy withdrawal with a threat of her own death.

Volumnia's corruption of nurture into aggression is strikingly emblematized by her assertion that

> The breasts of Hecuba
> When she did suckle Hector looked not lovelier
> Than Hector's forehead when it spit forth blood
> At Grecian sword, contemning.
>
> (1.3.41–4)

Janet Adelman[1] interprets this grotesque comparison as an image of Volumnia's emotional starvation of her son, and relates it to the patricians' denial of grain to the plebeians as parallel instances of Rome's life-denying ethos. There is also implicit in it hostility to her child's dependency (to which Martius also reacts);[2] as Stanley Cavell puts it, 'the suckling mother is presented as being slashed by the son-hero, eaten

---

[1] Janet Adelman, ' "Anger's My Meat": Feeding, Dependency, and Aggression in *Coriolanus*', in David Bevington and Jay Halio, eds., *Shakespeare, Pattern of Excelling Nature* (1978), 108–24, revised as part of Chap. 6 in her *Suffocating Mothers: Fantasies of Origin in Shakespeare's Plays, 'Hamlet' to 'The Tempest'* (1992), 146–64.

[2] Cf. such writers as: Melanie Klein, *Envy and Gratitude* (1957); Christiane Olivier, *Jocasta's Children: the Imprint of the Mother*, trans. George Craig (1988); Maud Mannoni, *The Child, His 'Illness', and the Others* (1967, trans. 1973). See David B. Barron, '*Coriolanus*: Portrait of the Artist as an Infant', *American Imago*, 19 (1962), 171–93.

by the one she feeds':[1] lactating breast is equated with bleeding forehead, Hector's sucking mouth with 'Grecian sword'. And it is also, of course, an image of equivalency: for Volumnia's 'milk' (i.e. love and approval) Martius must shed his blood in battle (as he literally does in Act 1). But when she uses a similar image in 'Thy valiantness was mine, thou suck'st it from me' (3.2.131) the metrical stress on 'from' suggests that Martius has taken from her what was rightfully her own (cf.3.2.129–30). As Sicinius' 'Are you mankind?' (4.2.18) puts it bluntly later, there is a challenging 'masculine' ability about Volumnia that she resents having to satisfy through Martius' surrogacy.[2]

Interpreted in this way, Volumnia provides a classic example of the widow of an apparently loveless marriage, left with an only son whom she uses to vindicate her own sexuality and to 'master' a patriarchal system that denies her other outlets. So D. W. Harding sees her as 'Shakespeare's most blood-chilling study of the destructive consequences of a woman's living out at someone else's expense her fantasy of what manhood should be. . . . She gains control through [Martius] of the sort of person she believes she could be if only she were a man.'[3] And Philip Slater, discussing similar situations in early Greece, emphasizes the inevitable ambivalence of such a mother's feelings: 'Her need for self-expression and vindication requires her both to exalt and belittle her son, to feed on and destroy him.'[4] As Menenius fears about 'renownèd Rome', there is the likelihood that Volumnia 'like an unnatural dam' will 'now eat up her own' (3.1.293–6).

This view is certainly more perceptive than uncritical idealization, and will probably remain the main way of interpreting Volumnia for some time to come; but it is by no means the full truth either. It needs to be qualified by at least three

[1] Stanley Cavell, ' "Who does the wolf love?": *Coriolanus* and the Interpretations of Politics', in Patricia Parker and Geoffrey Hartman, eds., *Shakespeare and the Question of Theory* (1985), p. 254. Adelman (see p. 51 n. 1), however, equates the sword with the breast, the sucking mouth with wounds; the image cuts both ways.

[2] M. C. Bradbrook suggests that Volumnia's role was probably played by a man rather than a boy; *Shakespeare: The Poet in his World* (1978), p. 214.

[3] Harding, p. 252.

[4] Philip E. Slater, *The Glory of Hera* (1968), p. 133.

considerations. A skilled actress will always look for opportunities to play against her character's main 'line', and the obvious way to do this for Volumnia is to find occasion to reassert her 'womanliness' (to borrow a term from Edith Evans, who played the role in 1959 to Olivier's Coriolanus[1]). In cultural terms, moreover, Volumnia is as much the victim as the agent of Rome's emphasis on *virtus*; so instead of dismissing her without sympathy as a neurotic virago, it is fairer to see her as someone struggling to interpret motherhood in terms of her society. The difficulty Lady Macbeth has in 'unsexing' herself (with a comparable distortion of breast-feeding to child-murder) can provide a clue to Volumnia's predicament;[2] and the alliance between Volumnia and Virgilia to attack the Tribunes in 4.2, then threaten Martius with their joint suicide in the pleading scene (5.3.125–8), should encourage us to re-evaluate not only Virgilia but Volumnia as well.[3] The two women are not so unlike by the end of the play as they seemed to be in the early sewing scene.

This leads to the third consideration. Dramatically, Volumnia is a vivid character in her own right, not just an explanation for Coriolanus' inadequacies; and she too can be observed to change during the course of the play.[4] Thus, her impatience with Virgilia in 1.3 is less unsympathetic if we interpret it as a reaction to the expression of emotions she herself has had to struggle to suppress; and her exaggerated bellicosity in that scene can be understood as a way of pre-empting what she fears the most—overstatements to deceive herself as much as others. Her excitement in 2.1 is as plausibly interpreted as exhilaration at Martius' safety as gratification of her own ambition; and by beginning that scene with Menenius and the Tribunes and keeping the former as a running commentator throughout the triumph, Shakespeare establishes a comic tone for the whole scene, to which Martius' teasing greetings conform. Martius' reaction to his

[1] Cited in Stanley Wells, *Royal Shakespeare: Four Major Productions at Stratford-upon-Avon* (1977), pp. 15–16.

[2] Harding, p. 245.

[3] Cf. Norman Rabkin, *Shakespeare and the Common Understanding* (1967), p. 126.

[4] This is discussed by Christina Luckyj, 'Volumnia's Silence', *SEL*, 31 (1991), 327–41, to whose arguments I am indebted.

mother is constantly softened by humour: he even teases her in 4.1, where he specifically emphasizes that her tears and solicitude now differ from her normal persona and relate her to the weeping Virgilia ('these sad women', 4.1.26); and Christina Luckyj notes illuminatingly that, though 3.2 is undoubtedly invented to anticipate 5.3, the two scenes have quite different tones. Whereas in 3.2 Volumnia is cynical, and even parodic in her demonstrations of flattery, and Martius' submission retains an edge of mocking impertinence, in 5.3 both are deadly serious. Volumnia's shabby dress, to which she draws attention, recalls Martius' significant costume changes earlier (see 'Original Staging'); this time she allows Virgilia to go first; and she appeals strongly to Martius' love of family, as she did not do before. She now pleads for all 'Romans', moreover, not just for the patricians; and the mother who boasted of sending her sixteen-year-old to 'cruel war' now pleads for 'th'interpretation of full time' to allow her grandson opportunity to mature.

It remains unclear whether Volumnia realizes Martius will not return to Rome—that depends upon our interpretation of the question (and speaker) that prompts his enigmatic 'Ay, by and by' (5.3.203 n.)—so her behaviour in the triumph of 5.5 can justifiably be shaded in many ways (see 'Structure'); but her complete silence now—not only in 5.5 but also after Martius' submission in 5.3—is so different from her characteristic volubility that it must mark some definite change in her; and grief would seem to be the most plausible explanation for it. She is facing the reality of a sacrifice she glibly exaggerated in 1.3; and, if she realizes this, her fate too is tragic.

Coriolanus himself has a similar complexity. Besides falsifying her own character, overemphasis on Volumnia's destructiveness also has the effect of diminishing Martius' tragedy to the case history of an abused child, the pathetic 'boy of tears'. It is imperative to balance against this the play's forcible presentation of him as a hero, with impressive, even attractive, qualities.[1] There are his 'great services to Rome',

---

[1] Useful defences of Martius' virtue despite his obvious defects can be found in: Ellis-Fermor, pp. 60–77; Brian Vickers, *Shakespeare: Coriolanus* (1976); John Bligh, 'The Mind of Coriolanus', *English Studies in Canada*, 13 (1987), 256–70; and the Sanders essay below. Cf. also Reuben Brower, *Hero and Saint:*

for instance, which the action of the play confirms and which not even his enemies dispute. The battle scenes of Act 1 are treated at such length partly to impress the audience with Martius' glamour and charisma as a warrior (see 'Original Staging'); and Shakespeare has also endowed him with terse wit so that 'we laugh and are complicit'.[1] 'Choler', which contemporaries would recognize as Martius' dominant 'humour' (cf. 3.1.86, 87; 3.3.25),[2] was believed to be the emotional source not just of strife but also of mankind's creativity and urge to self-transcendence;[3] and Martius' ideals of self-sacrifice for Rome and devotion to the truth, while they may be naïve and doomed to fail historically, are nobler than the other characters' self-serving 'policy' and readiness to lie. Aufidius, for example, who is the sort of hero Volumnia and Menenius (and even some modern critics) would seem to prefer, stands in relation to Martius as Laertes does to Hamlet, or Pompey and Octavius Caesar to Mark Antony: an almost great man is faced with the real thing, whose superiority he resents but never fails to recognize. And most important of all, there is an inarticulate tenderness between Martius and Virgilia which suggests a deeper, more emotionally sensitive level to Coriolanus than publicly—perhaps even consciously— he ever will admit. Martius consistently exhibits unease about the damage war does to women and children; and his succumbing to the women's plea is never really in doubt because, at first sight of Virgilia's 'dove's eyes', he admits, 'I melt, and am not | Of stronger earth than others' (5.3.27–9). He also recognizes his self-created identity as a revenger for what it

Shakespeare and the Graeco-Roman Heroic Tradition (1971), pp. 354–81, and James C. Bulman, *The Heroic Idiom of Shakespearean Tragedy* (1985), *passim*.

[1] Wilbur Sanders, 'An Impossible Person: Caius Marcius Coriolanus', in W. Sanders and H. Jakobson, *Shakespeare's Magnanimity: Four Tragic Heroes, Their Friends and Families* (1978), p. 142.

[2] e.g. Dover Wilson, p. xxvi: 'he is Shakespeare's study of a choleric man'; John W. Draper, 'Shakespeare's Coriolanus: a Study in Renaissance Psychology', *West Virginia University Bulletin: Philological Studies*, 3 (1939), 22–36. Amongst other things, Martius (like Hotspur) exhibits the sudden fits of amnesia which were thought to be typical of this temperament.

[3] Cf. Francis Bacon in his essay 'Of Ambition' and Book 1 of *The Advancement of Learning*, in James Spedding, ed., *Works of Bacon* (1859–61) vi. 465, and iii. 318, respectively. Alfred Adler and Anthony Storr make the same point about 'aggression'.

actually is, a mere persona created to restore meaning to his actions: 'Like a dull actor now', he admits, 'I have forgot my part, and I am out | Even to a full disgrace' (5.3.40–2); as earlier he saw not only that any pretence of conciliating the plebeians was 'a part', but also, more profoundly, that 'the man I am' was also 'play[ed]' (3.2.15–6)—an insight with which Volumnia tartly agreed (3.2.19–20). There is always a sense of strain about Martius' 'macho' toughness, in fact, which increases as the play proceeds and progressively reveals the emotional need and hurt beneath it. In Thomas Africa's striking phrase about the 'Coriolanus complex' in general, he is 'a suit of armour inside of which is encapsulated a child'.[1] The 1973 RSC production conveyed precisely the same perception by beginning with a mime in which, by gradually donning his armour, a weedy, gangling, worried-looking Martius was transformed Brechtianly to a 'driven' killer.

These admirable and sympathetic factors in the character should carry considerable weight, particularly in performance; but what is most fascinating about Caius Martius is not his strengths, which we must accept as historical givens, but Shakespeare's insight into the nature of his weakness. His behaviour can be illuminated from many psychoanalytical approaches, but the most useful paradigm amalgamates Freud's discussions of narcissism, Object Relations theory, and Lacan's more recent linguistic refinements of Freud. According to this pattern, a child depends on erotic 'mirroring' by its mother to develop an initial sense of separate identity. This primary concept of itself is always very physical in nature because it predates language ('infans' literally means 'speechless'), and, even at best, is always to some extent both faulty and inadequate, leaving a residual 'desire' for the still absent 'Other'. If 'mirroring' is denied, moreover, or is manipulated by the mother to supply her own emotional deficiencies (as Volumnia uses Martius), this unsatisfied 'desire' will be augmented and distorted into neurosis, particularly when there are no siblings and no father to offset the mother's influence. Eroticism then becomes transformed into aggression—hence

[1] Thomas W. Africa talks of the 'Coriolanus complex' as typical of Rome in 'Portrait of an Assassin: a Psychoanalytical Study of M. Junius Brutus', *Journal of Interdisciplinary History*, 8 (1978), 599–626, esp. p. 611.

the interchange of sex and warfare in the imagery of *Coriolanus* (see 'Style'); a disturbed sense of identity will be reflected in images of physical fragmentation and suicidal demands on one's own body; and the overdependent (because needy) child is trapped in whatever model of behaviour the mother extorts as the price of recognition, while at the same time resenting this demand from her. In Martius' case, these reactions coalesce in his image of himself as a warrior: highly physical, distrustful of language (see 'Style'), self-sufficient, and self-consciously hardened against all softer emotions—particularly pity and fear, which produce tears—as weaknesses fit only for women, children, or beggars (cf. 3.2.114 ff.). Three aspects of this negative side to Martius' character are worth special attention: his increasing isolation, and his relationships to Aufidius and to the plebeians.

Coriolanus is never really self-sufficient. He cannot bear the actual solitude of exile, but needs constantly to see himself opposed to other people. Thus, the central, recurrent image of the play is Martius against the rest. He lacks almost any developed sense of comradeship, even with his fellow commanders. He prefers to do things *alone*—the word re-echoes through his speeches ('O, me alone!', 'Alone I did it'); and, as we have seen, Shakespeare alters Plutarch several times to emphasize this isolation. Martius seems at home only on the battlefield, and then only fully when he is in single combat. He refuses praise less from modesty than to keep his comrades at a distance; and forgetting the name of his 'kindly' Corioles host, he leaves him to his fate. The plebeians are mere raw material for his battles; 'rats'; a beastly 'herd'; or disembodied 'voices'. And even Aufidius, whom he sees too idealistically as his one chivalric equal, is rapidly pushed into second place when Martius joins him, taking over his command as earlier he had done Cominius' in spite of his oath to serve, which Shakespeare has so pointedly emphasized (1.1.236–7). This separation culminates as, feeling himself 'a kind of nothing' (5.1.13), he tries to 'stand | As if a man were author of himself' (5.3.35–6); then, faced with the demands of Volumnia and Virgilia, to retreat into a denial of communication that has been called 'the most massive silence in all drama'.[1]

[1] Sanders, p. 164.

Such an absence of relationship is awe-inspiring. 'He that is incapable of living in society', says Aristotle in Book 1 of the *Politics*, 'is either a god or a beast';[1] and both friends and enemies constantly compare Martius to a god. But the Coriolanus who is welcomed back to Rome like a deity (2.1.215, 261–2), is driven out again like a beast, a 'lonely dragon' relegated to 'the city of kites and crows'. And, even more illuminatingly, he is several times reified to a 'thing', a killing machine or monstrous blood-covered juggernaut (see 'Imagery and Themes'), like Menenius' opening description of the impersonal Roman state (1.1.64–9).

In an early essay on Leonardo da Vinci,[2] Freud noted that a son's over-attachment to a narcissistic mother often results in a flight from femininity and compensatory attraction to another male who is really a surrogate for himself, especially if the father is ineffectual or absent; and he develops this further in one of his key studies, *On Narcissism: An Introduction* (1914). 'We have discovered, especially clearly', he states in the latter, 'in people whose libidinal development has suffered some disturbance . . . that in their later choice of love-objects they have taken as a model not their mother but their own selves. They are plainly seeking *themselves* as a love object, and exhibiting a type of object-choice that must be termed "narcissistic".'[3] The love-object such a person seeks is usually an 'ego-ideal'—i.e. 'what he himself would like to be'—and Freud notes that this does not rule out love also for a woman.[4] The eager inquiries about each other by Martius and Aufidius and their speculative exchange of places (e.g. 1.1.226–30; 1.11.4–5) certainly reveal a mutual fascination; and it was this that Tyrone Guthrie fixed on as the key to his 1963 production at the Nottingham Playhouse. At 4.5.102, writes Guthrie, 'when Aufidius expresses his absolute belief in

[1] Cf. F. N. Lees, '*Coriolanus*, Aristotle and Bacon', *RES*, NS 1 (1950), 114–25.

[2] S. Freud, 'Leonardo da Vinci and a Memory of His Childhood' (1910), in James Strachey, trans., *Complete Psychological Works of Freud* (repr. 1978), xi. 63–138.

[3] S. Freud, *On Narcissism: An Introduction* (1914), in Strachey, xiv. 88.

[4] Though this is still likely to take the form of a preference for very young brides and an exaltation of female virginity (e.g. 5.3.65–7); cf. Karen Horney, 'The Dread of Women', *International Journal of Psychoanalysis*, 13 (1932), 348–60.

him, Coriolanus at last breaks down in tears, and Aufidius embraces him, like a father his wayward son.... The image of the career-rival now presents itself as a possible father or elder brother, something that has always been missing from his life.'[1] Earlier, in Michael Langham's 1961 production at Stratford, Ontario, Aufidius alone was represented as homosexual because it was noted that, whereas Martius, embracing Cominius, says only that he is still *as fit* for battle as he had been to love his bride (1.7.29–32), Aufidius' use of the same trope when he embraces Coriolanus later claims that '*more* dances my rapt heart | *Than* when I first my wedded mistress saw | Bestride my threshold' (4.5.117–18). The trope is a Renaissance commonplace, however, used also by Cominius, Volumnia, and Aufidius' servants; so for the Martius–Aufidius relationship it is more accurate to adopt Meredith Skura's term 'pseudo-sexuality', which she defines as an adolescent phase 'in which [a youth] perceives another person as separate, but only as a mirror of himself, or a projection of his own feelings, or a substitute for his frustrated ideal grandiose self' and so craves 'a primitive merger with [this] mirror image of himself'.[2] As Freud also recognized, the purpose of such an attraction is not *to love* but *to be loved* by the 'narcissistic object-choice',[3] so the attraction necessarily has a strong element of rivalry about it—or 'emulation', to use Aufidius' own term (1.11.12). Thus, it is always ambiguously mixed of love and hate, and the balance between them can shift disconcertingly. Freud never offers a satisfying analysis of why this should be so, but Lacan explains that competition is inevitable for both men, because in either case there is a struggle for recognition between the primary physical sense of identity and an 'ego-ideal' projected on to the other person, each being an inadequate but rival view of the self (cf. 1.1.257–9). The closer such rivals become, in fact, the more likely is an explosion of antagonism between them, as Martius recognizes about those 'who *twin* as 'twere in love'

---

[1] Tyrone Guthrie, *In Various Directions: A View of the Theatre* (1965), pp. 90–1, 92.

[2] *The Literary Uses of the Psychoanalytic Process* (1981), pp. 182, 211.

[3] Freud, *On Narcissism*, pp. 98 ff.; this is expanded in Chap. 8 of his *Group Psychology* (1921), in Strachey, xviii. 113 ff.

(4.4.15).[1] Thus, Aufidius' eagerness to welcome Martius at Antium, which some critics have condemned as irreconcilable with his earlier vow to 'Wash my fierce hand in's heart' (1.11.27),[2] is possible because Martius says clearly in that scene that he has come to *serve* Aufidius (4.5.89–91, 101–2), thus seeming to confirm the latter's superiority.[3] And Aufidius can swing so suddenly back to murderous rivalry because, as he also clearly explains (5.6.37–40), Coriolanus has begun to treat him as an inferior again. This rivalry emerges at its most basic level in the final quarrel. More than the accusation of 'traitor' or neglect to call him 'Coriolanus' (which Aufidius has never done anyway), what infuriates Martius is the accuracy of the appellation 'boy of tears'; and his stress on the whippings he has given Aufidius (5.6.109–10) picks up Menenius' earlier question, 'Has he disciplined Aufidius soundly?' (2.1.123) to suggest that it is Aufidius, not he, who must be the beaten child. What is at issue between them is clearly a struggle for self-worth through admitted superiority, not the satisfaction of more narrowly sexual drives.

This overlaps with Martius' attitude to the plebeians, 'my sworn brother, the people' (2.3.92).[4] Anthony Storr observes

---

[1] Cf. Anthony Storr, *Human Aggression* (1968, repr. 1985), p. 82, and Joel Fineman, 'Fratricide and Cuckoldry: Shakespeare's Doubles', in Murray Schwartz and Coppélia Kahn, eds., *Representing Shakespeare: New Psychoanalytic Essays* (1980), 70–109. According to Roman myth, the war-god Mars fathered twin sons named Romulus and Remus who were suckled by a she-wolf (possibly 'lupa', a whore). Having founded the city of Rome, Romulus killed his twin for venturing beyond the city walls. The 1967 RSC production emphasized this 'mirroring twinship' by having Martius and Aufidius made to look alike, with blond wigs and tanned faces; the 1972–3 RSC production began with an elaborate procession led by an effigy of the she-wolf suckling the Roman twins.

[2] e.g. A. C. Bradley (repr. in B. A. Brockman, ed., *Shakespeare, 'Coriolanus': A Casebook*, 1977, p. 68) and Virgil K. Whitaker, *The Mirror Up to Nature: the Technique of Shakespeare's Tragedies* (1965), p. 306. In the 1986 Kick Theatre production Aufidius was even played as a manic-depressive.

[3] Cf. Ralph Berry, 'Sexual Imagery in *Coriolanus*', *SEL*, 13 (1972), 301–16; p. 308: 'Dominance is what both seek. And, in conformity to a well-known principle of animal and human psychology, submission gains an access of good-will.'

[4] Interestingly, in *On Narcissism*, pp. 94 ff., Freud notes that the paranoid extreme of this self-regard suffers from 'scopophobia' (dread of being looked at) and horror of abstractly demanding 'voices': as in Coriolanus' attitude to the plebeians. King James had a similar dread of self-display and crowds, whom he frequently dispersed with Martius-like cursing: see *The Journal of Sir Roger Wilbraham*, ed. H. S. Scott, *Camden Society Miscellany*, 10 (1902), p. 59.

6. 'Make you a sword of me?' Nicol Williamson in the 1973 Royal Shakespeare Company production

that a person suffering from paranoid aggression is likely to choose a sibling or social sub-group that he can loathe as the embodiment of weaknesses in himself which he is struggling to repress, and for which he therefore sees himself as a superior chastiser (cf. 3.1.84–5); and, at its extreme, such paranoia comes to see all humanity as mere trash to be 'exterminated like wasps'[1] (cf. 4.6.98–9; 1.3.62–8). What Martius hates particularly about 'my sworn brother, the people' (2.3.92), besides the physicality of their smell, are their needy mouths and their cowardice in war. In the canvassing scene, he bids them 'wash their faces | And keep their teeth clean' (2.3.58–9) as though they are still children; and when they break their promise, sneers that they have given him 'children's voices' (3.1.32), while Menenius says the Tribunes' abilities are 'too infant-like' (2.1.35). Fascinatingly, he treats the plebeians just as his mother treats him: as inferiors to be disciplined, their gentler side ignored; mere means to his own glory who must *earn* the patricians' care by risking themselves in war, as he does; who must be threatened into unpalatable action, as his mother threatens him. He even tries the same tactic of abandonment: 'I banish *you* . . . thus I turn my back. | There is a world elsewhere' (3.3.124, 135–6)—and, echoing Volumnia's threats of her own death, trails off into exile with the classic little boy's comment 'I shall be loved when I am lacked' (4.1.16). Beneath the politics of state obviously lie the politics of the family: we are watching the indictment of a way of life, the perverting Roman emphasis on *virtus* where 'valour is the chiefest virtue' (2.2.82), not just one man's weakness.

Hence the tensions of the climactic persuasion scene before Rome, in which Volumnia denies the distinction her son is desperately trying to make between 'mother' and 'country'. If the class struggle were the only level of political interest in the play, this scene would not work as a climax. What is on trial is the Roman way of life itself. With allowances for a change in tone, the scene is a virtual replay of the previous browbeating scene. Volumnia pleads, cajoles, flatters, threatens, instructs the other pleaders, moves them about, then uses her ultimate weapon, withdrawal with the threat of suicide. And Coriolanus crumbles. On one level it is a scene of bitter irony, because we cannot be sure that Volumnia has any

---

[1] Storr, pp. 119, 132, 145; cf. 2.2.18–20.

real sense of what she is doing: she insists on treating as political 'honour' what is clearly psychological dependence, and—except (perhaps) by her silence at the very end—betrays no awareness of the damage she has done her son. Yet the surrender is also very moving: less because it is heroic than because it is a genuinely loving act on Martius' part, made not as a Roman but as a son and husband; and, though this may be undercut by Volumnia's silence as she goes off for her first personal triumph, and by Coriolanus' own apparent relapse into arrogance on his return to Antium, still, for one moment, he does realize, fully, what has happened to him and the price he is paying for it and will have to pay.

The phasing of this *anagnorisis* is interesting. After he has reached out and, weeping, held his mother 'silent' by the hand (a brilliant dramaturgical stroke whose devastating effect can be lost in just the reading), he bursts out metatheatrically with:

> O mother, mother!
> What have you done? Behold, the heavens do ope,
> The gods look down, and this unnatural scene
> They laugh at. O my mother, mother, O!
>
> (5.3.183–6)

That word 'unnatural' cuts many ways (see 5.3.185 n.). It is bad in so far as it can be interpreted as Martius' ultimate surrender to his social and familial conditioning, since, as R. D. Laing explains:

The 'deeper' social laws are implanted in us, the more 'hard-programmed,' the more 'pickled' into us, the more like 'natural' laws they come to appear to us to be. Indeed, if someone breaks such a 'deeply' planted social law, we are inclined to say that he is 'unnatural.'[1]

Coriolanus had tried to live 'As if a man were author of himself', but confronted with his mother's obduracy and his own unassuaged need for her, he has to accept her definition of him again, even knowing it will destroy him. As Laing would put it, he is playing out a scenario written generations before

[1] R. D. Laing, *The Politics of the Family: Massey Lectures 1968* (1969), p. 22.

he was born. Yet the cry must be taken at its face value too. The mutual kneeling of parent and child recalls the similar scene in *King Lear*, and Martius' decision to put his feelings for his family above all else—despite their warping, and despite his mother's lack of reciprocity—is an affirmation at the same level of relationship that Lear too finally comes to rest on.

And so the play achieves a measure of tragedy—and the more so if Volumnia is seen not wholly as a monster. Not because in Coriolanus we have a sacrificial victim for our own repressed social hatreds;[1] nor even because Coriolanus' salvation of Rome offsets his private defeat, in an inversion of the usual tragic formula (though this is closer to the truth). It is tragic because, though—as in *King Lear*—it will not last, and nothing can be built upon it, Coriolanus' decision is an affirmation of the familial link on which, since Aristotle, it has been recognized that a healthy society must be built and which Shakespeare has come to see as the truly *political* core of human society set against the constant flux of history and 'th'interpretation of the time'. It is an insight to which, I have argued, Shakespeare worked through for himself in many plays, but—as Ernst Cassirer shows in his *Myth of the State*[2]—it aligns him with the Renaissance Neoplatonists, who also set against the static body-politic ideal on the one side, and Machiavelli's endless power struggle on the other, their own belief that man's instinct for society was a good thing, rationally dynamic, not static, and based not on endless competition but on an extension of the reciprocities of family life. So, though Plutarch's values of *patria* and *pietas* are heavily qualified by Shakespeare's alterations, they still remain as stunted positives in the play; and for the audience the result is a sort of emotional *quantum*, the painful coexistence of contradictory responses.

Existential. Neither the political nor the psychological interpretations advanced so far help explain the coda of 5.6,

---

[1] Kenneth Burke, '*Coriolanus*—and the Delights of Faction', *Hudson Review*, 19 (1966–7), p. 201.

[2] E. Cassirer, *The Myth of the State* (1946), Chap. 6.

however, or prevent Coriolanus' murder from seeming anti-climactic. We must dig deeper to an existential level.[1]

On the face of it, Coriolanus' death lacks inevitability, and to understand its tragic significance we must return to the battle sequences of Act 1. When Cominius' men respond to Martius' call for volunteers at 1.7.76.1–3, the Folio directs that '*They all shout and wave their swords, take him up in their arms, and cast up their caps*', and Martius himself gives the exultant, much-debated cry 'O, me alone! Make you a sword of me?', besides referring to himself for the first time in the self-dramatizing third person with the emphatic short line, 'And follow Martius'. This gesture is one of the key thematic statements of the play (as I interpret it). Its significance is clarified by Elias Canetti's comments on 'survival' in his study *Crowds and Power*. 'The moment of *survival*', says Canetti,

is the moment of power. Horror at the sight of death turns into satisfaction that it is someone else who is dead ... Whether the survivor is confronted by one dead man or many, the essence of the situation is that he feels *unique*. . . . and when we speak of the power which this moment gives him, we should never forget that it derives from his sense of uniqueness and from nothing else.[2]

Here, then, is an important clue to Martius' sense of uniqueness, his ability to act alone and wish to see himself as *causa sui*—to 'stand | As if a man were author of himself | And knew no other kin' (5.3.35–7). Martius' exultant sense of uniqueness, in other words, is not only a cause of prowess in war but itself a result of war, of surviving many confrontations with death. Against the knowledge of one's personal mortality that existentialist philosophers and psychologists believe to be a distinguishing characteristic of human (as distinct from animal) consciousness, one of the best forms of defence, as Canetti points out, is attack:

[1] Similar conclusions are arrived at independently by James L. Calderwood, *Shakespeare and the Denial of Death* (1987), especially Chap. 3, and Kirby Farrell, *Play, Death, and Heroism in Shakespeare* (1989), especially Chap. 6. The common influence is Ernest Becker, *The Denial of Death* (1978). See also E. A. M. Colman, 'The End of Coriolanus', *ELH*, 34 (1967), 1–20, esp. pp. 17–20.

[2] Elias Canetti, *Crowds and Power*, trans. Carol Stewart (1962), p. 227.

The lowest form of survival is killing. . . . This moment of confronting the man he has killed fills the survivor with a special kind of strength. There is nothing that can be compared with it, and there is nothing which more demands repetition [a point to which we must return]. The man who achieves this often is [thought to be] . . . favoured of the gods. (pp. 227–8)

This syndrome is intensified in Coriolanus by an almost suicidal intensity in the demands he repetitively makes upon himself—demands that are the natural outcome of his having been thrust into confrontation with death at too early and vulnerable an age, and also (a psychoanalyst would say) from 'introjection'—that is, the turning in upon himself of feelings of rage and resentment against Volumnia for placing him in such a position instead of, more naturally, protecting him. This peeps out unintentionally when he chides her for weeping at his banishment: 'My mother, you wot well | My hazards still have been your solace' (4.1.28–9), but is later voiced more consciously after Volumnia has dissuaded him from attacking Rome, without, apparently, realizing what this will mean for him. He calls this situation 'unnatural', as we have seen, and again uses the curiously distanced form 'my mother'—'O my mother, mother, O!' (5.3.186)—which has a remonstrative nuance of 'you, who are my *mother*!' Of the actors I know who have played Coriolanus, only Nicol Williamson seems to have emphasized this element of punitive self-fashioning, when he took over the role in the RSC production of 1973, though there was also more than a touch of it in Alan Howard's narcissistic reading for the RSC in 1977.

When Cominius' soldiers hoist him aloft, it must be remembered that Martius has been reported dead to them but has reappeared unrecognizably soaked in blood. Only one director that I know of and extraordinarily few critics have gone nearly far enough with this:[1] in productions he is given at most some smears of blood on face and arms and often there

[1] Exceptions are the Ashland, Oregon, production in 1980, directed by Jerry Turner; and, critically, Leo Kirschbaum, 'Shakespeare's Stage Blood and its Critical Significance', *PMLA*, 64 (1949), p. 535, and Joseph Weixlmann, ' " . . . action may | Conveniently the rest convey . . .": Some Key Presentational Images in Shakespeare's *Coriolanus*', *Forum of Texas*, 12 (Houston, 1974), 9–13.

is no blood at all (e.g. in Olivier's performances). But the text describes Coriolanus with sickening explicitness as 'a thing of blood' who looks 'as he were flayed'; and repeated references in the later battle scenes drive home the extreme frightfulness of his appearance—even to Jacobeans, who were used to public bloodshed. When this bloodiness is combined with his exultation at being 'alone' and odd self-description as their 'sword', and we remember that the soldiers who lift him are not his own men but have just suffered a humiliating defeat under Cominius, it seems obvious that what Shakespeare has provided here is a striking stage emblem of the glamour and charisma of survival from death, that seeming invulnerability which Canetti says has extraordinary power over crowds, and which ordinary men's wish to share has here converted (with perversely phallic symbolism) into a fetish—an erectile, blood-soaked sword for further aggression.

These implications of that charismatic *gest* also add another dimension to Martius' refusal to show his wounds in public to the voters—which is another Shakespeare addition. His refusal stems not just from class pride (he walks out of the Senate too), nor even from his belief that honour is intrinsic and not to be bestowed by others' approval. At a deeper level, it also reflects the denial of vulnerability on which his sense of unique 'aloneness' is built, rejection of those gashes—mere 'Scratches with briers' (3.3.49), as he dismisses them—into which (again with sexual, but also sacramental, overtones) the voters wish to put their tongues in order to share by confirming ('we are to put our tongues into those wounds and speak for them', 2.3.6–7).

The implications of this early battle scene are a key to the significance of 5.6, the scene of Martius' death. As was discussed earlier ('Structure'), this is virtually an ironic reprise of the whole play and, on the face of it, seems anticlimactic. Like Troilus and Lear, Martius seems to have relapsed from his sharp moment of truth when Volumnia overpersuaded him in the pleading scene. Rationally, there is no need for him to return to Antium at all (Livy, in fact, reports a version of the story in which Coriolanus survived into disillusioned old age). His family seems to have expected him to return home with them, and the relieved and joyful Romans, we have already learned in 5.5, are quite prepared to 'unshout' his banishment. And, although he does not share our knowledge of Aufidius' intended treachery, he has recognized that the situation his mother has created may prove 'most mortal' to him. Yet he still insists on going back, and Shakespeare provides no soliloquy or speech to tell us why. Loyalty to Aufidius is presumably one element in his decision. He may also be proving to himself that he retains his honour by returning to face punishment (like the hero Regulus), or, alternatively, by trying to reconcile Rome and the Volscians, as his mother advised in her persuasion speech—though he seems no more convinced of this than when she sent him back to mollify the Roman voters in 3.2. He may also have noted sadly that all the deputations asked him to spare Rome but none specifically urged his own return (a detail Shakespeare has cut from Plutarch). And there is surely also an element of fatalism in his behaviour (Cicero's *Brutus* reports a version in which Martius committed suicide): 'But let it come', he says stoically like Hamlet, after warning Volumnia that her victory may prove 'most mortal' to him. This element was clear earlier in his first braving of Aufidius alone in Antium, when, baring his breast, he said that if the Volscian leader would not receive him as an ally,

> then, in a word, I also am
> Longer to live most weary, and present
> My throat to thee and to thy ancient malice,
> Which not to cut would show thee but a fool.
>
> (4.5.95–8)

There was a Richard III-like daring about this in that earlier scene, but when he utters similar provocative remarks in 5.6 the element of bluff has gone. Only defiance remains, and he may not even bother to draw his sword for the final confrontation (5.6.130). Again Canetti's *Crowds and Power* can supply a possible subtext for Martius' complex state of mind here.

A drawback of Renaissance 'Self-fashioning'—(that urge to stand 'as if a man were author of himself')—as Stephen Greenblatt has recognized,[1] is that this can never be done

---

[1] *Renaissance Self-Fashioning: From More to Shakespeare* (1980); cf. also Michael Goldman, 'Characterizing Coriolanus', *Acting and Action in Shakespearean Tragedy* (1985), pp. 140–68.

once and for all; it requires constant repetition; especially, Canetti says, when it involves the sense of uniqueness induced by facing death: 'The satisfaction in survival . . . can become a dangerous and insatiable passion . . . The careers of heroes and soldiers suggest that a kind of addiction ensues, which in the end becomes incurable' (p. 230). The description of young Martius chasing a butterfly in 1.3 (another Shakespeare invention) emblematizes this process. Like Freud's description of his little grandson learning to master the external world by concealing, then revealing a cotton-reel in a 'fort-da' game,[1] Young Martius is described in 'one on's father's moods' as catching a butterfly, letting it go, then catching it once more, over and over again—like a cat with a mouse—till he revenges an unexpected tumble by 'mammocking' it.

In addition to this pattern of compulsive repetition, Canetti also points out that, though most men try to avoid the threat of death, the hero has always prided himself on a second way of coping with this basic human fear:

He has sought out danger and confronted it . . . Out of all possible situations, he has chosen the one involving risk and then enhanced that risk . . . This is the way of the *hero*. What does the hero really want? . . . It is assumed that glory is [his] sole motive, but it is more likely that [he is] originally seeking for . . . the evergrowing sense of invulnerability which can [only] be won this way.   (pp. 228–9)

As Menenius puts it: 'being angry, he does forget that ever | He heard the name of death' (3.1.261–2). After the humiliation of yielding his revenger's *causa sui* project to Volumnia, it is psychologically inevitable that Martius should seek to regain self-respect by deliberately risking death again, once more confronting the sort of peril that for him confirms 'uniqueness'. Again, for a third time, he will brave the Volscians single-handedly, and thus recover his identity.

It is this that saves 5.6 from becoming a satiric anticlimax, although there is certainly an ironically spurious quality about Martius' behaviour at first. His Volscian entry is quite unlike his triumph in 2.1: a contrast that was probably emphasized by parallel staging. The stage direction reads, *Enter Coriolanus, marching with drum and colours, the Commoners*

---

[1] S. Freud, *Beyond the Pleasure Principle* (1920), in Strachey, xviii. 14–15.

being with him. He is now relying on the support of citizens of the kind he has hitherto scorned. Moreover, this man who could not bear even his mother to praise him and scorned material gain, now disingenuously trumpets his own achievements, emphasizes the booty he returns with, and uses the 'generalissimo's plural'[1] of 'we' and 'our'. (In 1984 Ian McKellen even ran a victory lap around the stage, like a winning athlete, while the Volscian citizens patted him on the back and kissed him.) And, as will be argued (see 'First Production'), I also think he is intended to be resplendently dressed. Moreover, his immediate loss of self-control in the face of Aufidius' provocations suggests as much a revulsion from bad faith as the almost ludicrously programmed 'pride' it is usually reduced to. 'Cut me to pieces, Volsces,' he urges scornfully; then continues ambiguously, 'Men and lads | *Stain* all your edges on me' (5.6.112–13). Martius does not die fighting; nor commit suicide; nor accept death stoically; nor submit to being sacrificed. His death is a last act of aggression, his final humiliation of Aufidius. He dies as he has lived.

Plutarch has Coriolanus murdered before he can speak at all in his defence; but, in addition to his hollow justifications for sparing Rome, Shakespeare gives him a final striking speech of self-assertion—his deliberately provocative 'eagle fluttering the dovecote' reminder of former victory, with its characteristic vaunt, '*alone* I did it'. In performance, despite the weaknesses Martius has revealed and the falseness of his present situation, one cannot help but empathize with this last, defiant gesture, because Martius stands suddenly again for what he has always represented at the deepest level of the play: an appeal to what William Blissett once brilliantly described as 'the solitary achiever, whatever is unsocial and not to be educated, alone and raging in each of us'.[2] The heart of Martius' tragedy, suggests Michael Goldman, lies in his attempt to be true to himself: 'Character lies in the interpretation of the time, as Aufidius puts it, and is thus susceptible to change and falsehood. And yet it is the most

---

[1] Vickers, p. 51.

[2] William Blissett, 'Coriolanus and the Helms of [the] State', in Patricia Brückmann, ed., *Familiar Colloquy: Essays Presented to Arthur Barker* (1978), p. 159.

enduring thing about us. Perhaps this is what tragedy is about—that there is such a thing as human character.'[1]

Thus *Coriolanus*, like *King Lear*, has two levels of tragedy. Though Aufidius' behaviour and the ironies of the funeral cortege will dilute it yet again (see 'First Production'), the play ends as a Senecan tragedy of stoic individualism, turning death to self-assertion: a private, 'negative' victory to offset the public, more 'positive' assertion of self-sacrifice and family love at the end of Volumnia's pleading, producing a characteristically 'Roman' double-ending in which both levels have been heavily qualified by irony.[2]

Style

Because it has little conventional lyricism, *Coriolanus* has often been dismissed as lacking 'poetic atmosphere', but actually its style is very precisely fitted to character and action. T. S. Eliot even goes so far as to claim that *Coriolanus* is, 'with *Antony and Cleopatra*, Shakespeare's most assured artistic success'.[3]

Public Dimension. The opening cry of 'Hear me speak!' establishes the public nature of the play's style, its quality as rhetorical persuasion and self-display in a society where there is little privacy and even the most personal relationships must be conducted in the presence of others. This public dimension can be seen in Shakespeare's incorporation of several set-pieces almost verbatim from the source—Menenius' belly-fable, Martius' denunciations of corn doles and the tribunate, his plea to Aufidius in 4.5, and Volumnia's to him in 5.3—which Plutarch has structured according to the elaborate schemes and figures of formal Roman rhetoric;[4] and also in the heavy use of hyperbole, which *Coriolanus* shares with Shakespeare's other Roman plays but which it focuses much

[1] Goldman, *Acting and Action*, p. 163.

[2] See Introduction, p. 12 and n. 3. This double effect is analysed by Sheldon P. Zitner, 'Shakespeare's *Coriolanus* and the Aristotelian modes of pathos', in Martin Cropp, E. Fantham, S. E. Sully, eds., *Greek Tragedy and its Legacy* (1986), 295–312.

[3] T. S. Eliot, 'Hamlet', *Selected Essays* (1932), p. 124.

[4] Cf. Robert Miola's discussion of the Ciceronic division of Menenius' belly fable and the traditional epideictic structure of Cominius' eulogy: *Shakespeare's Rome* (1983), pp. 181 ff.

more intensely on the protagonist himself: either positively, as in Cominius' encomium or the frequent comparisons of Martius to various gods, or negatively, as in Menenius' malicious description of Coriolanus' stubbornness in 5.4.

Not surprisingly, therefore, there is very little soliloquy in the play—only thirty-six lines in all[1]—and what exists is significantly non-introspective, with a 'strangely hobbled quality'[2] that suggests discomfort with thought. Martius' solo lines at 2.3.108–19 (which are probably overheard by Third Citizen cf. 2.3.80.1 n.) merely express irritation at canvassing in a series of proverbial phrases whose triteness is emphasized by rhyme; and his one true soliloquy in 4.4 is constructed on an illogical, extended antithesis which betrays his inability to understand the impulse that is drawing him to Aufidius. Instead of soliloquies, Shakespeare experiments with a fascinating variety of *semi-soliloquy*: speeches, that is, which begin as conversations with other characters but develop into areas of personal obsession in which the speakers, for a while at least, seem to forget the presence of their listeners. Aufidius has two examples of this highly dramatic device: his early determination to defeat Martius by treachery in 1.11.17 ff., and his abortive attempt to understand the contradictions in Coriolanus' character in 4.7.28 ff. Martius' own reaction to the women's embassy at 5.3.22 ff. has the same semi-private quality about it, though clearly Aufidius overhears it; and Volumnia's eerily incantatory lines at 2.1.154–7, rising suddenly into verse from her previous prose, give public expression to very personal myth-making. This curious effect of seeming almost inadvertently to 'think out loud' can be made much more noticeable in performance.[3]

[1] In the 1983 BBC-TV version, Elijah Moshinsky tried to compensate for this by using frequent close-ups for Coriolanus' speeches: see Henry Fenwick in John Wilders *et al.*, *Coriolanus: BBC-TV Shakespeare* (1984), p. 22. Other television productions of the play have been mounted by the American 'Studio One' series in 1951, by BBC-TV in 1963 as part of its *Spread of the Eagle* series, and by Irish TV in 1972; and the BBC has broadcast radio versions in 1933, 1948, 1959, and 1979.

[2] Carol M. Sicherman, '*Coriolanus*: The Failure of Words', *ELH*, 39 (1972), 189–207; p. 201.

[3] Coriolanus and Aufidius delivered their semi-soliloquies straight out to the audience in the 1977 RSC production, as Volumnia did her lines at Stratford-upon-Avon in 1959.

Perhaps the chief characteristic of Rome's public style is its argumentativeness—in the sense of noisy contention, rather than Enright's more mannerly term, 'debate'.[1] Its characteristic idiom is assertive and combative: 'language that is spoiling for a fight'.[2] This too is established in the opening scene, by lines such as: 'He's one honest enough. Would all the rest were so!', 'Your belly's answer—what?', or 'What then? | 'Fore me, this fellow speaks! What then, what then?' (1.1.50–1, 111, 116–17). This abrasiveness of tone is heightened by jagged disruptions in grammar and syntax and by eccentricities of metre, and at its worst degenerates to outright abuse. There is a lot of name-calling in *Coriolanus*, not least by Martius himself. Besides the explicit direction '*Enter Martius, cursing*' (1.5.0.1–2), he is given three extraordinary tirades in the body of the play (1.1.165 ff., 3.1.69 ff., 93 ff.), and Shakespeare alters Plutarch to give him a final diatribe at his death. He seems to alternate between stubborn silence and furious outbursts, compulsively repeating words that have offended him—corn, shall, traitor, boy—and piling up derogatory comparisons in incremental lists.[3] Menenius blames this on Martius' military training (3.1.323–5), but Martius himself says he learned it from his mother (3.2.8–13). Volumnia certainly demonstrates the same penchant, not only capping Martius' invective at 3.2.23–4 but also cursing the Tribunes in her own right after Coriolanus' banishment and bringing her son himself to heel with stinging abuse at 5.3.179–83. This rhetorical likeness between mother and son is often pointed in performance: at Ashland in 1980, for instance, Martius silently mouthed along with Volumnia her brag 'Thy valiantness was mine, thou suck'st it from me' (3.2.131) to show how often he had heard her make that claim before.[4]

Another example of her influence on him occurs in 4.1, when at his departure into exile Martius rehearses the stoic

[1] D. J. Enright, '*Coriolanus*: Tragedy or Debate?', *Essays in Criticism*, 4 (1954), 1–19.

[2] Carol Rutter, 'Coriolanus Study Notes' (National Theatre, London, 1984), p. 11.

[3] John Porter Huston relates this habit of listing to Martius' desire for impenetrable self-sufficiency: *Shakespeare Sentences: A Study in Style and Syntax* (1988), pp. 160, 161–2.

[4] Alan Dessen, review in *SQ*, 32 (1981), p. 273.

'precepts' Volumnia has taught him previously; and this exemplifies another characteristic of the play's 'public' style: its heavy use of proverbs and semi-proverbial phrases, with their implication of rigidly conventional thought. Martius rightly mocks the plebeians for this kind of style (1.1.202–6), but he is no less prone to it himself; and the simplistic nature of his thinking can also be gauged from the platitudes with which he cheers on Cominius' troops at 1.7.68 ff. and his awkward speeches of embarrassed modesty in 1.10. The mechanicalness of such rote wisdom is often emphasized by rhyme, as in such a desperately defensive jingle as 'Not of a woman's tenderness to be | Requires nor child nor woman's face to see' (5.3.130–1) at the height of his mother's plea for Rome; and a more sinister example winds up Aufidius' bewildered attempt to comprehend Martius in 4.7. This also is riddled with proverbial phrasing, and ends with two brutally reductive couplets:

> One fire drives out one fire, one nail one nail;
> Rights by rights falter, strengths by strengths do fail.
> Come, let's away. When, Caius, Rome is thine,
> Thou art poor'st of all; then shortly art thou mine.
>
> (4.7.54–7)

Rhetorical Conventions. Aufidius' speech also demonstrates the use of antithesis, which is the play's central rhetorical figure, supported by such related forms of contradiction as oxymoron, paradox, and dilemma.[1] Again this is established at a simple, almost parodic level in the plebeians' opening speeches: 'I speak this in hunger for bread, not in thirst for revenge', 'Let us revenge this with our pikes ere we become rakes', or 'We are accounted poor citizens, the patricians good . . . our sufferance is a gain to them' (1.1.22–3, 21–2, 13–14, 20–1). The figure recurs constantly (e.g. 1.7.70–2, 2.3.148–9, 4.4.23–4); and in passages where the intention is to persuade, like Martius' denunciation of free corn and the tribunate in 3.1 or Volumnia's plea in 5.3, the style is particularly stiff with it. Antitheses also cluster whenever there is an attempt to

[1] See M. Doran, p. 189: 'the whole tissue of *Coriolanus* is antithetical'; R. F. Hill, '*Coriolanus*: Violentest Contrariety', *Essays and Studies*, NS 17 (1964), 12–23.

analyse behaviour: as in the 'whether-x-or-y' sequence of Aufidius' musings about Martius' character (4.7.37–49), or, more complexly, in Martius' own motive-hunting in the soliloquy before Antium of 4.4, with its specious balance of friends-who-become-foes with foes-who-become-friends, emphasized by superlatives and blatant alliteration: 'So fellest foes . . . shall grow dear friends' (4.4.18–21). Antitheses pointed by hyperbole or its opposite, litotes, are central to much of the play's invective, with a particularly interesting group used to express the almost hysterical horror Martius feels at the unnaturalness of Volumnia kneeling to him (5.3.58–62).

Besides conveying the unimaginative, binary limitation of Roman (and Volscian) thought, this emphasis on balanced contradiction contributes more generally to a sense of mental violence, a kind of intellectual 'noise'—or what Granville-Barker calls 'a banging about of contraries, like so many boxes on the ear'[1]—that parallels the other levels of conflict in the play. This relates to a second major rhetorical effect of *Coriolanus*: the sense it gives of overpackedness, of details overriding the regular patterns of metre, syntax, and grammar. This not only conveys the way that passion keeps breaking through inadequate expression, but also helps to create the impression that *Coriolanus* is a crowded urban play, where individuality is invaded by the pressures of community and by the physical city itself: a kind of stylistic agoraphobia.

A syntactical distortion such as Menenius' 'If you'll bestow a small—of what you have little— | Patience a while' (1.1.122–3) can be seen as part of his deliberate delaying tactics, but, more typically, the play's obscurities reflect the speakers' inability to find adequate formulation for passions that they do not really understand. Coriolanus, whose speech characteristically has the clipped, asyndetic abruptness traditionally associated with the laconic (i.e. Spartan) style of soldiers (e.g. 1.1.164–85, 1.10.82–7), has several examples of such grammatical confusion. The obscurity of his lines about the 'parasite's silk' (1.10.42–7), for instance, conveys the incoherence of his indignation at being cheered for repudiating booty he despises. The way language fails him is

---

[1] Granville-Barker, p. 174.

explicit at 2.3.47–9; and at 3.3.89–91 his anger overrides grammar by switching from a parallelism of the nouns 'death ... exile ... flaying' to the telescoped past-participle construction, 'pent to linger | But with a grain a day'. Aufidius' speech at 1.11.17–27 is another good example of the kind of irregularity which mirrors mental confusion. 'My valour, poisoned | With only suff'ring stain by him, for him | Shall fly out of itself' is obscure because the sentence twists twice the same way and plays on 'only' and 'stain' to convey Aufidius' acknowledgement of a double yet contradictory disgrace: his valour is already 'stained' by being defeated by Coriolanus 'only', but this is not its 'only' 'stain' because his decision to be treacherous contradicts that valour and makes it 'fly out of itself' (there is a similar pun on 'stain' at 5.6.113). In the sentence that follows, the verb 'lift up' is itself delayed by all the impediments to treachery that Aufidius says he is determined to ignore—sleep, sanctuary, naked, sick, fane, Capitol, prayers, sacrifice, all embargements of fury—thus creating a choked, passionate effect in the sentence structure, with 'Being naked, sick', moreover, paralleled ungrammatically to a list of nouns, and with the metre of the lines broken up to produce a 'peculiar lurching articulation'[1] that follows closely the emotional desperation of the speaker's thought.

This clumsiness combines, in fact, with a driven sense of energy, resolutely pushing to get through despite grammatical obscurities: what Traversi describes as strong feeling 'involved in a struggle against constraint, forcing itself to the surface in passionate and often distorted outbursts of narrow and concentrated emotion'.[2] Similarly, Michael Goldman has drawn attention[3] to the highly dramatic sense of 'attack' in many of Coriolanus' speeches, the way he seems to *fight* his way through language in such speeches as 3.1.69–77 or 3.3.121 ff, so that they provide a rhetorical equivalent of his conduct on the battlefield or in 3.3 (where successive counsels of restraint merely spur him recklessly on to speak his mind in full). Such 'driven' syntax contrasts strikingly with the

[1] F. H. Langman, '*Coriolanus*: the Poetry and the Critics', *Critical Review*, 9 (Melbourne and Sydney, 1966), pp. 92–105; 96.

[2] D. A. Traversi, *Shakespeare: the Roman Plays* (1963), p. 207.

[3] Goldman, *Acting and Action*, pp. 150–4.

Ciceronic fullness, use of subordinate clauses (hypotaxis), and careful use of connectives in the public style of Menenius and the Tribunes¹ and especially in the 'copious' loquacity of Volumnia.

A second effect of this packed disjunctiveness is to give imaginative specificity to the sense of encroachment by the city. The play is dense with references to the buildings and fabric of Rome—not only the Capitol, Senate, and market-place, which are locales for action, but also walls, gates, ports, streets, conduits, temples, storehouses, mills, shops, stalls, windows, leads, roofs, and foundations—as well as to its multifarious inhabitants—nurses, mechanics, cobblers, tailors, apron-men, actors, orange-wives, faucet-sellers, harlots, ballad-makers, mountebanks, veiled dames, and flamens, with their spits, trenchers, spoons, bats, clubs, cushions, chamber-pots, cobbled shoes, greasy caps and aprons, etc. Cumulatively, the effect is of an almost Jonsonian specificity of 'acrid and oppressive realism',² evoking a city environment that is the objective correlative of Martius' agoraphobia. An excellent example of this unpleasant but brilliantly metonymic style is Brutus' description of the crowds welcoming Coriolanus at 2.1.201–14, which has an extra ironic edge because it is spoken so contemptuously by one of their own Tribunes.³ Words are jammed together in this speech like the buildings along the route of Martius' triumph or the spectators swarming over them, and there is great particularity of detail; the verbs—clambering, prattling, chats, puff, smothered, horsed, press—are clumsily kinetic; and the alliteratively antithetical pun 'Her richest lockram 'bout her reechy neck' (l. 205) conveys intensely the wealthy Brutus' fastidious revulsion from such a juxtaposition of cheap finery with filthy skin. This is quite a different style from the lyrical, metaphoric quality

---

¹ Trevor Nunn, director of the 1972–3 RSC production of *Coriolanus*, remarks: 'We are also aware that the tribunes are speaking aristocratic speech, which is beautifully judged by Shakespeare': in Ralph Berry, *On Directing Shakespeare* (1989), p. 77.

² Langman, 'Repeated Action', p. 326. For the play's ambivalence to the city, see Gail Paster, *The Idea of the City in the Age of Shakespeare* (1985), *passim*.

³ Langman, 'Poetry and the Critics', pp. 102–4, illuminatingly contrasts this to a similar passage in the first scene of *Caesar*.

that we usually value in Shakespeare's poetry, but it is imaginative writing of the first order.

Imagery and Themes. A similar skill is manifest in the imagery of the play. It is a commonplace to note that *Coriolanus* is much less figurative than is customary in Shakespeare, and that the imagery that does exist usually takes the form of simile, not the imaginatively more suggestive form of metaphor. However, it is not true to assume that because of this the play lacks 'poetic atmosphere'. Though it has little of the transcendental reference and nature imagery usually thought of as 'Shakespearian', it does possess an intricate network of thematic correspondences based on three main image clusters: grain/nurture/cannibalism, body/blood/sex, and language/acting. Moreover, paralleling the antithetical rhetorical structure just discussed, it has the peculiar characteristic of reversing nearly all the main images so that they are made to serve quite contradictory purposes according to whichever side is using them. This prevents tidy allegorizing and to some extent compensates for the sparseness of metaphor.

The corn riot of Scene 1 establishes image clusters of corn–harvest–burning and of food–eating, with the latter ramifying into cannibalism–animals and the perversion of nurture to aggression. Grain becomes equated with the rebels who demand it, so that they are described as 'musty' and 'fusty' (1.1.223–4, 1.10.7)—i.e. mouldy and malodorous—the spoiled corn which Rome wishes to 'vent' in war. Alternatively, they represent the 'dry stubble' which the 'fire' of Martius' insolence may kindle to the Tribunes' advantage (2.1.253–4); or the 'cockle [i.e. weeds] of rebellion' (3.1.73–5) contaminating the corn—in fact, according to Coriolanus, it was the free dole of corn itself which 'nourished disobedience' and merely 'fed | The ruin of the state' (3.1.115–20). And, at a further remove, they are 'rats' who must be set on to attack the Volsces' granaries (1.1.247–8, 159). Later, however, when Martius marches vengefully on Rome, he has come to believe *all* Romans are spoiled corn[1], to be burned

---

[1] Coriolanus' wish to burn grain and weeds indiscriminately contradicts Christ's teaching in Matthew 13: 24–30, that wheat must be separated from 'tares' and only the latter burned.

without regard for any wholesome grains that may survive (5.1.25–32). The figure is extrapolated further by Volumnia's comparison of him to a 'thresher' who, like a day-labourer, must relentlessly finish the whole job before he is paid (cf. 1.3.37–8 n.); and later one of Aufidius' servants similarly gloats that Martius 'will mow all down before him, and leave his passage polled' (4.5.206–7). Behind these comparisons looms the traditional image of death as the 'grim reaper'.

War is also represented as a 'feast' where the combatants 'eat' one another. '[May] The present wars devour him' (1.1.256), is Brutus' wish for Martius, and his rebellious soldiers let him be trapped in Corioles with the callous dismissal, 'To th' pot, I warrant him' (1.5.20). When he comes to rescue Cominius, the latter marvels, 'Yet cam'st thou to a morsel of this feast, | Having fully dined before' (1.10.10–11); Cominius himself, however, is 'too full | Of the wars' surfeits' (4.1.46–7) to accompany his rescuer into exile; and when Martius joins Aufidius while the latter is feasting prior to a renewed attack on Rome, the success of their campaign will be 'a parcel of their feast, and to be executed ere they wipe their lips' (4.5.221–2), with the Volscian soldiers exulting in Coriolanus as their 'grace fore meat, | Their talk at table, and their thanks at end' (4.7.3–4).

This overlaps with cannibalism, a frequent Shakespeare image for social breakdown which is here used by both sides. The plebeians complain that, 'If the wars eat us not up, [the patricians] will' (1.1.81–2), claiming that Martius in particular would 'Be every man himself' (3.1.267). Martius indeed calls them 'you fragments' (1.1.220) and wishes to make a 'quarry' (i.e. heap of dead deer) of their bodies (l. 195); and a Volscian servant says 'before Corioles he scotched [Aufidius] and notched him like a carbonado'—i.e. like meat prepared for a barbecue—to which a second responds, 'An he had been cannibally given, he might have broiled and eaten him too' (4.5.191–4). Martius, on the other hand, claims that it is the plebeians whom the Senate must keep 'in awe, which else | Would feed on one another' (1.1.184–5); Menenius says a wolf only loves a lamb 'to devour him, as the hungry plebeians would the noble Martius' (2.1.9–10); and Martius tells Aufidius only his name 'Coriolanus' remains to him because

Rome 'hath devoured the rest' (4.5.77). One implication of the constant reference to the citizens as 'mouths', 'tongues', and 'teeth', in fact, is that 'For Coriolanus the belly is not the patricians but the plebeians'.[1] This culminates in the Volscian crowd's wish to tear him to pieces, which was sinisterly foreshadowed by the story of Young Martius setting his teeth to mammock a butterfly (1.3.63–8; cf. 4.6.98–9, 5.4.11–14).

The same obsession with eating dictates the play's dense sequence of animal imagery (for which it is second only to *Troilus and Cressida* in the Shakespeare canon).[2] Coriolanus, Aufidius, and the patricians are represented as noble predators —lion, bear, eagle, osprey, tiger, even dragon (though this is an ambivalent image)—while the plebeians are either non-aggressive animals who serve as prey—hares, geese, asses, mules, camels, mice, sheep, goats, and deer—or inferior, scavenging predators—rats, crows, wolves, cats, kites, foxes— with the epithets frequently paired for contrast, as in Martius' opening speech (1.1.168 ff.). The most insulting comparison is to dogs, hounds, curs, or 'rascals' (ill-bred dogs) applied mostly to Martius' enemies but again also turned against himself (e.g. 1.1.26, 2.1.253); and the plebeians' multiplicity is reflected by unflattering comparisons to herds, spawn, minnows, and particularly the 'hydra' or 'many-headed monster' (2.3.10–18, 3.1.95–7, 4.1.1–2) which was a traditionally derogatory image for the have-nots in society.[3]

The most perverse eating images, however, are references to eating—or, alternatively, starving—the self. Menenius is worried lest Rome become an 'unnatural dam' who eats up 'her own' (3.1.295–6), and Volumnia rejects his invitation to dinner with the paradoxical 'Anger's my meat: I sup upon myself | And so shall starve with feeding', an image that interestingly relates her both to traditional emblems of *Invidia* (see 4.2.53–4 n.) and to other self-starvation imagery in the

[1] Poole, p. 57.

[2] See J. C. Maxwell, 'Animal Imagery in *Coriolanus*', MLR, 42 (1947), 417–21.

[3] Cf. Christopher Hill, 'The Many-headed Monster...', in Charles H. Carter, ed., *From Renaissance to the Counter-Reformation* (1965), 296–324; C. A. Patrides, 'The Beast with Many Heads: Renaissance Views on the Multitude', SQ, 16 (1965), 241–6.

play (2.1.53–4, 2.3.109–10, 3.3.90–1; cf. 1.3.24–5), including Martius' decision to change allegiance for 'Some trick not worth an egg' (4.4.21). The most striking perversion of nurturing, however (as was discussed earlier: see 'Interpretation'), is Volumnia's equation of Hector's bloody forehead with Hecuba's suckling breasts (1.3.41–4), a grotesque conjunction that resonates ironically with her claim that Martius sucked his valiantness from her (3.2.131), with her insistence that both she and Rome are 'nurses' whom his attack is violating, and climactically with her self-cancelling sneer, 'This fellow had a Volscian to his mother' (5.3.179).

There are similar perversions of the ideas of marriage and sex. The trope of greeting a fellow soldier or, more dramatically, an ex-enemy as more welcome even than one's bride is used by Martius, Aufidius, Volumnia, Cominius, and one of the Volscian servants; and, conversely, there is a sense that war does violence especially to women and the family ties they represent (2.1.166–7, 4.4.2–4, 5.6.122–3, 152), with a specific likelihood of rape (4.5.231–2, 4.6.85–7; cf. 1.5.12). More obliquely, the same perversion surfaces in Volumnia's brag that she would prefer to have eleven sons dead for their country than 'one voluptuously surfeit out of action' (1.3.24–5), and in Martius' rejection of political flattery as a 'harlot's spirit' that will reduce his 'throat of war' and 'drum' (symbolizing martial virility, as in *All's Well*) to the small 'pipe' of a 'eunuch' or 'virgin' and fill his eyes with 'schoolboys' tears' (3.2.114–18). Such imagery suggests that one source of aggression is perverted virility.[1]

This relates to the second major figurative cluster in *Coriolanus*: imagery that centres on the human body as an emblem for the unified or divided state (with cognate imagery of disease and drastic surgery), and as a way of concealing the deadliness of war and glamorizing the institutions that depend on it. Though the point of Menenius' long belly fable is to argue for unity in both body and state, the political reality of Rome is one of warring factions; and this is reflected in recurrent images of the body's fragmentation, exploiting the rhetorical figure of synecdoche (using a part for the whole, or

[1] See Ralph Berry, p. 59 n. 3.

vice versa). Thus, the plebeians are constantly referred to as separate physical parts (e.g. 1.1.57–8, 71, 152, 2.1.265–8), and especially as mouths, tongues, breath, and voices: not only because of their demand for food and the noise of their rebellion, but also because of their dangerous power to vote (e.g. 3.1.23, 38, 273–4). But, interestingly, the same imagery of bodily fragmentation also twists back to apply to Coriolanus himself (cf. 2.1.143–8, 2.2.89), and it is this figure that Martius uses to express his own loss of integrity if he obeys his mother's order to dissemble with the voters (3.2.114–22): he is afraid, he says, lest 'my body's action teach my mind | A most inherent baseness' (3.2.124–5)—a key statement for understanding the psychology of his objection to acting, as we shall see.

A cognate cluster of imagery, traditionally accompanying the body politic trope, represents the body as diseased and suggests extreme measures to cure it—also, incidentally, conveying that revulsion from any physical limitation of the will which is part of the patrician mystique. Martius' first lines identify the plebeian grievances with an 'itch' they rub until they make themselves 'scabs', and compare their 'affections' to 'a sick man's appetite', desiring what will merely 'increase his evil' (1.1.162–3, 174–6). Such imagery accumulates with references to 'contagion of the South', boils, plagues, plastered o'er, infected, agued, decayed lungs, impoisoned, palsied, apoplexy, lethargy, sores, murrain (strictly a cattle disease), cicatrices, red pestilence, and hoarded plague, with a specially heavy concentration of the figure in 3.1 and a return to it at the end of the play (5.6.8, 10, 45, 72–3). And, as is typical of *Coriolanus*, the imagery cuts both ways. Martius urges the patricians to 'jump [i.e. shock] a body with a dangerous physic | That's sure of death without it' (3.1.156–7), only to have the image turned back against himself when the Tribunes say Menenius' counsels of moderation 'are very poison | Where the disease is violent' (3.1.221–2), and that, like a gangrened foot, Coriolanus is 'a disease that must be cut away … Lest his infection … Spread further' (3.1.297, 308–9, 312–13), though Menenius has urged, 'O, he's a limb that has but a disease; | Mortal to cut it off, to cure it easy' (3.1.298–9).

In *The Body in Pain: The Making and Unmaking of the World* (1985), Elaine Scary discusses the conflict between physical pain and man's language-based sense of reality, and particularly the way that in torture as in war the pain of others is interpreted in ways that support the institutions that cause the pain. Thus, in order to validate war, military societies have conventionally obscured fighting by discussing it in imagery of hunting (cf. 1.1.233–4), sport (1.4.1–7), and harvesting (1.3.37–8, 4.5.206–7), and dramatized it to personal antagonism between leaders who are mythologized into superhuman colossi—as Menenius describes Coriolanus as 'a thing | Made by some other deity than nature, | That shapes men better' (4.6.94–6)—or reified into killing machines (2.1.156–7, 2.2.105 ff.) who serve an equally impersonal state that is placed beyond question (1.1.64–9). In particular, wounds and blood are talked of as if they were by-products of war, instead of its essence, yet are used to validate—to 'embody'—such abstractions as the 'state' and to ratify the status of non-combatants: as in the scene where Menenius and Volumnia calculate the number of Martius' wounds. Mutilation has been converted from its painful subjective reality (cf. 1.10.28–9, 2.2.67–8) to a form of currency in Rome, where it can be exchanged for plebeian 'voices' (votes) in precisely the body/language transfer that Scary describes. Another tactic is to talk of war in terms of weaponry (cf. 4.5.109–10, 121–6), and twice in the play blood and weaponry are glamourized together. Volumnia evokes Martius wiping his 'bloody brow | With his mailed hand' (1.3.35–6), in stark contrast to the tender body mentioned a few lines earlier (l. 6); and, pre-eminently, there is Coriolanus' identification of his own blood-soaked body as itself a sword, when the cheering soldiers raise him shoulder-high—'Make you a sword of me?' (1.7.77)—thus emblematizing Titus Lartius' earlier praise that Martius 'sensibly outdares his senseless sword' (1.5.26). While exploiting the human fascination with physical violence, then (see 'Original Staging'), *Coriolanus* ruthlessly exposes its protective rhetoric.

This overlaps with the last main thread of imagery in the play which clusters metatheatrically round language and acting. Martius' denial of 'kindly' relationship to all but a chosen few is connected to his 'linguistic idealism' and distrust of rhetoric. As Stanley Fish points out, 'Part of Coriolanus' tragedy is that he is forever seeking a level of intention deeper... than that stipulated by the public conventions of language'.[1] Just as he 'rewards | His deeds with doing them' (2.2.125–6) and among the Volsces 'What he bids be done is finished with his bidding' (5.4.22–3), so he expects language to be immediately denotative, the *signifier*, that is, equating wholly with its *signified*. In his own case, 'His heart's his mouth' (3.1.259), and behind his magnificently futile 'I banish you! ... There is a world else-where' (3.3.124, 136) lies a kind of 'magical' belief that what he says will in fact happen.[2] This is of a piece with Shake-speare's emphasis (which is not in Plutarch) on the importance Martius also puts on keeping promises (cf. 1.1.236–7, 259 ff., 1.9.1–2, 3.1.32, 3.3.87): a trait that gives an extra irony to his own betrayals, first of what he promised to his family and friends when going into exile, then of Aufidius.

Martius' naïvety about language focuses particularly on the antinomy he sets up between 'name' and 'voice'.[3] He wants 'name' to represent what one actually *is*, not something for which one is reputed: he himself is a 'carbuncle entire' (1.5.28) who wishes 'Not to be other than one thing' (4.7.42). 'Voice', on the other hand, is merely public opinion, of which he is dismissive and contemptuous; though Volumnia, Menen-ius, the Tribunes, and Aufidius all realize that such opinion is effectively the price of power.[4] Their acceptance of the fabricated, agreed-on nature of society is one aspect of the play's heavy use of legal tropes mentioned earlier under 'Con-temporary Background'.[5]

---

[1] Stanley Fish, *Is there a text in this Class?* (1980), p. 212; cf. Lawrence Danson, *Tragic Alphabet: Shakespeare's Drama of Language* (1974), pp. 146–62.

[2] Cf. *On Narcissism*, Strachey, xiv. 75.

[3] See D. J. Gordon, 'Name and Fame: Shakespeare's *Coriolanus*', *Papers, Mainly Shakespearian* (1964), 40–57; cf. Leonard Tennenhouse, '*Coriolanus*: History and the Crisis of Semantic Order', *Comparative Drama*, 10 (1977), 328–46.

[4] 'Voices' itself is used 54 times in the canon, 36 of which are in *Coriolanus* with 27 in 2.3 alone: Marvin Spevack, *A Complete ... Concordance to ... Shakespeare* (1968–80), vol. 5.

[5] See G. E. Tanselle and F. W. Dunbar, 'Legal Language in *Coriolanus*', *SQ*, 13 (1962), 231–8, who find 'at least 194 words and phrases of legal significance in the play'.

The actual instability of 'names' (and hence of identity conceived of as essence) is emphasized by the way that, in the very scene in which he gains the honorific 'Coriolanus'— 'In *sign* of what you *are*' (1.10.26, my italics) Cominius tactfully emphasizes—Martius forgets the name of his Corioles host; Menenius too discovers that with the Volscian sentinels his 'name' is powerless (5.2.10–14, 29, 93–4); and whenever names are *over*-used, as when Aufidius harps on 'Martius' (4.5.102, 107, 127, 148) or Martius on 'Aufidius' (5.3.191, 192, 194), there is a sense of disingenuousness, emotional bad faith. This focuses particularly on Martius' own 'name'. When Aufidius fails to recognize him at Antium and six times demands his name (4.5.54–65), Martius finally identifies himself as 'Caius Martius', but then goes on to say that Rome has 'devoured' his personal name and patronymic so that only his honorific 'Coriolanus'—which Shakespeare calls his 'surname'—now remains (4.5.72 ff.). Aufidius, none the less, calls him 'Martius' throughout the scene, and Martius accepts this without demur though later he flies into a rage because Aufidius uses 'Martius' instead of 'Coriolanus'. Yet earlier, rebuffing Cominius, he had refused to reply to 'Coriolanus' either, declaring himself 'a kind of nothing, titleless, | Till he had forged himself a name o' th' fire | Of burning Rome' (5.1.11–15).[1] Clearly, his sense of identity is closely bound to insistence on his 'name', but the significance of that name is shown to be woefully unstable.

Such slipperiness of language is persistently equated with acting, which is a major image motif in the play.[2] It is particularly dense in the persuasion scenes with Volumnia. Having protested that canvassing 'is a part | That I shall blush in acting' (2.2.143–4) and deliberately parodied the process 'most counterfeitly' (2.3.96; cf. 2.3.153 ff.), he insists that he wishes only to 'play | The man I am' (3.2.15–16)—a more ambiguous phrase than he realizes—when he is pres-

---

[1] Revenge as a tactic of self-recreation is discussed by Richard W. Hillman, 'Meaning and Mortality in Some Renaissance Revenge Plays', *Univ. of Toronto Quarterly*, 49 (1979), 1–17.

[2] See Charney, pp. 169 ff.; Thomas Van Laan, *Role-playing in Shakespeare* (1978), pp. 212–15; Alexander Leggatt, *Shakespeare's Political Drama* (1988), pp. 189–213.

sured to return to the voters; only to have Volumnia retort, 'You might have been enough the man you are, | With striving less to be so' (ll. 19–20) and insist that now he 'seem | The same you are not' (ll. 48–9). Protesting that she herself would not hesitate to dissemble (l. 64), she gives him an elaborate lesson in the rhetoric and gestures of hypocritical public relations; and when Martius again protests 'You have put me now to such a part which never | I shall discharge to th' life' (ll. 107–8), Cominius offers to 'prompt' him (l. 108) and Volumnia says 'To have my praise for this, perform a part | Thou hast not done before' (ll. 111–12). The same metatheatrical imagery clusters again in 5.3: as the women approach, Martius, feeling his role of revenger threatened, admits, 'Like a dull actor now | I have forgot my part' (5.3.40–1), and, having succumbed, cries out, 'Behold, the heavens do ope, | The gods look down, and this unnatural scene | They laugh at' (5.3.184–6). The significance of this revulsion from acting and the symbolic contingency of words is more profound than merely a man-of-action's 'Spartan' preference for deeds before words (e.g. 2.2.69–70).[1] For Martius to act symbolically sets body against mind, so that he fears 'Lest I surcease to honour mine own truth, | And by my body's action teach my mind | A most inherent baseness' (3.2.123–5); and he sees such self-betrayal in sexual terms as a 'harlot's spirit' that undermines his manhood and reduces him to the weakness of a eunuch, virgin, or schoolboy (3.2.114 ff.).[2]

Thus *Coriolanus* has a density and sophistication of rhetoric, theme, and imagery that equal those of any other play by Shakespeare, but this is appreciable only in relation to the action and the subtlety of characterization. There is little that will seem impressive if anthologized out of context, and to

[1] Cf. Brockbank, pp. 46–7; Anne Barton, 'Shakespeare and the Limits of Language', *ShS*, 24 (1971), 27–8.

[2] A suggestive nexus for Martius' emphasis on the physical basis of personality (body-ego), distrust of language and socially imposed roles, emulative rivalry with Aufidius, lack of a father, and rejection by his mother can be found in the theory of Jacques Lacan: see his 'The Mirror Stage as Formative of the Function of the I', in *Écrits: a Selection*, trans. Alan Sheridan (1977), pp. 1 ff., and *The Language of Self*, trans. Anthony Wilder (1968), *passim*.

understand it fully it must also be seen in relation to the performance dimension of the play, its staging.

First Production

Date and Venue. Deciding the date and theatre for *Coriolanus'* first production is complicated by two important events: the King's Men's leasing of Blackfriars Theatre as a 'winter house' on 10 August 1608, a major decision in which Shakespeare would most certainly have had a voice; and severe visitations of plague that closed the public theatres for the second half of 1608 and most of 1609. These events make it possible that *Coriolanus* was one of Shakespeare's first plays to be tried out at the Blackfriars.

By 1608 the established procedure to control infection from the plague was to shut the theatres down whenever mortality bills for the city and suburbs rose over forty deaths a week—though one cannot rely on this being strictly adhered to because the city authorities always wanted to shut the theatres early and then to delay their reopening.[1] On this basis, theatres would have been officially closed from the end of July 1608 to the end of November 1609;[2] so Schoenbaum concludes, quite reasonably, 'By the late autumn of 1609 . . . the King's Men had probably begun operations in their new house in the heart of London.'[3]

An earlier, if temporary, use of Blackfriars is suggested, however, by a lawsuit of Kirkham vs. Painton, in which Burbage and Heminges both testified that by 1612 they had shared in profits from the presentation of plays at Blackfriars for four years; and if the plague rules were indeed applied fairly, there were at least two, possibly three, weeks when playing could have recommenced in the middle of March 1609,[4] though, as this coincided with Lent, it is unlikely that the theatres

---

[1] See F. P. Wilson, *The Plague in Shakespeare's London* (rev. edn. 1963), pp. 54–5, and Barroll (p. 3 n. 3), pp. 217–26, '*Appendix 2*: Plague Figures for Shakespeare's Stuart Period: 1603–1610'.

[2] Besides Wilson, pp. 125–7, see E. K. Chambers, *Elizabethan Stage*, iv. 350–1.

[3] Schoenbaum, p. 240.

[4] See Barroll, pp. 225–6; Bernard Beckerman, *Shakespeare at the Globe* (1962), p. 232 n. 4.

were reopened then. More intriguingly, the King's Men were granted special royal subsidies of £40 and £30 respectively for the winters of 1608–9 and 1609–10, 'by way of his Majesty's reward for their private practice in the time of infection that thereby they might be enabled to perform their service before his Majesty in the Christmas holidays', as the 1608–9 award puts it.[1] This was in addition to their remuneration for performing twelve unnamed plays at Court during the 1608–9 holidays, and seems too high a payment merely for rehearsals. F. P. Wilson suggested that this 'private practice would be perhaps at the private theatre in the Blackfriars'; and, remembering the earlier Boys' Company tactic of using such 'rehearsals' as an occasion for exclusive performance, E. K. Chambers cautiously extended Wilson's hypothesis with the speculation that 'Possibly this did not exclude the admission of spectators.'[2]

Failing production at Court or in such 'private practice' during the winter of 1608–9, the earliest date that the plague would have allowed *Coriolanus* to be performed in London is the winter season of 1609–10, beginning probably early in December 1609.[3] But again this is more likely to have been at the company's new 'winter house' than at the Globe because of the continuing severity of the weather—though later it would, of course, also have played at the latter. Certainly when *Coriolanus* was allocated to Killigrew's company at Drury Lane on 12 January 1669, it was listed among plays 'formerly acted at the Blackfriars'.[4]

The possibility (I would even say likelihood) that *Coriolanus* was composed from the start with the newly acquired Blackfriars in mind and subsequently annotated for what would

[1] The depositions are printed in Chambers, *Elizabethan Stage*, Appendix B, iv. 175, 176. Note that even the phrase about 'service before his Majesty' was dropped in the 1609–10 entry; and that 'private practice' was not mentioned in a similar award for 1603–4, when the King's men lacked the Blackfriars.

[2] See F. P. Wilson, p. 127 n. 1; E. K. Chambers, i. 78, and *Elizabethan Stage*, i. 133 n. 1.

[3] See Barroll, p. 226, and cf. *State Papers Venetian* XI, 427, for a statement in February, 1609–10 that the City had not for a long time been as free of the plague 'as it was all this winter'.

[4] See Allardyce Nicoll, *A History of English Drama, 1660–90* (1952), i. 353.

amount to a try-out in that house rather than the Globe throws certain aspects of its tone, dramatic technique, and stage directions into new relief. The elaborateness of its stage directions might be expected for an élite playhouse the company was not yet used to, especially if these were partly composed when Shakespeare was out of town at Stratford, as has been suggested.[1] The play's sardonic tone, long passages of constitutional debate, and heavy use of legal terminology are well suited to a sophisticated audience with a high proportion of Inns of Court men. And the two standard arguments against associating *Coriolanus* with the Blackfriars—its audience's objection to noisy, martial plays, and the smaller size of its stage—can both be easily countered. Though Ben Jonson parodied 'drum and trumpet' plays with Otter's entertainment in 4.2 of *Epicoene* as early as 1609, this may have been precisely in personal response to *Coriolanus*, like his mockery of 2.2.99 with 'You have lurched all your friends of the better half of the garland' (*Epicoene* 5.4.203–4).[2] There is really no evidence for a distinction of taste in this matter between public and private theatres until nearly twenty years later, in the Caroline period. Productions were exchanged freely between the Globe and Blackfriars at least till Burbage's death in 1619,[3] and as Andrew Gurr has emphasized,[4] the opening of *The Tempest* is quite as noisy as anything in *Coriolanus*. Similarly, though it is true that the Blackfriars stage was less than half the size of the Globe's and would also have had half a dozen gallants sitting on stools to either side

[1] J. Dover Wilson, *Coriolanus, A Facsimile of the First Folio Text* (1928), p. 1.

[2] *Epicoene*'s parody can be interpreted as Jonson's reaction to Shakespeare having stolen a march on him in the newly reopened private theatres towards which Jonson's own ambition was bent. This would agree neatly with his rewording of 2.2.99 as 'You have *lurched* all *your friends* of the *better half* of the garland' (*Epicoene* 5.4.203–4; *my italics*), his own play having been mounted later and at the other, less prestigious private theatre in Whitefriars.

[3] G. E. Bentley, *The Jacobean Stage* (1968), vi. 3–44; Andrew Gurr, *Playgoing in Shakespeare's London* (1987), pp. 167–8.

[4] 'The Tempest's Tempest at the Blackfriars', *ShS*, 41 (1989), p. 102. It is also possible that the Folio's 'Cornet' directions were *added* at the end of 1.10, the opening of 3.1, and also at 2.2.153.1 because the cornett was especially favoured as a private-theatre instrument: see George Cowling, *Music on the Elizabethan Stage* (1913), p. 54; Brockbank, p. 5 n. 2 and 1.10.0.1 n.; George, p. 492.

of it, this does not mean that it would have been difficult to
accommodate the play's crowd and battle scenes. It merely
means that we should forget the late eighteenth and nineteenth centuries' taste for pictorialism and crowds of supernumeraries.[1] Soldiers, citizens, and senators would be easy
to double because they require little acting,[2] so *Coriolanus*
could have been mounted with a comparatively small cast—as
has certainly proved feasible in such modern productions as
those by the RSC in 1977 and the Kick Theatre in 1989.
Much of the crowd noise is specifically identified in the
Folio text as coming from off-stage (eg. 1.1.43.1, 5.4.48, 57;
5.6.48), with on-stage crowds described as merely 'clusters';
and except for the 1.9 duel between Martius and Aufidius,
the fighting could logically be confined to spaces in front of
the stage doors. Moreover, if *Coriolanus* was written with the
new theatre at least in mind, which seems more likely than
not, then the theatrical occasion itself—the public theatre's
first invasion of a socially exclusive location—could emblematize a main theme of the play, with the shocking eruption
of rebellious citizens at the very top of Scene 1 providing a
striking example of the private theatre's (and Shakespeare's)
taste for metatheatre.

Original Staging. Questions of space and taste apart, not much
difference in staging would be needed between Blackfriars and
the Globe, as acting locations were roughly the same in both
houses. Exploitation of the delay between entering from the
tiring house and walking to a position downstage indicates
the type of thrust stage that could be found at either. Thus,
Menenius changes from placating the rioters in the first scene
to a provocative 'Rome and her rats are at the point of battle'
three lines before he actually greets Martius, whose precipitous, angry entrance with news of the Tribunes' election we
may assume he has already noticed; or, to give another
example, in 3.2 Martius wonders why his mother should now
disapprove of his treating the plebeians arrogantly six and a
half lines before he turns to her directly with 'I talk of you',

[1] See John Ripley, '*Coriolanus*'s Stage Imagery on Stage, 1754–1901', *SQ*,
38 (1987), p. 339.
[2] See Alice Venezsky, *Pageantry on the Shakespearean Stage* (1951), p. 21.

and most actors of the role assume (I think rightly) that he intends her to overhear all of his complaint as she walks towards him from her entrance. '*Enter two Senators with others on the walls of Corioles*' (1.4.12.1–2) shows that a balcony was used in the battle scenes, so probably later too; and directions such as '*Enter at one door, Cominius with the Romans; at another door, Martius, with his arm in a scarf*' (1.10.0.1–3) indicate the usual doors at either side of the stage. It seems likely, too, that a central recess (or possibly a free-standing central booth) was used as the entrance to Aufidius' off-stage dining-hall in 4.5 (with the servants using one side door as a route to the kitchen and cellars, and Martius entering through the other as though from the outside). Such a recess would also be likely for Coriolanus' tent before Rome in Act 5, and would be especially useful to represent the gates of Corioles in Act 1, though it is also possible that city-gates were an habitual, free-standing property on the Elizabethan stage.[1] The triumphant processions of 2.1 and 5.6 (and possibly 5.5) would have been more impressive from such a central entrance, though a side door would have been equally as practicable.

Such staging would be suitable for either the Globe or Blackfriars, but the latter's seating in the space before the stage would make less probable suggestions by Allardyce Nicoll, Joseph Weixlmann, and Francis Berry[2] that certain scenes (1.4, 5.3, and 5.5) may have used the theatre yard for entrances and exits. On the other hand, Blackfriars would make more plausible what seems to be a subtly ironic relation to the audience in 5.5. It is not often noticed that the directions for neither Martius' triumph in 2.1 nor Volumnia's in 5.5 indicate any entrance for the citizens—they are *not*, in fact, crowd scenes (Macready in the nineteenth century was the first to add the citizens for Martius' triumph, after Kemble had swelled the

---

[1] See Chambers, *Elizabethan Stage*, iii. 83; Irwin Smith, ' "Gates" on Shakespeare's Stage', *SQ*, 7 (1956), 159–76; Glynne Wickham, *Early English Stages, 1300–1600* (1959) ii. part 1, pp. 206–9.

[2] Allardyce Nicoll, ' "Passing Over the Stage" ', *ShS*, 12 (1959), pp. 47–55; Joseph Weixlmann, 'How the Romans Were Beat Back to Their Trenches ...', *NQ*, NS 21 (1974), pp. 133–4; Francis Berry, 'Shakespeare's Stage Geometry', *Deutsche Shakespeare-Gesellschaft Jahrbuch 1974* (Heidelberg, 1974), p. 170; J. W. Saunders, 'Vaulting the Rails', *ShS*, 7 (1954), 69–81.

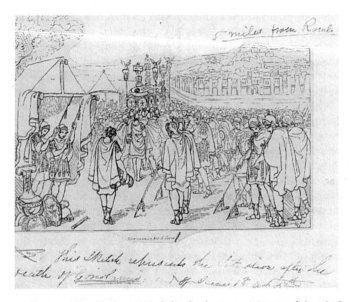

7. George Scharf's drawing of the final scene in Macready's 1838 production at Covent Garden, annotated for a prompt-book of Edwin Forrest's 1863 production in New York

procession with extra soldiers and choristers); but, whereas the off-stage crowd is vividly described by Brutus in 2.1 but not included in the dialogue or stage directions, the Senator's speech which constitutes nearly all of the very brief 5.5 is addressed directly to the plebeians, bidding them 'Call your tribes together' to praise Volumnia as Rome's saviour and 'Unshout the noise that banished Martius'. Despite cheering off-stage and the loud music that accompanies it (which is both heard and described in detail),[1] the effect of this scene is bound to be ironic if only a few anonymous 'Lords' are actually on stage, and will be doubly so if the Senator has to deliver his

[1] See E. H. Naylor, *Shakespeare and Music* (1896), p. 175; G. H. Cowling, *Music on the Shakespearean Stage* (1913), p. 55. Beethoven's *Coriolan* overture is not based on Shakespeare's play, but for a full account of music for productions of *Coriolanus* as well as operatic and other special settings, see Bryan N. S. Gooch, David Thatcher, *et al.*, eds., *A Shakespeare Music Catalogue* (1991), i. 219–36.

exhortation out towards the audience, which has just watched Martius crumble under Volumnia's emotional pressure and is aware of Aufidius' intention to 'potch at him'. The irony may remind us only too uncomfortably of Volumnia's own comment before Martius' triumph earlier: 'Before him | He carries noise, and behind him he leaves tears' (2.1.154–5).

Whether Blackfriars or the Globe was used, the staging shares four basic difficulties (besides the Act divisions, already discussed under 'Structure'). At 1.4.29.1–2 the Folio has the direction, '*The Romans are beat back to their trenches. Enter Martius cursing.*' These 'trenches' come straight from North's translation of Plutarch, but they raise the questions of whether they were staged and, if so, how. Francis Berry suggests that the Roman soldiers 'vaulted the rails' around the perimeter of the thrust stage to take refuge in the area known in Victorian theatres as the 'orchestra pit', with the height of the stage and its railing protecting them like a palisaded trench. Martius' advance to the lip of the stage to look down and curse them, Berry argues, would make him tower impressively 'like a great sea-mark' above the audience, before following the retreating Volscians up the full depth of the stage to be shut into the tiring-house façade.[1] This is an attractively vivid suggestion, but is not really practicable. For one thing, the soldiers would find it very difficult to clamber back on stage—the rails were designed precisely to keep people from doing so; for another, their important acerbities about Martius would be muffled and obscured for most of the audience. Gary Taylor has shown[2] that for such scenes of rout, the convention was for the retreating army to be beaten out through one side door and to re-enter through the other as though exhausted from long flight. Presumably the soldiers could then throw themselves and their equipment wearily down at the stage lip (as they usually do in modern productions); and, as far as the audience is concerned, Martius standing over them to curse would be just as impressive visually as he would be in Berry's suggestion.

Some modern productions have also had Martius strike or even kill one of his own soldiers at this point, to establish the

[1] Francis Berry, p. 170.   [2] See *Textual Companion*, p. 595.

berserker fierceness of his rage, but there is no warrant for this in the text. What *is* important is that, as we have seen, Shakespeare altered Plutarch to emphasize the alienation of Martius' soldiers, thus establishing an early, unforgettable impression of his 'aloneness'. This creates its own staging problems, however. When Martius reappears from the city— '*Enter Martius bleeding, assaulted by the enemy*' (1.5.34)— where on the Elizabethan stage would Martius have entered from? The usual assumption is that he comes back through the city gates; but, as William Empson has pointed out, since Shakespeare has eliminated his companions, it is implausible to have Martius opening a large door at the same time that he is fighting off several of the enemy. In 1977 the RSC solved this problem by stylization: Alan Howard straddled the production's tall metal gates towards their top and forced them open with spread-eagled arms and legs, while smoke billowed out beneath him; this hardly follows the direction's 'assaulted by the enemy', however. Empson's own suggestion is that Martius should reappear up on Corioles' walls as though fighting pursuers on the stairs behind him, and that Lartius should lead his rescue party up the siege ladders he has so pointedly called for forty lines earlier (1.4.22).[1] The gates could then be opened to admit the rest of the assault party; or, alternatively, the heartened Romans could break them in with battering rams, as they did in Bridges-Adams's 1933 production. A modern version of such staging was used in John Hirsch's provocative updating of the play at San Diego in 1989: firing his automatic rifle at Sandinista enemies below, an Oliver-North-like Martius was swung up from behind the walls clinging to the hook of an enormous crane, from which he lobbed grenades to blow a gap in the defence wall, the smoke from their explosions covering the small set change this required. However, this whole problem vanishes if we abandon the idea of practicable 'gates', and assume a non-representational curtain instead.

Another, more pervasive difficulty is in identifying particular Roman plebeians or Volscian servingmen. Many speeches

---

[1] William Empson, *Essays on Shakespeare*, ed. David Price (1986), pp. 177–83.

have the heading 'All', and there is no knowing whether in Shakespeare's day such speeches were delivered chorically (as Peter Hall claims is still possible today) or were split up between several speakers, as is more common modern practice. Orthodox stage history claims that the tactic of controlling mass effects by dividing the crowd into various groups, each with its own leader, was pioneered by the Duke of Saxe-Meiningen's company in late nineteenth-century Germany, but Menenius' 'Here come the clusters' when 'a troop of Citizens' enters at 4.6.136 suggests that Elizabethans may have already used the same method.[1] Certainly, Shakespeare identifies spokesmen for various views in the crowd by numbering particular citizens, but the trouble in *Coriolanus* is that he seems to have numbered each scene afresh, so that the aggressive First Citizen of 1.1 becomes the no-less arrogant Third Citizen in 2.3. Editors and directors usually regularize such numbering to maintain stage consistency for these characters.

There is similar confusion among the entrances and exits of Aufidius' servants at the beginning of 4.4, and a particularly tricky mix-up in the canvassing scene of 2.3, at the end of which Third Citizen is made to quote lines he cannot possibly have heard—including parts of Martius' brief soliloquy, spoken in a lull between meeting groups of voters. Directors have coped with this problem by having First Citizen enter a little behind the other two at '*Enter three of the Citizens*', and, after Martius' rebuff for his single, telling comment 'The price is to ask it kindly' (2.3.59, 71), having First Citizen break away from the discussion to hide somewhere that allows him to spy on Martius' subsequent canvassing. This helps to explain why Martius calls the three citizens who first enter 'a brace' and only counts their votes as *two* (2.3.59, 76–7), and also solves the problem of how a Citizen can later quote ideas that Martius spoke when he thought himself alone.

Finally, there are two problems of locale. Though Martius leaves Act 2 claiming to be heading for the Senate-house

[1] It is safest to assume that '*All.*' was interpreted in a variety of ways; see E. A. J. Honigmann, 'Re-enter the Stage Direction . . .', *ShS*, 29 (1976), 117–25; cf. Ralph Berry, 'Casting the Crowd: *Coriolanus* in Performance', *Assaph*, Sec. C: Studies in the Theatre, 4 (1988), 111–24.

(2.3.141, 144) and it is to the Capitol that the Tribunes and their followers leave to intercept him (2.3.250, 256), it is to that rival focus of Roman life, the market-place, that First Senator and Cominius say Martius is heading when the confrontation between the two parties actually occurs (3.1.33, 114). This is probably only a slip, but just possibly Shakespeare intended both 3.1 and 3.3—the crucial scenes of political confrontation—to be understood as happening somewhere between the two locations that identify the city's rival power blocks. A similar confusion at the end of the play is more puzzling. According to Plutarch, after sparing Rome Coriolanus returned to Antium, the Volscian capital which was also Aufidius' birthplace. The conversation between Aufidius and his Conspirators that begins 5.6 similarly makes clear that it is to Antium that Martius is returning in the play. 'Your native town', says one of the Conspirators to Aufidius,

> you entered like a post [i.e. courier],
> And had no welcomes home; but he returns
> Splitting the air with noise.
>
> (5.6.49–51)

Yet a few lines later, when Coriolanus objects to Aufidius addressing him unceremoniously as 'Martius', Aufidius replies,

> Dost thou think
> I'll grace thee with that robbery, thy stol'n name
> 'Coriolanus', in Corioles?
>
> (5.6.90–2)

Again, this may be a slip; or Shakespeare may have been unable to resist the massive irony of the line, and gambled that his audiences would not notice (as, in fact, few do). But alternatively, he may have intended the identification, in order to emphasize a thematic significance in the play's pattern of repetition. As we have noted, a recurrent situation in *Coriolanus* is of Martius deliberately setting himself against a variety of crowds so that a basic rhythm of the play is (to use a phrase from Michael Goldman)[1] the 'systole and

---

[1] Michael Goldman, *Shakespeare and the Energies of the Drama* (1972), p. 116.

diastole' of angry or enthusiastic mobs, with Martius refusing to be associated with either. One aspect of this rhythm is the repeated situation of him marching on a city, as its conqueror or its hero: Corioles, Rome, Antium, Rome again, and finally perhaps (exploiting the non-locationary quality of the thrust stage) Antium-conflated-with-Corioles, because in relation to Martius all cities have come to stand for the same challenge to his integrity —an identification made all the easier because the theatre's tiring-house façade would have to stand for all of them.[1]

It is also possible to deduce more general aspects of the original staging without reference to any particular theatre. Costume, for example, would almost certainly have been a mixture. Ordinary Jacobean working clothes would be worn by the plebeians, with an emphasis on their greasy aprons and on the 'caps' which they and the soldiers are so frequently bidden to throw aloft. This was an Elizabethan rather than Roman custom, and in the play is confined to the lower classes—except, interestingly, for Menenius, who also throws his cap up at the news of Martius' return (2.1.102). According to Livy, 'the commons liked [Menenius] as he was one of themselves',[2] but there is no other indication of this in the play; perhaps he has become a little *déclassé* like Falstaff? The patricians, on the other hand, would wear a formalized version of Roman garb that, it is generally accepted, by 1608 was likely to have been more accurate than that depicted in Henry Peacham's famous sketch for *Titus Andronicus* of 1595, both as regards patrician togas and the moulded breastplates, tunics, greaves, and feathered helmets of Roman armour.[3]

There are also two specific costuming refinements: how Volscians are likely to have been distinguished from Romans; and the occasionally emblematic significance of dress. Modern productions have tried to represent the Volsces as a less 'civilized' people by dressing them as Asiatics, Aztecs, North

---

[1] See David Bevington, *Action is Eloquence: Shakespeare's Language of Gesture* (1984), p. 106.

[2] Livy, *The Early History of Rome*, trans. A. de Selincourt (1960), p. 141.

[3] The Peacham drawing is reproduced in *ShS*, 1 (1948), facing p. 32. For comment on its limited usefulness, see W. M. Merchant, 'Classical Costume in Shakespearian Productions', *ShS*, 10 (1957), 71–6; Charney, pp. 208–9; Martin Holmes, *Shakespeare and his Players* (1972), pp. 150–4; Arthur Humphreys, ed., *Caesar* (1984), pp. 50–1.

8. The warrior's 'gressus': Coriolanus (Tino Carraro) greets Cominius (Cesare Polacco) in Strehler's 1957–8 production at the Piccolo Teatro, Milan

American Indians, Scottish Highlanders, Russians, or, more recently, Nicaraguan freedom fighters; but Antium in fact was only twelve miles from Rome—they were not opposite civilizations like Rome and Egypt—and it is more ironically effective to stress their likeness than their difference. Sufficient differentiation to guide an audience can easily be achieved by colour coding (in the 1954 Old Vic production, for example, the Romans dressed in red and the Volscians in bluey-green) and possibly by differences of accent: recent British productions have exploited Lancashire, Welsh, and Scots. As for emblematic effects: the shabby dress of the women petitioners to which Volumnia draws attention at 5.3.95–7 was conventionally represented in nineteenth-century productions by elaborate mourning dress, but this misses its important but ambiguous parallels to Coriolanus' 'gown of humility' in 2.3 (which hypocritically hides his pride) and the 'mean apparel' in which he appeared before Aufidius in 4.4 and 5 (representing a more genuine submission that was still, however, to some degree a 'disguise'). Volumnia talks of power itself as a garment (3.2.16–18), and each stage of Martius' career has been accompanied by significant costume changes, visually contradicting his fierce wish for integrity: patrician street-dress is followed by blood-soaked armour, the oak garland of triumph, the 'gown of humility' for canvassing, the consul's robe—too hastily donned—in which ironically he is banished, and the 'mean apparel' in which he arrives at Antium. In Act 5 he must be splendidly, even showily dressed. Plutarch says, 'he was set in his chair of state, with a marvellous and unspeakable majesty'; Menenius sneers that he looks like a 'thing made for Alexander' (5.4.22), who wore golden armour; and Cominius' earlier comment 'he does sit in gold' (5.1.63, punning in Elizabethan pronunciation on the heraldic phrase 'enguled' or blood-coloured, like the 'total gules' of Pyrrhus in *Hamlet*) may refer to his chair of state, or, more probably I think, to a red-gold cloak or golden breastplate.[1] Splendid regalia would now appropriately reflect his hollow new assertiveness, like the golden armour concealing corruption that betrays his ancestor, the heroic Hector in *Troilus and Cressida* (cf. the 'gilded butterfly' chased by Young Martius, 1.3.63), and would anticipate and contribute to the doomed flamboyance of his entry into Antium in 5.6.

The properties required are very simple: mainly seating—stools, 'cushions' for the Senate scenes (which would be like the wool sacks used in the Jacobean House of Commons), a 'chair of state'; weapons—bats, clubs, rakes, pikes, and other tools for the plebeians; pikes, swords, shields, and siege ladders for the solders; and occasional handprops: Titus Lartius' crutch in 1.1, the items of loot specified in 1.6, the wine called for by Martius in 1.10, the letter he gives Menenius, and his 'scroll' of 5.6.84. Again some props would carry quasi-emblematic significance: the women's sewing would not only be recognized as specifically Roman but might also draw upon its association in Christian allegory with the Virgin Mary,[2] so that Virgilia's patient needlework would contrast all the more with Volumnia's imitations of Martius' ferocity; and the fact that Aufidius enters 4.5 from a feast would probably be indicated by the emblematic convention of a napkin in his hand or thrown across his shoulder.

[1] Cf. Jean MacIntyre, 'Word, Acts, and Things: Visual Language in *Coriolanus*', *English Studies in Canada*, 10 (1984), 8–9.

[2] Cf. Bevington, p. 49.

The blocking of the action shows exceptionally heavy reliance on the ceremoniousness of mass entries and especially processions. Hence the importance of the Tribunes' indecorous entrance first at 1.1.224, which elicits from Martius an ironic 'See, our best elders' and prompts Titus Lartius' concern for proper precedence at the exit a few lines later. There are seven 'procession' scenes or entries: Martius' triumph in 2.1, followed by the formal entrance of the Senate in 2.2; his procession to become consul in 3.3, which is interrupted by the Tribunes; the procession of women in 5.3; Volumnia's brief triumph in 5.5; Martius' entry into Antium in 5.6, and the final cortège. As was suggested earlier, these repetitions give maximum opportunity for irony, which was probably pointed by deliberate parallelism in staging.[1]

Coriolanus has more directions for music than any other Shakespeare play[2] (which may also indicate that it was marked up for performance). Mostly this comprises the martial sounds of drums, trumpets, and cornetts. These are skilfully deployed to clarify for the audience the locales and advances or retreats of the off-stage battles in Act 1, with trumpets perhaps associated with the Roman troops and cornetts with the Volscians (though such a distinction ends after Act 1).[3] These seem mostly to have been sounded off-stage, and provide the basis for much critical comment on the clangorous nature of the play.[4] Only three scenes use non-martial music

[1] See Ripley, 'Stage Imagery on Stage', p. 339.

[2] Cecile de Banke, *Shakespearean Stage Production, Then and Now* (1953), pp. 269–70; cf. Thelma N. Greenfield, 'Non-vocal Music: Added Dimension in Five Shakespeare Plays', in Waldo F. McNeir and T. Greenfield, eds., *Pacific Coast Studies in Shakespeare* (1966), 106–21.

[3] See R. W. Ingram, ' "Their Noise Be Our Instruction": Listening to *Titus Andronicus* and *Coriolanus*', in John C. Gray, ed., *Mirror Up to Shakespeare . . .* (1984), p. 284.

[4] e.g. G. Wilson Knight in both *The Imperial Theme* (1931), pp. 154 ff. and *The Shakespearean Tempest* (1932), pp. 206–10. Modern productions often try for the same effect with atonal, heavily percussive 'musique concrète' or electronically amplified 'rock music' whereas 19th-century productions went in for massed choirs, with Kemble's productions, for example, accompanying Martius' victory parade of 2.1 with 'See the Conquering Hero Comes'—a tendency parodied in James Morgan, *Coriolanus, A Burletta* (1846), p. 35, and 'Coriolanus at the Seaside', W. C. Day, *Behind the Footlights* (1885), pp. 31–47 (where 'There is a world elsewhere' is accompanied by a rendition of 'Paddle your own canoe').

(plus the possibility that Volumnia may enter singing to illustrate 1.3.1). The first of these is for Aufidius' feast at 4.5.0.1, which not only emphasizes Martius' isolation as an outsider but may also have had ominous overtones because, conventionally, off-stage music was used to convey 'uneasiness of some sort'.[1] The second is the music for Volumnia's triumph in 5.5, which is not only the loudest in the play, but also mixes martial and non-martial instruments. Wilson Knight interprets this mixture as a sign of reconciliation and new harmony,[2] but it can equally well be interpreted as the musical equivalent to Volumnia's conflicted feelings in that scene (see 'Structure'). Lastly, there is the Dead March for which Aufidius specifically calls to end the play (as a dead march also ends *King Lear*), with ironies that are obvious.[3]

Such a heavy use of music contributes to the clamour of what has been called 'Shakespeare's noisiest play'.[4] This noisiness is especially true of Act 1, which is unique in Shakespeare's canon in opening with a rioting crowd; it then continues with noisy scenes of battle and the soldiers' rhythmic cheering of Coriolanus in 1.7 and 1.10. Similarly, in 3.3 the plebeians, at Sicinius' instigation, drown out Martius and his friends by chanting 'It shall be so! It shall be so!' in unison (rubbing in Martius' objection to Sicinius' 'absolute shall' at 3.1.90); they also cheer 'Hoo-hoo!' when Martius is banished (3.3.138), and are instructed by the Tribunes to follow Martius and hoot him out of the city, presumably off-stage (cf. 4.5.78–9, 4.6.130–2, 5.5.4: see 'Structure'). They also provide loud 'noises off' for the triumphs of 2.1 and 5.5 but are not directed to be on stage for those scenes. Towards the end of 3.3, however, a 'rabble' of plebs is brought on to augment the noisy quarrel between Martius and the Tribunes; and in 5.6, after 'great shouts of the people', again off-stage, Martius enters with enthusiastic Volscian 'Commoners' who fifty lines later are howling 'Tear him to pieces'. Thus

---

[1] R. W. Ingram, 'Musical Pauses and the Vision Scenes in Shakespeare's Last Plays', in McNeir and Greenfield, p. 242.

[2] *The Shakespearean Tempest*, p. 209.

[3] Cf. Michael Neill, 'Exeunt with a Dead March: Funeral Pageantry on the Shakespearean Stage', in David Bergeron, ed., *Pageantry in the Shakespearean Theatre* (1985), 153–93.

[4] Poole, p. xii.

9. Olivier's death fall from the Shakespeare Memorial Theatre's 1959 production

Coriolanus' habit of referring to the plebeians as 'mouths' and 'voices' is emphasized in performance.

The antithesis to such noise is a complex use of silence. This can be positive in its implication, as in Martius' lovely greeting to Virgilia, 'My gracious silence, hail!' (2.1.171), which signifies, like Cordelia's 'love and be silent', both honesty in a society which misuses language for deceit, and feelings that are too profound for words, including the inarticulateness of grief. Silence has been described as a way of retreating to a core of personality that cannot be spoken and will not surrender,[1] but, as with revengers such as Iago, or Hieronimo in *The Spanish Tragedy*, this can have sinister implications. The Tribunes' resentful silence when Cominius and Menenius accuse them of responsibility for the Volscians' renewed attack has this negative quality, as, even more powerfully, Aufidius' ominous silence has throughout 5.3— like Bolingbroke's, as that 'silent king' watched Richard II uncrown himself. Thus, Martius' silence throughout Volumnia's long plea for Rome, which is emphasized by four demands for him to speak, is less silence than 'white noise', suggesting a gamut of probable emotions—despair, stubbornness, grief, need, and love—and the '*silent*' which Shakespeare adds to '*Holds her by the hand*' leaves that gesture fraught with contradictory meaning: weak surrender, new humility, grief (as with Macduff), strength of family affection, and a deeper, more mysterious affirmation, as though the heart of his mystery were something inalienably bound up with the physical bond itself. And its richness is particularly evident when the gesture is recognized as the culmination of a series of such hand-clasps throughout the play.

There are many acting cues in *Coriolanus*, some explicit in stage directions, others buried in the text. Because Martius' isolation is so crucial, instances when he touches others physically take on special significance. Thus, he leaves 2.1 with Volumnia and Virgilia holding either hand (2.1.190), a gesture that may be ironically repeated at the end of 5.3, though it is not explicit there; and he takes Menenius' hand with a word-play on 'foot' for an ironic farewell at the end of 4.1. The key hand-clasps, however, are those with Aufidius at 4.5.148 and with Volumnia at 5.3.183. For Laurence Olivier acceptance of Aufidius' hand began Coriolanus' col-

---

[1] Cf. M. Neill, ed. *John Ford: Critical Revisions* (1988), pp. 166–7.

lapse,[1] and it is ironized in the text by Second Servingman's immediate false oath 'By my hand' and Third Servingman's comment that Aufidius 'makes a mistress of him, sanctifies himself with's hand' (4.5.200–1)—as well as by a possible parallel to the earlier spy scene if Adrian and Nicanor also leave for supper hand in hand (cf. 4.3.36, 42, 45). The climactic holding of Volumnia's hand is ironized by this parallel to Aufidius' earlier clasp, and by her own entrance to 5.3 with 'in her hand | The grandchild to her blood' (23–4); also perhaps by the fact that, unlike Plutarch (and in striking contrast to Martius' rapturous greeting of Virgilia), it still does not amount to an embrace. Actual embracing, as we have noted (see 'Imagery and Themes'), is accompanied by imagery that makes it emblematize the interconnection of sexuality and aggression, and rivalry between marriage and male bonding.

Another important gesture that runs throughout the action and dialogue of the play is kneeling, which, as in *King Lear*, can express genuine contrition or its contrary, a resentful mockery of submission. Menenius tells the plebeians that knees, not 'arms', must appeal to the gods (1.1.71); Coriolanus kneels to his mother in 2.1 (an addition to Plutarch that prefigures his kneeling in 5.3); Volumnia implores Martius to kneel to the voters, and even mimics the gesture for him; in 4.5 Coriolanus kneels to submit his life to Aufidius; at 4.6.24 the plebeians promise that their wives and children shall kneel in gratitude to the Tribunes; Menenius sneers that the Tribunes must now 'knee | The way into [Martius'] mercy' (5.1.5–6); a few lines later (65) Cominius describes the fruitlessness of his own kneeling; and the same bitter experience is sometimes used in performance to explain Menenius' later gibe that Coriolanus himself is more than a 'creeping thing' (5.4.14 n.), though there is no actual direction in 5.2 for Menenius to kneel. This series reaches its stage climax in a sequence of kneelings in 5.3. First Martius kneels to his

---

[1] Laurence Kitchin, *Mid-century Drama* (1960), pp. 135–6. This foreshadowed Martius' greater collapse when he took Volumnia's hand in 5.3: cf. Alan Howard, in Daniell, pp. 166–7: 'When they shake hands it is a diabolical moment. Coriolanus knows that in that agreement he will go to his death—but it will be worse for Aufidius. . . . Between two Samurai, honour has been compromised.' Cf. also 2.3.76 n.

The Funeral pyre we rear
The Funeral dirge we sing
For you we shed a tear
For you the trophies bring

Farewell, farewell, farewell
Son of the mighty Mars
Thy body to the flames we give
Thy soul unto the Stars.

10. The dirge and staging plan for Forrest's added scene of Coriolanus' cremation, from his prompt-book (Folger no. 20)

mother, as he did earlier in 2.1, but Volumnia, to his horror, tells him to stand up and kneels herself (which is not in Plutarch either); when Martius raises her in turn, Volumnia first calls for Young Martius' 'knee', then bids the other petitioners to 'shame' her son by joining her to kneel once more. The gesture is thus both submissive and aggressive, sincere and challenging, blending contradictions that even in *King Lear* were kept apart. The point when Volumnia finally rises from her knees is also important: if she remains kneeling (as in the Oxford text) till Martius' 'O mother, mother', this considerably weakens the threat of her last lines; whereas if, as seems to me more probable, she rises with the others at 'Come, let us go' (l. 178), this emphasizes her tactic of withdrawal (seen earlier in 3.2) and makes Coriolanus' hand-clasp more significant because it prevents her leaving, as earlier in the scene she had to prevent him (l. 132)—cf. 5.3.185 n.

Many acting cues are also embedded in the dialogue.[1] These can be straightforward description, like Martius' comment on the petitioners' behaviour at 5.3.22–33, but in most cases are implicit or oblique. For example, Volumnia's repetitions of 'thus' when she conjures up a picture of her son in battle—'Methinks I see him stamp thus, and call thus' (1.3.33)—obviously cue her gesture and vocal delivery, as does Martius 'thus I turn my back' (3.3.135); and Menenius, trying to quell the tumult when Martius hears the people have revoked their votes, cannot help but gasp the lines,

> What is about to be?—I am out of breath.—
> Confusion's near.—I cannot speak.—You tribunes,
> To th' people!—Coriolanus, patience!—
> Speak, good Sicinius.

$$(3.1.190-3)$$

Metre guides the actor here as clearly as the lines' descriptions of breathlessness; and, though one must be careful with this text because its lineation is particularly unreliable, there are several occasions when the metrical shortness of a line signals a significant pause. For instance, in 3.3, when

[1] Cf. my 'A Tale of Three Cities: Staging in *Coriolanus*', in A. L. Magnusson and C. E. McGee, eds., *The Elizabethan Theatre*, XIII (Toronto: P. D. Meany and Co., 1994), pp. 119–45.

Coriolanus has reluctantly been forced back to the plebeians and Sicinius has responded to his question about their change of vote with a bullying 'Answer to *us*', (3.3.61) the choppy shortness of Coriolanus' response indicates a struggle to keep his temper: 'Say then!—'Tis true, I ought so' (which is three syllables short of a pentameter). The pause that indicates his struggle, however, could come at the beginning of the line, or (as delivered by Laurence Olivier) could accompany a change of tone after an initially snapped out 'Say then'.

Minor parallels of staging are used to strengthen the play's ironic emphasis on repetition (see 'Structure'). Acting imagery, for instance, is actualized by Third Citizen's indignant imitation of Martius' burlesque courtesy earlier (2.3.95 ff., 162 ff.), a device that was elaborated for its humour in Kemble's productions and became a fixture in the play's stage history for over a hundred years.[1] But Martius' burlesque, in turn, merely anticipates Volumnia's cynically mimed instructions in 3.2; just as earlier his conduct on the battlefield is anticipated by her admiring demonstrations of it in 1.3, in a way that curiously distances his behaviour because he does and says so precisely what she has already described. Similarly, we see the Tribunes *rehearsing* the plebeian rioters and the Conspirators their leader Aufidius.

There is also a series of delayed exits which would be more noticeable in staging and which cumulatively leave an impression of characters caught up, for good and ill, in events they cannot control. In 2.1, for instance, Volumnia keeps urging that they go to greet the victorious Martius but is so excited talking about his success that the entry of the triumph catches her still on stage. Martius himself is almost Hamlet-like in his vacillations in 3.2 and in his reluctance to leave his mother to face the voters (3.2.112, 122, 133, 136); and the plebeians for their part show a similar collapse of confidence in their indecisive repetitions of 'Come, let's home' when they hear of the Volscians' renewed attack (4.6.158, 160, 162, 165). More complexly, the panicky Tribunes are several times ordered away, then physically prevented from leaving by the angry Volumnia and Virgilia at 4.2.9, 12, 16,

[1] See 2.3.162–9 n.

17, 24–5, 39–41, 46–7. In 4.6 it takes four successive messengers to disabuse the Tribunes of their determination to believe that Rome at last is safe; Menenius makes three ineffectual attempts to pass the Volscian guards; Aufidius has to ask the incredulous Martius six times what his name is, before the latter reluctantly tells him; and Volumnia interrupts her pleading four times, with increasing exasperation, to demand a response that Martius stubbornly denies her. Most grotesquely painful of all in stage terms is Menenius and Cominius' discovery that they are as helpless as Sicinius and the plebeians to make Coriolanus budge physically at the end of 3.3: foes, then friends, beat against his embattled obstinacy no fewer than eleven times, like ineffectual waves against his 'great sea-mark'.

Coriolanus himself must certainly have a dominating stage presence, so the role was probably created by the company's chief tragedian, Richard Burbage,[1] a crack swordsman who in 1608–9 was forty and certainly no 'boy'. He must be sufficiently imposing in person to make the audience flinch like the plebeian rioters themselves at his first abrasive appearance, thus literally 'fleshing out' the play's pervasive body imagery. He is very much a 'tear throat'. The loudness of his voice, which dominates the riots and battles of this very noisy play, is mentioned many times, as are his habitual 'grim looks' (1.5.31, cf. 1.1.253 n.)—which must surely be more aggressive than Kemble's statuesque hauteur (which made him look, says Hazlitt,[2] like a man about to sneeze). He must also be something of a strutter, I think. At one point Brutus inveighs against Martius' godlike 'posture' (2.1.215–17) and in a 1989 production in New York Christopher Walken gave the character a 'macho' swagger that—whencesoever derived—was well suited to the dominating *'gressus'* (i.e. step, way of walking) which all well-born Roman males were taught, and which Cicero says was borrowed more from the

---

[1] J. P. Collier, *New Particulars Concerning Shakespeare* (1836), p. 27, claimed to have seen an elegy on Burbage which included the lines, 'Brutus and Marcius henceforth must be dumb | For ne'er thy like upon our stage shall come' (quoted Furness, p. 726); cf. Holmes, *Shakespeare and Burbage*, pp. 192–7.

[2] *Complete Works of Hazlitt*, ed. P. P. Howe (1934), v. 350.

11. James Quin as Coriolanus

wrestler's movements than the dancer's.[1] Its contemporary equivalent was the 'majestic strut' that Anthony Esler says 'Elizabethan courtiers and captains affected',[2] and it may be such an arrogant gait that Aufidius' servant refers to when he talks so puzzlingly of 'sprightly walking' as characteristic of war (4.5.227). Martius must also obviously be impressive as a fighter—which is where Edmund Kean's diminutive stature betrayed him, despite his frenetic agility and the flaming torch with which he supplemented his sword. One of Aufidius' servants remarks in awe, 'What an arm he has! He turned me about with his finger and his thumb as one would set up a top' (4.5.153–5); and Shakespeare would have known that

[1] *De Oratore*, III.vix.220; cf. Quintilian, *Institutio Oratorio*, I.xi.18–19; Statius, *Silvae*, II.i.108. One meaning of 'hubris' was an insulting air of superiority which in itself constituted a civil offence (Burke, p. 185).

[2] Esler, p. 123; cf. Ulysses' description of Diomedes's gait in *Troilus*, 4.6.15–17. See Fig. 8.

12. John Philip Kemble as Coriolanus at the house of Aufidius, 1798, engraved by R. Earlham from the painting by Sir Francis Bourgeois, RA, in Sir John Soane's Museum

Plutarch says Martius preferred engaging his foes in hand-to-hand combat (Spencer, p. 297), relying more on muscle than on weapons and armour; so the duel with Aufidius—which again Shakespeare has added to his source—should probably take the form of very physical grappling. The dreams which Aufidius recounts to Martius in 4.5 can provide a detailed choreography for this, besides (not incidentally) making clear the homoerotic, 'rough trade' element of the relationship. This element of the duel was stressed in the 1981 production at Stratford, Ontario, where the stationary straining combatants were lit from below to look like George Bellows's expressionistic paintings of New York prizefighters, while in Hirsch's San Diego version, despite the modern setting, the knife struggle between Martius and Aufidius was so savage that one reviewer compared it to two grizzlies grappling in Montana.[1] These battle sequences would be all the more impressive because of Martius' bloody appearance, already remarked on;

---

[1] Jeff Smith, *The Reader* (18 Aug. 1988), p. 24.

and it is perhaps worth noting that it is blood covering his *face* that is especially emphasized (cf. 1.1.238; 1.3.35–6, 43; 1.7.29, 69–70; 1.9.9–10; 1.10.47–8, 68–70, 93), with Martius himself calling it a 'mask' (1.9.10) and contrasting it to 'blushing', which he despises as a juvenile weakness (1.10.68–70; cf. 2.2.144).

In our age of on-the-spot television, wide-screen cinema, and the fear of global disaster, it is difficult for directors and actors to recreate an adequate sense of enthusiasm and awe for Martius' prowess as a warrior—that 'lively and well spirited action' which Thomas Heywood considered inspiring:

> ... to see a soldier, shaped like a soldier, walk, speak, act like a soldier: to see a Hector all besmeared in blood, trampling upon the bulks of kings. . . . Oh these were sights to make an Alexander . . . so bewitching a thing is lively and well spirited action, that it hath power to new mould the hearts of the spectators and fashion them to the shape of any noble or notable attempt.[1]

The audience, in other words, must have been expected to feel some of the same enthusiasm as Cominius' men who cheer and lift Martius shoulder high. Kemble avoided this problem by cutting all the battle scenes except Martius' arrival to aid his fellow commander and his naming as 'Coriolanus'; and Kean was criticized for reintroducing the scenes not only because of his unimpressive physique but also because it was already being argued that battles can be more vividly imagined than realistically represented on the stage. Modern directors tend to represent the fighting in a stylized, slow-motion fashion, often obscured by smoke or flickering strobe lights, but this produces an abstract, 'Brechtian' effect that is quite different from the frisson of 'real' blood and glamour of expert swordsmanship with which Burbage would have thrilled his audiences in 1608–9.

Failure to establish a battle charisma for Martius in Act 1 strengthens the negative, satiric elements in Shakespeare's portrayal so that, even if the pleading scene works, there is real danger that his murder in 5.6 will seem anticlimactic. To avert this possibility actors and directors have invented many ways to make his death a spectacular *coup de théâtre*. The nineteenth-century stars, Kemble, Macready, and Phelps, who all presented

---

[1] *An Apology for Actors* (1612), ed. R. H. Perkinson (1941), B3 verso–B4 recto.

an idealized, wholly heroic Coriolanus, were stabbed from behind and collapsed with impressive abruptness. 'In the midst of the exclamation about Tullus Aufidius', wrote Sir Walter Scott of Kemble, 'he dropped as dead and as flat on the stage as if the swords had really met in his body. We have repeatedly heard screams from the female part of the audience when he presented this scene, which had the most striking resemblance to actual and instant death we have ever witnessed.'[1]

A similar effect was exploited by Richard Burton, in the 1954 Old Vic production. After figures had lunged from the shadows to stab him from all sides, Burton remained upright and motionless in a long pause, clutching at a door post for support, then crashed face downward on to the stage; his assassins fled back into the shadows; and the play ended with only Martius' body spread-eagled on the stage, its red cloak caught by a spotlight and a single drum-tap diminishing as the half-light gradually faded. Everything after the death was cut, to leave the audience with this powerful last image of isolation and loss.[2]

Other actors have considered that Coriolanus could only be overwhelmed by the people as a whole (though this goes against the text). In productions by the nineteenth-century American actor Edwin Forrest, for example, 'the crowd rush on him, cover him from the view of the audience, and in the melee he is slain—but the manner of his death is left to the imagination'.[3] While in 1981 at Stratford, Ontario, instead of being slain by the Conspirators, Coriolanus 'delivered his final challenge from the upper stage to the Volscians assembled below, and Aufidius came up the stairs to stab him from behind. As Coriolanus pitched into the crowd, they turned in upon him and rent him', then, parting to disclose his body grotesquely crumpled into the shape of a swastika, they 'turned out towards the theatre . . . with looks of candid complicity',[4] associating the audience with their crime.

Other interpreters have wanted to suggest that death is Martius' own heroic—or despairing—choice. At Stratford-upon-Avon in 1933 Anew McMaster died 'with sardonic

[1] *Quarterly Review*, 34 (1826), 224.
[2] Roger Wood and Mary Clarke, *Shakespeare at the Old Vic* (1954), i. 40–1.
[3] *The Evening Post* (New York), 25 Apr. 1855.
[4] Ralph Berry, review in *SQ*, 33 (1982), 202.

mirth, even as the Volscian swords ran through him';[1] and in the 1977 RSC production Alan Howard deliberately impaled himself on his own abandoned sword which Aufidius had picked up, a gesture that was given homoerotic implications in the BBC televised version of 1983. More heroically, the Coriolanus of the 1980 Ashland Festival was repeatedly stabbed by all classes of Volscians but fought his way through them to gain the upper stage, then, throwing aside his sword, leapt down among the rabble to his death.

This was an adaptation of the most spectacular death of all: that of Laurence Olivier at Stratford-upon-Avon in 1959, in his second interpretation of the role. Peter Hall, the director, believed that Coriolanus died not heroically but in total despair, not even wanting to fight; and looking for 'something really nasty' as a model (to use his own words), he and Olivier fixed on the ignominious end of Mussolini, whose corpse the Italian partisans hung upside down on a meat-hook. In Olivier's performance, as described by Kenneth Tynan, 'the over-mothered general ... leaps up a flight of precipitous stairs to vent his rage. Arrived at the top, he relents and throws his sword away. After letting his voice fly high in the great swingeing line about how he "fluttered your Volscians in Cor-i-o-li," he allows half a dozen spears to impale him. He is poised, now, on a promontory some twelve feet above the stage, from which he topples [backwards], to be caught by the ankles so that he dangles, inverted, like the slaughtered Mussolini. A more shocking, less sentimental death I have not seen in the theatre; it is at once proud and ignominious, as befits the titanic fool who dies it.'[2] And as he dangled, Aufidius stabbed him in the belly, then had to be restrained from trampling on the fallen, crumpled corpse.

Though many of these death scenes were theatrically successful, they all simplify in one way or another.[3] The

---

[1] *Birmingham Post*, 25 Apr. 1933.

[2] *Curtains* (1961), p. 241. The RSC productions of 1967 and 1972–3 both featured sadistic killings of Coriolanus, in line with the directors' belief that his return to Antium was masochistic.

[3] Cf. Thomas Clayton, ' "Balancing at Work": R(evoking) the Script in Performance and Criticism', in Marvin and Ruth Thompson, eds., *Shakespeare and the Sense of Performance* ... (1989), 228–49.

nineteenth-century foregrounding of heroism and family ignores the lonely, self-deluding aspects of Coriolanus' death; yet too exclusive an emphasis on that isolation—as in the Burton rendering—lacks recognition of his public service and historical importance; while emphasizing the ignominy of the killing, its suicidal or sadistic dimensions, or the inevitable victory of *realpolitik* and historical necessity, all divert attention on to contributory but secondary issues and lose that sense of re-affirmed integrity which, in spite of Coriolanus' inadequacies and mistakes, gives the end its necessary intensity.

Shakespeare's alteration of Plutarch to give Martius a final speech of self-assertion makes it probable that the death scene was spectacular in 1609 too, but he also adds the disingen-uities of Martius' boastful entry into Antium and specious self-defence, and complicates responses not only by his shock-ing added stage direction '*Aufidius stands on him*', but also by Aufidius' sudden change of heart and by the ironies implicit in the final funeral cortège. The Oxford editors' directions for other Conspirators to stand on the body with Aufidius has nothing to recommend it. Whether they do it all together or one after another, the effect is bound to be theatrically farc-ical; moreover, it confuses the sequence of commands from the Volscian Third Lord that follows (ll. 134–5); and worst of all, destroys the psychological insight of the original stage business—Aufidius' special, highly physical, love–hate rivalry with Martius (who Volumnia had promised should be the one to tread on Aufidius' neck: 1.3.47–8). This gesture trans-gresses the play's repeated direction for kneeling in respect to a standing figure, and represents an ultimate indignity to the hero's body, which has been a focus of symbolic worth throughout the play, since Menenius' body-politic parable and Volumnia's itemizing of its wounds. In Canetti's terms, the gesture can be interpreted positively as the triumphant flourish of a hunter who has killed a lion—Aufidius himself was earlier described by Martius as 'a lion | That I am proud to hunt' (1.1.233–4). Alternatively, like Vittoria and Zanche's treading on Flamineo's supposed corpse in *The White Devil* (Revels, 1960: 5.6.118.1–2), it can be seen as an expression of vindictive spite, by a coward who dared not act openly or alone—though this makes it hard to believe that Aufidius' immediate change of heart can be in any way sincere. The most startling version of the gesture occurred in Tyrone Guthrie's homosexually oriented production at Nottingham in 1963, where Ian McKellen (playing Aufidius) stamped on the dead Martius' groin, then with a moan of grief threw himself prostrate on to the body.[1]

The sincerity of Aufidius' volte-face is again a matter for disagreement: another of those over-determined choices on which the play is silent. It must partly be interpreted, I think, as Machiavellian policy, anticipating the inevitable swing of popular feeling as Octavius does in *Julius Caesar* and *Antony and Cleopatra*; but to the extent that Aufidius shares the psychology suggested for Martius, a genuine revulsion is also possible (without postulating homosexuality), because Aufidius must realize not only that Martius has shamed him yet again but also that he has destroyed the challenge that gave his own life special meaning. In the 1984 National Theatre production, before 'My rage is gone' Aufidius turned the body over to stare for a long moment at Martius' dead face, thus skilfully adding a gesture to motivate his change of mood.

The general effect of the conclusion, however, cannot escape the diminished note of the Second Lord's 'Let's make the best of it' (5.6.147); in A. P. Rossiter's sharp phrasing, it is 'flat, hurried, twisted off and depressing'.[2] And this surely must be the tone of the final cortège as, with reversed pikes instead of flourished swords, it leaves the stage to the muffled drum beats of the Dead March. Nineteenth-century productions went in for elaborate mourning processions in which, improbably, the Romans and Volscians marched together with Volumnia at their head; and Edwin Forrest even added a trick cremation scene in which, to the keening of massed choirs, a 'strange fowl' representing Martius' soul rose from the flames to seek refuge in the fly gallery.[3] The text, however, indicates that Martius, like Hamlet, is given a soldier's funeral that is thick with ironies. Such funeral processions were

---

[1] 'EAB', *Theatre World*, 60 (1964), 31.

[2] Rossiter, p. 233.

[3] *The Albion*, 25 Apr. 1855. For a prompt-book diagram of this, see the Folger copy listed as item 22 in Charles Shattuck, ed., *The Shakespeare Promptbooks: A Descriptive Catalogue* (1965). See Fig. 10.

traditionally connected with Roman triumphs,[1] and Martius' cortège inverts not only his triumph in 2.1 but also his heroic disappearance through the gates of Corioles earlier: 'He will be carried, covered with his *own* blood, through one more gate to end the play.'[2] Moreover, it is his murderer who speaks his eulogy; and as his blood-soaked corpse is borne aloft by Aufidius himself and 'three o'th' chiefest soldiers'—presumably the three Conspirators—it reflects ironically that earlier emblematic gesture in 1.6, when an equally blood-soaked Martius was brandished like a sword by beaten Roman soldiery as their fetish against defeat. A good proportion of the original audience would have been likely to know that, in a very short space of time (as Plutarch and Livy both report), the Volscians were to be crushed forever, Aufidius slain, and Rome consolidated for four and a half centuries as one of history's first successful democracies. This is the ultimate irony of Shakespeare's original staging, his final comment on power.

Stage History

Though *Coriolanus* is habitually described as one of Shakespeare's least 'popular' plays, it has had in fact a considerable and very varied stage history, enjoying about two-thirds as many revivals as the evergreen *Julius Caesar*, according to John Ripley[3] who has compiled stage histories of both. In addition, it has inspired numerous 'offshoots'—both adaptations and independent works of literature. And, as G. C. D. Odell remarked in 1922, it seems 'destined to be launched with new trimmings, during or after each of England's successive politico-civic upheavals'[4]—an observation that is even more pertinent now than when it was written, and need no longer be confined to England. Two full-scale stage histories of *Coriolanus* are nearing completion,[5] and a useful

[1] See, for example, Sir William Segar, *Honor Military and Civil, Contained in Foure Bookes* (1602), p. 138.

[2] Robert N. Watson, *Shakespeare and the Hazards of Ambition* (1984), p. 206.

[3] See John Ripley, review of Daniell's *'Coriolanus' in Europe*, in James Redmond, ed., *Drama and Symbolism*: Themes in Drama IV (1982), p. 209.

[4] Odell, i. 59.

[5] By John Ripley for CUP, and by David George as part of the New Variorum *Coriolanus*, ed. Thomas Clayton *et al.*; in addition, Marion Trousdale

summary of major productions between 1945 and 1984 has
been edited by Daniel J. Watermeier.[1]

Ideological Approaches. The probable relation of *Coriolanus* to
events in the early years of James I's reign has already been
discussed; and among the first items in its later stage history are two adaptations with specifically contrary intentions.
Nahum Tate's *The Ingratitude of a Commonwealth; or, The Fall
of Coriolanus* (1681)[2] was written to protest against the anti-
Catholic riots caused by false rumours of a 'Popish Plot' to as-
sassinate Charles II; while John Dennis's adaptation, *The Invader
of his Country: or, The Fatal Resentment* (1719)[3] was written in
response to the Jacobite Rebellion of 1715 in order to muster
patriotic sentiment against a threat of Catholic take-over.

Similarly, the second Jacobite Rebellion of 1745 stimulated
an original, neo-classical play about Coriolanus by James
Thomson,[4] the poet of *The Seasons*, written in 1747 and
produced two years later by James Quin at Covent Garden, after
Thomson's death. This was amalgamated with Shakespeare's
original by Thomas Sheridan under the title of *Coriolanus: or
The Roman Matron*, with the first four acts of Shakespeare
compressed into two, followed by three acts of Thomson with
a few Shakespearian interpolations. The resulting hybrid was
mounted at the Smock Alley Theatre of Dublin in 1752,
transferred, with alterations, to Covent Garden in 1754, and
revived there six times over the next fourteen years.[5] It also

is analysing six key productions of the play for Methuen's *Shakespeare in
Performance* series. For a collation of acting editions and prompt-books, see
William P. Halstead, *Shakespeare As Spoken* (1978), vol. 9, items 653c–6530,
and Charles H. Shattuck, *The Shakespeare Promptbooks*, pp. 73–80.

[1] In Samuel L. Leiter, ed., *Shakespeare Around the Globe: A Guide to Notable
Postwar Revivals* (1986), 83–102; cf. also William Babula, *Shakespeare in
Production, 1935–1978. A Selective Catalogue* (1981), pp. 44–51; and Ralph
Berry, 'The Metamorphoses of *Coriolanus*', *SQ*, 26 (1975), 172–83, repr. in
his *Changing Styles in Shakespeare* (1981), 18–36. The entries in Gooch and
Thatcher, eds., *A Shakespeare Music Catalogue* (1991), i. 219 ff., though not
exhaustive, are particularly helpful for modern European productions.

[2] See Cornmarket Press Facsimile edition (1969).

[3] Also in a 1969 Cornmarket Press Facsimile edition.

[4] James Thomson, *Works*, ed. P. Murdoch (1773) iv. 268 ff.

[5] Both the 1752 and 1754 versions are available as Cornmarket Press
Facsimile editions (1969); cf. Esther K. Sheldon, 'Sheridan's *Coriolanus*: An
18th-century Compromise', *SQ*, 14 (1963), 153–61.

became the basis for John Philip Kemble's further adaptation of 1789, which kept the same title and effectively determined ideology for the play throughout the nineteenth century.[1]

There were also some eighteenth-century attempts to revive Shakespeare's original text. On 11 November 1754, David Garrick produced a much shortened but unadulterated version of Shakespeare's play at Drury Lane, with Mossop as Coriolanus.[2] This ran for only eight performances, with a single revival in April 1755. Earlier there had been a series of entries for '*The Tragedy of Coriolanus*. By Shakespeare' at John Rich's theatre in Lincoln's Inn Fields, in which James Quin may have played the title role.[3] The first of these, in December 1718, provoked John Dennis's ire for false advertising;[4] and subsequent entries for 1719, 1720, 1721, and 1722 have two peculiarities about them. The entries for 14 November 1719 and 1 January 1720 mischievously use Dennis's title, *The Invader of his Country*, but credit it still to Shakespeare; and playbills for the productions list no actors for the principal roles but go into detail about six minor, invented roles played by the comedians of the company (e.g. 'Robsack the Miller—Bullock Snr.'). These anomalies suggested to A. H. Scouten that the Lincoln's Inn Fields version must, in fact, have been played as farce,[5] which would certainly be consistent with Rich's policy and might also help to explain the outrageous costuming of Quin in the only picture we have of him as Coriolanus (see Fig. 11).

[1] Kemble's 1789 and 1806 acting editions are both available as Cornmarket Press Facsimiles (1970); his 1811 prompt-book appears in Charles Shattuck, ed., *John Philip Kemble's Promptbooks*, vol. 2 (1974).

[2] The text is reprinted in *Bell's British Theatre* (1774), vol. xi.

[3] This was first suggested by John Genest, *Some Account of the English Stage, 1660–1830* (1832), iii. 55; and is accepted by Dover Wilson (p. xliii), Brockbank (p. 78), and C. B. Hogan, *Shakespeare in the Theatre, 1701–1800* (1952), p. 101.

[4] On 13 December 1718 the Theatre at Lincoln's Inn Fields advertised '*Coriolanus*. By William Shakespeare' as 'Not Acted these Twenty Years,' to which Dennis objected (26 Mar. 1719): 'there was no Occasion to tell them that [it] had not been acted in twenty Years, and that when it was brought upon the Stage twenty years ago, it was acted twenty Nights together': *Critical Works of Dennis* (1939–43), ii. 164–5. On this rather flimsy evidence, *The London Stage, Part I* (1964), clx, 502, lists a production of *Coriolanus* for 1699 'sometime in September'.

[5] Letter to RBP, 8 Oct. 1986.

Right-wing Interpretation. In reaction against the French Revolution, John Philip Kemble was a staunch supporter of established government; and the production of *Coriolanus* he
opened at Drury Lane on 7 February 1789, with his sister
Sarah Siddons as Volumnia,[1] presented an interpretation in
which Martius, Volumnia, and even Aufidius were idealized,
the Tribunes vilified, and the plebeians represented as clownish, ineffectual dolts. After the storming of the Bastille later
that year, Kemble temporarily suspended performances to
avoid occasion for public disturbance, and again when there
were new French uprisings in 1792; and from 1796 to his
farewell gala performance in 1817 he increasingly sharpened
the conflict between Martius and the Tribunes.[2] As a neo-
classicist, Kemble held that art should present universals,
not idiosyncratic detail, and the 'ruling passion' he found
for Martius was justifiable aristocratic pride, expressed in
slow, sonorous speech, commanding gesture, and statuesque
poses—as in the celebrated discovery of him on Aufidius'
hearth, standing haughtily in a great black cloak beneath a
statue of the war god Mars, of which Sir Francis Bourgeois
and Sir Thomas Lawrence both painted portraits (see Fig. 12).
He also established a stage tradition for the play of elaborate
antiquarian scenery—though, typically, he selected the Imperial period of Rome, not its more appropriate early years—
and of massive, ceremonial processions for Martius' triumphant
entry into Rome, Volumnia's plea, and Coriolanus' funeral,
with over two hundred people on stage including a troop of
soldiers from the Life Guards. Because of Kemble's enormous
popularity in the role over nearly three decades, and the fact
that he was the first methodically to publish acting versions
of his productions, it was this interpretation that was spread
throughout England and America by his numerous imitators:
Cooper, Vandenhoff, Conway, Phelps, Hamblin, the brothers

---

[1] For a description of Sarah Siddons's spirited acting in 2.1, see Julian
Charles Young, *Memoirs of Charles Mayne Young* (1871), i. 61–2; quoted in
Ripley, 'Stage Imagery on Stage', p. 342.
[2] See David Rostron, 'Kemble's *Coriolanus* and *Caesar*. An Examination of
the Prompt Copies', *Theatre Notebook* 23 (1968), pp. 26–34, and 'Contemporary Political Comment in Four of J. P. Kemble's Shakespearean Productions',
Theatre Research, 12 (1972), 113–19.

J. W. and H. Wallack, Butler, Young, and Dillon, to mention only the most prominent.

The only actor to attempt a quite different interpretation was Edmund Kean, who at Drury Lane early in 1820 tried to restore Shakespeare's text 'with omissions only', with no better fortune than Garrick earlier.[1] Kean's production failed after only four performances, for a variety of reasons: audiences had grown accustomed to the Sheridan–Kemble 'refinements'; the 'spectacle' was meagre in comparison with Kemble's; Kean himself was too small to be convincing as an unbeatable warrior; and there were too few 'supers', inadequately drilled, to take seriously in the restored battle scenes— but, most of all, because, instead of Kemble's 'marble pride', Kean emphasized the driven, overachieving 'boy' in Coriolanus, literally stuttering with passionate feeling, laughing hysterically, and delivering 'I banish you' with 'the rage of impotent despair':[2] a psychologically acute reading that was at least a hundred years ahead of its time.

The successful heir-apparent was William Charles Macready, who produced a cautious, very Kemble-like *Coriolanus* towards the end of 1819, the great success of which encouraged him to revive the play fifteen times in five several seasons, the last two—1838 and 1839—under his own management at Covent Garden, when he seems to have felt confident enough at last to branch out more originally. Besides the restoration of a text that was more fully Shakespearian than any since Garrick's, Macready's main contributions to *Coriolanus* lay in elaboration of its staging and his own Romantic interpretation of the title role. Abandoning Imperial Rome, he put the play back into its correct historical period, with several more sets than Kemble had provided, including an atmospheric view of Antium by starlight for the restored 4.4 and a beautiful tiered set for the interior of the Roman Senate; and his processions were even more elaborate than Kemble's, with a hundred extra people on stage.[3]

[1] See David George, 'Restoring Shakespeare's *Coriolanus*: Kean versus Macready', *Theatre Notebook*, 44 (1990), 101–18.

[2] Hazlitt, *Works*, xviii. 290.

[3] See A. J. Bassett, 'Macready's *Coriolanus*: An Early Contribution to Modern Theatre', *Ohio State University Theatre Collection Bulletin*, 13 (1966), 14–26.

13. Coriolanus' triumphant entry into Rome, in John Hirsch's 1988 production (Coriolanus: Byron Jennings; Roman Citizen: Mike Genovese)

As an actor, he endeavoured to combine Kemble and Kean, noting in his diary that he studied 'various attitudes from the antique . . . intent on mastering the patrician's outward bearing, [but] under that giving vent to the unbridled passions of a man';[1] and far from Kemble's accumulative 'ruling passion', he was praised for the variety and emotional range he could find in every speech, often by startling vocal shifts. Ideologically, however, his *Coriolanus* was still conservative, though between 1819 and 1838 there was a small but significant shift of political emphasis in his handling of the crowd. Even in his first production he had increased awareness of the plebeians by including them as palm-waving spectators of Martius' triumph; but in 1838, after the Reform Act, Chartism, and the Depression of 1837, he not only increased their numbers further but also individualized and armed them and directed them to behave realistically without regard to the audience, so they lost any resemblance to Kemble's clowns and became instead a genuine political threat. The reviewer for *John Bull* optimistically saw this as a recognition of 'men who have spied their way to equal fran-

---

[1] Macready's *Diary*, quoted in Furness, p. 730.

chise and are determined to fight their way to the goal',[1] but others saw it rather as a reaction to the danger of the nineteenth century's industrialized proletariat.

It was the negative possibility of Macready's emphasis that was mostly adopted by others. His bitter rival, Edwin Forrest, the first native-born American theatre star, kept more closely to the line laid down by Kemble. His sets reverted to Imperial Rome, and his processional and crowd effects were elaborated to popular but ludicrous proportions, including the extra scene, already mentioned, where Martius is cremated and his soul flies up to heaven. The plebeians were once more comic poltroons—according to one commentator, Forrest 'calmly looked them reeling backwards'[2]—but to suit the egalitarian prejudices of an American audience, he represented Martius as a kind of frontier hero, dominant because of sheer physical strength (Forrest was a fanatical body-builder, with a stentorian voice) and 'not so much patrician by status as by mind', shrinking by nobility of instinct, not training, 'from too familiar contact with natures that are vulgar'.[3] A dozen years later an equally Romantic though very different interpretation was given by the Italian star Tommaso Salvini on his fourth American tour in 1885. Salvini made Coriolanus conform to his own genially self-confident, humorous, and warmly affectionate personality.[4]

A specific class element remained strong in English productions throughout the century, however. Henry Irving had planned a production of *Coriolanus* as early as 1879, but by 1902, when it finally occurred as his last revival at the Lyceum Theatre, he was already sixty-three and, never athletic, was by then also in poor health. Alma-Tadema's 'Etruscan' sets were the most historically authentic and beautiful

---

[1] *John Bull's Magazine*, 19 Mar. 1838, quoted in Odell, ii. 212–13.

[2] W. R. Alger, *Life of Edwin Forrest* (1877, repr. 1972) ii. 763.

[3] New York *Sunday Mercury*, 8 Nov. 1863. Forrest's interpretation was continued for several years by another physically imposing American actor, John McCullough.

[4] See Marvin Carlson, *The Italian Shakespearians* (1985), pp. 122–7. Just previously in 1883 another visitor, the 'darkly handsome' Ludwig Barnay of the famous Meiningen Company, had given the role an heroic, 'Siegfried'-like interpretation with a New York German company. Salvini's text was published by J. J. Little and Co. (New York, 1885).

ever created for the play,[1] but the production was a dismal failure. Irving played Martius incongruously as an introverted, disillusioned military intellectual; Ellen Terry was equally miscast as an ultra-feminine, over-bedizened Volumnia,[2] who looked younger than her 'son'; the text was cut to the bone to fit into three acts; and though the small crowd was well rehearsed, it seems to have been comically bewildered, in the Kemble manner, rather than politically a threat.

Frank Benson's crowds, on the other hand, were described from the first as a 'frowning, sullen, malignantly threatening mob, full ripe for wholesale murder and reckless destruction'.[3] Benson's first production at Stratford-upon-Avon in 1893 was one of the most popular since Kemble's retirement, and he repeated it there for seven subsequent seasons between 1898 and 1919, as well as in two London productions in 1901 and 1910. One of the greatest assets of Benson's version was the superb Volumnia of Geneviève Ward, which made the pleading scene a high point; Benson's own depiction of Martius was as a boyish, public-school prefect, rather than a soldier; and his denigration of the plebeians and their Tribunes was unrelenting. Brutus was usually represented as the 'rough, scowling, uncouth mouthpiece of the mob',[4] but Sicinius, especially as played by Oscar Asche, was more grimly humorous and formidable: 'strong, coarse-minded, selfish and cunning, ... I can still see him, after the expulsion of Coriolanus, seated on a stone in the Roman street, contentedly peeling and eating an orange'.[5] And by the 1910 production, the crowd was directed to strangle and 'hack the intriguing Tribunes to pieces in a scene of popular frenzy introduced at the end of act four'.[6]

---

[1] The sets are reproduced in Sybil Rosenfeld, 'Alma-Tadema's Designs for Henry Irving's *Coriolanus*', *Deutsche Shakespeare-Gesellschaft West Jahrbuch* (1974), 84–95, and Cary Mazer, *Shakespeare Refashioned: Elizabethan Plays on Edwardian Stages* (1981); Irving's text was published by the Chiswick Press (London, 1901).

[2] Max Beerbohm said she reminded him of 'a Christmas tree decorated by a Pre-Raphaelite', *The Saturday Review* (27 Apr. 1901), p. 537.

[3] *Stratford-upon-Avon Herald*, 25 Aug. 1893.

[4] *The Era*, 16 Feb. 1901.

[5] R. Dickins, *Forty Years of Shakespeare on the English Stage* (1907), p. 98, quoted in Furness, p. 735.

[6] *The Stage*, 21 Apr. 1910.

Though productions at Stratford and the Old Vic after World War I restored yet more of Shakespeare's text and started to use simplified, non-realistic settings of platforms, curtains, and arches,[1] an anti-popular bias continued. It was especially strong in Bridges-Adams's 1933 production (with Anew McMaster as Coriolanus), which, coming hard upon a General Strike in England and the rise of Fascism in Europe, had a particularly fierce and clamorous mob, swarming from the orchestra pit up the long sweep of steps that constituted the set before the audience realized the play had even begun, and turning against their Tribunes at the end to exact a summary, savage vengeance in the true Bensonian manner. Almost simultaneously in Paris there occurred the most remarkable incident in *Coriolanus'* whole complicated stage history. A new translation by René-Louis Piachaud at the Comédie Française was used by royalist and fascist groups as a focus for demonstrations against the Daladier left-wing government; the latter made the situation worse by replacing the Comédie's popular director with the ex-head of the Sûreté Nationale, who had been forced to resign for involvement in the Stavisky financial scandal; and the theatre was shut down by the police after rioting disrupted a performance on 4 February 1934.[2] When it reopened early in March, however, performances of *Coriolanus* aroused no further demonstrations; and Piachaud's innocuous text has since been remounted several times—at Fouvière (1953), the Isle de Bendor (1956), Nîmes (1955), the Comédie Française (1957), and at festivals in Aubervilliers and Avignon (1964)—without political repercussions.

In Germany, where the play had been used to query militarism,[3] the Nazis banned Hans Rothe's 1932 translation for radio and exiled the author, then adopted *Coriolanus* as a

---

[1] A pioneer in this simple staging was André Antoine at the Paris Théâtre de l'Odéon in 1910. There were also occasional 'Elizabethan' productions with 17th-century costumes on an approximation of the Shakespearian stage: e.g. by Nugent Monck at Maddermarket, Norwich in 1928 and by Ben Iden Payne at Stratford-upon-Avon in 1939.

[2] Cf. Daniell, pp. 61–4, Ruby Cohn, *Modern Shakespearean Offshoots* (1976), pp. 10–16, Felicia Hardison Londré, 'Coriolanus and Stavisky: The Interpenetration of Art and Politics', *Theatre Research International*, NS 11, no. 2 (1986), 119–32.

[3] Cf. Bernard Kytzler, *Shakespeare Jahrbuch*, 57 (1921), p. 163; Martin Brunkhorst, *Shakespeares 'Coriolanus' in Deutscher Bearbeitung* (1973), p. 157.

schoolbook to demonstrate to Hitler Youth the unsoundness of democracy and to idealize Martius as an heroic *führer* trying to lead his people to a healthier society, 'as Adolf Hitler in our days wishes to lead our beloved German father-land'.[1] Consequently, in the early years of occupation after World War II, the American army banned the play; and when it began to be produced again in 1953, a Munich critic is reported as saying poignantly that returning German exiles, 'embittered and home-sick, felt horror and understood an outcast who wanted to take revenge on his native country, his former father-land' but could not do so because it was also 'a great mother, with the sweet-pain of the mother-tie'.[2]

Traditional, 'heroic' interpretations continued to appear after the Second World War but in muted, more 'liberal' forms. In Byam Shaw's 1952 production at Stratford-upon-Avon, for example, Anthony Quayle appealed to the audience's war nostalgia by representing Martius as a simple professional soldier, rough-tongued but boyishly well-intentioned, with 'The frightening rabble [as] the real star';[3] Michael Langham's avowedly non-political production at Stratford, Ontario, in 1961, which was set in France at the period of the Directoire, opposed Paul Scofield's genuinely noble Martius with the fierce *sans-culottes* of the French Revolution; and even more negative mobs were represented at the American Shakespeare Festival at Stratford, Connecticut, in 1965 and the Utah Shakespeare Festival in 1977. The hallmark of such liberal-conservative productions tends to be a Menenius who is reliable and wise. For a modern reactionary interpretation, however, we have to turn to one of *Coriolanus*' more recent 'offshoots', John Osborne's adaptation, *A Place Calling Itself Rome* (1971).[4] This transposes the action to Britain in the seventies, where greedy labour confronts ineffectual management over bargaining tables, demonstrations block the London squares, the Volscian war takes place with sub-machine-guns in some

---

[1] Quoted in Brunkhorst, p. 157.
[2] Quoted in Daniell, p. 137
[3] *Daily Herald*, 14 Mar. 1952.
[4] Published by Faber, 1973; cf. Cohn, pp. 22–6. Osborne seems to have been partly influenced by T. S. Eliot's two *Coriolan* poems, *Collected Poems, 1909–1962* (1963), pp. 137–43.

Northern Irish town like Derry, and chanted slogans and incoherent political rhetoric characterize a society without identity or communal purpose, from which the rebarbative protagonist feels totally alienated. The company's Literary Adviser of that time tells me that this play was turned down for production at the RSC on grounds that it was too like Shakespeare's original,[1] a judgement that would have startled previous generations.

Anti-heroic Interpretation. It is necessary to distinguish between interpretations which aim to 'deconstruct' the idea of Martius' heroism from those which are actively pro-plebeian; and though Ralph Berry was premature in declaring that British productions after World War II were not interested in politics, at the time he wrote he was essentially correct in saying that most of them till then had been more interested in exploring the flaws in Martius' psychology.[2]

Picking up Kean's insight, Laurence Olivier had presented a Martius who was emotionally overdependent on his mother in a performance at the Old Vic in 1938 which established him as his generation's leading actor; and he returned to deepen and expand this interpretation in a production directed by Peter Hall at Stratford-upon-Avon in 1959. Olivier managed to combine an energetic warrior, whose ferocious scorn in dismissing the plebeians gave Laurence Kitchin the bizarre impression of one man lynching a mob,[3] with the sulky, teasing rebelliousness of a difficult 'child'; and he exploited Martius' own awareness that often he is 'acting' to discover an extraordinary vein of humour in the character, which not only bridged its psychological contradictions but also established a sympathetic collusion between Olivier and his audience without sacrificing one jot of Martius' harshness. There had been an element of hapless youth in Richard Burton's reading of the role in Michael Benthall's 1954 production at the Old Vic, but Burton's boyishness was more charming (in

---

[1] I am obliged to my colleague Ronald Bryden for this information. In 1973 Bretton Hall College in Wakefield, Yorkshire, produced a modernized version of *Coriolanus* set in Northern Ireland which sounds very like Osborne's play.

[2] Berry, *Changing Styles*, pp. 27 ff.

[3] See Kitchin, p. 148.

the earlier Benson manner), less edgily ironic and could be reduced much more easily to tears by Volumnia's disapproval. Subsequently, in the RSC's 1973 revival at the Aldwych Theatre, Nicol Williamson gave a related but more desperately overachieving and anguished dimension to the painful link between Martius and his mother.

Extrapolating from Freud's connection between over-mothering and the narcissistic idealization of other men, Tyrone Guthrie concentrated his 1963 production at the Nottingham Playhouse on a homosexual attraction between Martius (John Neville) and Aufidius (Ian McKellen). This had been anticip-ated two years before by Guthrie's protégé, Michael Langham, at Stratford, Ontario; and twenty years later, in 1981, Brian Bedford's 'rough trade' production in the same theatre over-emphasized this element at the expense of Volumnia and Virgilia, who were reduced to emotional ciphers. Bedford's production in turn may have influenced Alan Howard's per-formance in the 1983 BBC television production directed by Elijah Moshinsky, which was far more homoerotic than his fascinating stage interpretation for the RSC six years before.

The RSC production of 1972 aimed to exploit a more general narcissism, with Ian Hogg portraying Martius, not very successfully, as a temperamental, spoiled young sporting star;[1] but this more solipsistic interpretation was then de-veloped brilliantly by Alan Howard for the RSC production of 1977.[2] Howard's narcissism had a rapt, almost mystical, black-leather machismo, which was self-worshipping but also eerily self-destructive—an edge which Christopher Walken's similar black-leather, but more bullying and twitchily neur-otic, portrayal lacked in a 1988 production directed by Steven Berkoff at the New York Shakespeare Festival. Interestingly, for the 1984 production of the National Theatre Ian McKellen said that he derived this streak of narcissism in Martius from the element of arrogant unreliability he found necessary for

---

[1] See Ian Hogg, 'Coriolanus', in Roger Sales, ed., *Shakespeare in Perspective* (1985), ii. 240–50.

[2] See Howard's own comments in Daniell, pp. 165–6; J. R. Mulryne, 'Coriolanus at Stratford-upon-Avon: Three Actors' Remarks', *SQ*, 29 (1978), 323–32; and John Higgins's interview with Terry Hands, *The Times*, 19 Oct. 1977, p. 11.

his own charisma as an actor;[1] though, in the production as a whole, this aspect was subordinated to Peter Hall's concern with the play's political dimension. Obviously, any interpretation that raises doubts about the nature of Coriolanus' heroism can easily coincide with a pro-plebeian attitude to class-war in the play.

Left-wing Interpretation. There was a series of productions of *Coriolanus* in Germany between 1911 and 1920 which aimed to question that country's militarism, but it was not until the 1930s that overtly left-wing interpretation began to appear; and, as might be expected, this first showed up in the communist countries of Eastern Europe. These invariably interpreted the play as a 'tragedy of individualism', idealizing the plebeians and Tribunes, and criticizing Martius as a proto-dictator, a would-be 'superman who has detached himself from the people and betrayed them'.[2] This was the interpretation of productions at Moscow's Maly Theatre in 1934 and the Grand Theatre in Leopol, Poland, in 1935, and in 1959 a production in the Army Theatre in Prague was still following the same party line.[3] Our record of productions in East Europe is sketchy, but there was an interesting—perhaps premonitory—surge of interest in *Coriolanus* in the early 1980s among satellite nations of the USSR. Dinu Cernescu directed it expressionistically at the Nottara Theatre in Bucharest in 1978;[4] there were three productions in 1979: one in Georgia at the Kutaissi 'Lado Meskvishile' Theatre in Tbilisi, which visited Moscow in 1981; an Armenian production directed by R. Kaplanyan at the 'Gabriele Sundukyan' Theatre in Yerevan, which visited Berlin and Weimar in 1980 and Moscow in 1981;[5] and a Czech production at the Tyl Theatre

---

[1] See Ian McKellen, 'Crunching Butterflies: Ian McKellen Talks to Christopher Edwards about *Coriolanus*', *Drama*, 155 (1985), p. 22, and Lawrence O'Toole, interview with McKellen, *New York Times Magazine* (6 Apr. 1992), p. 28. In some performances, for example, he 'flashed' the audience by opening his coat in the canvassing scene.

[2] Robert Speaight, *Shakespeare on the Stage* (1973), p. 200.

[3] Bretislav Hodek, review in *ShS*, 14 (1961), p. 118.

[4] Ilea Berlogea, review in *SQ*, 31 (1980), 407.

[5] Armin-Gerd Kuckhoff, review in *Shakespeare Jahrbuch*, 117 (Weimar, 1981), pp. 155 ff.

in Pilsen. According to Otto Roubiack, this was the tenth production of *Coriolanus* in Czechoslovakia; and two more quickly followed, one at the Checheno-Ingustian 'Nuradilov' Theatre in 1981, the other in 1984 at the Workers' Theatre in Most; and there were also a Polish production in Warsaw in 1982 and a Hungarian production at the National Theatre in Komarno in 1985. Of these, the Bucharest and Yerevan versions seem to have been the most innovative, with the former much influenced by Antonin Artaud, and the latter using moving walls expressionistically and presenting a Martius (played by Horen Abrahamjan) whose struggle to maintain integrity was now recognized as genuinely noble though he was still shown to be wrong to alienate himself from the people.[2]

The most celebrated communist reading of *Coriolanus*, however, is the adaptation that Bertolt Brecht was working on at his death in 1956.[3] Brecht believed in thorough rewriting, and had completed a version of the last act in which, instead of being demoralized by Martius' attack the plebeians are organized by the Tribunes into a defence force, and it is smoke from their armouries, rather than Volumnia's plea on behalf of the patricians, that persuades Coriolanus to end the siege of Rome, because 'Irreplaceable | Thou art no longer: now merely a threat | Mortal to all'. This was Brecht's main ideological point, and it was driven home by also altering the conclusion. Instead of Aufidius' eulogy and the funeral cortège, Brecht's version ends with the Roman Senate voting down a proposal to honour the women's embassy, and Menenius' request that Coriolanus' family at least be granted permission to mourn publicly vetoed by Brutus with one curt word, 'Refused'.

A version of this, cobbled up with passages from Dorothea Tieck's standard translation, was mounted briefly by Heinrich

---

[1] Otto Roubiack, review in *Ceske divadlo*, 8 (1983), pp. 169 ff.

[2] Reviewed by Kuckhoff (p. 127 n. 5), and by Hans Jochem Gemzel, *Die Weltbühne*, 16 (1980), 505–7, and Jochem Gleiss, *Theater der Zeit*, 35 (1980), 50–1.

[3] See Cohn, pp. 370–4, Christopher Innes, *Modern German Drama* (1979), pp. 52, 55–6, 193–5; for the subsequent productions, see Harry Carlson, interview with members of the Berliner Ensemble, *The Drama Review*, 12, no. 1 (1967), 112–17, and the 1975 essay by Manfred Wekwerth and Joachim Tenschert in *Introductions to Shakespeare . . . in the Folio Society Edition 1950–76* (1977), 204–10.

Koch at Frankfurt in 1962,[1] but the 'official' Berliner Ensemble version, completed by Manfred Wekwerth and Joachim Tenschert, did not appear till 1964, with Brecht's widow, Helene Weigel, as Volumnia and his son-in-law, Ekkehard Schall, as 'Coriolan'. This toured Europe and visited the UK and the USA with considerable success, and received further attention when Günther Grass produced his *The Plebeians Rehearse the Revolution* (trans. Ralph Mannheim, 1966), which purports to show Brecht rehearsing *Coriolanus* in 1953 but ignoring an East Berlin workers' protest that was happening in real life. Wekwerth and Tenschert were invited to England in 1971 to give Shakespeare's original a Brechtian production at the National Theatre (with Anthony Hopkins as Coriolanus); and drab Brechtian costuming and distancing stage techniques—especially the slow-motion, balletic battle sequences choreographed for Brecht by the Japanese martial-arts expert, Kuta Kanze—have been copied in many productions since, whether left-wing or not.

The most important independent interpretation influenced by Brecht, however, was Giorgio Strehler's 1957 version at the Piccolo Teatro in Milan, in a new translation by Gilberto Tofano.[2] Brecht's advice to see the play as radically dialectic, with Coriolanus as a once essential warrior now bypassed by history, became the core of Strehler's interpretation, which also incorporated many 'epic' staging techniques: the division of the text into twenty-three sequences, each introduced by a projected caption to summarize and comment on its significance; constant bright lighting; and a simple, non-representational set, with scenes changed openly by 'supers'. Instead of presenting the Volsces as a more primitive tribe than the Romans, however, which is the line most modern directors have taken, Strehler saw them rather as 'decadent'; and their more elaborate armour, with extremely brief tunics, and a certain preening, dapper quality in Aufidius himself, subtly conveyed a sense of homoeroticism without this ever

[1] See *The Stage*, 13 Dec. 1962.

[2] Cf. Giorgio Strehler, '*Coriolan* de Shakespeare 1957', in *Un Théâtre Pour La Vie*, trans. Emannuelle Genevois (1986), 250–9. See my '*Coriolanus* at the Piccolo Teatro of Milan, 1959', in Renzo Crivelli and Luigi Sampietro, eds., *Il passagiere italiano: saggi sulle letteratura di lingua inglese in onore di Sergio Rossi* (Rome: Bulzone editore, 1994), pp. 245–68.

being overt. Strehler went well beyond Brecht's interpretation in many ways: he insisted that there are at least three interacting levels of dialectic, with the class-conflict paralleled by a conflict between public and private values and the clash of emotions within Martius himself caused by his overdependence on his 'monstrous' mother; and tried to ensure that events were seen throughout from a psychoanalytical angle no less than a political, with the former gaining predominance in the second half of the play. Moreover, at the end he pessimistically sensed the presence of what he calls the 'black dog' of human experience—man's constant, self-destructive resort to violence, summed up in Aufidius' acceptance that 'one fire drives out one fire'—which undercuts the ideological positives of Martius' brief moment of recognition. This was probably the most subtle of left-wing interpretations so far; though, more recently, a 1989–90 production by the RSC has tried to historicize the view of Martius as a man who could not accommodate himself to historically inevitable progress by interpreting the play through Livy and Machiavelli's comment-ary on Livy, rather than through Plutarch.

Historical Relativity. An obvious way to emphasize the political level of the play is to set it in another historical setting, particularly in modern dress. An ingenious example of the latter was Dominic Roche's production for the Manchester Repertory Company during election week in November 1935, which combined protest against the effects of the Depression in England with criticism of Mussolini's rise in Italy. Martius was dressed in a white drill cavalry uniform, with solar topi, and shiny revolver belt; Aufidius was vaguely oriental; the Tribunes wore red ties, with Sicinius made up to resemble Lenin; and the battle scenes were conveyed by news flashes over a public loudspeaker system, interspersed with martial music, and the headlines of newspaper vendors. Paul Barry's version for the New Jersey Shakespeare Festival in 1973 set the play in Italy during the allied invasion of World War II, with a set of barbed wire, ruins, and burned-out tanks, the Volsces costumed as Nazis, the plebeians as Italians, and the Roman patricians and soldiers as American officers and servicemen, with Coriolanus himself made up to resemble

General George Patton (as portrayed in a recent film by George C. Scott).[1] In 1965 the New York Shakespeare Festival staged its patrician–plebeian confrontations in terms of racial tensions in that city, pointing divisions within the plebeians themselves by mixing black and hispanic actors; while the 1991 Folger Shakespeare Company at Washington, DC, exploited the recent 'Desert Storm' war against Iraq for battle scenes in Act I, though its generally eclectic costuming overlapped into the 'post-modern' category of production.[2] Perhaps the cleverest of these modern dress versions was John Hirsch's very successful production at the Old Globe Theatre of San Diego in 1989. This updated the Volscian war to the United States' struggle against the Sandinistas of Nicaragua, with Coriolanus identified with Colonel Oliver North giving evidence before a Senate tribunal, Volumnia and Virgilia associated with Rose and Ethel Kennedy (the former lethal in a wheelchair), and Menenius as a southern, white-suited, 'pork-barrel' senator; and the play's concern with the falsifications of acting and public image was brilliantly updated by having the action televised by on-stage 'news' crews, with their takes appearing simultaneously on banks of television screens to each side of the stage, interspersed with inappropriate commercials and patriotic music. Hirsch's plebeians mixed suggestions of New York street people with 'Solidarnos' strikers from the Gdansk shipyards in Poland; and these latter were also used in Michael Bogdanov's production for the English Shakespeare Company, with Michael Pennington as Coriolanus, which was playing on tour in 1990–1 just as the Soviet Union began to collapse.

Another device has been to set the play in different historical periods where there were comparable political problems. This was William Poel's original idea for his experimental, single performance of *Coriolanus* at the Chelsea Palace Theatre on 11 May 1931, which was intended to be in the period of the

---

[1] See Babula, p. 49; Patricia Lyles, review in *SQ*, 24 (1973), 447. A similar updating to the war in Vietnam was used at the Champlain Shakespeare Festival 1982.

[2] These two productions also shared a particularly impressive interpretation of Volumnia by the coloured actress Jane White (for which she won the 1965 Obie award as Best Actress of the Year).

French Directoire 'to show the ageless spirit of militarism',[1] though it ended up by mixing several periods; and Poel's idea was borrowed by Michael Langham for his 1961 production at Stratford, Ontario, and Tyrone Guthrie at the Nottingham Playhouse in 1963. In 1970 Hans Hollman set the play among the 'patriotic' clubs and haute bourgeoisie of nineteenth-century Germany, to criticize the connections between national-ism, capitalism, and militarism.[2] At the Villanova Summer Shakespeare Festival of 1980, it was produced like a Group Theatre's 1930 production of Odets's *Golden Boy*, with strik-ing workers and their union leaders, the patricians as fascist brownshirts, the Volsces as Al Capone gangster types with machine-guns concealed in violin cases, and Coriolanus as a champion boxer on a set that resembled a gymnasium.[3] And of particular interest was Richard Digby Day's production at the Nottingham Playhouse in 1983, which extrapolated the early Stuart tensions of Shakespeare's play to a period about 1639, just before the Civil War, with the patricians as Cava-liers, the plebeians and their Tribunes as Puritans, and the Volsces as highland Scots with kilts, feathered bonnets, bagpipes, and thick Scottish accents.[4] Unhappily, the actual produc-tion did not live up to its clever concept, and gave particular offence in trying to get crowd effects by having the actors mingle with the audience—a device that overlaps with our final and currently most fashionable mode of staging *Coriolanus*.

Post-modernist Interpretation. The distinguishing characteristics of post-modernist productions are their insistence on the play as 'theatre', not an Aristotelian 'imitation of life'—which often involves attempts to co-opt the audience directly into the performance—with an emphasis on non-verbal elements of production as levels of semiotic significance independent of (and frequently contradicting) the author's words. There can

[1] Poel's program note, quoted in J. C. Trewin, *Shakespeare on the English Stage 1900–1964* (1964), p. 131.

[2] Joachim Kaiser, review in *Theater Heute* (Sept. 1970), 22–5. Similar pre-1914 German settings were used by the National Youth Theatre of Britain, 1964, and the Liverpool Playhouse, 1970.

[3] See Cary Mazer, review in *SQ*, 32 (1981), 202: the boxing-ring motif was extended to the battle scenes.

[4] See Roger Warren, review in *SQ*, 35 (1984), 335.

be considerable overlap with expressionism and epic theatre, however, so it is not always easy to categorize interpretations such as Dinu Cernescu's 1978 production in Bucharest which combined the influences of Brecht and Artaud, or Jane Howell's arena stage production for the Young Vic in 1989, with Corin Redgrave as Coriolanus and his real-life mother, Rachel Kempson, as Volumnia, which had a straightforward interpretation of the characters' relationships and costumed them consistently in the Victorian period, but set the play in an arena surrounded by steel mesh, on which a gridiron of bars descended for battle scenes and Coriolanus' murder, thus literally converting the arena to a cage. This was an extremely noisy production, with constant clashing of weapons on the metal mesh, against a background of loud rock music; 'blood' was represented by red confetti; the whole set was doused luridly in red light for the final assassination; and actors constantly infiltrated the audience, not only by processing through the aisles but also by using the balcony for Corioles' walls and seating some 'Senators' among the audience to listen to Cominius' eulogy in 2.2.

Self-conscious theatricalism was even more obvious in a stripped-down version directed by Deborah Warner for the Kick Theatre of Islington in 1986 in almost rehearsal-room conditions: the 'set' was merely twelve orange crates ranged in a circle, by which the actors knelt when not performing and used intermittently for drums; 'costume' was floppy pyjamas for everyone; and battles and Coriolanus' murder were merely mimed; but again character interpretation was straightforward (with Aufidius interestingly portrayed as a manic-depressive) and the minimal staging allowed nearly the whole script to be performed uncut.

European directors, on the other hand, are apt to be very cavalier about Shakespeare's script, possibly because they are dealing with it only in translation. Hans Hollman's second production, at the Thalia Theatre in Hamburg in 1977, used monstrous caricatures of the *Ubu Roi* type;[1] while the Comédie Française's second production of the Piachaud translation in 1957 combined a very noisy 'constructivist' set of

---

[1] See Daniell, pp. 92–3.

white-painted lumber, on which the actors did gymnastics, with odd costuming (the Volsces were in black bathing-suits), and again there was obtrusive involvement of the audience. A production at the Théâtre de Gennevilles in 1983 took place in a ruined theatre, littered with wheelbarrows, cement-mixers, scaffolding pipes, and miscellaneous rubble, with everyone wearing similar beige tunics except for the women who wore orange and red (which extended to their eyebrows and hair), though at Aufidius' house the Volscians were unexpectedly dressed as Russians being served by Parisian café waiters. The whole theatre was used as an acting area, with spectators once more absorbed into the 'Senate'; and slow-motion, balletic battles were conducted with toy wooden swords, painted green with purple spots for 'blood', in dead silence despite the dialogue's references to drums and trumpets.[1]

Another hallmark of post-modernism is to mix costumes eclectically from several historical periods to create an effect of timeless or recurrent relevance. This was how Poel's 1931 experiment ended up, though originally he had intended it all to be in the early Napoleonic period (Coriolanus' first costume, however, was a lion's skin). And an elaboration of such eclecticism could be seen in Steven Berkoff's 1988 production for the New York Shakespeare Festival, which relied less on different historical periods than on a range of Hollywood stereotypes, performing on a black and white, unlocalized, art deco set. Gangsters in 'zoot-suits' mixed with Volscians in South American guerilla fatigues and 1930s 'Bowery boys' (armed literally with baseball 'bats'); the women all wore medieval costume; and Martius and his fellow generals had black shirts and long black leather coats which managed to seem simultaneously Hollywood 'Nazi' and contemporary urban chic. Plebs, patricians, soldiers, and Volsces were all played by the same nine-person 'chorus', who did song and dance numbers to relentlessly percussive music; occasionally scenes were acted in slow motion; and there was extensive use of dance mime of the kind associated with the choreographer Agnes de Mille: not only for the battles and the final assassination but also for the opening riot (with the plebs

---

[1] See Leonore Leiblein, review in *Cahiers Elisabéthains*, 24 (1983), 96–7.

running vigorously on the spot) and for a Roman 'cavalry' attack on Corioles.[1]

The reductiveness and semiotic confusion of this production show the obvious dangers of a post-modernist approach, yet one interpretation of major importance has certainly been directed in this style. This was Peter Hall's left-wing production at the National Theatre in 1984, mounted in reaction against the Thatcher government's cuts in social services and bellicosity about the Falklands war. Hall's set was a circular sand-pit backed by great double-doors, with a minimum of furniture brought on and off by actors. The audience was involved not only by the usual processing through the aisles but also by seating part of them on bleachers on the stage at each side of the sand-pit, and co-opting them to represent part of the plebeian crowd. Predictably in practice this failed to work, but it was theoretically possible because the play's costuming was a mixture of Roman and contemporary modern, with Coriolanus himself, for instance, wearing a suit and white overcoat, yet going into battle with a broadsword. The production had a considerable (though qualified) success,[2] but would not have worked without the traditional acting skills of its distinguished company and Hall's own scholarly familiarity with Shakespeare's text.

'*Coriolanus* is perhaps the least dated of Shakespeare's plays' (see p. 1 n. 2); and reflecting the political upheavals and psychological stresses of the late twentieth century, it has been very frequently performed since the end of World War II, with more than a dozen major productions in English alone over the last two decades, including five by the Royal Shakespeare Company. (Yet another is in rehearsal by the Renaissance Theatre Company at Chichester as this paragraph is being written in the Spring of 1992.) Such a rediscovery is very gratifying, because the play is undoubtedly a major achievement. But in so far as revivals of *Coriolanus* in the past

[1] A similar, though more restrained, eclecticism characterized Robert Lepage's Théâtre Repère production of a new translation and adaptation by Michel Garneau at the 1993 Festival de théâtre des Ameriques in Montreal: see the Toronto *Globe and Mail*, 13 May 1993.

[2] Cf. Roger Warren, review in *SQ*, 37 (1986), 114–20; Nicholas Shrimpton, review in *ShS*, 39 (1987), pp. 191–3; and Kristina Bedford's full-length study, '*Coriolanus*' at the National: '*Th'Interpretation of the Time*' (1992), *passim*.

have heralded periods of social upheaval, it may also be a little ominous. 'Pity a society that needs heroes', says Bertolt Brecht. Pity even more a society that delights to see them sacrificed.

The Folio Text

Coriolanus first appears in the Stationers' Register on 18 November 1623 as part of a global entry made for 'Master [Edward] Blounte and Isaac Jaggard' of sixteen previously unpublished plays.[1] It is listed among the texts 'not formerly entred to other men' and there is no evidence of a quarto printing, so the definitive text for the play is that of the 1623 Folio (F). F's table of contents and the play's own quire signatures and pagination show that it was intended to begin the collection's group of 'Tragedies', but subsequently *Troilus and Cressida* was inserted before it, with anomalous signatures and without pagination except for independent numbering (79 and 80) on two early pages.

F is a folio in sixes, with the text in double columns on each page, and was set by formes, not seriatim, so that its copy must have been cast off before composition. The main compositor was the workman traditionally designated as B, with some help from his more accurate colleague A, who set seven and a quarter of the play's thirty pages. There seems to have been practically no stop-press correction;[2] but one hiatus did occur, when the two outer sheets of quire bb— i.e. pp. 13, 14, 15, 16 (2.3.113–3.1.296) and 21, 22, 23, 24 (4.2.44–4.6.161)—were printed out of order, two weeks later than they should normally have been. Hinman (ii. 164) suggests that 'some kind of warehouse disaster' may have destroyed a first printing of these sheets; in which case, the pages as they now exist in F 'may be wholly or partly a reprint of a first setting'.[3] There seems to be nothing else remarkable about them, however.

---

[1] Arber, iv. 10; reproduced in S. Schoenbaum, *William Shakespeare: Records and Images* (1981), p. 221.

[2] See Charlton Hinman, *The Printing and Proof-reading of the First Folio of Shakespeare* (1963), ii. 134–94; and i. 284–5, where Hinman finds only one, unimportant press variant in the whole play. For compositors, see S. W. Wells *et al.*, *Textual Companion*, pp. 151–4.

[3] Ibid, p. 593.

By and large, F's text is good. As the division between Acts 3 and 4 seems to be faulty (see 3.3.144 n.), the act divisions were probably done by someone other than Shakespeare, either for production at the Blackfriars when the King's Men moved into that theatre in 1608-9 or, less probably, for the Folio printing later.[1] The scene divisions were introduced much later, when Edward Capell refined previous partitionings by Rowe and Pope for his edition of 1768, with the division between 5.5 and 5.6 added in the nineteenth century by Alexander Dyce and that between 1.4 and 1.5 by the editors of the Oxford Shakespeare as recently as 1986.

About a dozen speeches are wrongly assigned in F, probably because the compositors misread abbreviated speech-headings which either closely resembled each other in the manuscript or were unclearly aligned along its margins.[2] However, problems with the designation of speeches for numbered but unnamed Citizens in 1.1 and 2.3 and numbered Servingmen in 4.5 probably derive from confusions in the copy-text itself, as do inconsistent references to the character Titus Lartius, who is referred to in stage directions as *Titus Lartius, Titus Latius*, or merely *Titus* (see 1.1.237 n.) and in speech-headings very variously as *Tit., Lar., Lart., Titus Lartius, Titus Latius*, and *Latius*, with one reference to 'Titus Lucius' within the text at 1.1.237 which is almost certainly a misreading of the copy-text's 'Latius'. The variant spellings Lartius/Latius are not compositorial but can be traced to Shakespeare's use of the 1595 edition of North's Plutarch, which had 'Latius' incorrectly in the text but 'Lartius' in the marginal glosses,[3] while the erratic behaviour assigned to Lartius in the play (see 1.4.25 n. and 1.10.75-6 n.) may well have affected the variety of speech-headings used for the character.

---

[1] Cf. Wilfred T. Jewkes, *Act Division in Elizabethan and Jacobean Plays, 1583-1616* (1958), pp. 97-8; Emrys Jones, *Scenic Form*, pp. 71-6. In 1984 NT, Peter Hall experimented with an intermission after 4.1.

[2] Cf. Thomas Clayton's 'Today We have Parting of Names: A Preliminary Inquiry into Some Editorial Speech-(be)headings in *Coriolanus*', in *Today*, 15 February 1986.

[3] See Honigmann, *Stability*, p. 148; he also argues that passages with the 'Latius' spelling must have been composed first, even though this may cut across their sequence in the action of the play.

There are also other variant speech-headings—between Plebeians/Citizens, for example, and Patricians/Nobles/Senators—which provide one good reason for believing the copy-text may have been close to the author's working manuscript, an assumption that is borne out by the text's two main peculiarities. Almost ten per cent of the lineation is irregular, with a much greater preponderance of short lines than is usual in Shakespeare (except for other plays of about this date), plus one of the highest percentages in the canon of contractions, colloquial clippings, and sense pauses. And, like *The Tempest* which begins the 'Comedies' section of F, *Coriolanus* has many elaborate, rather 'literary' and occasionally permissive stage directions, some of which seem to be duplicated by terser, more explicit instructions.

Copy-text. Scholars are generally agreed that the copy underlying the text of *Coriolanus* was close to Shakespeare's manuscript, but opinions differ as to whether this could have been the author's foul papers, not yet fully revised; or foul papers in whose margins the theatre bookholder had jotted down occasional supplementary directions, as he prepared it for fair copying as a prompt-book; or an authorial fair copy, already so carefully prepared for the theatre that it may have served as a prompt-book, though there is no specific evidence that this was so; or a scribal copy of the author's manuscript which possibly was also annotated by the bookholder for use as a prompt-book.[1]

The clearest evidence of F's closeness to Shakespeare's manuscript is the presence in it of several of his eccentric spelling preferences, plus mistakes that are readily traceable to peculiarities of his cursive secretary hand known to us from Hand D in *The Book of Sir Thomas More*. One typically Shakespearian spelling is the unusual 'sc' beginning 'Scicinius', which is retained some thirty times by the more faithful compositor A, but only occurs twice in the much larger stint set by B where the spelling is usually regularized to 'Sicinius'. There is also evidence of Shakespeare's habit of using upper-

[1] See, respectively, Charlton Hinman, ed., *The First Folio of Shakespeare* (1968), p. xv; Dover Wilson, pp. 130–7; Greg, pp. 405–7; *Textual Companion*, pp. 593–4.

case Cs improperly in mid-sentence, which produces confusions at 4.1.5, where F has 'common. Chances', the absurd mistake of '*with Cumaljis.*' at 3.3.136.2, and 'sword. *Contenning*' at 1.3.42, which also illustrates the minim confusions that were another characteristic of his hand. Similarly, his capital I, which resembled an A or arabic 4,[1] was responsible for three errors: '*Annius*' for '*Junius*' at 1.1.224, '*Athica*' for '*Ithaca*' at 1.3.87, and 'foure shall' for 'I shall' at 1.7.85. His spelling 'one' for 'on' produced errors at 1.1.15, 1.2.4, 2.2.79, and 3.1.145; his preference for '- les' as a suffix rather than '-less' resulted in 'Naples' at 2.1.230 instead of 'napless'; and his carelessness about abbreviation marks led to misreadings of 'tongue' for 'toge' at 2.3.111 and 'Through' for 'Throng' at 3.3.36, and probably also the curtailment of 'lamentation' to 'lamention' at 4.6.36. Hand D's preference for 'oo' spellings can be traced in F's 'shoot' (for 'shout') at 1.1.211, 1.10.50, and 5.5.4, 'strooke' (for 'struck') at 1.7.4, 4.1.8, 4.2.21, and 4.5.220, and 'too' (for 'to'), especially in the form 'too't' which occurs nine times. Other errors typical of misreadings of his hand can be seen in 'taintingly' for 'tauntingly' at 1.1.107, 'Lessen' for 'Lesser' at 1.7.71, 'one' for 'our' at 3.1.290, 'things' for 'tryings' at 3.2.21, 'fiue' for 'fine' at 5.3.150, and 'change' for 'charge' at 5.3.153. At 4.4.23, 'have' for 'hate' may be a misreading or a foul case error. And, finally, the very light pointing characteristic of Hand D seems to have stimulated both compositors to introduce their own punctuation, which is frequently wrong. There is a heavy use of colons and brackets in F that is totally atypical of Hand D, and in particular, as A. H. Gomme notes, a habit of switching mid-line and end-line punctuation (e.g. F's 'most charitable care | Have the Patricians of you for your wants.' at 1.1.62–3) that relates to the most tricky bibliographical aspect of all: the text's irregularity of lining and, in particular, its heavy use of mid-line pauses and short lines.

Lineation. There are several factors to be taken into account before deciding how many of the play's more than 300

---

[1] See the last 'I' on Plate VII of Sir Edward Maunde Thompson's *Shakespeare's Handwriting* (1916).

irregular lines need correcting. Some of the factors are external to the meaning of the text, others are intrinsic. In the first category come certain manuscript habits in the *More* extract which show how easy it would be to misline Shakespeare's holograph when he was composing with the fluency on which both Ben Jonson and the Folio editors comment. Hand D shows him running long lines over into the next line; beginning a new verse line in the space left at the end of a short line; omitting the capital letters which might indicate where each new line began; and cramming additional lines or revisions into narrow margins, which confuses the lineation further. These difficulties within the copy-text would be compounded for the compositors of F because they had to accommodate the verse to a double-column format that was frequently too narrow for a full pentameter line, and were also working from cast-off copy which occasionally required that the text be 'crowded' or, alternatively, 'spread' to fit the page lengths predetermined for each forme. A good example of spreading can be seen on sigs. aa5, recto and verso, of F (pp. 9–10) where speeches that amount to sixteen lines in the present edition have been spread to take up twenty-one lines (2.1.176–87, 196–8, with two lines more spun out of 2.1.206–7, 233–4). An example of crowding can be seen at 3.1.119–20 where the text that editors divide as 'I say they nourished disobedience, fed | The ruin of the state' is rendered as a single line.[1]

It is difficult to be certain of such adjustments, however, because of the intrinsic irregularity of all of Shakespeare's late blank verse, in which, to quote the editor of the *London Shakespeare*, 'Shakespeare, like a composer, with the rhythm in his head, was at times apt to be unmindful of exact line division'.[2] This late verse is full of elisions and metrical slurrings, contractions, and what A. C. Partridge has called Shakespeare's 'new technique of colloquial clipping',[3] which he may have learned from the example of Ben Jonson. He

---

[1] See Brockbank, p. 11 nn. 1 and 2 for lists of all F passages that may possibly be crowded or spread. A large proportion of these, however, he identifies as 'trivial and dubious'.

[2] John Munro, *The London Shakespeare* (1958), vi. 1210.

[3] *Orthography in Shakespeare and Elizabethan Drama* (1964), p. 116. Partridge notes that Shakespeare is haphazard about using apostrophes for such abbreviations.

writes lines that are both longer and shorter than iambic pentameter, with extra syllables at mid-line and in double endings, with run-ons or enjambment, and, in particular, with heavy mid-line syntactical pauses which, combined with the frequent enjambment, give a Donne-like counterpoint of metrical and grammatical stress, in which a phrase often ends in mid-line and a line correspondingly in mid-phrase. This is accompanied by what George Wright calls 'rashes of short-line exchanges that hover between verse and prose', producing 'a rhetoric that virtually abandons the flowing sentence for brief and abrupt bursts of staccato phrases that seem almost, at times, in their jagged discourse, to mock both line and phrase'.[1] Not unnaturally, these occur particularly in short volleys of dialogue, especially where there is a mixture of verse and prose, as in the exchanges between patricians and plebeians, and also at the start or conclusion of long speeches—though Fredson Bowers has shown that they are far more likely to occur at the end of such speeches than at the beginning.[2] Compositor A has been taken to task[3] for lining in a fashion that sacrifices metre to syntactical division, but, considering his general faithfulness to copy and the overall effect of Shakespeare's late verse, it seems equally probable that in this he may have reproduced Shakespeare's own manuscript, before a fair copy was made.

Although he set less than one quarter of F's *Coriolanus*, Compositor A is responsible for nearly half of its irregular lines, and in this he seems to coincide with a general critical perception that, even among Shakespeare's late plays, *Coriolanus* is remarkable for its deliberately unmusical, compressed, cacophonous, and jagged style, where syllables 'are crushed into the lines like fuel to stoke a furnace'.[4] This happens especially in Coriolanus' own passionately energetic lines,

---

[1] George T. Wright, 'The Play of Phrase and Line in Shakespeare's Iambic Pentameter', *SQ*, 34 (1983), p. 155; see also his *Shakespeare's Metrical Art* (1988), pp. 116–42.

[2] F. T. Bowers, 'Establishing Shakespeare's Text: Notes on Short Lines and the Problem of Verse Division', *Studies in Bibliography*, 33 (1980), 74–130.

[3] e.g. Brockbank, pp. 13–14, 16; *Textual Companion*, p. 593; Paul Werstine, 'Line Division in Shakespeare's Dramatic Verse: An Editorial Problem', *Analytical and Enumerative Bibliography*, 8 (1984), 73–125.

[4] Granville-Barker, p. 172. See p. 75.

where, speaking 'thick' like Hotspur, he loses semantic control and 'utters a string of words which are neither grammatical, logical, nor at times, even coherent',[1] and occurs also, to a lesser extent, in Aufidius' speeches, as he tries to grapple with defeat or confront the contradictions in Martius' character and his own ambiguous response to them. Because such a style is appropriate for this harsh, uncompromising play, G. B. Harrison and several other editors[2] have argued that F's irregular lineation should be preserved, as representing Shakespeare's probable intention; but so wholesale a conservation ignores passages where compositorial crowding or spreading are obvious, or where F's lining creates obscurities unrelated to the speakers' mental confusion or to turmoil in the action.

An especially interesting feature of lineation in this play is the frequent occurrence of three short lines in sequence, with the middle 'amphibious' line able to be joined with equal propriety to either of the other two in order to produce a regular pentameter. In such cases, the Oxford editors have determined to retain the Folio's metrical ambiguity,[3] and the present edition has (with a few exceptions discussed in the Commentary) followed their example. Such a device seems appropriate for a play where 'taints and honours' are so equally mixed in characterization, where there are so many enigmatically 'over-determined' silences, and the audience's sympathy is kept oscillating between rival points of view.

This edition neither consistently regularizes metre nor leaves the lineation exactly as in F, therefore, but tries to judge each irregularity separately, within the context of its own particular variables. It has a bias towards conserving F (particularly in the matter of short lines), but also a willingness to adjust when such a change seems possible without sacrificing other values. The relation of metre to sense is ultimately very subjective, and Shakespeare himself seems to have varied between metrical and phrasal emphases during the course of composition.

Obviously, one of the factors that must influence a decision here is whether the manuscript beneath the text appears to

[1] G. B. Harrison, p. 250.
[2] e.g. George Gordon (1912); M. R. Ridley (1934); G. B. Harrison (1947).
[3] See Gary Taylor in *Textual Companion*, pp. 637–9.

be a final version, or a draft that still required revision. The weight of the evidence seems to favour the latter. Besides the length of the play, which, at over 3,400 lines, is 'longer than would be normal for an acting version'[1] and is exceeded in the canon only by *2 Henry IV*, *Troilus and Cressida*, *Richard III*, and *Hamlet*, there are many anomalies that would probably need to be corrected for performance, including some the author himself might want to clarify before submitting a fair copy.

Some of these have already been touched on. There are confusions of identity among the Citizens and Servingmen who are represented only by number in 1.1, 2.3, and 4.5; variations in speech-headings and stage directions for Plebeians/ Citizens and Patricians/Nobles/Senators/Gentry and for Titus Lartius; and obscurity in the latter's behaviour, particularly his appearance in the ovation at 2.1.149.1 and 174 before his return from Corioles has been ratified by the Senate at 2.2.36, and his improbable lack of involvement in the riot of 3.1, though ostensibly he is present in that scene (see 3.1.21 n.). To these may be added the variant spellings of Corioles (Coriolas, Carioles, Cariolus, Corialus); reversal of the hero's first two names at 1.10.65, 67, 2.1.160, 168, and 2.2.44; descriptions of Cominius as 'the Generall' at 2.1.157.1 and 178 but as 'the Consul' at 2.2.34.3; misascription of speeches at 3.1.50, 204, 231–2, 237, 238, 240, 4.1.38 (and possibly 4.2.15, 27–30), some of which may be authorial; contradictions in the numbers of Citizens specified at 2.3.59 and of Conspirators at 5.6.8, 131.1; confusions of place in 3.1 and 5.6; two incorrect directions to 'Enter', one at 2.1.200.2 for the Tribunes who earlier at 93 were said merely to have stood 'Aside', the other at 4.5.148.2 for two Servingmen who have clearly heard the previous conversation on stage; and finally, perhaps, the omission of several key stage directions, such as the point where Volumnia rises from her knees in the pleading scene 5.3—though such omissions are characteristic of all texts. However, we are here encroaching on the text's second main peculiarity, which needs separate consideration.

---

[1] Maurice Charney, in S. W. Wells, ed., *Shakespeare: Select Bibliographical Guides* (1973), p. 216.

Stage Directions. The stage directions of *Coriolanus* are much more elaborate than usual, possibly because Shakespeare was already in semi-retirement at Stratford and wanted to be sure that, in his absence, the company in London fully understood his intentions in their new theatre at the Blackfriars, or conceivably because Heminges and Condell wished *Coriolanus*, like *The Tempest*, to appear especially impressive as the first play of its section in the Folio. Scholars are agreed that, despite some gaps and confusions, 'The directions are always expert, devised by someone who has visualized the action very clearly',[1] but disagree about whether they all derive from the author's manuscript or were occasionally supplemented from elsewhere (and if so, by whom).

Typically authorial are such 'permissive' directions as 'Enter Tullus Auffidius bloudie, with two or three Souldiors' (1.11.0.1–2), 'Enter seuen or eight Citizens' (2.3.0.1), 'Enter three or foure Citizens' (4.6.21.1), and 'Enter 3 or 4 Conspirators of Auffidius Faction' (5.6.8). Also likely to be authorial are such discursively elaborate directions as 'Enter Martius, Titus Lartius, with Drumme and Colours, with Captaines and Souldiers, as before the City Corialus' (1.4.0.1–4),[2] 'A Sennet. Trumpets sound. Enter Cominius the Generall, and Titus Latius [*sic*]: betweene them Coriolanus, crown'd with an Oaken Garland, with Captaines and Souldiers, and a Herauld' (2.1.157.1–3), 'A Sennet. Enter the Patricians, and the Tribunes of the People, Lictors before them: Coriolanus, Menenius, Cominius the Consul: Scicinius [*sic*] and Brutus take their places by themselves: Coriolanus stands' (2.2.34.1–6), or 'Enter Coriolanus marching with Drumme, and Colours. The Commoners being with him' (5.6.70.1–2). These ceremonial entrances are a recurrent element in the dramaturgy of the play and are very carefully specified: hence the bare, anonymous direction for Volumnia's ovation in 5.5.0.1–2, 'Enter two Senators, with Ladies, passing ouer the Stage, with other Lords', gains significance by contrast to the other, much more detailed triumphs in the play, and there appears to be

[1] Granville-Barker, p. 190.

[2] Cf. also such 'advisory' directions as: '*Enter Cominius as it were in retire, with soldiers*' (1.7.0.1–2), '*Enter two Officers, to lay Cushions, as it were, in the Capitoll*' (2.2.0.1–2), '*Enter Menenius to the Watch or guard*' (5.2.0.1).

an attempt to counter its sparseness with reiterated emphasis
on the clamorous music which announces, then accompanies
it ('Trumpets, Hoboyes, Drums beate, altogether', 5.4.48). The
directions also carefully name supernumerary characters, including specifically 'the yong Nobility of Rome' at 4.1.0.2,
recalling Plutarch's distinction between the older patricians
who were prepared to sacrifice Martius and the younger ones
who supported him—a detail the play does not otherwise
develop. There is a constant concern for sound effects in the
text, from the drums, trumpets, and cornetts of the simulta-
neous battles in Act 1, where 'we heare their Larum, & they
Ours' (1.4.9), to the 'dead March' called for at the conclusion. The directions often bias response by a literary choice
of words: 'Citizens steale away' (1.1.248), for instance, 'Enter
a rabble of Plebeians with the Ædiles' (3.1.181), 'They all
bustle about Coriolanus' (3.1.186.1—using Richard of Gloucester's word for civil disorder), or 'Martius fights til they be
driuen in breathles' (1.9.13.3). And as the last example also
demonstrates, the directions often contain extra detail about
acting or props of a kind usually left to the actor in Elizabethan play texts: 'Enter Volumnia and Virgilia, mother and
wife to Martius: They set them downe on two lowe stooles
and sowe' (1.3.0.1–3), 'Alarum, the Romans are beat back
to their Trenches[.] Enter Martius Cursing' (1.4.29.1–2,
1.5.0.1–2), 'They all shout and waue their swords, take him
vp in their Armes, and cast vp their Caps' (1.7.76.1–3), 'Enter
at one Doore Cominius, with the Romanes: At another Doore
Martius, with his Arme in a Scarfe' (1.10.0.1–3), 'A long
flourish. They all cry, Martius, Martius, cast vp their Caps
and Launces: Cominius and Lartius stand bare' (1.10.40.1–3),
'Holds her by the hand silent' (5.3.183), and 'Draw both the
Conspirators, and kils [*sic*] Martius, who falles, Auffidius
stands on him' (5.6.131.1–2).

There is also evidence for what may be duplication in the
stage directions, however. The most striking is a terse 'Enter
the Gati' (i.e. Gates) three lines after the more expansive and
premature direction 'Another Alarum, and Martius followes
them to gates, and is shut in' (1.5.13.1–3), with 'followes' in
the text immediately before the latter also possibly a wrongly
assimilated stage direction. Similarly, at 3.1.229.1–2 a marginal

Exeunt is followed by 'In this Mutinie, the Tribunes, the
Ædiles, and the People are beat in' which merely glosses its
meaning. There are also several cases where two music cues
seem to come together: 'A flourish. Cornets' (1.10.94.1), 'A
Sennet. Trumpets sound' (2.1.157.1, 4), 'Flourish. Cornets'
(2.1.192.1), where the specification of instruments may possibly reflect production of the play at Blackfriars.[1] The Oxford
editors also instance four entry directions in which a descriptive 'the two tribunes' stands unnecessarily in apposition
to their names,[2] while a similar objection has been made to
the redundancy of place-name in 'as before the City Corialus
[*sic*]' and 'on the Walles of Corialus [*sic*]' at 1.4.0.3–4 and
1.4.12.0.2, respectively.

Neither singly nor cumulatively do these examples prove
later revision, however: 'Flourish Cornets', undivided by a
period, also occurs at 2.2.153.1; and 'A Sennet. Trumpets
sound' marks two different movements in the action (see
2.1.157.1 n.) and was probably misplaced because 'Trumpets
sound' was in the margin. Moreover, among critics who argue
for non-authorial intervention, there is no agreement about
where this intervention came from. Following Philip Williams,
the Oxford editors postulate an intervening scribe, on the
grounds that the direction 'Enters' (1.8.0.3) 'does not elsewhere appear in texts thought to be set from Shakespeare's
papers', that the high incidence of parentheses and apo-
strophied 'ha's' and 'do's' is not usually associated with
Shakespeare, that the favoured spelling 'Oh' runs against
Shakespeare's preference for 'O' (ignoring the fact that 36 of
these 'Oh's' are set by B, whose preference it was), and that
29 examples of 'a'th' ' make this contraction three times more
frequent in *Coriolanus* than in any other Shakespeare play.[3]
Such evidence leaves a decision about scribal intervention
with the Scottish verdict of 'not proven'; and one remembers
Greg's cautions against postulating transcripts between foul

[1] See *Textual Companion*, p. 594; Brockbank compares *Merchant* 2.7.1 ff.
where several cornett flourishes are prescribed in the F text only. See p. 88
n. 4 above.
[2] *Textual Companion*, p. 593.
[3] Philip Williams, 'Textual Problems in Shakespeare', *Studies in Bibliography*,
8 (1956), p. 6; *Textual Companion*, p. 593.

papers and the prompt-book: 'speculation on these lines, however ingenious and plausible in the abstract, is at too great a remove from concrete probability to carry conviction'.[1]

More widely held is the theory that some of the duplicate or redundant stage directions in F may reflect sophistication that derives from the theatre, either because the bookholder partially annotated the manuscript, or because the Folio editors elaborated their *Coriolanus* text by consulting its prompt-book or, possibly, the 'Plot' summary which hung backstage in Elizabethan theatres for quick reference by the actors and is thought to have been particularly concerned with elaborate stage entrances, the identification of supernumeraries, provision of precise music cues, and clarifications of unusually elaborate stage business.[2]

Each of these theories is possible, but none is really necessary. On the principle of Occam's razor, I agree with Brockbank and Dover Wilson that 'both the virtues and the vices of the Folio text [of *Coriolanus*] are more readily assignable to the hand of Shakespeare than another's',[3] remembering the speed with which he composed and the great likelihood that he imagined staging simultaneously with the text (particularly if he wrote the play at Stratford and had Blackfriars in mind as well as the Globe Theatre). Whatever difficulties remain will dissolve if we assume the copytext manuscript was not his fair copy (which would probably have become the company's prompt-book and not have been surrendered to the press if an alternative was available), but, rather, a penultimate draft in which he was still to some extent 'thinking through' the play. This would explain its length, and certain roughnesses in its continuity, such as the behaviour of Titus Lartius or confusions among the speeches (and characterization) of the Citizens, Servingmen, and Conspirators identified only by numbers. The elaborate stage directions would reflect

---

[1] Greg, p. 467; cf. also William B. Long, '*John a Kent and John a Cumber*: An Elizabethan Playbook and Its Implications', in W. R. Elton and W. B. Long, eds., *Shakespeare and the Dramatic Tradition* (1989), p. 127.

[2] For 'plots', see W. W. Greg, *Dramatic Documents from the Elizabethan Playhouses* (1931), ii. 1–11; and Bernard Beckerman, 'Theatrical Plots and Elizabethan Stage Practice' in Elton and Long, 109–24.

[3] Dover Wilson, p. 131.

his initial imaginings of the action, with terser directions added *currente calamo* to indicate exactly where an important event should occur, to add a further staging idea, or to specify particular instruments for music cues when these have a particular semiotic importance. And the 'rashes' of half-lines would convey his sense of the semantic (as distinct from metrical) rhythm of the play, that disjunctive, enigmatically over-determined, ambiguous and ultimately mysterious quality of *Coriolanus* about which there is such general agreement.

EDITORIAL PROCEDURES

THIS edition aims to provide a modernized text according to the principles published by Stanley Wells in 'Modernizing Shakespeare's Spelling' in Wells and Gary Taylor, *Modernizing Shakespeare's Spelling, with Three Studies in the Text of 'Henry V'* (1979) and the procedures laid out in Gary Taylor's edition of *Henry V* (1982), pp. 3–36. Spelling and punctuation are modernized without annotation unless they affect meaning, in which case they are recorded in the Collation, with an indication of their provenance and any variant readings from other editions. Such modernization extends also to quotations from other early texts referred to in the Introduction, Commentary notes, and Appendix B, 'Sources and Analogues', though these are not annotated. It is a convention of the series to render unstressed past participle endings as 'ed' and stressed endings with an accented 'èd'. Speech-headings are normalized silently and only recorded in the Collation if there is a question about who is speaking; act divisions are as in the 1623 Folio text, but scene divisions are all collated because they were added by later editors.

Stage directions are added or expanded as seems necessary to clarify the action. All 'asides' or directions to speak 'to' a particular person are the responsibility of this edition, and have not been noted unless there is disagreement about them. Other editorial changes in the stage directions are not indicated in the text, but are noted in the Collation, again with provenance and other editors' alternatives; while directions that seem probable but not certain are indicated by broken brackets (⌈ ⌉). As lineation is a special problem in *Coriolanus* all changes of that sort have been recorded separately in Appendix A. Both stage directions and lineation are analysed under 'The Folio Text' in the Introduction; and changes of particular significance are also discussed in the Commentary notes.

Abbreviations and References

Line numbers and references to other Shakespeare plays are from *The Complete Works*, ed. Stanley Wells, Gary Taylor, *et al.* (1986). Titles are normally given in modern spelling. F1 is only specified when the First Folio needs to be distinguished from the later folio editions.

EDITIONS OF SHAKESPEARE AND TEXTUAL COMMENTARIES

F, F1	The First Folio, 1623
F2	The Second Folio, 1632
F3	The Third Folio, 1663
F4	The Fourth Folio, 1685
Alexander	Peter Alexander, *The Complete Works* (1951)
Arden	W. J. Craig and R. H. Case, *Coriolanus*, The Arden Shakespeare (1922)
Brockbank	Philip Brockbank, *Coriolanus*, revised Arden Shakespeare (1976)
Brooke	C. F. Tucker-Brooke, *Coriolanus*, The Yale Shakespeare (1924)
Brower	Reuben Brower, *Coriolanus*, Signet Classic Shakespeare (1966)
Cambridge	W. G. Clark and W. A. Wright, *Works*, The Cambridge Shakespeare (1865); 2nd edn., ed. W. A. Wright (1892)
Capell	Edward Capell, *Works of Shakespeare* (1768)
Chambers	E. K. Chambers, *Coriolanus*, The Warwick Shakespeare (1898)
Clarendon	W. A. Wright, *Coriolanus*, The Clarendon Press Shakespeare (1878)
Collier	J. P. Collier, *Works of Shakespeare* (1844)
Collier 1858	J. P. Collier, *Works*, 2nd edn. (1858)
Collier 1876	J. P. Collier, *Works*, 3rd edn. (1876)
Collier MS	J. P. Collier, *Notes and Emendations to the text of Shakespeare's Plays, from early manuscript corrections, in a copy of the Folio, 1632* (1853); in Furness
Craig	W. J. Craig, *Works of Shakespeare*, The Oxford Shakespeare (1892)
Delius	N. Delius, *Shakespeare Werke* (1854)
Dyce	Alexander Dyce, *Works of Shakespeare* (1857)
Dyce 1866	Alexander Dyce, *Works of Shakespeare*, rev. edn. (1866)

Edwards	T. Edwards, *Canons of Criticism*, 3rd edn. (1750)
Furness	H. H. Furness Jr., *Coriolanus*, The New Variorum Shakespeare (1928)
Globe	W. G. Clark and W. A. Wright, *Works of Shakespeare*, The Globe Shakespeare (1864)
Gomme	A. H. Gomme, *Coriolanus*, Shakespeare Workshop (1969)
Gordon	George S. Gordon, *Coriolanus* (1912)
Hanmer	Thomas Hanmer, *Works of Shakespeare* (1744)
Harrison	G. B. Harrison, *Coriolanus*, The Penguin Shakespeare (1947)
Hibbard	G. R. Hibbard, *Coriolanus*, New Penguin Shakespeare (1967)
Hudson	H. N. Hudson, *Works of Shakespeare*, The Harvard Shakespeare (1880)
Johnson	Samuel Johnson, *Plays of Shakespeare* (1765)
Keightley	T. Keightley, *Plays of Shakespeare* (1864)
Kemball-Cook	B. H. Kemball-Cook, *Coriolanus*, The New Clarendon Shakespeare (1954)
King	A. H. King, 'Notes on *Coriolanus*', *English Studies* (1937–8) 19–20
Kinnear	Benjamin G. Kinnear, *Cruces Shakespearianae* (1883)
Kittredge	G. L. Kittredge, *Works of Shakespeare* (1936); rev. Irving Ribner (1971)
Knight	C. Knight, *Works of Shakespeare*, Pictorial Shakespeare (1838–43)
Leo	F. A. Leo, *Coriolanus* (1864)
Malone	Edmond Malone, *Plays and Poems of Shakespeare* (1790)
Mason	John Monck Mason, *Comments on Several Editions of Shakespeare's Plays* (1807; combining his *Comments on the last edition of Shakespeare's Plays*, 1785, and *Additional Comments on the Plays of Shakespeare*, 1797)
Munro	John Munro, *Works of Shakespeare*, The London Shakespeare (1958)
Neilson	W. A. Neilson, *The Complete Dramatic and Poetic Works of Shakespeare* (1906); rev. edn. with C. J. Hill (1942)
Oxford	Stanley Wells, Gary Taylor, *et al.*, ed. John Jowett, in *The Complete Works* (1986). Textual notes appear in Stanley Wells, Gary Taylor, *et al.*, *William Shakespeare: A Textual Companion* (1987)

Pope	Alexander Pope, *Works of Shakespeare* (1723)
Pope 1728	Alexander Pope, *Works of Shakespeare* (1728)
Rann	Joseph Rann, *Dramatic Works* (1786–94)
Reed	Isaac Reed, *The Dramatic Works of Shakespeare* 'with notes by Samuel Johnson and George Steevens' (1803)
Rowe	Nicholas Rowe, *Works of Shakespeare* (1709)
Rowe 1714	Nicholas Rowe, *Works* (1714)
Schmidt	A. L. Schmidt, *Coriolanus* (1878)
Singer	S. W. Singer, *Dramatic Works of Shakespeare* (1826)
Singer (1856)	S. W. Singer, *Dramatic Works* (1856)
Sisson	C. J. Sisson, *New Readings in Shakespeare*, vol. 2 (1956)
Staunton	H. Staunton, *Plays of Shakespeare* (1858)
Steevens	Samuel Johnson and George Steevens, *Plays of Shakespeare* 'with the Corrections and Illustrations of Various Commentators' (1773)
Steevens 1778	Samuel Johnson and George Steevens, *Plays* (1778)
Steevens–Reed	Samuel Johnson, George Steevens and Isaac Reed, *Plays* (1785)
Steevens–Reed 1793	George Steevens and Isaac Reed, *Plays of Shakespeare* (1793)
Textual Companion	See Oxford, above
Theobald	Lewis Theobald, *Works of Shakespeare* (1733)
Theobald 1740	Lewis Theobald, *Works* (1740)
Tyrwhitt	T. Tyrwhitt, *Observations on Shakespeare* (1766)
Verity	A. W. Verity, *Coriolanus*, Students' Shakespeare (1905)
Warburton	W. Warburton, *Works of Shakespeare* (1747)
White	R. G. White, *Coriolanus* (1861)
Wilson	J. Dover Wilson, *Coriolanus*, New Shakespeare (1960)

OTHER ABBREVIATIONS

Abbott	E. A. Abbott, *A Shakespearian Grammar* (1879)
Arber	Edward Arber, *A Transcript of the Register of the Company of Stationers of London,* 1554–1640, 5 vols. (1875–94)

Bullough	Geoffrey Bullough, *Narrative and Dramatic Sources of Shakespeare*, vol. 5 (1964)
Chambers, *W. S.*	E. K. Chambers, *William Shakespeare: A Study of Facts and Problems*, 2 vols. (1930)
Charney	Maurice Charney, *Shakespeare's Roman Plays: The Function of Imagery in the Drama* (1961)
Daniell	David Daniell, *'Coriolanus' in Europe* (1980)
ELR	*English Literary Renaissance*
Granville-Barker	Harley Granville-Barker, *Prefaces to Shakespeare*, 5th series (1947)
Kantorowicz	Ernst H. Kantorowicz, *The King's Two Bodies: A Study in Medieval Political Theology* (1957)
Leggatt and Norem	Alexander Leggatt and Lois Norem, *'Coriolanus': An Annotated Bibliography* (1989)
MLR	*Modern Language Review*
North	Sir Thomas North, trans. of Plutarch, *The Lives of the Noble Grecians and Romans* (1595)
NQ	*Notes and Queries*
NT	The National Theatre, London
Odell	G. C. D. Odell, *Shakespeare—from Betterton to Irving*, 2 vols. (1920), repr. with a new introduction by R. H. Ball (1966)
OED	*The Oxford English Dictionary*, 13 vols. (1933) and Supplements 1–4 (1972–86)
Onions	C. T. Onions, *A Shakespeare Glossary* (1911, revised by Robert D. Eagleson, 1986)
OV	Old Vic Theatre, London
Palmer	John Palmer, *Political Characters of Shakespeare* (1945)
Poole	Adrian Poole, *Coriolanus*, Harvester New Critical Introductions to Shakespeare (1988)
RES	*Review of English Studies*
RSC	Royal Shakespeare Company
Schoenbaum	S. Schoenbaum, *William Shakespeare: A Compact Documentary Life* (rev. edn., 1987)
SEL	*Studies in English Literature*
ShS	*Shakespeare Survey*
SMT	Shakespeare Memorial Theatre at Stratford-upon-Avon

SQ	*Shakespeare Quarterly*
Spencer	T. J. B. Spencer, ed., *Shakespeare's Plutarch* (1964)
Tilley	M. P. Tilley, *A Dictionary of the Proverbs in England in the Sixteenth and Seventeenth Centuries* (1950)

The Tragedy of Coriolanus

THE PERSONS OF THE PLAY

Caius MARTIUS, later called CORIOLANUS
MENENIUS Agrippa, his elderly friend
COMINIUS, Consul and Commander-in-Chief
Titus LARTIUS, a general
VOLUMNIA, Coriolanus' mother   patricians of Rome
VIRGILIA, his wife
YOUNG MARTIUS, his son
VALERIA, a chaste lady of Rome

SICINIUS Velutus } tribunes
Junius BRUTUS   } of Rome
CITIZENS of Rome   plebeians of Rome
SOLDIERS in the Roman army

Tullus AUFIDIUS, a general of the Volscian army
His LIEUTENANT
His SERVINGMEN
CONSPIRATORS with Aufidius
Volscian LORDS
Volscian CITIZENS
SOLDIERS in the Volscian army

ADRIAN, a Volscian spy
NICANOR, a Roman traitor
A Roman HERALD
MESSENGERS
officers of the Roman Senate
Aediles

A Gentlewoman, an Usher, Roman and Volscian Senators and
Nobles, Captains in the Roman army, Lictors

The Tragedy of Coriolanus

1.1 *Enter a company of mutinous Citizens with staves,*
    clubs, and other weapons

FIRST CITIZEN Before we proceed any further, hear me
speak.

ALL Speak, speak.

FIRST CITIZEN You are all resolved rather to die than to
famish?   5

ALL Resolved, resolved.

FIRST CITIZEN First, you know Caius Martius is chief
enemy to the people.

ALL We know't, we know't.

FIRST CITIZEN Let us kill him, and we'll have corn at our   10
own price. Is't a verdict?

ALL No more talking on't, let it be done. Away, away.

SECOND CITIZEN One word, good citizens.

FIRST CITIZEN We are accounted poor citizens, the patricians good. What authority surfeits on would relieve   15

THE PERSONS OF THE PLAY] *after* OXFORD; *not in* F; *first given, imperfectly,* by ROWE
1.1] F (*Actus Primus. Scaena Prima.*)   7 First, . . . know] DYCE (*conj.* Cornwall); ~∧ . . .
~, F   15 on] F (one). *Similarly at 1.2.4.*

1.1 According to Roman mythical history, Martius captured Corioles in 493
BC

1.1.0.1 This boisterous opening, with the
citizens swarming on to the stage
through every entrance, instantly
engages the audience's attention and
establishes both the danger of the mob
and the fact that Shakespeare has
made starvation the chief cause of
their rebellion.

1–6 **proceed ... hear ... resolved ...**
Resolved, resolved Legal phraseology,
in a trial: cf. also 'Verdict' (l. 11),
'proceed' (24). This establishes a
recurrent motif. See Introduction,
p. 83 n. 5, 88.

4–5 **You ... famish?** Cf. the Stratford
labourers who, told that grain cost

nine shillings a bushel, declared they
would rebel since 'they were as good
be slain in the market place as starve'
(J. M. Martin, *Midland History,* 7
(1982), p. 30).

10–11 **corn ... price** Not in Plutarch, but
reflecting such contemporary London
situations as an apprentices' riot at
Southwark in 1595 in which shop-
keepers were forced to sell food at the
rioters' prices.

14 **poor** Playing on 'impoverished' and
'bad', as a protest against the mercantile evaluation of men according to
'productivity' and wealth.

15 **good** well-to-do, therefore presumed to
be worthy; cf. 'dear', l. 18
authority those in authority, the patricians

us. If they would yield us but the superfluity while it
were wholesome, we might guess they relieved us humanely, but they think we are too dear. The leanness
that afflicts us, the object of our misery, is as an inventory to particularize their abundance; our sufferance is   20
a gain to them. Let us revenge this with our pikes ere
we become rakes; for the gods know, I speak this in
hunger for bread, not in thirst for revenge.

SECOND CITIZEN Would you proceed especially against
Caius Martius?   25

ALL Against him first. He's a very dog to the commonalty.

SECOND CITIZEN Consider you what services he has done
for his country?

FIRST CITIZEN Very well; and could be content to give him
good report for't, but that he pays himself with being   30
proud.

⌈SECOND CITIZEN⌉ Nay, but speak not maliciously.

FIRST CITIZEN I say unto you, what he hath done famously, he did it to that end. Though soft-conscienced

---

26 ALL] F; *First Cit.* HUDSON (*conj.* Malone); THIRD CITIZEN Against . . . first. FOURTH
CITIZEN He's . . . commonalty. OXFORD   32 SECOND CITIZEN] MALONE (*2. Cit.*); *All.* F;
OXFORD *reads* FIFTH CITIZEN

16–17 **If . . . humanely** Not from Plut-
     arch, but an echo of *Lear*, 3.4.33–6,
     4.1.61–5.
17 **guess** think, understand
     humanely out of fellow-feeling, as
     human beings (cf. kindly, 2.3.71)
18 **dear** a play on 'expensive', and
     'attractive to them as we are'
19 **object** sight, spectacle
19–20 **as an inventory . . . abundance** like
     a calculator to itemize their own con-
     trasting plenty
20 **sufferance** suffering
21 **pikes** Playing on 'lances' and 'pitch-
     forks', the latter being an agricultural
     (rather than urban) tool that combines
     with 'rakes'. The English food riots of
     1607 were in the countryside.
22 **rakes** 'As lean as a rake' is proverbial:
     cf. 1.1.202 ff. for Martius' sneer at the
     Citizens' habit of using proverbs.
26 ALL See Introduction, pp. 94 n. 1.
     a very dog i.e. pitilessly cruel; cf. *Two
     Gentlemen* 2.3.10–11, 'no more pity in
     him than a dog'. This is the first
     example of the play's recurrent animal
     imagery; cf. Introduction, p. 79.

commonalty common people
30 **pays himself** 'i.e. for his services to the
     country' (Wilson)
32 SECOND CITIZEN This is not a comment
     that could be made by '*All*' (F), and it
     is Second Citizen who goes on to de-
     fend Martius at l. 38.
     maliciously (a) with ill-will; (b) with
     the deliberate ill-will, 'malice prepense',
     that in law distinguishes a crime from
     a tort (*OED*): cf. 'It is a purposed thing,
     and grows by plot' (3.1.40). 'Malice',
     'malicious', and 'maliciously' are key
     terms in the play, recurring at 1.1.85;
     2.1.51, 224; 2.2.20, 31; 2.3.185;
     4.6.43.
33 ff. **I say unto you . . .** This is the first
     of many analyses of Martius' person-
     ality by other characters; it sets up all
     the 'explanations' that are sub-
     sequently explored: honour, fame, pa-
     triotism, pride, and desire to please his
     mother.
33–4 **famously** in a way that won him
     fame
34 **to that end** i.e. to win fame
     soft-conscienced soft-headed, easy-going

men can be content to say it was for his country, he   35
did it to please his mother and to be partly proud—
which he is, even to the altitude of his virtue.

SECOND CITIZEN What he cannot help in his nature you
account a vice in him. You must in no way say he is
covetous.   40

FIRST CITIZEN If I must not, I need not be barren of
accusations. He hath faults, with surplus, to tire in
repetition.

    Shouts within

What shouts are these? The other side o'th' city is
risen. Why stay we prating here? To th' Capitol!   45

ALL Come, come.

    Enter Menenius Agrippa

FIRST CITIZEN Soft, who comes here?

SECOND CITIZEN Worthy Menenius Agrippa, one that
hath always loved the people.

FIRST CITIZEN He's one honest enough. Would all the   50
rest were so!

35-6 he ... to please ... partly proud] F; he ... to please ... partly to be proud HAN-
MER; he ... partly to please ... to be proud CAPELL; 'he ... to please ... proud' (*making
it dependent on* say) OXFORD   36 partly] F; portly STAUNTON *conj.*; pertly LETTSOM
conj. (*in* Cambridge)   42 accusations. He] ROWE; ~‿ he F   46.1 *Enter ... Agrippa*] *after*
I.47 F

36 **to be partly proud** partly from pride
(see Abbott §20 for the construction):
First Citizen, shrewdly, now puts even
more stress on Martius' wish to please
his mother than on his pride. The ambiguity of the construction reflects the
recurrent difficulty that commentators
in the play have in analysing the contradictions of Martius' character: cf.
Aufidius' servants at 4.5.156 ff. and
Aufidius himself at 4.7.37 ff. and
5.6.147–54.
  proud (a) self-valuing, (b) disdainful of
others

37 **even to the altitude of** i.e. as pre-
eminent as; to the same high degree
as
  virtue valour (cf. 2.2.81–2)

39–40 **no ... covetous** Cf. Martius' contempt for booty at 1.6.4–8 and
1.10.37–40, and Cominius' comment
on this, 2.2.122–7.

42–3 **tire in repetition** tire one out in re-
counting them

43.1 **within** i.e. 'off-stage, in the tiring
house'

44 **other ... city** Cf. 'in these several
places of the city' (1.1.182); North
does not speak of trouble specifically 'on the other side' of the city till
later.

45 **Capitol** The Capitoline Hill on which
stood the temple of Jupiter, where
Shakespeare assumes throughout the
play that the Senate meeting-house is
located (though, in fact, the Senate's
Curia was in the Forum beneath the
hill; cf. 3.1.33). Shakespeare's use of
Roman topography is symbolic rather
than exact: the power base of the patricians is set against the market-place
in which the plebeians forgather, so
that, as *John Bull* (18 Mar. 1838) com-
mented about Macready's production,
'The rude magnificence of the Capitol
is ever in contrast with the turbulent
commotion of the Forum.'

47 **Soft** stay, wait a moment

MENENIUS

What work's, my countrymen, ~~in hand?~~ Where
go you
With bats and clubs? The matter? Speak, I pray you.

⌈FIRST⌉ CITIZEN Our business is not unknown to th'
Senate; they have had inkling this fortnight what we   55
intend to do, which now we'll show 'em in deeds.
They say poor suitors have strong breaths; they shall
know we have strong arms too.

MENENIUS

Why, masters, my good friends, mine honest neighbours,
Will you undo yourselves?   60

⌈FIRST⌉ CITIZEN We cannot, sir; we are undone already.

MENENIUS

I tell you, friends, most charitable care
Have the patricians of you. For your wants,
Your suffering in this dearth, you may as well
Strike at the heaven with your staves as lift them   65
Against the Roman state, whose course will on
The way it takes, cracking ten thousand curbs

---

53 matter?] THEOBALD; ~ˌ F; ~. OXFORD   54 FIRST] CAPELL *and throughout the rest of the scene*; 2 F   63 you. For ... wants,] ROWE (*after* F4); ~ˌ for ... ~. FI   65 heaven] F; heavens MASON *conj.*

---

52 ff. **What work's ... Menenius'** measured
blank verse, though colloquial in
syntax and vocabulary, immediately
contrasts with the prose of the plebs.
52 **work's** (a) 'work is', with 'my
country-men' as vocative; (b) less
probably, 'work has', with 'my
countrymen' as plural subject of the
singular verb
countrymen Menenius seems to accept
a relationship that Martius denies
(3.1.238–40), though cf. l. 159.
in hand The implication is that they
should be working: cf. 4.6.83, 92,
100–1, 123–4.
53 **bats ... clubs** Cudgels were the weapons of London's riotous apprentices,
whose rallying cry was 'Clubs'.
54 (*and throughout the rest of the scene*)
FIRST Up to this point First Citizen has
been belligerently hostile to the patricians, while Second Citizen has de-

murred and acted as peacemaker;
Capell's alterations maintain this consistency of character: see Introduction,
p. 94.
54–5 **not ... Senate** Brockbank draws attention to North's comment that 'The
Senate met many days in consultation
about it: but in the end they concluded
nothing.'
57 **suitors** petitioners, beggars
strong breaths A frequent gibe in
Shakespeare; cf. 3.1.69, 3.3.121–2,
4.6.102, 139. First Citizen continues
with a play on 'strong arms' that gives
a quasi-proverbial air to his comment.
60 **undo** ruin
63 **For** as for (cf. 1.1.69, 'For the dearth')
66 **will on** will keep on, will continue
(Abbott §405)
67 **curbs** restraints or hindrances: literally
the chain which is part of a horse's
bit, hence 'link' (l. 68).

Of more strong link asunder than can ever
Appear in your impediment. For the dearth,
The gods, not the patricians, make it, and   70
Your knees to them, not arms, must help. Alack,
You are transported by calamity
Thither where more attends you; and you slander
The helms o'th' state, who care for you like fathers,
When you curse them as enemies.   75
⌈FIRST⌉ CITIZEN Care for us? True, indeed! They ne'er
cared for us yet: suffer us to famish, and their store-
houses crammed with grain; make edicts for usury,
to support usurers; repeal daily any wholesome act
established against the rich, and provide more piercing   80
statutes daily to chain up and restrain the poor. If the
wars eat us not up, they will; and there's all the love
they bear us.
MENENIUS Either you must
Confess yourselves wondrous malicious   85
Or be accused of folly. I shall tell you
A pretty tale. It may be you have heard it,
But since it serves my purpose, I will venture
To stale't a little more.

---

76 indeed! They] THEOBALD; ~, they F   89 stale't] THEOBALD; scale't F

---

69 **your impediment** hindrance or obstruction that you make
70 **The gods ... it** This is the play's only
reference to the Tudor explanation of
dearth by the doctrine of 'God's judgements'.
72 **transported** carried away
calamity i.e. the famine and its consequences
73 **Thither** i.e. towards insurrection
attends awaits
74 **helms** (a) helmsmen, pilots, (b) helmets (cf. 4.5.126), i.e. 'heads (plural)
of state'? Cf. a similarly abstract use of
'casque' (4.7.43).
fathers i.e. they take paternal care of
you, as befits City Fathers (*patres* =
originally senators, hence *patricians*)
78–81 **make ... poor** This summarizes
the main grievances behind the plebeians' first rebellion in Plutarch: see
Introduction, p. 33.

80 **piercing** oppressive, severe
82 **wars ... will** The first of an important
series of cannibalism images; cf. Introduction, p. 78. Such imagery was a
commonplace in anti-Enclosure literature.
87 **pretty** apt, well calculated to the cir-
cumstance of the telling; Furness notes
that 'pretie' is used of the account of
Menenius' tale in North's translation
of the *Fables of Bidpai, The Morall Philo-
sophie of Doni*, 1570 (ed. Jacobs), p. 64,
although this account has no other
close parallels to Shakespeare's version.
It ... it. Menenius' tale is recognized
in Sir Philip Sidney's *Apology for Poetry*
(ed. J. Van Dorsten, 1966, pp. 41–2)
as a famous sophistry: 'for the tale is
notorious, and as notorious that it was
a tale'.

⌈ FIRST ⌉ CITIZEN Well, I'll hear it, sir; yet you must not   90
think to fob off our disgrace with a tale. But an't please
you, deliver.

MENENIUS
There was a time when all the body's members,
Rebelled against the belly, thus accused it:
That only like a gulf it did remain   95
I'th' midst o'th' body, idle and unactive,
Still cupboarding the viand, never bearing
Like labour with the rest; where th'other instruments
Did see and hear, devise, instruct, walk, feel,
And, mutually participate, did minister   100
Unto the appetite and affection common
Of the whole body. The belly answered—

---

100 And,] MALONE; ~_∧ F   101 appetite_∧] F4; ~; FI   102 answered—] CAPELL;
~. F

89 **stale't** make it stale (by repetition). Editorial attempts to justify F's 'scale' as
'disperse', 'weigh and apply', or 'peel,
strip' are not as plausible in context as
a confusion of 't' for 'c' in secretary
hand.

90 **Well, I'll** Brockbank suggests that this
may have been the compositor's false
correction of his copy's 'We'll' or
'Wele'.

91 **fob off** get rid of by a trick. No such
suspicious (and accurate) reaction to
Menenius can be found in North's
Plutarch or Livy. By adding it, Shakespeare alerts us to be wary of Menenius' motives.
disgrace (a) injury; (b) degrading mis-
fortune

91–2 **an't . . . deliver** i.e. 'if you want to,
go ahead'

93 ff. **There was . . .** The probable sources
for this tale are discussed in the Introduction, p. 18.

93 **There . . . time** Brockbank notes that
Sidney's version of the tale begins with
the same traditional phrase.

95 **gulf** whirlpool. In Camden's version
the stomach is called a 'swallowing
gulf' and in Averill 'a bottomless
whirlpool'.

96 **unactive** 'The only instance of this
word (there is none of its modern

equivalent *inactive*) in Shakespeare'
(Arden).

97 **Still** always, continually
cupboarding hoarding, stowing away
unused. Averill has an analogous
'Pantry'.
viand food; elsewhere plural in Shakespeare. The singular occurs in Averill
too.

98 **where** whereas
instruments organs

99 **devise** ponder, deliberate. The distinction of particular functions probably
comes from Camden's translation of
John of Salisbury, since the versions
by North and Livy do not go into such
detail.

100–2 **minister . . . body** North's phrasing
is close: 'careful to satisfy the appetites
and desires of the body' (Spencer,
p. 303).

100 **participate** 'participant or particip-
ating' (Malone): Arden cites *Twelfth
Night* 1.5.256, where 'reverberate'
means 'reverberating'. Camden's 'all
parts performed their functions' seems
to be the source for the phrase 'mutually participate', though the actual
word 'participate' occurs only in
Averill.

101 **appetite** needs
affection inclination, wishes

⌈FIRST⌉ CITIZEN
  Well, sir, what answer made the belly?
MENENIUS
  Sir, I shall tell you. With a kind of smile,
  Which ne'er came from the lungs, but even thus—   105
  For, look you, I may make the belly smile
  As well as speak—it tauntingly replied
  To th' discontented members, the mutinous parts
  That envied his receipt; even so most fitly
  As you malign our senators for that   110
  They are not such as you.
⌈FIRST⌉ CITIZEN   Your belly's answer—what?
  The kingly, crownèd head, the vigilant eye,
  The counsellor heart, the arm our soldier,
  Our steed the leg, the tongue our trumpeter,
  With other muniments and petty helps   115
  In this our fabric, if that they—
MENENIUS   What then?
  Fore me, this fellow speaks! What then, what then?

---

104 you. With] THEOBALD (*subs.*); ~‿ with F   107 tauntingly] F4; taintingly F1;
tantingly F2   111 answer—what?] HANMER; ~: What‿ F; ~? What! DYCE (*conj.* Collier)
112 kingly, crownèd] This edition; ~‿ crown'd F; ~‿ crownèd OXFORD; kingly-crowned
THEOBALD 1740

104 **With . . . smile** This derives from North's elaboration of Plutarch, 'the belly . . . laughed at their folly'.
104–5 **a kind . . . lungs** a disdainful smile, not a hearty laugh
105 **thus—** Menenius mimics such a smile, either by ludicrously contorting his face or somehow by manipulating his belly; modern actors often belch. This talking down to the plebeians sparks First Citizen's impatient response.
107 **tauntingly** mockingly (to go with the belly's disdainful smile); F's 'tainting-ly' is more probably a minim error than the equivalent of 'attaintingly'
109 **envied his receipt** envied it for what it received
  fitly justly (used ironically here)
111 ff. **Your belly's . . .** First Citizen matches Menenius' blank verse and shows that he is well acquainted with this received political wisdom.
112 **kingly, crownèd head** cf. Introduction, pp. 44–5.
113 **counsellor heart** 'The heart was con-

sidered by Shakespeare as the seat of understanding' (Malone): cf. 1.1.133 n. and 2.3.199–200. Camden's version has the body's members desiring 'the advice of the Heart' and being answered by 'Reason'.
115 **muniments** supports or furnishings, but literally 'fortifications': the whole speech has an underlying military metaphor of the body as a town under siege, which is appropriate to the speaker's desperation and contrasts ironically with the digestive and provisioning metaphors that underlie Menenius' use of the trope. Ironically, each speaker seems to be using the other's preferred imagery: see Introduction, p. 19.
116 **fabric** body; continuing his metaphor of the body as a building (though OED 3 has no example in this sense before 1695)
117 **Fore me** upon my soul, on my word (on the analogy of 'Fore God')
  speaks i.e. 'can certainly talk' (ironic flattery)

⌈FIRST⌉ CITIZEN

   Should by the cormorant belly be restrained,

   Who is the sink o'th' body—

MENENIUS   Well, what then?

⌈FIRST⌉ CITIZEN

   The former agents, if they did complain,   120

   What could the belly answer?

MENENIUS   I will tell you,

   If you'll bestow a small—of what you have little—

   Patience a while, you'st hear the belly's answer.

⌈FIRST⌉ CITIZEN

   You're long about it.

MENENIUS   Note me this, good friend:

   Your most grave belly was deliberate,   125

   Not rash like his accusers, and thus answered:

   'True is it, my incorporate friends,' quoth he,

   'That I receive the general food at first

   Which you do live upon, and fit it is,

   Because I am the storehouse and the shop   130

   Of the whole body. But, if you do remember,

   I send it through the rivers of your blood

   Even to the court, the heart, to th' seat o'th' brain;

---

119 body—] ROWE; ~. F   122–3 small—of . . . little— | Patience‸] CAMBRIDGE; small (of . . . little) | Patience‸ F; small of . . . little— | Patience—OXFORD   123 you'st] F; you'll ROWE 1714   124 this,] F4; ~‸ FI   133 court,] F; court of KEIGHTLEY *conj.* heart,] F; ~.—MALONE   o'th'] F; the RANN (*conj.* Tyrwhitt)   brain;] THEOBALD; ~, F

---

118 **cormorant** greedy, insatiable: a frequent epithet in the 'moral economy' literature against hoarding: see Introduction, pp. 35–6.

  restrained First Citizen's vocabulary is full of quasi-legal phrasing: cf. 'agents . . . complain . . . answer' (ll. 120–1); see 3.3.30.1–2 n.

119 **sink** cesspool

122 **small** 'a small quantity or amount' (*OED* 35)

123 **you'st** you'll: a provincialism perhaps conciliatory but, in context, more likely to be mocking; cf. 1.1.202 n.

125 **Your . . . belly** i.e. 'this most serious belly we are talking about' (another colloquialism)

127 **incorporate** A legal term, meaning that they are all united in one body as if they had received a corporate franchise; here comically literalized.

132–7 **I . . . live** Probably suggested by the source passage from Holland's Livy.

133 **Even . . . brain** In 'humours' physiology, blood was sent from the stomach to the heart where it was 'concocted' to 'vital spirits' which were then sent on to the brain and other organs. Characteristically, Menenius' syntax obscures the traditional distinction between the brain, the 'seat' of King Reason, and the heart, the 'court' of his understanding counsellors. J. C. Maxwell notes that the 'o' is that of definition (*OED* 23), so that 'as the court is the heart, so the brain is the "seat" (or throne)': *NQ*, 198 (1953), 329.

And through the cranks and offices of man
The strongest nerves and small inferior veins   135
From me receive that natural competency
Whereby they live. And though that all at once,
You, my good friends'—this says the belly, mark me—
⌈FIRST⌉ CITIZEN
Ay, sir, well, well.
MENENIUS   'Though all at once cannot
See what I do deliver out to each,   140
Yet I can make my audit up that all
From me do back receive the flour of all
And leave me but the bran.' What say you to't?
⌈FIRST⌉ CITIZEN
It was an answer. How apply you this?
MENENIUS
The senators of Rome are this good belly,   145
And you the mutinous members. For examine
Their counsels and their cares, digest things rightly
Touching the weal o'th' common, you shall find
No public benefit which you receive
But it proceeds or comes from them to you,   150
And no way from yourselves. What do you think,
You, the great toe of this assembly?

---

134 man₍] OXFORD; ~, F; ~; POPE   137–8 once, | You ... friends'—... belly, ...
me—] ROWE (subs.); once₍ | (You ... Friends, ... Belly) ... me. F; once'— | You ...
friends, ... belly, ... me—OXFORD   142 flour] KNIGHT; Flowre F; flower CAPELL
147 cares, digest] CAMBRIDGE; Cares; disgest F

134 **cranks** winding corridors: *OED* 1
  quotes North's translation of Plutarch's 'Life of Theseus': 'How he
  might easily wind out of the turnings
  and cranks of the Labyrinth'.
  offices 'The parts of a house or buildings
  attached to a house, specially devoted
  to household work or service' (*OED* 9).
135 **nerves** (a) sinews (Latin *nervus*),
  (b) nerves in the modern sense: both
  usages occur in Shakespeare but
  (a) predominates.
136 **natural competency** supply proper to
  their nature
138 **You ... me—** This syntax seems
  preferable to F's, which would have
  'You, my good friends' addressed by
  Menenius to the Citizens instead of by

the belly to the members. Menenius is
perceptibly dragging the story out.
142 **flour** F's spelling allows a play on
  'flower' (meaning 'the best'; cf.
  1.7.33) and 'flour'
143 **bran** indigestible, excremental part of
  the corn
147 **digest** punning on 'understand, interpret' and the physical sense
148 **weal o'th' common** general welfare
  of all
152 **great toe** Cf. 3.1.297, 308–10, where
  Sicinius compares Martius himself to a
  gangrened foot that must be ampu-
  tated; and *Hamlet* 5.1.136–7: 'the toe
  of the peasant comes so near the heel
  of the courtier he galls his kibe'.

⌈FIRST⌉ CITIZEN
    I the great toe? Why the great toe?
MENENIUS
    For that, being one o'th' lowest, basest, poorest
    Of this most wise rebellion, thou goest foremost.   155
    Thou rascal, that art worst in blood to run,
    Lead'st first to win some vantage.
    But make you ready your stiff bats and clubs:
    Rome and her rats are at the point of battle;
    The one side must have bale.
        Enter Caius Martius

                            Hail, noble Martius!   160
MARTIUS
    Thanks.—What's the matter, you dissentious rogues,
    That, rubbing the poor itch of your opinion,
    Make yourselves scabs?
⌈FIRST⌉ CITIZEN   We have ever your good word.

---

160 bale] F (baile)

156–7 **Thou ... vantage** 'Thou that art a
    hound, a running dog of the lowest
    breed, lead'st the pack, when anything
    is to be gotten' (Johnson).
156 **rascal** (a) one of the common rabble,
    (b) an ill-bred dog: cf. 1.7.45 and
    Timon 5.1.114, 'rascal dogs'
    in blood by breeding. Two other inter-
    pretations are possible: (a) when roused
    to courage (cf. 4.5.216, 4.2.49–51):
    i.e. 'least likely to hunt by reason of
    high spirit'; (b) during battle: i.e. 'most
    likely to run away in a real battle'
    (cf. Martius' complaints later).
158 **stiff bats** stout cudgels (see 1.1.53 n.).
    Menenius plays on 'bats ... battle ...
    bale'.
159 **rats** Cf. 1.1.247; Coriolanus is the
    'dog' (1.1.26) who harasses these
    'rats'.
160 **bale** (a) harm, injury, (b) possibly
    a misprint for 'bane', meaning rat-
    poison, which would certainly fit the
    imagery of the passage: cf. *Measure*
    1.2.121
    Caius Martius The individual name or
    praenomen is here followed by the
    nomen or clan name (see 2.3.233–41),

then later in the play by 'Coriolanus',
an *agnomen* or extra identifying name
based on some notable characteristic
or achievement. F uses the speech
prefix *Martius* until 2.1.164, then *Coriolanus*; cf. 1.10.68 n. Instead of correcting to Plutarch's Marcius, Shakespeare
retains North's misspelling (also found
in Holland's translation of Livy) and
plays upon its significance 'pertaining
to Mars' at 4.5.119 and 5.6.102–3.
noble This word occurs more often in
Coriolanus than in any other Shakespeare play.
161–3 **Thanks ... scabs** Both Martius'
    curt reaction to compliment and
    his intolerance of the plebeians are
    immediately registered; also his
    terrible eagerness for violent confronta-
    tion.
161 ff. **What's the ...** Martius is out of
    temper, because he has just heard
    of the election of tribunes (cf. ll.
    207–18).
162 **opinion** self-conceit
163 **yourselves scabs** (a) scabs on your-
    selves, (b) yourselves into 'scabs', sores
    on the body of society

MARTIUS

He that will give good words to thee will flatter
Beneath abhorring. What would you have, you curs   165
That like nor peace nor war? The one affrights you,
The other makes you proud. He that trusts to you,
Where he should find you lions finds you hares,
Where foxes, geese. You are no surer, no,
Than is the coal of fire upon the ice,   170
Or hailstone in the sun. Your virtue is
To make him worthy whose offence subdues him,
And curse that justice did it. Who deserves greatness
Deserves your hate, and your affections are
A sick man's appetite, who desires most that   175
Which would increase his evil. He that depends
Upon your favours swims with fins of lead,
And hews down oaks with rushes. Hang ye! Trust ye?
With every minute you do change a mind,
And call him noble that was now your hate,   180
Him vile that was your garland. What's the matter,
That in these several places of the city
You cry against the noble Senate, who,
Under the gods, keep you in awe, which else

---

169 geese. You are, no] THEOBALD (*subs.*); Geese, you are: No F   178 Hang ye! Trust
ye?] CAMBRIDGE; Hang ye: trust ye? F

---

164 **thee** Dyce changed to the plural 'ye',
but Wilson notes the theatrical effect-
iveness of having Coriolanus turn directly on the obstreperous First Citizen
and cow him.

166 **nor peace** neither peace
   The one i.e. war

167 **proud** (a) insolent, overweening,
(b) high spirited (and therefore un-
governable)?

169 **geese. You are** F's reading makes
sense but is less satisfactory than
Theobald's emendation. Martius also
calls them 'geese' at 1.5.5; cf. 5.3.35,
163–4.

170 **coal . . . ice** See Introduction, p. 5.
This imagery of fire, water, and melting will be applied to Martius himself
in the pleading scene of 5.3.

171–3 **Your . . . it** i.e. 'Your characteristic

quality is to honour a man who has
deserved to be punished and to curse
the justice that does so.'

173 **Who** he who

174 **affections** inclination

176 **evil** 'disease, malady' (*OED* B7)

178 **Hang ye! Trust ye?** Wilson notes that
Coleridge 'plausibly' conjectured that
these phrases had been transposed, but
the meaning is clear anyway

180 **now** just now

181 **vile** F's spelling 'vilde' was a common
alternative (cf. 3.1.10)
   garland (a) hero (who in Rome was
awarded a garland, cf. 1.3.14–15 n.,
1.10.60), (b) ornament?

182 **several places** Cf. 1.1.44 n. North
says nothing about riots in different
parts of the city.

Would feed on one another?
(*To Menenius*)   What's their seeking?   185

MENENIUS

For corn at their own rates, whereof they say
The city is well stored.

MARTIUS   Hang 'em! They say?
They'll sit by th' fire and presume to know
What's done i'th' Capitol, who's like to rise,
Who thrives and who declines; side factions and give
    out   190
Conjectural marriages, making parties strong
And feebling such as stand not in their liking
Below their cobbled shoes. They say there's grain
    enough!
Would the nobility lay aside their ruth
And let me use my sword, I'd make a quarry   190   195
With thousands of these quartered slaves as high
As I could pitch my lance.

MENENIUS

Nay, these are all most thoroughly persuaded,
For though abundantly they lack discretion,
Yet are they passing cowardly. But I beseech you,   200

---

197 pitch] ROWE; picke F   198 all most] SINGER 1856 (Collier MS); almost F

---

185 **Would ... another** The same idea oc-
    curs in Hand D of *More* and, in a
    slightly different context, in *Lear*; it
    was a commonplace (see F. P. Wilson,
    'Shakespeare's Reading', *ShS*, 3
    (1950), pp. 19–20).
187 **city ... stored** This idea of domestic
    hoarding is different from the Roman
    situation, where 'great store of corn'
    was imported from abroad to solve the
    famine.
188 **They'll ... fire** Wilson compares
    North's 'the home-tarriers and house
    doves that keep Rome still'. For the
    'They say' (l. 187) formula for report-
    ing public complaint, cf. the 'Septem-
    ber' eclogue of Spenser's *Shepherds'
    Calendar* (1578), and *2 Henry VI*
    3.2.250 ff.
190 **side** take sides with
192 **feebling** disparaging

193 **cobbled** roughly mended, patched
194 **ruth** pity
195 **quarry** 'A heap of the deer killed at
    a hunting' (*OED* 2), here applied to
    humans: cf. the hunting imagery at
    1.1.233–4.
196 **quartered** butchered; literally, 'cut
    into four pieces' like a slaughtered an-
    imal (or an executed traitor); with a
    possible play on 'quarter' as a measure
    of grain (*OED* II. 4)
197 **pitch** F's 'pick' is described as 'A
    collateral form of PITCH' in *OED*, v.
198 **all most** F's 'almost' is possible but
    does not agree as well with the sense
    of the two next lines
199–200 **discretion ... cowardly** Menen-
    ius is playing on the proverbial 'Dis-
    cretion is the better part of valour'
200 **passing** exceedingly, surpassingly

What says the other troop?

MARTIUS   They are dissolved. Hang 'em!
They said they were an-hungry, sighed forth proverbs—
That hunger broke stone walls, that dogs must eat,
That meat was made for mouths, that the gods sent not
Corn for the rich men only. With these shreds   205
They vented their complainings, which being answered,
And a petition granted them—a strange one,
To break the heart of generosity
And make bold power look pale—they threw their caps
As they would hang them on the horns o'th' moon,   210
Shouting their emulation.

MENENIUS   What is granted them?

MARTIUS

Five tribunes to defend their vulgar wisdoms,
Of their own choice. One's Junius Brutus,
Sicinius Velutus, and I know not. 'Sdeath,

---

203 hunger broke] F3 (Hunger); Hunger-broke F1   211 Shouting] POPE; Shooting F
213 Brutus,] F; Brutus, one HIBBARD (*conj.* Walker *in* Hudson); Brutus, another KEIGHTLEY

---

201 **other troop** Cf. 1.1.44
202 **an-hungry** Like Menenius at
   1.1.123, Martius is mocking the
   Citizens' homely manner of speech
   (and goes on to mock their reliance on
   proverbs). The word is not found elsewhere in Shakespeare, though 'a-hun-
   gry' appears with a similar parodic
   effect in *Twelfth Night* 2.3.123, and
   Merry Wives 1.1.251.
203 **hunger ... walls** A frequently used
   proverb; see Tilley H811.
   dogs must eat Tilley D533 and D487
   (*Dignet canis pabula*, 1580); Furness
   also quotes Ray's *Collection of English
   Proverbs*, 'he's an ill dog that deserves
   not a crust', and Arden Matthew
   15: 27.
204 **meat ... mouths** Cf. Tilley M828;
   Arden cites also 'All meats to be eaten,
   and all maids to be wed' from Heywood's *Proverbs*.
204–5 **gods ... only** Quasi-proverbial;
   Brockbank neatly terms it 'an emer-
   gent slogan'
205 **shreds** Arden compares *Richard III*
   1.3.335, 'old odd ends, stol'n forth of
   Holy Writ'.
206 **vented** expel, get rid of; but with the

sense also of 'excrete' (cf. 1.1.223)
208 **To ... generosity** 'to give the final
   blow to the nobles' (Johnson); 'generosity' from Latin *generosus*, of noble
   birth. This is the first indication of a
   split in the ranks of the nobility.
209 **power** This word (in its political
   sense) is central to the play: it is used
   38 times, compared to 18 in its closest
   competitor, *Richard II*.
   threw their caps A recurrent gesture
   of joy in this play: cf. Introduction,
   p. 96.
211 **Shouting** F's 'shooting' is a known
   Shakespearian spelling preference; see
   Introduction, p. 139.
   their emulation (a) i.e. 'each of them
   striving to shout harder than the rest'
   (Malone); (b) less probably, 'malicious
   triumph' (Verity)
212 **Five** As in Plutarch and Livy. Only
   two are named in North, and Shakespeare 'cleverly turns the omission into
   an illustration of Coriolanus' contempt
   for the people' (Verity); cf. his forgetting of his host's name in 1.10.
214 **'Sdeath** God's (i.e. Christ's) death (an
   anachronistic oath)

The rabble should have first unroofed the city   215
Ere so prevailed with me! It will in time
Win upon power and throw forth greater themes
For insurrection's arguing.

MENENIUS

This is strange.

MARTIUS (*to the Citizens*) Go get you home, you fragments.   220
        Enter a Messenger hastily

MESSENGER

Where's Caius Martius?

MARTIUS   Here. What's the matter?

MESSENGER

The news is, sir, the Volsces are in arms.

MARTIUS

I am glad on't. Then we shall ha' means to vent
Our musty superfluity.—

        Enter Sicinius Velutus, Junius Brutus; Cominius, Titus
        Lartius, with other Senators

                    See, our best elders!

---

215 unroofed] THEOBALD (unroof'd); vnroo'st F   224 *Enter ... Senators*] *as* SISSON; *after*
elders F   *Junius Brutus; Cominius*] F4; *Annius Brutus Cominisn* F   224 See,] ROWE; ~∧ F
elders!] This edition; ~. F

215 **unroofed the city** This anticipates the
    imagery of 3.1.199, 204–7.
217 **Win upon power** (a) take advantage
    of the power won to win more, (b) get
    the better of those in authority?
218 **For ... arguing** (a) as arguments in
    favour of insurrection, (b) 'for insur-
    gents to debate upon' (Malone)?
220 **fragments** (a) food scraps, (b) parts of
    a dismembered carcass? Olivier (1959
    SMT) pointed it humorously with a
    pause before 'fragments'.
223 **vent** (a) sell, market (musty corn), (b)
    cast out, excrete (as also implied by
    Menenius' 'bran', 1.1.143), cf. 206 n.
    The latter image is explicit in North
    where the Romans are said to have
    used war 'to clear the [city] of many
    mutinous and seditious persons, being
    the superfluous ill humours that griev-
    ously fed this disease'. The ideas of
    war as a riddance of extra population
    (cf. 4.5.228) and as a way of diverting
    insurrection were both commonplaces:
    cf. C. G. Cruickshank, *Elizabeth's Army*

(1946), pp. 9–10.
224 **Enter ... Senators** See Introduction,
    p. 99.
224 *Sicinius Velutus* Shakespeare follows
    North's error in the *nomen*, which in
    Plutarch is *Bellutus*. He is an old man
    (cf. 3.1.178–9) and, according to
    North, the 'cruellest and stoutest' of
    the Tribunes.
    Junius Brutus Junius Brutus was an
    earlier Roman leader against Tarquin;
    according to Dionysius of Halicarnas-
    sus, this later tribune was only called
    Lucius Junius but added the name Bru-
    tus to strengthen his political image.
    At 4.6.168–9 Shakespeare suggests
    that Brutus is wealthy. Both Tribunes
    are called 'bald' (3.1.166) and said to
    have beards (2.1.84–6).
    Junius F's misreading *Annius* probably
    occurred because the manuscript's
    capital I resembled a '4': see Introduc-
    tion, p. 139.
    Cominius The final *us* ligature is
    turned in F.

FIRST SENATOR

Martius, 'tis true that you have lately told us.   225

The Volsces are in arms.

MARTIUS   They have a leader,

Tullus Aufidius, that will put you to't.

I sin in envying his nobility,

And were I anything but what I am,

I would wish me only he.

COMINIUS   You have fought together!   230

MARTIUS

Were half to half the world by th'ears and he

Upon my party, I'd revolt to make

Only my wars with him. He is a lion

That I am proud to hunt.

FIRST SENATOR   Then, worthy Martius,

Attend upon Cominius to these wars.   235

COMINIUS (*to Martius*)

It is your former promise.

MARTIUS   Sir, it is,

And I am constant. Titus Lartius, thou

Shalt see me once more strike at Tullus' face.

What, art thou stiff? Stand'st out?

LARTIUS   No, Caius Martius.

---

230 together!] F(~?); ~. CAPELL   237 Lartius] ROWE; *Lucius* F   239, 243 LARTIUS] F (*Tit.*) (*cf. 1.10.11*)

---

225 **that** that which
  lately told us Johnson notes that this implies prior knowledge on Martius' part (cf. 1.2:4–6): the first reference to a persistent theme of spying in the play.

227 **Tullus Aufidius** Plutarch does not mention Aufidius until Coriolanus goes to join the Volsces; see Introduction, p. 27.
  to't to the test

229–30 **And ... he** Aufidius has a similar comment at 1.11.4–5: each imagines the other as his ideal.

230 **together!** F's question mark must indicate an exclamation here; Cominius could not have been ignorant of the fact (cf. 1.11.7–8).

231–3 An ironic anticipation; cf. 1.5.10–11 n.

231 **by th'ears** fighting (like animals)

232 **party** side

237 **I am constant** I keep my word (cf. 1.9.1–2, and 1.1.259–74 n.). See Introduction, p. 83 for the emphasis Martius consistently puts on keeping promises.
  Lartius See Introduction, p. 137: *Lartius* and *Latius* occur in both the 1595 and 1603 editions of North at the point when Cominius divides his army into two commands, and E. A. J. Honigmann has argued that this suggests that 2.1.157 ff. and 3.1, and possibly parts of 1.1, were written out of sequence, before Shakespeare spotted the misprint in his copy of North (*The Stability of Shakespeare's Text*, 1965, pp. 146–7). The evidence is too slight to be conclusive.

239 **stiff** (a) with either wounds or age; playing on (b) obstinate. If Titus is

---

I'll lean upon one crutch and fight with t'other   240
Ere stay behind this business.

MENENIUS   O true bred!

⌈FIRST⌉ SENATOR
Your company to th' Capitol, where I know
Our greatest friends attend us.

LARTIUS (*to Cominius*)   Lead you on.
(*To Martius*) Follow Cominius. We must follow you,
Right worthy your priority.

COMINIUS   Noble Martius.   245

⌈FIRST⌉ SENATOR (*to the Citizens*)
Hence to your homes, be gone.

MARTIUS   Nay, let them follow.
The Volsces have much corn. Take these rats thither
To gnaw their garners.   *Citizens steal away*
                        Worshipful mutineers,
Your valour puts well forth. (*To the Senators*) Pray follow.
                        Exeunt all but Sicinius and Brutus

SICINIUS
Was ever man so proud as is this Martius?   250

BRUTUS He has no equal.

242, 246 FIRST SENATOR] ROWE (*subs.*); *Sen.* F   245 your] F4; you F1   Martius] F;
Lartius THEOBALD *conj.*   248 *Citizens steal away*] *as* WILSON; *after* 1.249 *in* F   249.1]
OXFORD; *Citizens steale away. Manet Sicin. & Brutus.* F

aged enough to be on crutches yet is
still a valiant warrior, he contrasts
with Menenius who twice pleads age
as an excuse for not supporting Coriolanus, 3.2.32–5, 4.1.56–8.
Stand'st out? (a) Do you resist, refuse
to take part? (b) perhaps with a glance
at his leg or arm in a splint?

241 **true bred** i.e. bred to the wars; cf. *2
Henry IV* 5.3.67–8, 'a will not out; 'tis
true-bred'.

243–5 **Lead . . . priority** Cf. Introduction,
p. 99. Actually, in Plutarch Titus
Lartius was Cominius' second-in-
command, not Martius; Shakespeare's
change sharpens the effect of Martius'
take-over on the battlefield and its

parallelism to his later relationship
with Aufidius.

245 **Right . . . priority** you thoroughly
deserve to go first (as Sicinius and
Brutus did not at l. 225)

247 **Volsces . . . corn** Another detail from
North, who says that in later forays
against Antium, Coriolanus 'met with
great plenty of corn'.

248 **garners** granaries
Citizens . . . away Martius' comment,
'Worshipful . . . forth', is more pointed
if the citizens have already begun to
'steal away'. In 1959 SMT Olivier
turned to laugh at their cowardice before leaving the stage himself.

249 **puts well forth** promises well; literally, 'buds, burgeons' (*OED* 42g)

SICINIUS

When we were chosen tribunes for the people—

BRUTUS

Marked you his lip and eyes?

SICINIUS   Nay, but his taunts.

BRUTUS

Being moved, he will not spare to gird the gods—

SICINIUS Bemock the modest moon.   255

BRUTUS

The present wars devour him. He is grown

Too proud to be so valiant.

SICINIUS   Such a nature,

Tickled with good success, disdains the shadow

Which he treads on at noon. But I do wonder

His insolence can brook to be commanded   260

Under Cominius!

BRUTUS   Fame, at the which he aims,

---

256 him.] F (~,); ~! HANMER

---

252 ff. **When we ...** The Tribunes seem
even to think in tandem here, complet-
ing each other's phrases.

253 **his lip** Cf. 2.1.112; Arden notes that
drooping of the lip indicated contempt,
citing *Winter's Tale* 1.2.373–4 and
Twelfth Night 3.1.144. This is one of
many acting cues in the play: cf. Introduction, p. 107.

254 **moved** exasperated, moved to anger
gird sneer, scoff at (*OED* 4b)
gods Brockbank draws attention to
3.3.73–4 and 5.6.102 as possible
examples of such hubris, but neither
is properly a 'gird'

255 **modest** chaste and bashful; Martius'
compliment to Valeria, 5.3.65–7,
suggests quite the opposite attitude,
however. Neither of the Tribunes'
accusations is borne out by the text.

256–7 **The present ... valiant** (a) 'May
the present wars devour him! His
valour has made him too proud'; (b)
'May the present wars devour him!
Such valour coupled with such courage is dangerous'; (c) 'The present
wars are eating him up with increased
pride in being so valiant'. F's punctu-

ation (him,) allows any of these interpretations, but 'Too proud' makes the
first most likely.

258 **Tickled with** flattered by
success fortune, result

259 **noon** the height of success. At noon
shadows are smallest and, lying beneath the feet, can seem to be 'disdained'; but the implication is that
later they grow.

259–74 **But ... merit** not The Tribunes'
explanation of Martius' relation to
Cominius is wrong and reveals their
own deviousness, yet there is also an
ironic grain of truth in the comments:
Cominius thought it necessary to remind Martius of his promise (1.1.236),
and Martius does, in effect, take over
Cominius' command as later he does
Aufidius' (cf. 4.7.1–6, 12–16).

260–1 **to ... Under** to be under the command of

261–2 **Fame ... whom** 'Fame is thought
of at first as an object to be aimed at,
hence the use of "which"; then as a
goddess whose favours Martius has received, hence the use of "whom" '
(Hibbard).

175

In whom already he's well graced, cannot
Better be held nor more attained than by
A place below the first; for what miscarries
Shall be the general's fault, though he perform   265
To th'utmost of a man, and giddy censure
Will then cry out of Martius 'O, if he
Had borne the business!'

SICINIUS   Besides, if things go well,
Opinion, that so sticks on Martius, shall
Of his demerits rob Cominius.

BRUTUS   Come: 270
Half all Cominius' honours are to Martius,
Though Martius earned them not; and all his faults
To Martius shall be honours, though indeed
In aught he merit not.

SICINIUS   Let's hence and hear
How the dispatch is made, and in what fashion,   275
More than his singularity, he goes
Upon this present action.

BRUTUS   Let's along.   *Exeunt*

I.2   *Enter Tullus Aufidius, with Senators of Corioles*
FIRST SENATOR

So, your opinion is, Aufidius,
That they of Rome are entered in our counsels
And know how we proceed.

AUFIDIUS   Is it not yours?

I.2.0.1 *Corioles*] F (*Coriolus*)

266 **giddy censure** people of fickle judgement
269 **Opinion** Both (a) reputation, honour, and (b) the public opinion that confers it.
     sticks is set
270 **demerits** deserts, merits
     Come let's go further
274 **aught** anything
275 **dispatch** final arrangements
276 **More ... singularity** besides self-importance
I.2.0.1 *Tullus Aufidius* See Introduction, p. 27.

Corioles Though in Latin the correct form is 'Corioli', this is North's spelling and the usual spelling in F; see Introduction, p. 143.
2 **entered in** in the secret of, acquainted with. Aufidius' pragmatic concern for secrecy and spying contrasts unfavourably with the chivalric note on which Martius concluded I.1, though Aufidius' point is that the Romans also have spies (hence Volumnia's argument at 3.2.43–7). The play's emphasis on spying (cf. 4.3) is not in North.

What ever have been thought on in this state
That could be brought to bodily act, ere Rome   5
Had circumvention? 'Tis not four days gone
Since I heard thence. These are the words. I think
I have the letter here—yes, here it is.
(*He reads*) 'They have pressed a power, but it is not
    known
Whether for east or west. The dearth is great,   10
The people mutinous, and it is rumoured
Cominius, Martius your old enemy,
Who is of Rome worse hated than of you,
And Titus Lartius, a most valiant Roman,
These three lead on this preparation   15
Whither 'tis bent. Most likely 'tis for you.
Consider of it.'
FIRST SENATOR   Our army's in the field.
We never yet made doubt but Rome was ready
To answer us.
AUFIDIUS   Nor did you think it folly
To keep your great pretences veiled till when   20
They needs must show themselves, which in the
    hatching,
It seemed, appeared to Rome. By the discovery
We shall be shortened in our aim, which was
To take in many towns ere, almost, Rome
Should know we were afoot.
SECOND SENATOR   Noble Aufidius,   25

---

4 have] F1 ; hath F2   on] F (one), F3   9 *He reads*] THEOBALD (*Reading*); *not in* F

4 **have** F2 corrects to 'hath' but the F1
reading is acceptable if 'What' is interpreted as 'What things'
10 **east or west** The Volscian territories
stretched south-east and south-west of
Rome: Antium was to the south-west
and Corioles almost directly south.
13 **of** by
15 **preparation** prepared military force
19 **answer us** meet our attack
20 **great pretences** main plans
21 **in the hatching** (a) as soon as they
were made public, (b) while they were
still being contrived?
22 **appeared** became apparent
discovery disclosure
23 **shortened . . . aim** prevented from carrying out all we intended
24 **take in** capture
ere, almost (a) even before (Onions);
(b) however, because F puts 'almost'
in brackets, Percy Simpson suggests
that it must still be considered 'a qualifying expression or afterthought', not
an intensifier (*Shakespearean Punctuation*, 1911, p. 89).

Take your commission, hie you to your bands.
Let us alone to guard Corioles.
If they set down before's, for the remove
Bring up your army, but I think you'll find
They've not prepared for us.

AUFIDIUS   O, doubt not that.   30
I speak from certainties. Nay, more,
Some parcels of their power are forth already,
And only hitherward. I leave your honours.
If we and Caius Martius chance to meet,
'Tis sworn between us we shall ever strike   35
Till one can do no more.

ALL THE SENATORS   The gods assist you!
AUFIDIUS
And keep your honours safe.
FIRST SENATOR   Farewell.
SECOND SENATOR   Farewell.
ALL   Farewell.

Exeunt ⌈ *Aufidius at one door, Senators at*
                                        another door ⌉

1.3   *Enter Volumnia and Virgilia, mother and wife to*
       Martius. They set them down on two low stools
       and sew

VOLUMNIA I pray you, daughter, sing, or express yourself in a more comfortable sort. If my son were my hus-

---

27–8 Corioles. . . . before's,] F4 (Coriolus:); ~ₐ . . . ~: FI   28 the] F; their HUDSON
(*conj.* Johnson)   34 we] F; I THEOBALD *conj.*   36 ALL THE SENATORS] F (*All.*)   37.1–2]
OXFORD; *Exeunt omnes.* F

26 **bands** troops
27 **Let us alone** trust us
27–8 **Corioles . . . before's** F's punctu-
    ation, though possible, makes inferior
    sense
28 **set . . . before's** besiege us
    for the remove to raise the siege. Lines
    27–8 prepare the audience to under-
    stand the battle strategy of Scenes 4–10.
30 **prepared** Cf. l. 15 n.
32 **parcels** portions

37.1–2 **one door . . . another door** See
    Introduction, p. 90.
1.3.0.2–3 **two . . . sew** The stools and
    sewing establish the scene's domest-
    icity: see Fig. 3. The non-martial as-
    pect of clothing is used derogatively
    later in 'parasite's silk' (1.10.45) and
    'twist of rotten silk' (5.6.98).
  2 **comfortable sort** cheerful manner
  2–3 **If . . . husband** This is a psychological
    crux: see Introduction, p. 48.

band, I should freelier rejoice in that absence wherein
he won honour than in the embracements of his bed
where he would show most love. When yet he was but 5
tender-bodied and the only son of my womb, when
youth with comeliness plucked all gaze his way,
when for a day of kings' entreaties a mother should
not sell him an hour from her beholding, I, considering how honour would become such a person—that it 10
was no better than, picture-like, to hang by th' wall if
renown made it not stir—was pleased to let him seek
danger where he was like to find fame. To a cruel war
I sent him, from whence he returned his brows bound
with oak. I tell thee, daughter, I sprang not more in 15
joy at first hearing he was a man-child than now
in first seeing he had proved himself a man.

VIRGILIA But had he died in the business, madam, how
then?

VOLUMNIA Then his good report should have been my 20
son. I therein would have found issue. Hear me profess
sincerely: had I a dozen sons, each in my love alike,
and none less dear than thine and my good Martius, I
had rather had eleven die nobly for their country than
one voluptuously surfeit out of action. 25

1.3.8 kings'] THEOBALD; ~∧ F; king's JOHNSON 23 Martius] F; Martius' OXFORD

5–13 Cf. 2.2.85 and Introduction, p. 49.
8 **should** would
10 **such a person** 'one of such a goodly exterior' (Clarendon)
 it i.e. the person of goodly exterior
11 **hang ... wall** be merely ornamental
12 **renown ... stir** if (desire for) fame did not stir it into motion
13 **a cruel war** The war to expel the tyrant Tarquin, which ended with the Battle of Lake Regillus: cf. Cominius' account in 2.2.85–96. Though 'cruel' refers to 'war', by association it colours our reaction to Volumnia's own behaviour.
14–15 **brows ... oak** The *corona civica* (citizen's crown) was 'a garland of oaken boughs' awarded to a Roman who saved another citizen's life in

battle; according to North, Martius won his first one 'being but a stripling' at the age of sixteen. Shakespeare, however, seems to assume that the oaken garland was awarded to the bravest soldier in a battle (cf. 1.10.60, 2.1.121–2, 2.2.96, 99), though in fact the hero of a Roman 'triumph' wore a crown of bays and the hero of an 'ovation' a crown of fir.
23 **Martius** Oxford adds an apostrophe, to make 'son' a reference to Young Martius as well as to Martius himself
25 **voluptuously surfeit** enjoy sensual pleasure excessively: an interestingly sexual antithesis to dying in battle; cf. the similar ideas put forward by Aufidius' servants at 4.5.228–30, 232–3

Enter a Gentlewoman

GENTLEWOMAN (*to Volumnia*) Madam, the Lady Valeria is
come to visit you.

VIRGILIA Beseech you give me leave to retire myself.

VOLUMNIA Indeed you shall not.

Methinks I hear hither your husband's drum,   30
See him pluck Aufidius down by th' hair;
As children from a bear, the Volsces shunning him.
Methinks I see him stamp thus, and call thus:
'Come on, you cowards, you were got in fear
Though you were born in Rome!' His bloody brow   35
With his mailed hand then wiping, forth he goes,
Like to a harvest-man that's tasked to mow
Or all or lose his hire.

VIRGILIA

His bloody brow? O Jupiter, no blood!

VOLUMNIA

Away, you fool! It more becomes a man   40
Than gilt his trophy. The breasts of Hecuba

37 that's] F2 (thats); that F1

25.1 *Gentlewoman* Wilson remarks that
it is a sign of Volumnia's high rank
that she is attended by a Gentlewoman, not a servant
26 *to Volumnia* The house is Volumnia's;
it is she who answers the Gentlewoman at ll. 44–5 and greets Valeria
first at 50.
30 hither i.e. coming this way (Abbott
§322)
32 As . . . him A reversed construction:
'the Volsces shunning him as children
(recoil) from a bear'.
33–6 Volumnia's description accurately
forecasts Martius' actions in the
next two scenes: cf. 1.4.28–9; 1.5.0.2,
1–11.
33 thus . . . thus Cues for Volumnia to
mimic what she is describing: see Introduction, p. 105.
34 got begotten. It is obvious whence
Martius learned his contempt for plebeians and ordinary soldiers: cf. 3.2.8–
13 and Introduction, pp. 60–1.
35, 39, 43 bloody . . . no blood . . . blood
This blood will be startlingly emblematized by Martius in the battle scenes

to follow: cf. Introduction, p. 65.
37–8 tasked . . . hire i.e. 'compelled to
mow the whole harvest or not be paid
at all'. The sword–sickle comparison
is a commonplace, but in the context
of a corn dearth its perversion of
agrarian plenty gains extra significance: cf. 4.5.206–7 and 'husbandry'
(4.7.22). The comparison also typifies
Volumnia's insistence that her son
must earn his praise by wholesale
slaughter, or face rejection.
40 fool This can be a term of pity and
endearment (cf. *Lear* 5.3.281: 'my
poor fool is hanged'); Volumnia seems
to use it here with a mixture of pity
and exasperation.
41 gilt . . . trophy than gilding becomes
the monument to his triumphs: see
5.1.63 n.
41–4 The breasts . . . contemning See
Introduction, pp. 50–1.
41–2 Hecuba . . . Hector The queen of
Troy and her son, its champion, from
whose family the Romans claimed descent via Hector's brother Aeneas:
cf. 1.9.11–12.

When she did suckle Hector looked not lovelier
Than Hector's forehead when it spit forth blood
At Grecian sword, contemning.—
    (*To the Gentlewoman*)   Tell Valeria
    We are fit to bid her welcome.   *Exit Gentlewoman*   45
VIRGILIA
Heavens bless my lord from fell Aufidius!
VOLUMNIA
He'll beat Aufidius' head below his knee
And tread upon his neck.
    Enter Valeria with an usher and the Gentlewoman
VALERIA My ladies both, good day to you.
VOLUMNIA Sweet madam.   50
VIRGILIA I am glad to see your ladyship.
VALERIA How do you both? You are manifest house-
keepers.
    ⌈*To Volumnia*⌉ What are you sewing here? A fine spot,
    in good faith.   55
    (*To Virgilia*) How does your little son?

---

44 At] F; As LETTSOM *conj.* (*in* Cambridge) sword, contemning.—Tell] LEO; sword. *Contenning, tell* F; swords *contending*: tell F2; swords' contending.—Tell CAPELL; swords, contemning. Tell SINGER 1856 (Collier MS); sword, contemning't. Tell CAMBRIDGE *conj.*
45 Gentlewoman] F (*Gent.*)   48.1 *the*] OXFORD; *a* F   54, 56 s.d.'s] This edition; *not in* F

44 At . . . contemning i.e. 'the blood from Hector's forehead contemptuously spat upon the Grecian sword that wounded it'. F's reading suggests that the compositor thought *Contenning* was the name of Volumnia's Gentlewoman.

45 fit 'ready, prepared; or, in the ordinary sense, aimed at Virgilia, who wished to avoid the visitor. Cf. *Ham*[*let* 5.2.164]' (Arden).

46 bless guard, protect

48 tread . . . neck Cf. 5.6.131.2.

48.1 *Valeria* Coriolanus' effusive praise of Valeria's chastity (5.3.64–7) may mean that Shakespeare thought of her as a 'vestal virgin,' an aristocratic priestess of Diana; her worldliness and confidential information in 1.3 would be compatible with this.
   an usher an attendant who walked before a person of high rank to announce his or her presence: cf. 2.1.154.

50 housekeepers Valeria is making a joke: (a) good housewives (cf. 1.3.73), (b) stay-at-homes. Valeria's seemingly trivial chatter informs the audience about how Martius must have been raised and also about the battle strategy of the following war scenes, cf. ll. 99–103.

54 spot embroidered pattern, usually of small flowers or fruits

56 little son In Plutarch, Virgilia is not sewing but has Coriolanus' two infant children playing on her lap. Shakespeare uses only one older child and invents a personality for him that reflects ironically on the immaturity of his father: see Introduction, p. 23. Some productions have also brought Young Martius on stage in this scene, usually to play soldiers with his grandmother.

VIRGILIA

  I thank your ladyship; well, good madam.

VOLUMNIA He had rather see the swords and hear a
  drum than look upon his schoolmaster.

VALERIA O' my word, the father's son! I'll swear 'tis a   60
  very pretty boy. O' my troth, I looked upon him o'
  Wednesday half an hour together: 'has such a confirmed countenance! I saw him run after a gilded butterfly, and when he caught it he let it go again, and
  after it again, and over and over he comes, and up   65
  again, catched it again. Or whether his fall enraged
  him, or how 'twas, he did so set his teeth and tear it!
  O, I warrant, how he mammocked it!

VOLUMNIA One on's father's moods.

VALERIA Indeed, la, 'tis a noble child.   70

VIRGILIA A crack, madam.

VALERIA Come, lay aside your stitchery. I must have
  you play the idle housewife with me this afternoon.

VIRGILIA No, good madam, I will not out of doors.

VALERIA Not out of doors?   75

VOLUMNIA She shall, she shall.

VIRGILIA Indeed, no, by your patience. I'll not over the

---

62 'has] F (ha's); He's OXFORD

---

58 **swords** Arden notes that, by met-
onymy, this could also mean 'soldiers'.
62 **'has** he has
  confirmed determined: cf. descriptions
of his father's 'grim looks' at 1.5.31,
5.1.63–4, 5.4.17–18, 20.
63–4 **gilded butterfly** Cf. 4.6.98–9,
5.4.11–14: 'gilded' may mean no
more than light-coloured, but it seems
here also to imply the contempt for
frivolity in which both father and son
have been raised (cf. *Lear* 5.3.13), and
may also relate more obscurely to the
gold–blood–honour associations of 'sat
in gold'; see 5.1.63 n.
68 **mammocked** tore to pieces: one of the
play's recurrent images of dismember-
ment
69 **on's** of his
  moods specifically 'rages': cf. *Two
Gentlemen* 4.1.49, *Richard III* 1.2.228

70 **la** a rather affected exclamation, 'formerly used . . . to call attention to an
emphatic statement' (*OED*)
  noble Ironic in its implications, though
Valeria does not seem to intend it so
71 **crack** rogue (used here with deprecat-
ing affection, 'little devil'); cf. *2 Henry
IV* 3.2.30, where it is used about Falstaff as a boy
77 **by your patience** by your leave. It was
a Roman wife's duty to stay at home
while her husband was away, and Virgilia's firmness is emphasized by her
physical stillness as Volumnia and
Valeria move around gesticulating and
also by their contrasting speech
rhythms: Valeria has dragged the
scene back into rapid prose but Virgilia's lines still have a verse rhythm
behind them: 'Indeed . . . patience; |
I'll . . . lord | Return . . . wars'.

threshold till my lord return from the wars.

VALERIA Fie, you confine yourself most unreasonably.
Come, you must go visit the good lady that lies in. 80

VIRGILIA I will wish her speedy strength, and visit her
with my prayers, but I cannot go thither.

VOLUMNIA Why, I pray you?

VIRGILIA 'Tis not to save labour, nor that I want love.

VALERIA You would be another Penelope. Yet they say 85
all the yarn she spun in Ulysses' absence did but fill
Ithaca full of moths. Come, I would your cambric were
sensible as your finger, that you might leave pricking
it for pity. Come, you shall go with us.

VIRGILIA No, good madam, pardon me, indeed I will 90
not forth.

VALERIA In truth, la, go with me, and I'll tell you excellent news of your husband.

VIRGILIA O, good madam, there can be none yet.

VALERIA Verily, I do not jest with you: there came news 95
from him last night.

VIRGILIA Indeed, madam?

VALERIA In earnest, it's true. I heard a senator speak it.
Thus it is: the Volsces have an army forth, against
whom Cominius the general is gone with one part of 100
our Roman power. Your lord and Titus Lartius are set
down before their city Corioles. They nothing doubt
prevailing, and to make it brief wars. This is true, on

84 VIRGILIA] F3 (*Virg.*); *Vlug.* F1   87 Ithaca] F3; *Athica* F1   97 madam?] F4; ~. F1;
—ROWE

80 **lies in** expects a baby imminently. One
of the main effects of Valeria's inclusion here and in 5.3 is to give the
impression of a woman's sphere
banded together against the patriarchal ethos of Rome.

84 **want** lack

85–7 **Penelope . . . Ulysses . . . Ithaca** Penelope, wife of Ulysses, the King of Ithaca, was considered the model of a
dutiful wife because, while he was absent at the siege of Troy, she stayed at
home weaving and repelling suitors.

87 **Ithaca** For F's *Athica* see 1.1.224 n.

moths A teasing reference to (a) the
inutility of Penelope's weaving (to
delay choosing a suitor, she secretly
unravelled her work every night) and
(b) the suitors themselves (to avoid
whom the Roman matron stayed at
home).

cambric fine linen, named after Cam-
brai in north-east France

88 **sensible** sensitive
leave leave off, desist from

102–3 **They . . . wars** i.e. 'They are
confident that they will win and that
the war will be of short duration'.

mine honour; and so, I pray, go with us.

VIRGILIA Give me excuse, good madam, I will obey you   105
in everything hereafter.

VOLUMNIA (*to Valeria*) Let her alone, lady. As she is now,
she will but disease our better mirth.

VALERIA In truth, I think she would. Fare you well, then.
Come, good sweet lady. Prithee, Virgilia, turn thy solem-   110
ness out o' door and go along with us.

VIRGILIA No, at a word, madam. Indeed, I must not. I
wish you much mirth.

VALERIA Well then, farewell.

    Exeunt ⌈ Valeria, Volumnia, and usher at one
    door, Virgilia and Gentlewoman at another door⌉

1.4 *Enter Martius, Titus Lartius, with a drummer,*
   ⌈ *a trumpeter*⌉, *and colours, with captains and*
   Soldiers ⌈ *carrying scaling ladders*⌉, *as before the*
   city Corioles; to them a Messenger

MARTIUS

Yonder comes news. A wager they have met.

---

107 lady. As . . . now,] POPE (lady;); ~, ~ . . . ~. F1; ~, ~ . . . ~, F4 114.1–3] OXFORD;
Exeunt Ladies F

1.4.0.2 *a trumpeter*] OXFORD; *not in* F 0.3 *carrying scaling ladders*] OXFORD; *not in* F

---

107 **Let . . . now, she** F1's punctuation is
 possible but makes inferior sense.
108 **disease . . . mirth** i.e. 'spoil our enjoy-
 ment which will be better without
 her'; with the original meaning of 'disease' (*OED* 1) and 'better' used proleptically. Virgilia responds with a touch
 of sharpness at 'much mirth' (l. 113).
110 **thy** Valeria's sudden switch to the
 second person familiar may suggest
 either a certain sympathy (cf. 5.2.87,
 88, 90 n.) or perhaps an attempt to
 cajole.
112 **at a word** bluntly, once and for all
1.4–10 The next seven scenes present a
 much more complex sequence of tactics than can be found in any of Shakespeare's other plays because the action
 is closely based on Plutarch's historical
 account, except for the addition of
 1.9—the single combat between Mar-

tius and Aufidius—and small but significant adjustments to Martius' plea
 for his Corioles host at the end of 1.10:
 see Introduction, pp. 25, 84.
0.4 **to . . . Messenger** 'The side of the stage
 from which he enters will hence-
 forward represent the direction of
 Cominius' force, and alarums sounded
 by Cominius and Aufidius will come
 from that side' (Kemball-Cook).
1 **wager** This bet is Shakespeare's addition, suggested presumably by Plutarch's comment on the horse that
 Cominius gave Martius after the battle.
 It establishes the jocular, competitive
 attitude that the patricians take to
 war, a traditionally 'chivalrous' stance
 meant to convey their lack of fear and
 eagerness to be first in battle. Ram-
 bures tries to make a similar wager
 before Agincourt in *Henry V* 3.7.83–4.

LARTIUS

  My horse to yours, no.

MARTIUS   'Tis done.

LARTIUS   Agreed.

MARTIUS (*to the Messenger*)

  Say, has our general met the enemy?

MESSENGER

  They lie in view, but have not spoke as yet.

LARTIUS

  So, the good horse is mine.

MARTIUS   I'll buy him of you.   5

LARTIUS

  No, I'll nor sell nor give him. Lend you him I will,

  For half a hundred years.

  (*To the trumpeter*)   Summon the town.

MARTIUS (*to the Messenger*)

  How far off lie these armies?

MESSENGER   Within this mile and half.

MARTIUS

  Then shall we hear their 'larum, and they ours.

  Now Mars, I prithee, make us quick in work,   10

  That we with smoking swords may march from hence

  To help our fielded friends.

  (*To the trumpeter*)   Come, blow thy blast.

      They sound a parley. Enter two Senators, with others, on
      the walls of Corioles

  (*To the Senators*) Tullus Aufidius, is he within your
  walls?

FIRST SENATOR

  No, nor a man that fears you less than he:

---

14 nor ... that ... less] F; nor ... but ... less JOHNSON; but ... that ... less KEIGHT-
LEY; nor ... that ... more HUDSON (*conj.* Johnson)

1, 3 **met** met in battle

4 **spoke** fought

7 **Summon** i.e. summon to parley
(cf. 1.4.12.1). Interestingly, the trumpeter does not sound till Martius also
commands him at 1.4.12. As later
with Cominius and Aufidius, Martius is
establishing a natural dominance over
his co-commander, Lartius: cf. 1.4.25,
where he tells Lartius to advance.

8 **mile and half** Cf. 1.7.16 n.

9 **'larum** alarum, call to arms (in this
play usually on the drums); it sounds
off-stage at 1.4.19

11 **smoking** reeking (with blood);
cf. 2.2.117

12 **fielded** still on the battlefield

12.2 **walls of Corioles** i.e. the stage balcony: see Introduction, p. 90.

13 ff. **Tullus** ... This parley is not in
Plutarch.

14 **less** Grammatically, the sense requires

That's lesser than a little.
     Drum afar off
⌈*To the Volscians*⌉   Hark, our drums   15
Are bringing forth our youth. We'll break our walls
Rather than they shall pound us up. Our gates,
Which yet seem shut, we have but pinned with rushes;
They'll open of themselves.
     Alarum far off
(*To the Romans*)   Hark you, far off
There is Aufidius. List what work he makes   20
Amongst your cloven army.
                    ⌈*Exeunt Volscians from the walls*⌉
MARTIUS   O, they are at it!
LARTIUS
     Their noise be our instruction. Ladders, ho!
          Enter the army of the Volsces ⌈*from the gates*⌉
MARTIUS
     They fear us not, but issue forth their city.
     Now put your shields before your hearts, and fight
     With hearts more proof than shields. Advance, brave
          Titus.   25
     They do disdain us much beyond our thoughts,
     Which makes me sweat with wrath. Come on, my
          fellows.
     He that retires, I'll take him for a Volsce,
     And he shall feel mine edge.

---

17 up.] F3 (*subs.*); ~∧ FI   19 *Alarum far off*] F (*at end of line*)   21 *Exeunt ... walls*]
OXFORD; *not in* F   22.1 *from the gates*] OXFORD; *not in* F

'more', but Shakespeare frequently in-
tensifies a negative by substituting
'less' (cf. *Troilus* 1.1.27–8). Johnson
solved the obscurity by changing 'that'
to 'but'.

17 **pound us up** shut us up like animals
     in a pinfold (enclosure for stray cattle)
18 **pinned with rushes** only lightly bolted,
     easily opened
20 **List** hark, listen to
21 **cloven** (a) divided into two commands,

(b) cut to pieces (another dismember-
     ment image)
22 **our instruction** 'a lesson to us'
     (Hibbard)
22.1 **army** Not Aufidius' troops but a
     sortie by the defenders of Corioles.
25 **proof** of tested strength
     Advance ... Titus Since he re-enters at
     1.5.20.1, Lartius must leave the scene
     at some point. It could logically be
     here: cf. 1.4.7 n. and 1.10.75–6 n.
29 **edge** sword edge; cf. 5.6.113

*Alarum. The Romans are beat back⌈and exeunt⌉to
their trenches, ⌈the Volsces following⌉*

I.5   *Enter⌈Roman Soldiers in retreat, followed by⌉
Martius, cursing*

MARTIUS

All the contagion of the south light on you,
You shames of Rome! You herd of—Boils and plagues
Plaster you o'er, that you may be abhorred
Farther than seen, and one infect another
Against the wind a mile! You souls of geese   5
That bear the shapes of men, how have you run
From slaves that apes would beat! Pluto and hell:
All hurt behind! Backs red, and faces pale
With flight and agued fear! Mend and charge home,
Or by the fires of heaven I'll leave the foe   10
And make my wars on you. Look to't. Come on.

29.1 *and exeunt*] OXFORD; *not in* F   29.2 *the Volsces following*] OXFORD; *not in* F
I.5] *Scene divided as in* OXFORD   0.1 *Roman . . . by*] OXFORD; *not in* F   2 Rome! You
herd of—] JOHNSON; Rome: you Heard of, F; Rome: you herds of, ROWE; Rome, you!
Herds of, THEOBALD, POPE 1733; Rome, you herds, you! HANMER; Rome: you herds; of,
POPE   Boils] F (Byles); Biles F3, HARRISON

29.1 *exeunt* See Introduction, p. 92 n. 2.
29.2 *trenches* See Introduction, p. 92.
I.5.0.2 *cursing* North merely says 'with a loud voice' (Spencer, p. 306)
I **contagion . . . south** Cf. 2.3.27–30 for the idea that the warm, damp south wind brings fogs and pestilence: 'miasma' was thought to encourage the plague from which London was suffering at the time *Coriolanus* was written, and was associated with infection from 'bad breath' of which the plebeians are constantly accused.
2 **herd of—** Martius' anger makes him stumble from one favourite denigration to another, from an animal metaphor to imagery of infection. Similar abrupt switches of focus can be seen in his language at I.I.207–9 and I.7.43: the headlong effect is very like Hotspur's habit of speaking 'thick' and was considered typical of the 'choleric' temperament: cf. 3.3.28–30 for Brutus' comment on this characteristic. Here it may also cue a gesture.

Boils and plagues 'Boils' (buboes) were a symptom of bubonic plague
3–5 **abhorred . . . mile!** i.e. 'so that you will be shunned (on account of your stink) before you can be seen, and the infection be so strong as to carry a mile against a contrary wind' (Gomme).
8 **All hurt behind** It was accounted a disgrace to be wounded in the back because this betrayed the fact that one was running away: in *Macbeth* 5.11.12–13, Young Siward is praised because his hurts are all 'on the front'.
9 **agued** shivering, as though feverish with the ague (another plague symptom); cf. I.5.34
  Mend do better
  home to the goal aimed for; i.e. 'into the midst of the enemy'
10 **fires of heaven** The first use of fire imagery that will increasingly be associated with Rome's destruction.
10–11 **I'll . . . you** Ironically prophetic. There was a similar irony at I.I.231–3.

If you'll stand fast, we'll beat them to their wives,
As they us to our trenches. Follow's!
    Another alarum, and ⌜ *as the Volsces re-enter to*
    attack ⌝ *Martius* ⌜ *beats them back and* ⌝ *follows them to*
    the gates
So, now the gates are ope. Now prove good seconds.
'Tis for the followers fortune widens them,   15
Not for the fliers. Mark me, and do the like.
    He enters the gates
FIRST SOLDIER Foolhardiness! Not I.
SECOND SOLDIER Nor I.
    Alarum continues. ⌜ *The gates close, and* ⌝ *Martius is*
    shut in
FIRST SOLDIER See, they have shut him in.
⌜ THIRD SOLDIER ⌝ To th' pot, I warrant him.   20
    Enter Titus Lartius ⌜ *with soldiers carrying ladders* ⌝
LARTIUS
  What is become of Martius?
⌜ THIRD SOLDIER ⌝   Slain, sir, doubtless.
FIRST SOLDIER
  Following the fliers at the very heels,
  With them he enters, who upon the sudden

---

13 trenches. Follow's!] SISSON (*conj.* Collier); ~‸followes. F; ~‸ followed. F2; ~. Follow!
COLLIER 1858; ~. Follow me! DYCE 1866 (*conj.* Lettsom); trenches.‸ CLARENDON   13.1–3]
This edition (*after* OXFORD); *Another Alarum, and Martius followes them to gates, and is
shut in.* F   16.1] F (*Enter the Gati.*)   18.1–2] *as* OXFORD; *Alarum continues* (*after* in) F
20, 21 THIRD SOLDIER] OXFORD; *All.* F   20.1 *with soldiers carrying ladders*] This edition;
not in F   21 LARTIUS] F (*Tit.*)

---

12 **stand . . . beat them to their wives** The
    wording carries sexual overtones of
    rivalry and rape: cf. war as a 'ravisher'
    (4.5.231–2) and Cominius on the price
    of being conquered, 4.6.85–7.
    beat them to (a) drive them to with
    blows, (b) get to before them?
13 **Follow's** F's omission of the apost-
    rophe may have been influenced by
    follows in the succeeding stage direc-
    tion. The command continues the
    sense of 'Come on' two lines earlier,
    and is an accepted colloquialism. Al-
    ternatively, it can be interpreted as a
    stage direction analogous to '*Enters the
    gates*'.

13.3 **to the gates** F's '*and is shut in*'
    anticipates the explicit direction at
    1.5.16.1; see Introduction, p. 145.
14 **seconds**   supporters.   Shakespeare
    eliminates the soldiers who help Mar-
    tius in North; cf. Introduction, p. 25.
    This contrasts with the Volscians who
    come to Aufidius' aid unasked in 1.9.
15 **followers** (a) pursuers, (b) playing on
    'follow's'?
    widens them i.e. 'opens the gates'
16 **fliers** fugitives, those in retreat
20 **pot** stew-pot, with the implication of
    'cut to pieces' (cf. 5.6.112): cf. the
    idiom 'gone to pot'?
20.1 Cf. 1.4.25 n. and 1.5.34.1 n.

Clapped-to their gates. He is himself alone
To answer all the city.

LARTIUS   O noble fellow,   25
Who sensibly outdares his senseless sword
And, when it bows, stand'st up! Thou art lost, Martius.
A carbuncle entire, as big as thou art,
Were not so rich a jewel. Thou wast a soldier
Even to Cato's wish, not fierce and terrible   30
Only in strokes, but with thy grim looks and
The thunder-like percussion of thy sounds
Thou mad'st thine enemies shake as if the world
Were feverous and did tremble.

                Enter Martius bleeding, assaulted by the enemy

FIRST SOLDIER   Look, sir.

LARTIUS   O, 'tis Martius!
Let's fetch him off, or make remain alike.   35
                They fight, and all enter the city

---

24 Clapped-to] MALONE; Clapt to F   27 stand'st] F; stands ROWE   art lost,] SINGER
1856 (*conj.* Collier); art left﹀ F; artless﹀ BULLOCH *conj.* (*in* Cambridge)   27–8 Martius.
| A . . . entire, . . . art,] CAMBRIDGE (*subs.*); ~﹀ . . . ~: . . . ~﹀ F   29 Were] F (Weare)
30 Cato's] THEOBALD; *Calues* F

24 **himself alone** quite alone
25 **answer** deal with, encounter
25–34 **O . . . tremble** The clustering of
  difficult consonants gives this eulogy a
  harsh, barking sound. The premature
  obituary is one of the first examples of
  the play's deliberate use of ironic bad
  timing: see Introduction, p. 29.
26–7 **Who . . . up!** i.e. 'Who, though sensitive to pain, is braver than his sword
  which feels nothing, and stands firm
  when the sword bends': cf. 1.3.58 n.
  and 1.7.77 n., 1.4.24–5.
27 **stand'st** thou standest (looking back to
  the implied vocative in 'fellow')
  lost This agrees better than F's 'left'
  with the comparison to a carbuncle
  that follows, which Rome has 'lost'
  not 'left'.
28 **carbuncle** (a) a red-coloured gem,
  probably a ruby (agreeing with the
  imagery of Martius as a 'thing of
  blood'); (b) ironically, it can also mean
  'a boil' (cf. l. 2 n.).
  entire flawless, complete in itself:
  cf. *Othello* 5.2.152, 'one entire . . .
  chrysolite'

30 **Cato** Marcus Porcius Cato (234–149
  BC), known as the 'Censor', was remembered for his advocacy of the
  traditional military virtues of Rome.
  North's 'For he was even such another
  as Cato would have a soldier and a
  captain to be' has betrayed Shakespeare into an anachronism. Cf.
  2.1.113 n., 2.3.237 n., etc.
32 **thunder-like . . . sounds** For the loudness of Martius' voice, see Introduction, p. 107.
34 *Enter . . .* This creates a staging problem: see Introduction, p. 93.
  bleeding The first reference to one of
  the most striking stage images of the
  play: see Introduction, pp. 65–6.
35 **fetch him off** rescue (antedates *OED*
  16)
  make remain alike stay there like him
  ('remain' is a noun: *OED sb.*²)
35.1 *all . . . city* Gary Taylor (see *Textual
  Companion*, p. 595) notes that the staging of events throughout 1.4 and 1.5
  is very like that of a scene in Thomas
  Heywood's *1 Edward IV* (*Works*, i. 20),
  which may have influenced it.

1.6   *Enter certain Romans with spoils*

FIRST ROMAN This will I carry to Rome.

SECOND ROMAN And I this.

THIRD ROMAN A murrain on't, I took this for silver.

> *Alarum continues still afar off. Enter Martius,*
> ⌈*bleeding*⌉, *and Titus Lartius with a trumpeter*

MARTIUS

  See here these movers that do prize their hours
  At a cracked drachma! Cushions, leaden spoons,   5
  Irons of a doit, doublets that hangmen would
  Bury with those that wore them, these base slaves,
  Ere yet the fight be done, pack up. Down with them!
> ⌈*Exeunt Romans with spoils*⌉

  And hark what noise the general makes. To him!
  There is the man of my soul's hate, Aufidius,   10
  Piercing our Romans. Then, valiant Titus, take
  Convenient numbers to make good the city,
  Whilst I, with those that have the spirit, will haste
  To help Cominius.

1.6.3] *after* ROWE (*see l. 8.1*); *exeunt.* F   3.1–2] *as* F; OXFORD *adds* '*Exeunt Romans with spoils*'   3.2 *bleeding*] OXFORD; *not in* F   3.2 *Lartius*] *not in* F   *trumpeter*] F (*Trumpet*)   4 hours] F; honours ROWE 1714   5 drachma] SINGER 1856; Drachme F; dram STAUNTON   7 them, these] F3 (~, These); ~. These F1   8.1] KITTREDGE (*subs.*); *not in* F   9 him!] POPE (*subs.*); ~ˌ F1; ~, F3

1.6.1–3 **This ... this ... this** These 'spoils' are identified by Martius in ll. 5–6.

3 **murrain** cattle plague

3.2 *trumpeter* F's *trumpet* can have this meaning (*OED* 4); cf. *Henry V* 4.2.61

4 **movers** (a) active fellows (ironical), (b) removers (scavengers, looters)?
hours F's reading seems better than Rowe's 'honours': cf. 'Ere ... up', 1.6.8, and North's comment that Martius 'cried out on them that it was no time to look after spoil'. F has, however, a mark over the o of 'hours' that could be interpreted as an abbreviation bar.

5 **drachma** a Greek coin of small value, worth even less when cracked

6 **Irons** (a) weapons, (b) fire irons?
doit A Dutch copper coin (duit) worth only half an English farthing.

6–7 **doublets ... them** The clothes of people executed were the perquisite of the hangman; a doublet was the Elizabethan, not Roman, equivalent of a modern jacket or, without sleeves, a waistcoat.

8 **pack up** (a) make into a bundle, (b) quit (though Shakespeare has no other example in this sense)?

8.1 *Exeunt ... spoils* F gives the Roman soldiers no exit. To put this after 'Down with them!' (where 'them' means 'spoil', not 'movers') seems more logical than Brockbank's suggestion that they leave as Martius enters.

9 **the general** i.e. Cominius, who is also a consul (2.1.157.1, 2.2.34.3)

11 **Piercing** Cf. 'cloven' 1.4.21 n., which has the same ambiguity.

12 **make good** secure, complete the conquest of and establish defences for

LARTIUS   Worthy sir, thou bleed'st.
Thy exercise hath been too violent   15
For a second course of fight.
MARTIUS   Sir, praise me not.
My work hath yet not warmed me. Fare you well.
The blood I drop is rather physical
Than dangerous to me. To Aufidius thus
I will appear and fight.
LARTIUS   Now the fair goddess Fortune   20
Fall deep in love with thee, and her great charms
Misguide thy opposers' swords! Bold gentleman,
Prosperity be thy page.
MARTIUS   Thy friend no less
Than those she placeth highest. So farewell.
LARTIUS Thou worthiest Martius!   *Exit Martius*   25
Go sound thy trumpet in the market-place.
Call thither all the officers o'th' town,
Where they shall know our mind. Away.

                    Exeunt ⌜severally⌝

1.7   *Enter Cominius, as it were in retire, with*
         Soldiers

COMINIUS

Breathe you, my friends. Well fought. We are come off
Like Romans, neither foolish in our stands
Nor cowardly in retire. Believe me, sirs,

---

22 swords! Bold gentlemen,] JOHNSON; ~, ~~: F   25 *Exit Martius*] CAPELL; *not in* F
28.1] OXFORD; *Exeunt* F

16 **course** (a) passage at arms, bout
(*OED* I.5), (b) course of a banquet
(cf. 1.10.10–11)?
18 **physical** restorative, good for the
health; cf. 'exercise' and 'warmed me',
ll. 15, 17: another patrician trope concealing the mortality of war. Blood-
letting was a common Renaissance
medical treatment (particularly for the
over-choleric).
19–20 **To...fight** Martius' eagerness
to show his bloody body to Aufidius
contrasts with his later reluctance to
show even his scars to the plebeians.
21 **charms** magic spells

23 **Prosperity...page** success attend you
23–4 **Thy...highest** i.e. 'May she be no
less a friend to thee than to those, etc.'
(Globe)
28.1 *severally* i.e. they both go through
the central 'gates' but head in different
directions, Martius having left at l. 25
by the side door associated with the
noise from Cominius' battle.
1.7.1 **Breathe you** take your breath, rest
are come off have got clear. Cominius
is not very inspiring as a leader, but
he shows the same caution more profitably later in dealing with the plebeians.

We shall be charged again. Whiles we have struck,
By interims and conveying gusts we have heard   5
The charges of our friends. Ye Roman gods,
Lead their successes as we wish our own,
That both our powers, with smiling fronts encount'ring,
May give you thankful sacrifice!
      Enter a Messenger
                        Thy news?

MESSENGER
The citizens of Corioles have issued,   10
And given to Lartius and to Martius battle.
I saw our party to their trenches driven,
And then I came away.
COMINIUS   Though thou speak'st truth,
Methinks thou speak'st not well. How long is't since?
MESSENGER Above an hour, my lord.   15
COMINIUS
'Tis not a mile; briefly we heard their drums.
How couldst thou in a mile confound an hour,
And bring thy news so late?
MESSENGER   Spies of the Volsces
Held me in chase, that I was forced to wheel
Three or four miles about; else had I, sir,   20
Half an hour since brought my report.   ⌈*Exit*⌉
      Enter Martius, bloody
COMINIUS   Who's yonder,

1.7.6 Ye] HANMER; The F   9 *Enter a Messenger*] *at end of line* F   13 speak'st] ROWE; speakest F   16 briefly⌄] F; ~, THEOBALD   21 *Exit*] *not in* F   bloody] OXFORD; *not in* F

3 **retire** a mild term for 'retreat'
4 **struck** been striking blows
5 **By . . . gusts** carried on the winds at intervals
6 **Ye** Hanmer's emendation is clearer for a modern audience, though F's 'The' (MS 'Ye'?) could also be vocative; cf. 'give you', 1.7.9.
7 **Lead . . . successes** (a) guide their fortunes, (b) proleptically, 'lead them to good fortune, success'
8 **powers** armies
   fronts (a) front lines (of the armies), (b) faces

10 **issued** made a sortie
16 **'Tis . . . mile** At 1.4.8 it was a 'mile and half'; presumably Cominius' troops have retired towards the other Roman force.
   briefly not long since
17 **confound** waste
19 **that** so that
21 *Enter . . . bloody* Another striking entrance, because of our ironic expectation of it, the four-line pause for descriptive comment before Martius speaks, and his appallingly 'bloody' appearance.

That does appear as he were flayed? O gods!
He has the stamp of Martius, and I have
Before-time seen him thus.

MARTIUS   Come I too late?

COMINIUS

The shepherd knows not thunder from a tabor   25
More than I know the sound of Martius' tongue
From every meaner man.

MARTIUS   Come I too late?

COMINIUS

Ay, if you come not in the blood of others,
But mantled in your own.

MARTIUS   O, let me clip ye
In arms as sound as when I wooed, in heart   30
As merry as when our nuptial day was done,
And tapers burnt to bedward!
        ⌜ *They embrace* ⌝

COMINIUS

Flower of warriors! How is't with Titus Lartius?

MARTIUS

As with a man busied about decrees,
Condemning some to death and some to exile,   35
Ransoming him or pitying, threat'ning th'other;
Holding Corioles in the name of Rome
Even like a fawning greyhound in the leash,

---

24 Before-time] HANMER (*subs.*): Before time F   30 wooed, in heart] OXFORD (*conj.*
Theobald); ~‸ ~~; F   32.1 *They embrace*] OXFORD;   *not in* F

22 **flayed** i.e. as bloody as a newly skinned
carcass: not just lightly smeared but
soaked in blood. See Introduction,
p. 66.
23 **stamp** (a) impress, bearing, (b) stamp
of the foot, a cue for one of Martius'
characteristic gestures (cf. 1.3.33)?
25 **tabor** small drum
27 **man** i.e. 'man's': Malone compares
Cymbeline 4.2.253: 'Thersites' body is
as good as Ajax'.
29 **clip** embrace: cf. 4.5.110
30–2 **In ... bedward** Aufidius uses the
same marital imagery when he embraces Coriolanus at 4.5.115–19; con-

versely, Martius cannot embrace his
wife without thinking of war, 5.3.45:
cf. Introduction, pp. 58, 80.
30 **wooed, in heart** F's punctuation
makes inferior sense.
32 **to bedward** showing us it was time for
bed
33 **Flower of warriors!** F's punctuation
would make this vocative. The embrace should probably come after 'warriors!'.
36 **Ransoming ... pitying** releasing a
man for ransom or for pity
38–9 **Even ... will** The idea of the subjug-
ated city fawning on its all-powerful

193

To let him slip at will.

COMINIUS   Where is that slave

Which told me they had beat you to your trenches?   40

Where is he? Call him hither.

MARTIUS   Let him alone.

He did inform the truth—but for our gentlemen,

The common file—a plague! tribunes for them!—

The mouse ne'er shunned the cat as they did budge

From rascals worse than they.

COMINIUS   But how prevailed you?   45

MARTIUS

Will the time serve to tell? I do not think.

Where is the enemy? Are you lords o'th' field?

If not, why cease you till you are so?

COMINIUS

Martius, we have at disadvantage fought,

And did retire to win our purpose.   50

MARTIUS

How lies their battle? Know you on which side

They have placed their men of trust?

COMINIUS   As I guess, Martius,

Their bands i'th' vanguard are the Antiates,

Of their best trust; o'er them Aufidius,

Their very heart of hope.

MARTIUS   I do beseech you   55

By all the battles wherein we have fought,

---

42 truth—but . . . gentlemen,] HIBBARD (*anon. conj.*); ~: ~~, F   43 plague! tribunes]
ROWE; plague—Tribunes F1; ~ₐ ~ F3   46 think.] F (thinke:); think—ROWE; think it.
COLLIER 1858   53 vanguard] F (Vaward)   Antiates] POPE; Antients F

conqueror is a sado-masochist image
of some interest, but the use of 'slip'
seems imprecise since a greyhound is
let slip to hunt or race, which does not
seem appropriate here.

43 **file** Cf. modern 'rank and file': files of
ten men each were the units into
which Elizabethan foot soldiers were
organized: cf. 2.1.22.

44–5 **budge | From** flinch from, retreat
from; cf. 1.9.5

45 **rascals** See 1.1.156 n.

46 **think** think so (Abbott §64)
51 **battle** battle-formation
53 **vanguard** F's spelling 'Vaward' was
quite usual in the 17th century
Antiates i.e. men of Antium (the chief
city of the Volsces and Aufidius' home
town, cf. 5.6.49): a trisyllable, cf. F's
spelling 'Antiats' at l. 60.
55 **Their . . . hope** the man on whom all
their hopes depend
56–60 **By . . . Antiates** F's lineation pre-
serves a ceremonial parallelism

By th' blood we have shed together,
By th' vows we have made
To endure friends, that you directly set me
Against Aufidius and his Antiates,   60
And that you not delay the present, but,
Filling the air with swords advanced and darts,
We prove this very hour.

COMINIUS   Though I could wish
You were conducted to a gentle bath
And balms applied to you, yet dare I never   65
Deny your asking. Take your choice of those
That best can aid your action.

MARTIUS   Those are they
That most are willing. If any such be here—
As it were sin to doubt—that love this painting
Wherein you see me smeared; if any fear   70
Lesser his person than an ill report;
If any think brave death outweighs bad life,
And that his country's dearer than himself,
Let him alone, or so many so minded,
Wave thus to express his disposition,   75
And follow Martius.

⌈ *He waves his sword.*⌉ *They all shout and wave*
their swords, take him up in their arms and cast
up their caps

O, me alone! Make you a sword of me?

61–2 but, . . . advanced‸] ROWE; (but‸ . . . aduanc'd) F 71 Lesser] F3; Lessen FI; less
for ROWE   76.1 *He* . . . *sword.*] *after* OXFORD, *where it follows l. 74; not in* F   2–3 *take*
. . . *caps*] *as* F; *after l.* 77 BROCKBANK   77] *Line given to* 'All.' BROOKE (*conj.* Style),
BROCKBANK   O, me alone! Make . . . me?] ARDEN *subs.*; Oh me alone, . . . me: F; O'
me alone, make . . . me? OXFORD (*conj.* Marshall); O' me alone? Make . . . me? SISSON; O, me
alone! Make . . . me! BROCKBANK; O' me alone, make . . . me. HIBBARD

---

61 **delay the present** make any delay now
(Abbott §305)

62 **advanced** raised before them: cf.
2.1.157

63 **prove** put to the test; cf. 1.4.25 n.

69 **this painting** i.e. the blood with which
he is covered

71 **Lesser** less for

75 **thus** A cue for a gesture; cf. 1.7.76.1.

76 **And** . . . **Martius** For the first time Martius speaks of himself in the impersonal

third person.

76.2 **take** . . . **arms** See Introduction, pp.
65–6, 82.

76.3 **caps** Clearly these are Elizabethan
soldiers, cf. 1.10.40.2. Modern productions often substitute tossed pikes or a
fascist salute with clenched fists.

77 **O** . . . **me?** This is one of the two main
cruces of the play (see Introduction)
and can be interpreted as delight,
surprise, or protest. As presented by

If these shows be not outward, which of you
But is four Volsces? None of you but is
Able to bear against the great Aufidius   80
A shield as hard as his. A certain number—
Though thanks to all—must I select from all.
The rest shall bear the business in some other fight
As cause will be obeyed. Please you to march,
And I shall quickly draw out my command,   85
Which men are best inclined.
COMINIUS   March on, my fellows.
Make good this ostentation, and you shall
Divide in all with us.   *Exeunt*

1.8   *Titus Lartius, having set a guard upon Corioles, going*
          with drummer and trumpeter toward Cominius and
          Caius Martius, enters with a Lieutenant, other
          soldiers, and a scout

82 select from all] F; select HANMER   83–4 The rest ... fight | As cause ... obeyed.]
F (*subs.*); rest (as cause ... obey'd) shall bear | The ... fight: ROSSITER *conj.* (*in* Brock-
bank)   85 I] HUDSON (*conj.* Capell); foure F; forth KEIGHTLEY   88 Exeunt] F; *Exeunt
marching* OXFORD

Oxford, it is a battlefield joke: 'Do you
hold just me in the air like a sword
(when I asked you to wave your real
swords)?' Martius' mood is exultantly
teasing, however, not at all critical, as
the next lines make clear; so it seems
more likely that the first phrase should
be ecstatic, 'O, me alone!' (i.e. O, you
think I'm in a class by myself, you
value me uniquely!). As Michael Goldman says (*Acting and Action in Shakespearean Tragedy*, 1983, p. 155): 'It is
[Coriolanus'] happiest moment in the
play.'

78 **outward** mere appearance, superficial
79 **But** is that is not
82–4 **Though ... march** Rossiter's relining is also attractive: F puts 'As
cause will be obeyed' in brackets, so it
may well have been a marginal or
interlinear correction in the manuscript which the compositor misplaced.
84 **As ... obeyed** as occasion demands
85 **I** F's 'foure' is a misreading of Shake-

speare's capital I as the arabic num-
eral 4. See Introduction, p. 139.
draw out pick
command command-force, troop; with
'which men are best inclined' in apposition
87 **Make ... ostentation** verify the promise
of this show by your performance
88 **Divide in all** share all the booty. A
typically uninspired piece of leadership
(the same promise is made by Richard
III), to which Martius' contempt for
booty is diametrically opposed; cf.
1.6.4–8, 1.10.37–40.
1.8.0.1–4 **Titus ... scout** Greg (*Shakespeare First Folio*, 1955, p. 406) remarks that this direction really
summarizes what Lartius goes on to
say in the scene; he suggests it may
have been copied from the author's
plot or scenario into his foul papers.
The scene provides a rationale for Lartius' sudden appearance at 1.10.11,
but its main purpose is probably to
allow time for Martius to prepare for

LARTIUS (*to the Lieutenant*)

   So, let the ports be guarded. Keep your duties

   As I have set them down. If I do send, dispatch

   Those centuries to our aid. The rest will serve

   For a short holding. If we lose the field

   We cannot keep the town.   5

LIEUTENANT Fear not our care, sir.

LARTIUS Hence, and shut your gates upon's.

                       ⌈*Exit Lieutenant*⌉

   (*To the scout*) Our guider, come; to th' Roman camp

   conduct us.   *Exeunt*

1.9   *Alarum, as in battle. Enter Martius and Aufidius, at
several doors*

MARTIUS

   I'll fight with none but thee, for I do hate thee

   Worse than a promise-breaker.

AUFIDIUS   We hate alike.

   Not Afric owns a serpent I abhor

   More than thy fame and envy. Fix thy foot.

1.8.7 *Exit Lieutenant*] OXFORD; *not in* F   8 *Exeunt*] POPE; *Exit* F; *Exeunt towards
Cominius and Caius Martius* OXFORD

   1.9.4 fame‸ and] F; ~, ~ THEOBALD; fame I COLLIER MS envy] F; envy't KINNEAR
conj. (*in* Cambridge)

---

the single combat with Aufidius in 1.9;
cf. 1.10.75–6 n. It also provides an
ironic contrast between Martius' concern for personal glory and the grim
administrative chores of war.

1 **ports** gates
3 **centuries** companies of 100 men
(Latin *centuria*)
8 **guider** guide, scout
1.9 Shakespeare adds this scene as a
climax to the battle
0.1 *Alarum ... battle* F puts this at the
end of 1.8; it obviously refers to the
action following, bridging between
the 'scenes'
0.2 *at ... doors* i.e. Martius from one
side door, Aufidius from the other; cf.
1.10.0.1–2 and Introduction, p. 90.
1, 2 **hate ... hate alike** North's Plutarch
says that, because of the many encounters between Martius and Aufidius,

'besides the common quarrel between
them, there was bred a marvellous
private hate one against another'.
2 **Worse ... promise-breaker** See Introduction, p. 83: a splendid example of
dramatic irony.
3 **Afric ... serpent** To illustrate Africa's
reputation for serpents, Globe cites
Thomas Heywood, *The Silver Age*
(*Works*, ed. Shepherd, iii. 125–6) and
Arden Arthur Golding's translation of
Ovid's story of the Gorgon's head in-
festing Libya with snakes, *Metamorphoses*, iv. 756–63.
4 **fame and envy** (a) 'fame and the envy
it creates (in me)', (b) 'envy' may be
a verb paralleling 'abhor', (c) by hendiadys, 'detested fame', (d) malicious
hatred
   Fix thy foot i.e. as for the beginning of
a formal duel. Wilson compares *Antony*
3.7.66, 'fighting foot to foot'

MARTIUS

    Let the first budger die the other's slave,   5

    And the gods doom him after.

AUFIDIUS   If I fly, Martius,

    Holloa me like a hare.

MARTIUS   Within these three hours, Tullus,

    Alone I fought in your Corioles' walls,

    And made what work I pleased. 'Tis not my blood

    Wherein thou seest me masked. For thy revenge,   10

    Wrench up thy power to th' highest.

AUFIDIUS   Wert thou the Hector

    That was the whip of your bragged progeny,

    Thou shouldst not 'scape me here.

> *Here they fight, and certain Volsces come in the aid of*
> *Aufidius. Martius fights till they be driven in breath-*
> *less, ⌈ Martius following⌉*

    Officious and not valiant, you have shamed me

    In your condemnèd seconds.   *Exit*   15

1.10   *Alarum. A retreat is sounded. Flourish. Enter at one*
door Cominius with the Romans, at another door
Martius with his ⌈ left ⌉ arm in a scarf

COMINIUS (*to Martius*)

    If I should tell thee o'er this thy day's work

---

7 Holloa] F (hollow)   13.3 *Martius following*] OXFORD; *not in* F   15 condemnèd] F
(*subs.*); contemned JOHNSON (*conj.*)   *Exit*] OXFORD; *not in* F; *Exeunt.* HANMER
    1.10.0.1 *Alarum . . . Flourish.*] OXFORD; *Flourish. Alarum. A Retreat is sounded.* F

5 **budger** See 1.7.44–5 n.

7 **Holloa** hunt with shouts; cf. 1.1.233–4 and the hooting of Martius from Rome. Brockbank notes that Shakespeare frequently used the hare to emblematize timidity.

9–10 **'Tis . . . masked** This is not strictly true: cf. 1.6.14, 18–19.

10 **masked** Cf. 'mantled', 1.7.29: a theatre image used unintentionally by Martius (cf. 3.2.15–16: 'play | The man I am').

11 **Wrench . . . highest** Wilson compares *Macbeth* 1.7.60, 'screw your courage to the sticking-place'

11–12 **Hector . . . progeny** Cf. 1.3.41–2 n.

12 **whip of** the scourge belonging to: cf. *Hamlet* 3.1.72

    your bragged progeny (a) the ancestors you brag of, (b) your boastful race

(*OED, brag, v.* 2b)?

13.1–3 **Here . . . following** Again the direction summarizes what is to happen in the rest of the scene (cf. 1.8.0.1–4 n.): there has been a tendency in modern productions to interpret this duel in terms of Aufidius' homoerotic dream at 4.5.123–7. It makes sense to double these 'certain Volsces' with the Conspirators of 5.6 as Aufidius' special supporters.

13.3 **Martius following** F omits exits for either combatant, but it seems unlikely that Martius would let Aufidius go if he too had remained behind when the rescuers were driven in.

15 **In . . . seconds** by your damnable support: cf. 1.5.14 n.

1.10.0.1 **Alarum . . . Flourish** F puts

Thou't not believe thy deeds. But I'll report it
Where senators shall mingle tears with smiles,
Where great patricians shall attend, and shrug,
I'th' end admire; where ladies shall be frighted   5
And, gladly quaked, hear more; where the dull tribunes,
That with the fusty plebeians hate thine honours,
Shall say against their hearts 'We thank the gods
Our Rome hath such a soldier.'
Yet cam'st thou to a morsel of this feast,   10
Having fully dined before.

    Enter Lartius, with his power, from the pursuit

LARTIUS   O general,
Here is the steed, we the caparison.
Hadst thou beheld—

MARTIUS   Pray now, no more. My mother,

0.2 *left*] *This edition; not in* F   2 Thou't] F1; Thou'lt F4; Thou'ldst CAMBRIDGE (*conj.*
Capell)   11 *Lartius*] F (*Titus*)

Flourish before *Alarum*, but this is
probably the result of a misplaced marginal note since *flourish* usually her-
alds the entrance of victors (see E. W.
Naylor, *Shakespeare and Music*, 1896,
pp. 167–8).
retreat A trumpet call to fetch back
troops pursuing the enemy: cf. 1.10.11.
0.3 *left* cf. 2.1.143, 4.5.121
in a scarf in a sling. Martius' wounds
show his human limitation. They help
to excuse his irritation with Cominius'
lengthy praise and also his inability to
remember the name of his Corioles
host, and are crucial for the later vote-
begging scene.

2 **Thou't** thou wouldst: abbreviation of
the colloquial 'thou woot'
4 **attend** pay attention
shrug in disbelief—an interestingly unexpected comment
5 **admire** marvel, wonder
6 **gladly** (a) pleasurably, (b) willingly?
quaked agitated; cf. *Dream* 3.1.25–40,
5.1.219–20
dull spiritless
7 **fusty** mouldy-smelling: cf. 1.1.224
plebeians Accented here on the first
syllable.
10–11 **Yet … before** (a) 'You came to

take a part in the feast (of battle
against Aufidius) although you had
already dined fully (at Corioles)', cf.
4.5.220–1; (b) 'this feast was but a
morsel compared with the large dinner
you had eaten before (in Corioles)'
(Wilson, interpreting 'of' as 'in')? Surely Cominius is not just recognizing the
scale of Martius' valour, but also stak-
ing a tactful claim for his own part in
the battle before Martius arrived:
hence 'morsel of this feast'. Cf. 1.7.49–
50. See Introduction, p. 78.
11 *from the pursuit* Another purely
'literary' direction.
12 **Here … caparison** i.e. 'This man performed the action, and we only filled
up the show' (Johnson). Lartius' metaphor anticipates Cominius' gift of 1.10.
61–2, described by North as 'a goodly
horse with a caparison, and all the
furniture to him', and recalls the chivalric horse wager of 1.4.2–7; but
Johnson is correct in calling it an 'odd
encomium'.
13 ff. **Pray …** Martius' apparent modesty
here and in 2.2 is Shakespeare's addition to Plutarch and is very much part
of his characterization of the hero: see
Introduction, p. 56.

Who has a charter to extol her blood,
When she does praise me, grieves me.   15
I have done as you have done, that's what I can;
Induced as you have been, that's for my country.
He that has but effected his good will
Hath overta'en mine act.

COMINIUS   You shall not be
The grave of your deserving. Rome must know   20
The value of her own. 'Twere a concealment
Worse than a theft, no less than a traducement,
To hide your doings and to silence that
Which, to the spire and top of praises vouched,
Would seem but modest. Therefore, I beseech you—   25
In sign of what you are, not to reward
What you have done—before our army hear me.

MARTIUS

I have some wounds upon me, and they smart
To hear themselves remembered.

COMINIUS   Should they not,
Well might they fester 'gainst ingratitude,   30
And tent themselves with death. Of all the horses—
Whereof we have ta'en good, and good store—of all

31–2 horses— . . . store—of] ALEXANDER; Horses, . . . store of F; horses, . . . store, of
ROWE

14 **charter** prerogative, legal right
15–17 F's lineation has an appropriate
   parallelism which Hanmer's relining
   lacks. The shortness of l. 15 suggests
   a pause, and perhaps a change of tone
   from personal irritation to the public
   comradeliness of what follows.
16 **you** Martius is addressing Cominius
   and Lartius, not the rank and file
18–19 **He . . . act** 'He who has managed
   to carry out his good intentions has
   achieved more than I.'
20 **deserving** deserts
20–1 **Rome . . . own** This emphasizes that
   Martius is a creation of the society in
   which he has been reared: 'must' implies both (a) needs to, and (b) has a
   right to.
22 **traducement** slander, calumny (governed by ' 'Twere' and paralleling

'concealment' not 'theft')
24 **to . . . vouched** if proclaimed to the
   very heights
25 **but modest** only moderate praise
26–7 **In . . . done** 'as a token of your
   uniqueness, not as payment for your
   deeds'; cf. Martius' objection, l. 37. See
   Introduction, p. 84.
29 **not** i.e. not hear themselves remembered
30 **'gainst** in the face of
31 **tent . . . death** 'cure our ingratitude by
   killing you'. A *tent* was a roll of lint
   used to probe and clean wounds;
   cf. 3.1.236.
31–6 **Of . . . choice** This offer of booty, not
   in Plutarch, derives from Amyot's
   French translation.
32 **good, and good store** good ones and
   plenty of them

The treasure in this field achieved and city,
We render you the tenth, to be ta'en forth
Before the common distribution   35
At your only choice.
MARTIUS   I thank you, general,
But cannot make my heart consent to take
A bribe to pay my sword. I do refuse it,
And stand upon my common part with those
That have upheld the doing.   40

> *A long flourish. They all cry 'Martius, Martius!', cast-*
> *ing up their caps and lances. Cominius and Lartius*
> *stand bare*

May these same instruments which you profane
Never sound more. When drums and trumpets shall
I'th' field prove flatterers, let courts and cities be
Made all of false-faced soothing!
When steel grows soft as the parasite's silk,   45
Let him be made an ovator for th' wars!
No more, I say! For that I have not washed
My nose that bled, or foiled some debile wretch,

---

40 upheld] CAPELL; beheld F   40.1–2 *casting*] F (*cast*)   41 May] CAPELL; *Mar.* May F
43 courts and] F; camps, as THEOBALD (*conj.* Warburton)   46 an ovator] BROCKBANK
(*conj.* Hulme); an Ouerture F; a coverture STEEVENS 1778

---

35 **distribution** Pronounced as five syllables.
36 **At . . . choice** entirely as you choose
40 **upheld** sustained. F's 'beheld' does not agree with 'common part'.
40.1–2 **They. . . lances** Even when they support him, the crowds are usually at cross purposes with Martius.
40.2–3 **Cominius . . . bare** i.e. bare-headed, as a mark of respect: cf. 4.5.199 n., and Volumnia's instructions at 3.2.75–6.
44 **Made all** entirely given over to
   false-faced soothing hypocritically mollifying flattery; Martius is saying that, if even soldiers have started to flatter, they must expect civilian life (where flattery is usual) to become utterly corrupt.
45–6 **When . . . wars!** The play's second main crux, again the result of Martius' incoherence when in the grip of strong emotion; 'him' refers to 'parasite' (a Roman social and dramatic type who

earned his meals by flattery), 'ovator' (pronounced like 'overture': see Kökeritz, p. 271) was a Roman term meaning 'one who receives a public ovation' (*OED*), 'for' means 'in recognition of': thus, 'when steel (armour and behaviour of the battlefield) degenerates to the softness of a parasite's silk (clothing and flattery), may an ovation in recognition of (services in) the wars be given to a flatterer' (see Hilda M. Hulme, *Explorations in Shakespeare's Language*, 1962, pp. 155–6, 205–6). Martius is trying simultaneously to repudiate the troops' 'flattery' of himself and their assumption that his rejection of a larger share of booty was intended to flatter them.
47 **For that** because
48 **foiled** defeated
   debile feeble

Which without note here's many else have done,
You shout me forth   50
In acclamations ~~hyperbolical;~~
As if I loved my little should be dieted
In praises sauced with lies.
COMINIUS   Too modest are you,
More cruel to your good report than grateful
To us that give you truly. By your patience,   55
If 'gainst yourself you be incensed we'll put you,
Like one that means his proper harm, in manacles,
Then reason safely with you. Therefore be it known,
As to us, to all the world, that Caius Martius
Wears this war's garland, in token of the which   60
My noble steed, known to the camp, I give him,
With all his trim belonging; and from this time,
For what he did before Corioles, call him,
With all th'applause and clamour of the host,
Martius Caius Coriolanus!   65
Bear th'addition nobly ever!
          Flourish. Trumpets sound, and drums
ALL Martius Caius Coriolanus!
CORIOLANUS I will go wash,
And when my face is fair you shall perceive
Whether I blush or no. Howbeit, I thank you.   70

---

50 shout] F1 (shoot), F4   53 praises‸ sauced] HANMER; ~, ~ F   65, 67 Martius Caius]
F (*Marcus*), SISSON; Caius Martius ROWE   67 ALL] F (*Omnes*)   68, 79, 82, 90 CORIO-
LANUS] STEEVENS; *Martius.* F

49 **without note** unnoticed
50 **shout me forth** cry me up, acclaim me;
    cf. Introduction, p. 139, for F's spelling
    'shoot'.
52 **little** small achievement
52–3 **dieted | In** fattened on
53 **sauced** spiced, seasoned
55 **give** report
    By . . . patience by your leave
57 **means . . . harm** intends to injure him-
    self (a suicide image)
60 **Wears . . . garland** Cf. 1.3.14–15 n.
    These garland references may be one
    reason the Tribunes suspect that Mar-
    tius has ambitions to become the
    'kingly, crownèd head' (1.1.113).
62 **trim belonging** (a) the equipment that

goes with him, (b) fine trappings?
65 **Martius Caius Coriolanus** This order of
    names is not likely to be a compositor-
    ial or scribal error because it is re-
    peated at 2.1.160, and at 2.2.44. As
    F has the spelling 'Marcus' at 1.10.65,
    67, it is possible that, in spite of a
    page-long digression explaining Roman
    nomenclature in North's Plutarch,
    Shakespeare confused the *gens* name
    with the Roman first name 'Marcus'
    (cf. 4.5.68–9 n.).
66 **addition** extra title
68 CORIOLANUS F does not alter the hero's
    speech-heading till 2.1.164, but most
    editors change it here
69 **fair** clean

(To Cominius) I mean to stride your steed, and at all times
To undercrest your good addition
To th' fairness of my power.

COMINIUS   So, to our tent,
Where, ere we do repose us, we will write
To Rome of our success. You, Titus Lartius,   75
Must to Corioles back. Send us to Rome
The best, with whom we may articulate
For their own good and ours.

LARTIUS   I shall, my lord.

CORIOLANUS

The gods begin to mock me. I, that now
Refused most princely gifts, am bound to beg   80
Of my lord general.

COMINIUS   Take't, 'tis yours. What is't?

CORIOLANUS

I sometime lay here in Corioles,
At a poor man's house. He used me kindly.
He cried to me; I saw him prisoner;
But then Aufidius was within my view,   85
And wrath o'erwhelmed my pity. I request you
To give my poor host freedom.

---

71 *To Cominius*] *so* This edition; *not in* F; *before l. 68* OXFORD   83 At a poor] F (poore);
At a most poor CAPELL; And at a poor HANMER

72–3 **undercrest ... addition** i.e. 'treat my
new title as an heraldic crest and try
to live up to it'
73 **To ... power** 'as becomingly as I can'
(Arden)
75–6 **You ... back** Lartius' movements
remain obscure: cf. 1.4.25 n. Although ordered back to Corioles here,
he is present in Rome for the ovation
at 2.1.157.1 though Menenius says
the Senate has only determined to
send for him at 2.2.36. He then enters
Rome again with Martius and the
others at 3.1.0.2 with news of Tullus
Aufidius, and is finally welcomed
home at 3.1.21, yet uncharacteristically has no lines or moves in the riot
that ensues and is not provided with
an exit. He should probably leave immediately after his welcome. The prob-

lem is sometimes solved by giving him
lines in 3.1 that F assigns to various
Senators and Nobles.
77 **best** leading citizens of Corioles
articulate settle articles of a treaty
79 **The gods ... me** An anticipation of
5.3.185–6.
82 **lay** lodged
83 **poor man's** Plutarch says he was a
rich man; Shakespeare gives the situation more pathos and links this
Volscian to Rome's plebeians. Shakespeare also changes the timing of the
request so that Martius asks for his
host's life as a personal afterthought,
whereas in North it is presented as a
magnanimous public gesture in lieu of
booty.
used treated
kindly Cf. the citizen voter at 2.3.71.

COMINIUS   O, well begged!
Were he the butcher of my son, he should
Be free as is the wind. Deliver him, Titus.

LARTIUS
Martius, his name?

CORIOLANUS   By Jupiter, forgot!   90
I am weary, yea, my memory is tired.
Have we no wine here?

COMINIUS   Go we to our tent.
The blood upon your visage dries; 'tis time
It should be looked to. Come.

                              A flourish of cornetts. Exeunt

1.11   *Enter Tullus Aufidius, bloody, with two or three*
        Soldiers

AUFIDIUS   The town is ta'en.

A SOLDIER
'Twill be delivered back on good condition.

AUFIDIUS   Condition?
I would I were a Roman, for I cannot,
Being a Volsce, be that I am. Condition!   5
What good condition can a treaty find
I'th' part that is at mercy? Five times, Martius,
I have fought with thee; so often hast thou beat me,

94.1 *A flourish ... Exeunt*] OXFORD; *Exeunt* F
1.11.0.1–2 *Enter ... Soldiers*] OXFORD; *A flourish. Cornets. Enter Tullus Auffidius bloudie,
with two or three Souldiors.* F   2, 16, 29, 33 A SOLDIER] F (*Sould.*); *First Sol.* CAPELL
5 Condition!] F (~?)

90–2 **By ... here?** Shakespeare adds this
forgetfulness of Coriolanus. It is caused
by natural fatigue, but may also suggest that his request was more a matter of *noblesse oblige* than of genuine
fellow-feeling; see Introduction, p. 25.

94.1 *A ... cornetts* F puts '*A flourish, Cornets.*' at the beginning of 1.11, but, as
Granville-Barker points out, a triumphal
'flourish' suits the end of 1.10 but
is inappropriate to Aufidius' retreat;
cf. 1.10.0.1 n. It has also been suggested that 'Cornets' was a prompter's
marginal addition (Brockbank), and
that there may be a distinction in Act

1 between Roman trumpets and
Volscian cornetts: see Introduction,
p. 99.

1.11.2, 6 **good condition** The Soldier
means 'favourable terms,' but Aufidius
puns bitterly on the sense 'good
quality, sound state' (cf. 2.3.93).

4–5 **I ... am** Cf.   1.1.229–30 n.   and
3.2.15–16.

7 **part ... at mercy** defeated side that is
'absolutely in the power of the victor'
(*OED, mercy, sb.* 5b)

7 ff. **Five times** At 4.5.123 he emends
this to 'Twelve several times'; cf. Introduction, p. 25.

And wouldst do so, I think, should we encounter
As often as we eat. By th'elements,   10
If e'er again I meet him beard to beard,
He's mine, or I am his! Mine emulation
Hath not that honour in't it had, for where
I thought to crush him in an equal force,
True sword to sword, I'll potch at him some way,   15
Or wrath or craft may get him.

A SOLDIER   He's the devil.

AUFIDIUS

Bolder, though not so subtle. My valour, poisoned
With only suff'ring stain by him, for him
Shall fly out of itself. Nor sleep nor sanctuary,
Being naked, sick, nor fane nor Capitol,   20
The prayers of priests nor times of sacrifice—
Embargements all of fury—shall lift up
Their rotten privilege and custom 'gainst
My hate to Martius. Where I find him, were it
At home upon my brother's guard, even there,   25
Against the hospitable canon, would I
Wash my fierce hand in's heart. Go you to th' city.
Learn how 'tis held, and what they are that must
Be hostages for Rome.

A SOLDIER   Will not you go?

---

15 wáy,] F; ~, OXFORD   17–18 valour, poisoned, . . . by him,] POPE (*subs.*); valors,
~, . . . by him: F   21–2 sacrifice— . . . fury—] F (~: . . . ~,)   22 Embargements] OXFORD
(*conj.* Heath); Embarquements F; Embarkments ROWE; Embankments HANMER; Em-
barrments WARBURTON; Embalkments DANIEL *conj.* (*in* Cambridge)

9–10 **should . . . eat** Another of the play's
  persistent equations of food and aggression, here ironically foreshadowing the feasting context of 4.5.
12 **emulation** desire to equal or excel: see
  Introduction, p. 58.
13 **where** whereas
14 **in . . . force** on level terms
15 **potch at** poke at (a self-consciously
  vulgar word for a mean act)
16 **Or . . . or** Either . . . or
17–27 See Introduction, p. 75, for a discussion of Aufidius' speech.
18 **stain** disgrace; cf. 5.6.113
19 **fly . . . itself** betray its nature
20 **naked** defenceless

fane temple
22 **Embargements** 'placings under embar-
  go' (*OED*)
23 **rotten** corrupt with age; cf. Martius' similar disdain for custom in
  2.3.113–17
25 **upon . . . guard** under the protection of
  my brother
26 **the . . . canon** the law of hospitality
  (anticipating his welcome of Coriolanus in 4.5, then later treachery)
26–7 **would . . . heart** Cf. *Caesar*, 3.1.107–
  8: the image combines suggestions of
  a ceremonial 'lustration' and the execution of a traitor.

AUFIDIUS

    I am attended at the cypress grove. I pray you—   30
    'Tis south the city mills—bring me word thither
    How the world goes, that to the pace of it
    I may spur on my journey.

A SOLDIER   I shall, sir.

               Exeunt ⌐ Aufidius at one door, Soldiers
                              at the other door⌐

2.1   *Enter Menenius with the two tribunes of the people*
       Sicinius and Brutus

MENENIUS The augurer tells me we shall have news
    tonight.

BRUTUS Good or bad?

MENENIUS Not according to the prayer of the people, for
    they love not Martius.   5

SICINIUS Nature teaches beasts to know their friends.

MENENIUS Pray you, who does the wolf love?

SICINIUS The lamb.

MENENIUS Ay, to devour him, as the hungry plebeians
    would the noble Martius.   10

BRUTUS He's a lamb indeed that baas like a bear.

MENENIUS He's a bear indeed that lives like a lamb. You
    two are old men. Tell me one thing that I shall ask you.

SICINIUS *and* BRUTUS Well, sir?

33.1–2 *Exeunt . . . other door*] OXFORD; *not in* F; *Exeunt.* ROWE
    2.1] F (*Actus Secundus.*)   1 augurer] F1 (Agurer), F2   14, 23, 26, 40 SICINIUS *and*
BRUTUS] OXFORD; *Both* F

30 **attended** waited for
31 **south . . . mills** This is a London, not a
    Roman, detail: there were four flour
    mills near the Globe on the south bank
    of the Thames. It also ties in appropri-
    ately with the play's 'corn' theme.
31–3 **bring . . . journey** Cf. 4.7.49–50; for
    good and ill this readiness to temporize
    is what distinguishes Aufidius from
    Coriolanus.
2.1 This scene is almost entirely of Shake-
    speare's invention, including Martius'
    ovation which is the first of several
    processional scenes: see Introduction,
    p. 99.

1 **augurer** Strictly 'augur', a Roman offi-
    cial who foretold the future by study-
    ing omens derived from the behaviour
    of birds or the entrails of sacrificial
    victims.
6 **Nature . . . friends** This sounds proverb-
    ial, like much of the plebeians' rhetoric;
    it is immediately contradicted, how-
    ever, by Sicinius' predatory suggestion
    that the wolf's love is for the lamb.
13 **old men** (implying that they should
    therefore be wise)
14, 23, 26, 40 SICINIUS *and* BRUTUS F's
    Both. suggests that they speak
    together, a habit that usually amuses

MENENIUS In what enormity is Martius poor in that you   15
  two have not in abundance?
BRUTUS He's poor in no one fault, but stored with all.
SICINIUS Especially in pride.
BRUTUS And topping all others in boasting.
MENENIUS This is strange now. Do you two know how   20
  you are censured here in the city—I mean of us o'th'
  right-hand file? Do you?
SICINIUS *and* BRUTUS Why, how are we censured?
MENENIUS Because you talk of pride now—will you not
  be angry?   25
SICINIUS *and* BRUTUS Well, well, sir, well?
MENENIUS Why, 'tis no great matter, for a very little thief
  of occasion will rob you of a great deal of patience.
  Give your dispositions the reins, and be angry at your
  pleasures—at the least, if you take it as a pleasure to   30
  you in being so. You blame Martius for being proud?
BRUTUS We do it not alone, sir.
MENENIUS I know you can do very little alone, for your
  helps are many, or else your actions would grow wondrous single. Your abilities are too infant-like for doing 35

---

17 with all] F3; withall FI   24 Because͟] F; ~—OXFORD   now—] CAPELL; ~, F
30 pleasures—at the least,] KITTREDGE; ~ (at the least) F; ~; at the least, THEOBALD
31 proud?] CAPELL; ~. F

audiences. To prevent them seeming foolish, their joint speeches are often divided (e.g. l. 23: SICINIUS Why? BRUTUS How are we censured?); but by stressing that, far from being far-sighted Machiavels, they are often at a loss and need to look at each other in order to improvise, 1977 RSC retained this joint speaking without making them seem clownish.

15 In ... in A characteristic Shakespearian repetition (Abbott § 407).
  enormity irregularity of conduct, vice
  poor The sense would seem to require 'rich' (which is how Brutus takes it), but 'poor' here means 'to be the worse for'.
17 with all FI's 'withall' could equally mean 'withal', but F3's reading is stronger
19 topping surpassing

boasting This is obviously untrue of Martius until 5.6.
21 censured judged, criticized
22 right-hand file right-wing, i.e. the patricians; cf. J. W. Fortescue in S. Lee and C. T. Onions, eds., *Shakespeare's England* (1916) i. 114: 'the place of honour to military men has always been the right of the line, and accordingly a captain always drew up his best and choicest men in the right hand files of his company'.
26 Well ... well? See 2.1.52 n. for Menenius' mockery of the Tribunes' fondness for this word.
27 'tis ... matter (if you do get angry)
27–8 a ... you a trifling occasion will be a thief to rob you ('of' being a genitive of definition; *OED* 23)
35 single playing on the senses 'solitary' and 'feeble'

much alone. You talk of pride. O that you could turn
your eyes toward the napes of your necks, and make
but an interior survey of your good selves! O that
you could!

SICINIUS *and* BRUTUS What then, sir?   40

MENENIUS Why, then you should discover a brace of un-
meriting, proud, violent, testy magistrates, alias fools,
as any in Rome.

SICINIUS Menenius, you are known well enough too.

MENENIUS I am known to be a humorous patrician, and   45
one that loves a cup of hot wine with not a drop of
allaying Tiber in't; said to be something imperfect in
favouring the first complaint, hasty and tinder-like
upon too trivial motion; one that converses more with
the buttock of the night than with the forehead of the   50
morning. What I think, I utter, and spend my malice
in my breath. Meeting two such wealsmen as you are,
I cannot call you Lycurguses. If the drink you give me

---

49 upon too] ROWE 1714; ~, to F   52–3 are, I...Lycurguses. If] SPEDDING *conj.* (*in*
Cambridge); are (I...*Licurgusses,*) if F; are—I...Lycurguses—if CAMBRIDGE

36–8 **turn...selves!** turn your eyes in-
wards to examine yourselves: cf. *Hamlet* 3.4.79, 'Thou turn'st mine eyes
into my very soul'.

42 **testy** irritable
magistrates...fools Cf. 2.1.67–76.
See Introduction, p. 40.

44 **known...enough** i.e. notorious

45 **humorous** whimsical

46 **hot** (a) mulled; (b) heating; cf. *As You
Like It* 2.3.50 (Kemball-Cook)?

47 **Tiber** Rome's river, hence 'water' in
general. Because of famine, in 1598 the
Stratford-upon-Avon council ordered
alehouses to sell watered beer in order
to conserve barley, and there was a
Royal Proclamation to the same effect
on 12 December 1608: cf. ll. 53–4.

47–8 **something...complaint** somewhat
hasty in deciding in favour of the
plaintiff (who speaks first)

48 **hasty and tinder-like** too quick-
tempered and ready to flare up
motion cause, provocation

49–51 **converses...morning** 'is more used
to staying up late at night than rising

early in the morning'. Menenius uses
his characteristic comic body imagery;
cf. *L.L.L.* 5.1.84 'in the posteriors of
this day'. Sir Toby Belch (*Twelfth Night*
2.3.1–9) and Falstaff (1 *Henry IV*
1.2.1 ff.) invert time in the same way.

51–2 **spend...breath** expend my resentment in words, i.e. harbour no grudges
wealsmen (a) men 'devoted to the public good' (*OED*) used ironically, (b)
possibly a play on their fondness for
the ejaculation 'well', cf. 2.1.14, 26,
44 and 64?

53 **Lycurguses** Lycurgus was the legend-
ary lawgiver of Sparta and the source
of the Renaissance ideal of a *stato
misto*, in which the power of competing social classes is carefully balanced;
he may also have been suggested here
by a comment in North's Plutarch that
he was an *innovator*: 'Lycurgus...
began to devise how to alter the whole
government of the common weal'.

53–4 **If...it** i.e. 'if I disagree with what
you say, I show it in my face'; cf. l.
47 n.

touch my palate adversely, I make a crooked face at it.
I cannot say your worships have delivered the matter   55
well, when I find the ass in compound with the major
part of your syllables. And though I must be content to
bear with those that say you are reverend grave men,
yet they lie deadly that tell you have good faces. If you
see this in the map of my microcosm, follows it that   60
I am known well enough too? What harm can your
bisson conspectuities glean out of this character, if I be
known well enough too?

BRUTUS Come, sir, come, we know you well enough.

MENENIUS You know neither me, yourselves, nor any-   65
thing. You are ambitious for poor knaves' caps and legs.
You wear out a good wholesome forenoon in hearing
a cause between an orange-wife and a faucet-seller,
and then rejourn the controversy of threepence to
a second day of audience. When you are hearing a   70

---

55 cannot...have] CAPELL; can...haue   F,   BROCKBANK; can't...have   THEOBALD;
can...have not COLLIER   59 tell you] F; tell you, you POPE   62 bisson] THEOBALD;
beesome F

---

55 **cannot** Brockbank argues that F's 'can' is meant sarcastically, but this is surely in parallel with 'cannot' in l. 53.

56–7 **the ass...syllables** i.e. 'a large element of folly in most of what you say'. Conjectures that Menenius is mocking either some aspect of Latin grammar or the use of 'as' in legal documents are not sufficiently grounded in the text.

59 **deadly** excessively (*OED adv.* 4), punning on 'grave' (l. 58)
tell report that
good playing on 'honest' and 'handsome'

60 **map...microcosm** the face, which charts what is happening in the 'little world' of the man

61, 63 **known well enough** Menenius indignantly echoes Sicinius' phrase at l. 44; then Brutus compounds the offence with 'you are well understood' at l. 78.

62 **bisson conspectuities** blear-eyed insights. 'Conspectuities' is one of

Menenius' nonce-words (Latin, *conspectus*); cf. 'empiricutic' (l. 114) and ' 'fidiussed' (l. 128). Perhaps he is a little tipsy in this scene: cf. l. 102 n.

62 **character** character-sketch. There was a vogue for collections of such sketches at the time *Coriolanus* was written, with Joseph Hall's *Characters of Vices and Virtues* actually appearing in 1608: cf. 5.4.17–26 n.

66 **caps and legs** doffing of caps (cf. 1.10.40.2–3 n.) and bows or curtsies

67 **wholesome** 'which might be spent more profitably' (Schmidt)

68 **orange-wife** woman who sells oranges
faucet-seller (a) seller of pegs for keg taps; (b) street seller of water (or wine) from a keg? Presumably such people might be rivals in quenching the thirst of the public: an appropriate example for Menenius to use.

69 **rejourn** adjourn, postpone

70 **audience** hearing. If Menenius decides cases too promptly, the Tribunes drag disputes out.

matter between party and party, if you chance to be
pinched with the colic, you make faces like mummers,
set up the bloody flag against all patience, and in roaring for a chamber-pot, dismiss the controversy bleeding,
the more entangled by your hearing. All the peace you   75
make in their cause is calling both the parties knaves.
You are a pair of strange ones.

BRUTUS Come, come, you are well understood to be a
perfecter giber for the table than a necessary bencher
in the Capitol.   80

MENENIUS Our very priests must become mockers if they
shall encounter such ridiculous subjects as you are.
When you speak best unto the purpose, it is not worth
the wagging of your beards, and your beards deserve
not so honourable a grave as to stuff a botcher's   85
cushion or to be entombed in an ass's pack-saddle. Yet
you must be saying Martius is proud, who, in a cheap
estimation, is worth all your predecessors since Deucalion, though peradventure some of the best of 'em
were hereditary hangmen. Good e'en to your worships.   90
More of your conversation would infect my brain,
being the herdsmen of the beastly plebeians. I will be
bold to take my leave of you.

82–3 are. When ... purpose, it] F4 (*subs.*) ROWE; ~, when ... ~. It FI   93.1 *He ...
aside.*] OXFORD; *Bru. and Scic. Aside.* F

71 **party** litigant
72 **faces ... mummers** grimaces like actors in a dumb-show or mime
73 **set ... flag** the flag signalling battle; cf. *Henry V* 1.2.101, *Caesar* 5.1.14
74 **bleeding** (a) unhealed (applied to 'controversy'), (b) urinating blood (applied to the Tribunes). Menenius is comically conflating the play's legal, military, and disease imagery.
79 **giber ... table** wit at the dinner-table
79–80 **necessary ... Capitol** indispensable member of the Senate; 'bencher' could also mean 'magistrate or judge' and 'bench' a court, cf. 3.1.108, 168.
82 **subjects** (a) creatures, (b) topics
82–3 **are. When ... purpose,** F's punctuation is possible but less pointed than Rowe's
84–6 **beards ... cushion** A hackneyed

joke; Clarendon compares Lyly's *Midas* (ed. Bond), 5.2.170, 'A dozen of beards, to stuffe two dozen of cushions', and *Much Ado* 3.2.42–3.
85 **botcher** mender of old clothes
87–8 **in ... estimation** at a conservative estimate
88–9 **Deucalion** The equivalent of Noah in Greek mythology.
90 **e'en** Literally 'evening' but it could be used any time after noon; he is bidding them farewell: cf. 4.6.22.
91 **conversation** (a) talk, (b) society (*OED* 5)
92 **being** i.e. 'you being'
herdsmen Imagery of herds and herdsmen, applied to the plebeians and Tribunes, contrasts with hunting and chivalric imagery applied to the patricians.

⌈*He leaves*⌉ *Brutus and Sicinius, who stand aside.*
Enter Volumnia, Virgilia, and Valeria

How now, my as fair as noble ladies—and the moon,
were she earthly, no nobler—whither do you follow   95
your eyes so fast?

VOLUMNIA Honourable Menenius, my boy Martius approaches. For the love of Juno, let's go.

MENENIUS Ha, Martius coming home?

VOLUMNIA Ay, worthy Menenius, and with most pros-   100
perous approbation.

MENENIUS (*throwing up his cap*) Take my cap, Jupiter, and
I thank thee! Hoo, Martius coming home?

VIRGILIA *and* VALERIA Nay, 'tis true.

VOLUMNIA Look, here's a letter from him. The state hath   105
another, his wife another, and I think there's one at
home for you.

MENENIUS I will make my very house reel tonight. A
letter for me?

VIRGILIA Yes, certain, there's a letter for you; I saw't.   110

MENENIUS A letter for me? It gives me an estate of seven
years' health, in which time I will make a lip at the
physician. The most sovereign prescription in Galen is

94–5 my . . . nobler—] CAMBRIDGE; (my . . . Noble) Ladyes, and . . . Earthly, no Nobler: F
102 (*throwing up his cap*)] KEIGHTLEY (*conj.* Johnson); *not in* F   104 VIRGILIA *and*
VALERIA] CAPELL (*subs.*); 2. *Ladies.* F; *Vol. Vir.* DYCE

93.1 **Sicinius** For F's spelling 'Scicinius',
see Introduction, p. 138.
94 **the moon** i.e. Diana, goddess of chastity: cf. 1.1.255. This is probably
addressed to Valeria, anticipating Martius' 'moon of Rome' at 5.3.65–7.
95–6 **follow . . . fast?** An affected phrase
that serves nonetheless as a cue for the
ladies.
98 **Juno** Chief goddess in the Rome pan-
theon, to whom Volumnia compares
herself at 4.2.56 (cf. 5.3.46 n.); consort of 'Jupiter', to whom Menenius
throws his cap (2.1.102).
100–1 **prosperous approbation** confirmed
success. The tempo of the scene now
rises excitedly as Menenius, Volumnia,
Valeria, and Virgilia cap each other's
lines, Menenius poses question after
question without waiting for answers,
the exit announced twice at ll. 98 and

130 is progressively postponed, there
are frequent contractions and staccato
outbursts of monosyllables, and Volumnia and Menenius rush to corrobor-
ate Valeria's 'there's wondrous things
spoke of him' (l. 134), overriding Vir-
gillia's caution.
102 **Take . . . Jupiter** See Introduction,
p. 96. Menenius' bonhomie, neologisms,
easy vulgarity, sentimentality, and occasional spitefulnesses (e.g., 5.2.62–5)
give him a touch of the *déclassé*.
111 **gives . . . estate** endows me with (a
typically patrician property image)
112 **make a lip at** mock, scorn; cf. 1.1.253
n.
113 **Galen** Like the reference to Cato
(1.5.30), an anachronism: Galen was
a famous physician of the second century AD who was still regarded as an
authority in the Renaissance.

but empiricutic and, to this preservative, of no better
report than a horse-drench. Is he not wounded? He was   115
wont to come home wounded.

VIRGILIA O, no, no, no!

VOLUMNIA O, he is wounded, I thank the gods for't!

MENENIUS So do I, too, if it be not too much. Brings a
victory in his pocket, the wounds become him.   120

VOLUMNIA On's brows, Menenius. He comes the third
time home with the oaken garland.

MENENIUS Has he disciplined Aufidius soundly?

VOLUMNIA Titus Lartius writes they fought together, but
Aufidius got off.   125

MENENIUS And 'twas time for him too, I'll warrant him
that. An he had stayed by him, I would not have been
so 'fidiussed for all the chests in Corioles and the gold
that's in them. Is the Senate possessed of this?

VOLUMNIA Good ladies, let's go. Yes, yes, yes. The Sen-   130
ate has letters from the general, wherein he gives my
son the whole name of the war. He hath in this action
outdone his former deeds doubly.

VALERIA In truth, there's wondrous things spoke of him.

MENENIUS Wondrous, ay, I warrant you; and not with-   135
out his true purchasing.

VIRGILIA The gods grant them true.

VOLUMNIA True? Pooh-whoo!

---

116 wounded.] POPE; ~? F   120 pocket, the] HANMER; ~? The F   121 brows, Menenius.] THEOBALD (*subs.*); ~: ~, F   128 'fidiussed] F (fiddious'd)   138 Pooh-whoo] F (pow
waw)

114 **empiricutic** A nonce-word, combin-
ing 'pharmaceutic' and 'empiric' (i.e.
experimental) to imply 'hit or miss,
mere quackery'.
  to this preservative compared to this
  means of preserving life and health
115 **horse-drench** draught of horse
medicine
119 **Brings a** if he brings
121 **On's brows** Referring not to 'wounds'
(despite 1.3.35 ff) but to 'victory',
which is not 'in his pocket' but 'on
his brows' in the shape of 'the oaken
garland' (for which, see 1.3.14–15 n.).
123 **disciplined ... soundly** thrashed sound-

ly as a punishment: a revealing phrase,
cf. Introduction, p. 59.
127 **An** if
128 **'fidiussed** (a) a nonce-word, making
the past participle of a verb from Aufidius' name, (b) playing on the legal
term 'fidejussor', one who goes bail for
another
129 **possessed** informed
132 **name** (a) honour, credit, (b) the cognomen, 'Coriolanus'?
136 **purchasing** deserving, achieving
138 **Pooh-whoo** An exclamation of
amused scorn, spelled 'pow waw' in F.

MENENIUS True? I'll be sworn they are true. Where is he
    wounded? (*To the Tribunes*) God save your good wor-   140
    ships. Martius is coming home. He has more cause to
    be proud. (*To Volumnia*) Where is he wounded?
VOLUMNIA I'th' shoulder and i'th' left arm. There will be
    large cicatrices to show the people when he shall stand
    for his place. He received in the repulse of Tarquin   145
    seven hurts i'th' body.
MENENIUS One i'th' neck and two i'th' thigh—there's
    nine that I know.
VOLUMNIA He had before this last expedition twenty-five
    wounds upon him.   150
MENENIUS Now it's twenty-seven. Every gash was an
    enemy's grave.
      A shout and flourish
    Hark, the trumpets.
VOLUMNIA
    These are the ushers of Martius. Before him
    He carries noise, and behind him he leaves tears.   155
    Death, that dark spirit, in's nervy arm doth lie,

140–1 wounded? ... worships.] THEOBALD (*subs.*); ~, ... ~? F   148 nine] F; ten THEO-
BALD *conj.*   152.1 *A shout and flourish*] *after l.* 153 *in* F

141–2 more ... proud This recalls their
  criticism of Martius at 2.1.18.
144 cicatrices scars
  when Volumnia says 'when,' not 'if '
145 his place i.e. the consulship; our first
  indication of Volumnia's plan for her
  son
  Tarquin Tarquinius Superbus, the last
  king of Rome, finally defeated at the
  battle of Lake Regillus in 496 BC,
  when Martius first attracted attention;
  cf. 2.2.86–94 and 1.3.13 n.
148 nine It misses the point to regularize
  this counting between Volumnia and
  Menenius because the comedy comes
  from the competitive insensitivity of
  their gloating.
152.1 *A ... flourish* This direction is
  pointed by Menenius' comment 'Hark,
  the trumpets', then Volumnia shifts
  into an incantatory four lines with the

last two a couplet, building a cre-
scendo of anticipation for the final
entry at 157.1, 'A Sennet'. Similar directions of audience attention can be
found at 5.3.19; 5.4.48, 51, 57.
154–7 These ... die F misdivides the first
  two lines into three short units because the compositor had too much
  space to fill at the bottom of a column
  but needed to keep the last two lines
  as a rhyming couplet.
154 ushers Cf. 1.3.48.1 n.
155 The rhythm here parallels the sense.
  In Kemble's productions (and the
  many that copied him) the speech was
  cut off here to provide an *exeunt* line,
  so that Volumnia and her party (and,
  more strangely, the two Tribunes)
  might join the victory ovation that
  immediately followed.
156 nervy sinewy

Which being advanced, declines; and then men die.
> *A sennet. Enter Cominius the general and Titus*
> *Lartius: between them Coriolanus crowned with an*
> *oaken garland, with captains and soldiers, and a Her-*
> *ald. Trumpets sound*

HERALD

Know, Rome, that all alone Martius did fight
Within Corioles' gates, where he hath won
With fame a name to 'Martius Caius'; these   160
In honour follows 'Coriolanus'.
Welcome to Rome, renownèd Coriolanus!
> *A flourish sounds*

ALL

Welcome to Rome, renownèd Coriolanus!

157.1–4] This edition; *A Sennet. Trumpets sound. Enter . . . Herauld.* F; *Trumpets sound a sennet. Enter . . . Herald.* OXFORD   *Lartius*] F (*Latius*). *Similarly spelled in* F *at* 3.1.0.2 *and for the five speech-prefixes following.* 160 Martius Caius] F; Caius Martius ROWE   161 Coriolanus] STEEVENS; *Martius Caius Coriolanus* F   162.1 *A flourish sounds*] F (*Sound. Flourish.*)

157 **advanced, declines** raised, falls. Martius' arm has become a fatal sword, cf. 1.7.77 n.
and . . . die The four heavy stresses give an effect of inevitability.

157.1–4 *A sennet . . . Trumpets sound* Though F puts these two directions together, as though duplicated, it seems likely that the first (a ceremonial flourish) would accompany rather than announce the soldiers' entrance, then 'Trumpets sound' would introduce the Herald's speech which follows. Beginning with Sheridan in 1752 and lasting till 1920 OV, this entry was staged as a spectacular 'Ovation': see Introduction, p. 118.

157.1–3 *Cominius . . . garland* 'The elaborate s.d. shows how Shakespeare wished this tremendous moment to be staged. "Coriolanus" (as F terms him from now on), who went to the war Cominius' lieutenant returns as the main hero, flanked on either side by Cominius and Lartius' (Kemball-Cook).

157.1–2 *Titus Lartius* See 1.10.75–6 n. and 2.2.36. Hibbard remarks that it looks 'as though II.1, or at least part

of it, was composed at a different time from Act I and II.2'; alternatively, it may have been an open option in the foul papers that Shakespeare would have expected to clear up for the prompt-book.

160 **With** along with
to in addition to
Martius Caius See 1.10.65 n.

160–1 **these . . . 'Coriolanus'** i.e. the name 'Coriolanus' follows these (the names 'Martius Caius') as an honorific. Volumnia teases him about this at l. 170, but in 5.3.171, 179–80 her antagonism to any honour that does not arise from herself emerges when she criticizes the honorific as a source of family-forgetting pride. F's extrametrical repetition of 'Martius Caius' in l. 161 is an obvious example of dittography, and 'the third foot is completed by a pause, to give due emphasis to the resounding name which follows' (Chambers).

162.1 *A . . . sounds* F's *Sound. Flourish.* (with a gap between the two words) is another example where a clarifying direction may have been added.

CORIOLANUS

No more of this, it does offend my heart.

Pray now, no more.

COMINIUS   Look, sir, your mother.

CORIOLANUS (*to Volumnia*)   O!   165

You have, I know, petitioned all the gods

For my prosperity!

   He kneels

VOLUMNIA   Nay, my good soldier, up,

My gentle Martius, worthy Caius,

And, by deed-achieving honour newly named—

What is it?—'Coriolanus' must I call thee?   170

   ⌈*He rises*⌉

But O, thy wife!

CORIOLANUS (*to Virgilia*) My gracious silence, hail.

Wouldst thou have laughed had I come coffined home,

That weep'st to see me triumph? Ah, my dear,

Such eyes the widows in Corioles wear,

And mothers that lack sons.

MENENIUS   Now the gods crown thee!   175

⌈CORIOLANUS⌉

And live you yet? (*To Valeria*) O my sweet lady, pardon.

---

167 *He kneels*] F (*Kneeles.*)   170 it? . . . must] F (it (*Coriolanus*) must)   170.1 *He rises*] COLLIER 1858 (*subs.*) *after* wife! l. 171; *after* l. 168, OXFORD   174 wear] F (were)   176 CORIOLANUS] THEOBALD; *Com.* F   *To Valeria*] THEOBALD; *not in* F; *before* And live OXFORD

164 **Look . . . mother** A cue to focus audience attention on this key relationship.

167 *He kneels* This is not in Plutarch. In Shakespeare's time it was customary for children to kneel when greeting their parents. Hence the shock when the situation is reversed at 5.3.56, 173.

169 **deed-achieving** won by deeds

171 **But . . . wife!** Either Coriolanus has forgotten his wife here and needs reminding or, more likely, his attention is already swinging to her away from the embarrassment of his mother's praise; cf. other occasions when Volumnia tries to appropriate Virgilia as part of her own persona: 1.3 (*passim*); 4.2.44; 5.3.156–7.

  gracious (a) lovely, (b) spiritually beneficent?

silence See Introduction, p. 102.

172–5 **Wouldst . . . sons** This passage shows Coriolanus' uneasy awareness of the compassion his upbringing has denied (cf. 4.4.2–6), and l. 175 may also contain an oblique, not wholly conscious criticism of his mother's contrasting freedom from distress (cf. 4.1.28–9): in 1977 RSC Alan Howard deliberately 'played it off Volumnia' (Daniell, p. 165).

173 **Ah, my dear** A strong expression of affection; surprisingly, the only other person Coriolanus addresses this way is Valeria at 5.3.67.

174 **eyes . . . wear** Cf. 5.3.38 for another example of this unusual idiom.

176 CORIOLANUS F's *Com.* is an easy error for manuscript *Cor.*, and the change of

VOLUMNIA

I know not where to turn. O, welcome home!
~~And welcome, general, and~~ you're welcome all.

MENENIUS

A hundred thousand welcomes! I could weep
And I could laugh, I am light and heavy. Welcome!   180
A curse begin at very root on's heart
That is not glad to see thee. You are three
That Rome should dote on. Yet, by the faith of men,
We have some old crab-trees here at home that will not
Be grafted to your relish. Yet welcome, warriors!   185
We call a nettle but a nettle, and
The faults of fools but folly.

COMINIUS Ever right.

CORIOLANUS Menenius, ever, ever.

HERALD

Give way there, and go on.

CORIOLANUS ⌈ *to Volumnia and Virgilia* ⌉

Your hand, and yours.   190

Ere in our own house I do shade my head
The good patricians must be visited,

---

181 begin at] F; begnaw at CRAIG; begnaw the WILSON   182 You] F2; Yon FI
189 Menenius, ever] F; ~ˏ ~ALEXANDER   190 (*to Volumnia and Virgilia*)] CAPELL (*subs.*);
not in F

---

speech-heading from *Mar.* to *Cor.* probably contributed to the misreading. There
is no case for Cominius to speak here.
176 **And . . . yet?** Cf. Introduction, p. 24
n. 2.

177–87 **I know . . . folly** F's mislineation
is almost certainly caused by the
compositor's attempt to stretch the lines
to fill the rest of the page, the following
page having already been set up.
180 **light and heavy** joyful and sad
182 **You** F2's alteration of F1's 'Yon'
agrees better with 'your', l. 185
183, 184 **by the . . . We have** The metre
requires that these two phrases be
slurred.
184 **crab-trees** i.e. the Tribunes, who are
compared to sour crab-apple trees
185 **grafted . . . relish** altered (as a crab-
tree may be grafted to bear sweet

apples) to your taste (both to your way
of thinking and to a liking for you)
186–7 **We . . . folly** i.e. 'nuisances just
have to be accepted for what they are':
Menenius intends both 'nettles' and
'fools' to apply to the Tribunes, but the
context allows the latter to suppose
that, though he intends 'nettles' to
apply to them, he means himself by
'fools', a sly ambiguity that Cominius
uses for placation and that Martius
enjoys sardonically. Cf. Proverbs. 14:
24, 'the foolishness of fools is folly'.
190 **Give . . . on** Another example of the
play's use of a delayed exit to focus
audience attention, in this case on
Coriolanus' intervening exchange with
his mother in which he clearly states
his dislike for the political ambition she
has for him.
Your . . . yours See Introduction, p. 102.

From whom I have received not only greetings,
But with them change of honours.

VOLUMNIA   I have lived
To see inherited my very wishes,   195
And the buildings of my fancy. Only
There's one thing wanting, which I doubt not but
Our Rome will cast upon thee.

CORIOLANUS   Know, good mother,
I had rather be their servant in my way
Than sway with them in theirs.

COMINIUS   On, to the Capitol.   200

A flourish of cornetts. Exeunt in state, as before,
⌈*all but*⌉ *Brutus and Sicinius, who come forward*

BRUTUS
All tongues speak of him, and the bleared sights
Are spectacled to see him. Your prattling nurse
Into a rapture lets her baby cry
While she chats him; the kitchen malkin pins
Her richest lockram 'bout her reechy neck,   205

---

194 change] F; charge THEOBALD   200.1 A ... cornetts] OXFORD; *Flourish. Cornets.* F
200.2 all ... forward] THEOBALD (subs.); *Enter Brutus and Sicinius.* F

194 **change of honours** (a) fresh honours, (b) a new name?

195–6 **inherited ... fancy** i.e. 'come into possession of what I had wished for and imagined'. Like Menenius at l. 111, Volumnia uses a patrician property image for ambition: she sees her son as an heir who has come into the estate she had only dared hope would be his.

200 **sway with** (a) rule over, (b) go along with

200.1 *A ... cornetts* F again has the possibly duplicate form *Flourish. Cornets.* Nineteenth-century productions invariably ended the first of their three acts with this triumphant exit to the Capitol.

200.2 *who ... forward* F puts *Enter Brutus and Sicinius*, though at l. 93.1 it had *Bru. and Scic. Aside.* The only difficulty with *come forward* is that Brutus then gives the detailed description of the crowds welcoming Coriolanus that he has had no opportunity to see.

In production it is easy to have him slip out and return before 'crab-trees', l. 184 (his gloomy return might even prompt that remark).

201 **sights** eyesights

202 **spectacled** i.e. bespectacled. This is an anachronism, but the whole description is of a very Elizabethan crowd: cf. *Richard II* 5.2.5–21; *Caesar* 1.1.37–51. The sneering attitude to the women and priests in the crowd is very 'Roman', however.
Your The impersonal 'that I am talking of'; cf. 1.1.125 n., 5.4.12

203 **rapture** fit, paroxysm (*OED sb.* 5c)

204 **chats** gossips about
kitchen malkin slut (diminutive of Maud) who works in the kitchen

205 **lockram** coarse linen (named after a Breton village, *OED*); 'richest lockram' is thus an oxymoron
reechy greasy, sweat-stained; with a sound-play on 'richest' to emphasize the incongruity

Clamb'ring the walls to eye him. Stalls, bulks, windows
Are smothered up, leads filled and ridges horsed
With variable complexions, all agreeing
In earnestness to see him. Seld-shown flamens
Do press among the popular throngs, and puff   210
To win a vulgar station. Our veiled dames
Commit the war of white and damask in
Their nicely guarded cheeks to th' wanton spoil
Of Phoebus' burning kisses. Such a pother
As if that whatsoever god who leads him   215
Were slily crept into his human powers
And gave him graceful posture.

SICINIUS   On the sudden
I warrant him consul.

BRUTUS   Then our office may
During his power go sleep.

---

213 guarded] WILSON (*conj.* Lettsom); gawded F; gauded BROCKBANK   216, 245
human] F (humane), ROWE

206–9 Cf. Thomas Dekker's description of
James I's coronation procession
through London: 'the streets seemed to
be paved with men; stalls instead of
rich wares were set out for the children; open casements filled up with
women': John Nichols, *The Progresses,
Processions, and Magnificent Festivities
of King James the First* (1828), i. 342.
206 **Clamb'ring ... windows** This line is
too long for the folio double-column
format, so F divides it.
  bulks frameworks projecting from the
front of shops (*OED* 3)
207 **leads** lead-covered roofs (cf. 4.6.86)
  ridges horsed roof ridges with spectators sitting astride them
208 **variable complexions** various types;
'complexions' refers to the mixture of
the four basic 'humours'—sanguine,
choleric, melancholy, phlegmatic—
which were thought to constitute
character.
209 **Seld-shown flamens** priests rarely
seen in public
211 **vulgar station** place among the
crowd
  veiled veiled (a) for the sake of mod-

esty, (b) to protect their complexions
212 **war ... damask** A Petrarchan commonplace for women's complexions:
'damask' is pink, the colour of a Damask rose; cf. *Lucrece* 71–2, *Shrew*
4.6.31.
213 **nicely guarded** carefully protected;
F's 'gawded' may also mean 'covered
with cosmetics', but 'guarded' agrees
better with 'veiled'; cf. *Two Gentlemen*
4.4.150, 'sun-expelling mask'. A sun-
tan was socially unfashionable in
Shakespeare's day.
213–14 **spoil ... kisses** i.e. risk of sun-
burn. Another Petrarchan conceit
(used sardonically by Brutus),
'Phoebus' being the sun god.
214 **pother** turmoil, commotion
215 **As ... him** 'As if that god who leads
him, whatsoever god that be...'
(Johnson); cf. l. 262, 'As to Jove's
statue'.
217 **graceful posture** 'a bearing of divine
impressiveness'; Malone compares
Antony 4.9.24–6, 'He hath fought
today | As if a god, in hate of man-
kind, had | Destroyed in such a
shape'. Cf. Introduction, p. 107.

SICINIUS

   He cannot temp'rately transport his honours   220
   From where he should begin and end, but will
   Lose those he hath won.

BRUTUS   In that there's comfort.

SICINIUS   Doubt not
   The commoners, for whom we stand, but they
   Upon their ancient malice will forget
   With the least cause these his new honours, which   225
   That he will give them make I as little question
   As he is proud to do't.

BRUTUS   I heard him swear,
   Were he to stand for consul, never would he
   Appear i'th' market-place nor on him put
   The napless vesture of humility,   230
   Nor, showing, as the manner is, his wounds
   To th' people, beg their stinking breaths.

SICINIUS   'Tis right.

BRUTUS

   It was his word. O, he would miss it rather

---

221 and end] F; t'an end JOHNSON *conj.*; to the end HUDSON (*conj.* Seymour)   222 not‸]
KNIGHT; ~, F   230 napless] F (Naples), ROWE

---

220 **temp'rately ... honours** Cf. 4.7.36–
7, 'he could not | Carry his honours
even': 'transport' means both 'carry'
and 'exploit, develop'.

221 **From ... end** 'from what is actually
granted to an appropriate goal': i.e.
Coriolanus will not only overestimate
the honours paid him but, in trying to
push them too far, will lose even them

222–3 **Doubt ... they** 'doubt not but that
the commoners, whom we represent'

224 **Upon ... malice** out of their former
animosity

225 **which** i.e. which cause

227 **As** as that

230 **napless ... humility** 'Napless' means
threadbare; North's 'poor gown' and
'mean apparel' arise from a misunderstanding of Plutarch's comment that
candidates for the consulship wore a
toga with no tunic beneath, as a con-
venience for displaying scars and *per-*

haps as a sign of humility, cf. 'stand
naked', 2.2.136 n. Shakespeare seems
to have equated North's gloss with the
sheet worn by public penitents in Elizabethan times to create a powerful
revulsion in Coriolanus that is in
neither Plutarch nor North. See Introduction, p. 66.

232–9 **'Tis ... out** In F Compositor A
could well have spread the first four
lines to gain space but he had no
bibliographical reason to render Sicinius' subsequent verse as prose. It is
reasonable to suppose that the manuscript copy distinguished between
verse and prose only intermittently
and often unclearly, especially in the
Tribunes' speeches, and that the compositors could not always distinguish
between them.

233–4 **miss ... carry**   do   without ...
obtain

Than carry it, but by the suit of the gentry to him,
And the desire of the nobles.

SICINIUS   I wish no better   235
Than have him hold that purpose, and to put it
In execution.

BRUTUS   'Tis most like he will.

SICINIUS
It shall be to him then, as our good wills,
A sure destruction.

BRUTUS   So it must fall out
To him, or our authority's for an end.   240
We must suggest the people in what hatred
He still hath held them; that to's power he would
Have made them mules, silenced their pleaders,
And dispropertied their freedoms, holding them
In human action and capacity   245
Of no more soul nor fitness for the world
Than camels in the war, who have their provand
Only for bearing burdens, and sore blows
For sinking under them.

SICINIUS   This, as you say, suggested
At some time when his soaring insolence   250

---

240 authority's‸ for an end.] HIBBARD (*conj.* Thirlby); Authorities, ~~~. F; authorities.
For an end, POPE; authority's at an end; THIRLBY *conj.* (*in* Furness)   247 the] HANMER;
their F

234–5 **gentry ... nobles**   This   reflects
   English class divisions, rather than
   Roman;   cf.   3.1.0.1 n.,   l.   146,
   and 'commons',   'commoners'   at
   3.3.14 and 5.6.70.1–2.
234 **but ... him** 'in any other way than
   at the suit of the patricians' (Gomme)
238 **as ... wills** as our interest demands;
   'good' is a noun, in apposition to 'a
   sure destruction', l. 239
240 **To ... end** Hibbard's emendation is
   neater than the usual reading, 'To him
   or our authorities. For an end'; 'for'
   means 'destined for', as in *Antony*
   5.2.190. The more usual reading provides an interesting parallel with Martius' own perception at 3.1.111–14,
   however.

241 **suggest** suggest to, persuade
242 **still** always
244 **dispropertied** (a) dispossessed them of
   their freedom, as a person may be
   legally dispossessed of property (a legal
   phrase), (b) deprived of their essential
   nature?
247 **the** Brockbank's argument that F's
   'their' is an anticipation of 'their' later
   in the line seems most probable.
   Neither Chambers's suggestion that
   'their' refers to the patricians, nor Oxford's that it stands for impersonal
   'your' adjusted to indirect speech, is as
   plausible.
   provand provender, food
249 **them** i.e. burdens
   suggested insinuated

Shall touch the people—which time shall not want
If he be put upon't, and that's as easy
As to set dogs on sheep—will be his fire
To kindle their dry stubble, and their blaze
Shall darken him for ever.
    Enter a Messenger
BRUTUS   What's the matter?   255
MESSENGER
You are sent for to the Capitol.
'Tis thought that Martius shall be consul.
I have seen the dumb men throng to see him,
And the blind to hear him speak. Matrons flung gloves,
Ladies and maids their scarves and handkerchiefs,   260
Upon him as he passed. The nobles bended
As to Jove's statue, and the commons made
A shower and thunder with their caps and shouts.
I never saw the like.
BRUTUS   Let's to the Capitol,
And carry with us ears and eyes for th' time,   265
But hearts for the event.
SICINIUS   Have with you.   *Exeunt*

2.2 *Enter two Officers, to lay cushions, as it were in the Capitol*

FIRST OFFICER Come, come, they are almost here. How many stand for consulships?

251 touch] HANMER; teach F; reach THEOBALD   253 his] F; as CAPELL; the POPE

251 **touch** (a) threaten (a fencing term), (b) inflame, cf. *Henry V* 3.0.32–3. F's 'teach', meaning either 'teach the people the time (to revolt)' or 'give the people a reason (for revolt)', is also possible, but 'touch' (as in 'touchwood' or 'touch-paper') looks forward to the 'fire . . . kindle . . . blaze' of ll. 253–4, a major image in the play.
251–2 **which . . . upon't** 'which time is sure to come if he is provoked to it' (i.e. 'insolence', l. 250)
253–4 **his . . . stubble** 'the spark that setting him alight, will then kindle the people like dry stubble'. Both Coriola-

nus and the people are to be inflamed; cf. 2.3.186–7.
255 **darken** extinguish (as sunlight can put out a fire)
265 **carry . . . time** i.e. be alertly pragmatic. This is a characteristic they share with Aufidius, cf. 1.11.31–3 n.
266 **But . . . event** but committed to the outcome (i.e. the political conflagration they have just planned)
   Have with you (a) I agree, (b) let's go
2.2.0.1 **two Officers** These civil servants, familiar with the vagaries of the 'great', are another facet of the prismatic series of comments Shakespeare provides on

SECOND OFFICER Three, they say, but 'tis thought of
everyone Coriolanus will carry it.

FIRST OFFICER That's a brave fellow, but he's vengeance   5
proud and loves not the common people.

SECOND OFFICER Faith, there hath been many great men
that have flattered the people who ne'er loved them;
and there be many that they have loved they know not
wherefore, so that if they love they know not why, they   10
hate upon no better a ground. Therefore for Coriolanus
neither to care whether they love or hate him mani-
fests the true knowledge he has in their disposition,
and out of his noble carelessness lets them plainly see't.

FIRST OFFICER If he did not care whether he had their   15
love or no he waved indifferently 'twixt doing them
neither good nor harm; but he seeks their hate with
greater devotion than they can render it him, and leaves
nothing undone that may fully discover him their opposite. Now to seem to affect the malice and displeasure   20
of the people is as bad as that which he dislikes, to
flatter them for their love.

SECOND OFFICER He hath deserved worthily of his country,

2.2.7 hath] F1; have F4

his protagonist. Their comments draw
on Plutarch's 'Comparison between
Alcibiades and Coriolanus' (see Bullough, pp. 482, 544–5).
2.2.0.1 **cushions** Cf. 3.1.103 and especially Aufidius' comment that Coriolanus
may not be able to adapt from 'th'
casque to th' cushion', 4.7.43. Brockbank suggests that the cushions would
be of seat-size, like those in Parliament.

2 **stand for consulships** i.e. for selection
as the Senate's nominees, not for election by the people; see Introduction,
p. 41.
5 **vengeance** exceedingly, frightfully
7 **hath** The use of 'there is' or 'hath'
before a plural subject is common in
the period.
8–9 **who ... them ... they** Disagreeing
with Brockbank, I think 'who' refers
to 'great men' and 'them' to 'the
people', though 'they' in l. 9 does refer
to 'the people'. Such pronoun shifts

are common in Shakespeare, especially
in this play.
13 **in** of
14 **noble carelessness** (a) The speaker intends this to mean 'highminded *sprez-
zatura* and indifference to public
opinion', but (b) it also carries a negative shadow of 'aristocratic lack of sympathy'.
16 **waved** would waver (*OED v.* 2); using
an indicative for the subjunctive
(Abbott §361)
  indifferently impartially
16–17 **'twixt ... harm** Two constructions
are confused, 'he wavered indifferently
'twixt good and harm' and 'doing
them neither good nor harm' (Cambridge).
19 **discover** disclose: a legal term referring
to the process used before a trial to
bring into the open the evidence to be
used by the adverse party
19–20 **opposite** adversary, opponent
20 **seem to affect** give the impression of
preferring

and his ascent is not by such easy degrees as those
who, having been supple and courteous to the people,　25
bonneted, without any further deed to have them at all
into their estimation and report. But he hath so planted
his honours in their eyes and his actions in their hearts
that for their tongues to be silent and not confess so
much were a kind of ingrateful injury. To report other-　30
wise were a malice that, giving itself the lie, would
pluck reproof and rebuke from every ear that heard it.
FIRST OFFICER No more of him. He's a worthy man. Make
　way, they are coming.

> *A sennet. Enter the Patricians, and Sicinius and*
> *Brutus, the tribunes of the people, lictors before*
> *them; Coriolanus, Menenius, Cominius the consul.*
> ⌈*The Patricians take their places and sit.*⌉ *Sicinius*
> *and Brutus take their places by themselves.*
> *Coriolanus stands*

MENENIUS

Having determined of the Volsces, and　　　35

---

24 ascent] F1 (assent), F2   25–6 people, bonneted,] F; ~_∧ ~, HANMER; ~, unbon-
netted_∧ JOHNSON *conj.*   26–7 bonneted, ... report.] F (*subs.*); bonneted into their
estimation and report, without ... at all: HUDSON   26 deed ... at all] F; deed at all
to have them CAMBRIDGE (*anon, conj.*)   have] F; heave POPE   34.1–2 *Sicinius and
Brutus*] OXFORD; *not in* F   34.4 *The Patricians ... sit*] OXFORD; *not in* F

---

24 **ascent ... degrees** F1's 'assent' makes
　inferior sense and does not agree so
　well with 'degrees', meaning 'steps'
26–7 **bonneted ... report** 'went cap-in-
　hand and, without doing anything else
　whatever to earn them, won popu-
　larity and a good repute' (after Hib-
　bard). This comment prepares the
　audience for Coriolanus' behaviour at
　2.3.91–8 and Volumnia's advice at
　3.2.75–8; cf. 1.10.40.2–3 n.
34.1–6 **A ... stands** This procession and
　meeting of the Roman Senate might be
　staged with visual parallels to those of
　the Volscian Senate in 1.2.
34.2 **lictors** Attendants like mace-bearers
　who announced the entry of Roman
　magistrates by carrying before them
　the *fasces*, rods bound up with an axe
　in the middle which signified that
　Rome's strength lay in unity.
34.6 ***Coriolanus stands*** Because this dir-

ection seems to be contradicted by
'*Coriolanus rises*' at l. 64, Brockbank
suggests that it may be a prompter's
annotation. However, Menenius' 'thus
stood for his country' (l. 39) seems to
play off the direction, and Coriolanus
after all is a soldier not a regular senator, as seating him with the others
would suggest. As usual, he towers like
a 'sea-mark' separate from everyone
else; and it would be logical to motion
him politely to sit at l. 46, as his
sponsor, Menenius, sits down and First
Senator bids Cominius rise to give the
customary panegyric.
35–6 **Having ... Lartius** As Granville-
　Barker notes, these initial comments
　enlarge the situation in a typically
　Shakespearian way by making it seem
　in medias res, an 'after-meeting' (l. 37);
　'determined of' means 'settled what to
　do about'.

To send for Titus Lartius, it remains
As the main point of this our after-meeting
To gratify his noble service that
Hath thus stood for his country. Therefore please you,
Most reverend and grave elders, to desire   40
The present consul and last general
In our well-found successes to report
A little of that worthy work performed
By Martius Caius Coriolanus, whom
We met here both to thank and to remember   45
With honours like himself.

⌈*Coriolanus sits*⌉

FIRST SENATOR   Speak, good Cominius.
Leave nothing out for length, and make us think
Rather our state's defective for requital
Than we to stretch it out.
(*To the Tribunes*)   Masters o'th' people,
We do request your kindest ears and, after,   50
Your loving motion toward the common body
To yield what passes here.

SICINIUS   We are convented
Upon a pleasing treaty, and have hearts
Inclinable to honour and advance

---

44 Martius Caius] F; Caius Martius ROWE   45 met] F; meet HANMER   46 *Coriolanus sits*] NEILSON; *not in* F   48 state's] F4; states F1   50 ears and, after,] F3 (*subs.*); eares: ~ ᴧ ~ ᴧ F1; ears, ~ ᴧ ~ ᴧ BROCKBANK

---

38 **gratify** show gratitude for, reward
39 **stood for** defended, stood up for
42 **well-found** (a) fortunate, (b) found to be good, of approved report; cf. *All's Well* 2.1.101 (Brockbank)?
45 **met** assembled, convened (rather than 'encountered'); 'whom' depends on 'thank' and 'remember'
  remember acknowledge our debt to
46 **like himself** becoming to such a person
47 **for length** for fear of speaking too long
48–9 **Rather ... out** 'That our state has not means to reward him fully rather than that we are unwilling to strain it to do so'; 'stretch it out' picks up 'Leave nothing out for length', because, ironically, part of the reward is this very panegyric.

50 **after** afterward
51 **motion ... body** influence with the ordinary people; cf. *Antony* 1.4.44 for this meaning of 'common body'. By omitting the comma behind 'after' Brockbank gets the meaning 'in accordance with your solicitous disposition towards the common people,' with 'yield to' meaning 'report to'.
52 **yield** assent to
  convented (a) convened, summoned to meet, (b) agreed on (*OED* 4, a legal term)?
53 **treaty** matter to be treated of (*OED* 2). Sicinius' careful choice of words keeps open the possibility of negotiation, which Brutus' blunt continuation makes clear.

The theme of our assembly.
BRUTUS   Which the rather   55
    We shall be blessed to do if he remember
    A kinder value of the people than
    He hath hereto prized them at.
MENENIUS   That's off, that's off.
    I would you rather had been silent. Please you
    To hear Cominius speak?
BRUTUS   Most willingly,   60
    But yet my caution was more pertinent
    Than the rebuke you give it.
MENENIUS   He loves your people,
    But tie him not to be their bedfellow.
    Worthy Cominius, speak.
        Coriolanus rises and offers to go away
    (*To Coriolanus*)   Nay, keep your place.
⌈FIRST⌉ SENATOR
    Sit, Coriolanus. Never shame to hear   65
    What you have nobly done.
CORIOLANUS   Your honours' pardon,
    I had rather have my wounds to heal again
    Than hear say how I got them.
BRUTUS   Sir, I hope
    My words disbenched you not?
CORIOLANUS   No, sir, yet oft
    When blows have made me stay I fled from words.   70
    You soothed not, therefore hurt not; but your people,

65, 121, 129 FIRST SENATOR] ROWE; *Senat.* F   66 honours'] THEOBALD; Honors F;
honour's ROWE

56 **blessed** happy, glad
56–7 **remember . . . people** remember to
    evaluate the people more generously
58 **off** off the point, impertinent (in both
    senses)
62 **your** Menenius may be using the im-
    personal form, 'the people we are talk-
    ing about', or be identifying them with
    the Tribunes positively, 'the people
    you care about', or negatively, 'those
    people of yours' (after Brockbank).
63 **bedfellow** intimate; again a submerged
    sexual image, contradicting those of

1.7.29–32, 4.5.115–16
64 *offers* prepares to, tries to. This is not
    a gesture of politeness, however; quite
    the contrary.
69 **disbenched** caused you to leave your
    seat; significantly, the only instance in
    OED of the general use of a term ap-
    plied usually to losing one's member-
    ship in the Inns of Court. Sicinius and
    · Brutus resemble the lawyers who op-
    posed James I in Parliament; see Intro-
    duction, p. 40
71 **soothed** flattered; cf. 1.10.44 n.

I love them as they weigh—

MENENIUS   ~~Pray now, sit down.~~

CORIOLANUS

I had rather have one scratch my head i'th' sun
When the alarum were struck than idly sit
To hear my nothings monstered.   *Exit*

MENENIUS   Masters of the people,   75
Your multiplying spawn how can he flatter—
That's thousand to one good one—when you now see
He had rather venture all his limbs for honour
Than one on's ears to hear it? Proceed, Cominius.

COMINIUS

I shall lack voice; the deeds of Coriolanus   80
Should not be uttered feebly. It is held
That valour is the chiefest virtue, and
Most dignifies the haver. If it be,
The man I speak of cannot in the world
Be singly counterpoised. At sixteen years,   85
When Tarquin made a head for Rome, he fought
Beyond the mark of others. Our then dictator,
Whom with all praise I point at, saw him fight

---

75 *Exit*] F (*Exit Coriolanus*)   76–9 flatter— ... one— ... it?] CAPELL (*subs.*); ~? ...
~, ... ~. F; ~, ... ~? ... ~. ROWE   79 one on's] F3; on ones FI

---

72 **as . . . weigh** according to their worth
75 **monstered** (a) shown forth (French 'mon(s)trer'), (b) monstrously exaggerated, picking up the 'monster' imagery applied to the plebeians
76 **multiplying spawn** A literal translation of Latin *proletarii*; 'The lower classes of Romans were known as *proletarii*, good only to breed children (*proles*)' (Chambers).
79 **on's** of his
80 ff. **I shall . . .** Hibbard calls this 'laus' or formal speech of praise 'one of the finest pieces of epic poetry in English'; but, noting its reifications of Coriolanus and almost grotesque images of carnage at ll. 105–8, 117–18 (and perhaps nervous of their audiences' toleration of long formal addresses), modern directors often undercut it, either by making it comic or, more interestingly, by suggesting discomfort behind Cominius' exaggerations.

81–3 **It . . . haver** This comment on Roman values is closely based on Plutarch and is the ideological heart of the play.
85 **singly counterpoised** equalled by any other single person
   sixteen years North has 'being but a stripling'
86 **Tarquin** Cf. 1.3.13 n.
   made a head for raised an army against
87 **Beyond the mark of** beyond the capacity of. The image is from archery, where the 'mark' is the target.
   Our then dictator Not named in Plutarch, but according to Livy it was Aulus Posthumus Regillenius who was appointed in 499 BC after the battle of Lake Regillus.
88 **Whom . . . at** Chambers notes that this is 'a reminiscence of the common phrase in Latin *quem honoris causa nomino*'

When with his Amazonian chin he drove
The bristled lips before him. He bestrid   90
An o'erpressed Roman, and, i'th' consul's view,
Slew three opposers. Tarquin's self he met,
And struck him on his knee. In that day's feats,
When he might act the woman in the scene,
He proved best man i'th' field, and for his meed   95
Was brow-bound with the oak. His pupil age
Man-entered thus, he waxèd like a sea,
And in the brunt of seventeen battles since
He lurched all swords of the garland. For this last
Before and in Corioles, let me say   100
I cannot speak him home. He stopped the fliers,
And by his rare example màde the coward
Turn terror into sport. As weeds before

89 chin] F3; Shinne F1   103 weeds] F; waves ROWE

89 **Amazonian** beardless (the Amazons being a tribe of female warriors in classical myth); cf. l. 94 n. and 1.3. 5–9. The Romans did not consider a boy without facial hair (*impubes*) an adult.
90 **bestrid** stood over with legs astride. Brockbank notes that it derives from North's mistranslation of 'standing before' to 'straight bestrid', cf. 4.5.119 n.
92–3 **Tarquin's ... knee** This detail is added by Shakespeare; it contributes to the irony of the Tribunes' accusations against Martius at 3.3.1–2, 64–5.
93 **on his knee** on to his knee(s); cf. Introduction, p. 103.
94 **might ... scene** (a) was of an age to act a woman's role (his voice being unbroken, and boys acting the women's parts on the Elizabethan 'scene'), (b) young enough to have been excused for weeping at such sights?
95 **meed** reward
96 **brow-bound ... oak** See 1.3.14–15 n.
96–7 **His ... thus** (a) 'having started his apprenticeship in the style of one who had already completed it' (Hibbard), (b) 'being initiated into manhood while still in his minority' (Cambridge)
97 **waxèd ... sea** Usually an ominous

image in Shakespeare; cf. *Romeo* 5.3.37–9.
98 **brunt** (a) shock, violence, (b) assault, charge (*OED* 2): Martius is always on the attack
seventeen battles A number invented by Shakespeare that was probably suggested, as Gordon notes, by the seventeen *years* that Plutarch says Martius had been a soldier (which would put him in his early thirties at the time of the play).
99 **lurched ... garland** Probably (a) 'easily won the victor's crown from all competing soldiers' (where *lurch* means 'to gain an easy and sweeping victory at cards', *OED sb.*¹ 2), though possibly (b) 'robbed all the other soldiers of the victory garland' (where *lurch* means 'to get a start of (a person) so as to prevent him from obtaining a fair share of food, profit, etc.' (*OED*, *v.*¹ 2). See Introduction, pp. 3, 88 n. 2.
99–112 **For ... planet** To get this mythologizing rhetoric into perspective, one must realize that Cominius was not present at Corioles, whereas the audience has seen what actually happened there. Significantly, no mention is made of Titus Lartius, who saved the day.
101 **speak him home** find words to describe him adequately

A vessel under sail, so men obeyed
And fell below his stem. His ~~sword, death's stamp,~~   105
~~Where it did mark,~~ it took. From face to foot
He was a thing of blood, whose every motion
Was timed with dying cries. Alone he entered
The mortal gate of th' city, which he painted
With shunless destiny, aidless came off,   110
And with a sudden reinforcement struck
Corioles like a planet. Now all's his.
When by and by the din of war gan pierce
His ready sense, then straight his doubled spirit
Requickened what in flesh was fatigate,   115

---

106 took. ... foot₌ STEEVENS (*conj.* Tyrwhitt); tooke₌ ... ~: F, HIBBARD (*subs.*)
109 he₌] F; ~, OXFORD   110 destiny] FI; defamy F2

---

105 **stem** prow. This slightly incongruous
nautical imagery also appears at 4.1.
6–7, 4.5.62–3, and, most notably, at
5.3.74.
stamp tool or die for stamping a mark
on softer material

106 **took** (a) made its mark (following up
the 'stamp' metaphor), (b) destroyed?
took ... foot F's original punctuation
'took ... foot', has been defended,
most recently by Hibbard who sees it
as analogous to *Macbeth* 1.2.22, 'Till
he unseamed him from the nave to th'
chops'; but the rhythm of 'Where it
did mark, it took' re-enacts the
meaning; while the extremity of 'From
face to foot | He was a thing of blood'
agrees with Cominius' equally vivid 'as
he were flayed', 1.7.22: cf. the description of Pyrrhus in *Hamlet* 2.2.459–60:
'Head to foot | Now is he total gules,
horridly tricked | With blood of fa-
thers, mothers, daughters, sons, ...'

107 **thing** Cf. 4.5.117, 4.6.94, 4.7.42,
5.4.14, 22. This use of 'thing' suggests
both the difficulty of characterizing
Coriolanus and a dehumanizing reifi-
cation of him. It is also used contemptuously once of Sicinius, 3.1.180, and
several times of the plebeians, 3.2.9,
4.6.70, 155, 5.2.101.

108 **timed with** regularly accompanied by
(like clockwork)

109 **mortal** (a) threatening death to Coriolanus, (b) because it was the entrance

by which Coriolanus brought death
into the city

109–10 **painted | With shunless destiny**
marked with blood for a destiny it
could not avoid (like the red crosses
that identified houses stricken with
plague). Oxford's suggestion that it
was Coriolanus rather than the gate of
Corioles that was 'painted ... destiny'
is an attractive one that agrees with
the description of him covered with
blood but is grammatically awkward
in that it requires 'which' to mean
'from which'.

111 **reinforcement** (a) renewed assault,
(b) the troops who eventually went to
his aid?

112 **like ... planet** (a) like a thunderbolt
(Chambers), (b) like the malignant influence of a planet (which was thought
to bring plague)? Hibbard suggests that
the planet here 'is indubitably Mars'.
Now all's his. Wilson defends F's punctuation as meaning 'No sooner is all
his, when ...' This is possible, but as
the 'when ...' clause is followed by a
'then ...' clause, it creates a rhetorically clumsy sentence, besides losing
the authentically epic effect of 'Now
all's his' as a complete unit that creates the sense of a battle lull.

114 **ready** (a) keen, (b) eager
doubled i.e. doubled in strength

115 **Requickened** revivified, reanimated
fatigate weary

And to the battle came he, where he did
Run reeking o'er the lives of men as if
'Twere a perpetual spoil; and till we called
Both field and city ours he never stood
To ease his breast with panting.

MENENIUS　　　　　　　　　Worthy man.　　　　120

⌈FIRST⌉ SENATOR
He cannot but with measure fit the honours
Which we devise him.

COMINIUS　　　　　　Our spoils he kicked at,
And looked upon things precious as they were
The common muck of the world. He covets less
Than misery itself would give, rewards　　　125
His deeds with doing them, and is content
To spend the time to end it.

MENENIUS　　　　　　　He's right noble.
Let him be called for.

⌈FIRST⌉ SENATOR　Call Coriolanus.

OFFICER　He doth appear.　　　　130
　　　Enter Coriolanus

MENENIUS
The Senate, Coriolanus, are well pleased
To make thee consul.

CORIOLANUS　　　　　I do owe them still
My life and services.

MENENIUS　　　　　It then remains

121, 129 FIRST SENATOR] ROWE (*subs.*); *Senat.* F

117 **Run** A hunting image (see 'spoil',
l. 118 n.), with the same motholog-
izing implication of inevitability as
Menenius' earlier 'whose course will
on', 1.1.66.
　reeking smoking with blood; cf.
1.4.11, 'smoking swords'
118 **spoil** (a) spoliation, massacre, (b) a
hunting term for slaughter of the
quarry (cf. 1.1.195) that agrees with
'run reeking' and 'ease his breast with
panting'
120 **Worthy** i.e. worthy because heroic
121 **with measure** (a) appropriately,
(b) with moderation? Cf. Sicinius'
assessment of the kind of 'measure'

with which Coriolanus is likely to react
to new honours, 2.1.220 n.
125 **misery** (a) wretched poverty, (b)
miserliness (*OED* 4)?
128–30.1 Let ... *Coriolanus* This sum-
mons is elaborated, either (a) to focus
intense attention yet again on a Coriolanus entrance, or (b) to suggest a
moment of delay and hesitation as to
whether he will reappear. In 1984 NT
he was momentarily seen brooding
in the corridor beyond the Senate-
chamber's door, 'sweating it out'
(Peter Hall).
132 **still** as ever

That you do speak to the people.

CORIOLANUS   I do beseech you,
Let me o'erleap that custom, for I cannot   135
Put on the gown, stand naked, and entreat them
For my wounds' sake to give their suffrage.
Please you that I may pass this doing.

SICINIUS   Sir, the people
Must have their voices, neither will they bate
One jot of ceremony.

MENENIUS (*to Coriolanus*) Put them not to't.   140
Pray you, go fit you to the custom and
Take to you, as your predecessors have,
Your honour with your form.

CORIOLANUS   It is a part
That I shall blush in acting, and might well
Be taken from the people.

BRUTUS (*to Sicinius*)   Mark you that?   145

CORIOLANUS

To brag unto them 'Thus I did, and thus',
Show them th'unaching scars, which I should hide,
As if I had received them for the hire
Of their breath only!

MENENIUS   Do not stand upon't.—

---

137 suffrage] F (sufferage), F4   145 that?] ROWE; ~. F   146 'Thus ... thus,'] F 3;
(~ ... ~) FI; ~ ... ~; CAMBRIDGE; 'Thus ... thus!' ALEXANDER

136 **naked** (a) exposed (to view), defenceless, (b) naked beneath the gown (see
2.1.230 n.)
138 **pass** omit (let pass, pass over). This
protest against seeking plebeian approval is not in Plutarch.
139 **voices** (a) votes, (b) also, in practice,
right to question and discuss: cf. 2.3.41
n. and Introduction, pp. 42–3.
140 **One ... ceremony** The plebeians are
being conservative here, demanding a
traditional right, not a new privilege:
cf. 'might well | Be taken from the
people' (ll. 144–5) and 2.3.174–7. See
Introduction, p. 40.
Put ... to't i.e. 'don't push them to a
show-down'; cf. 1.1.227 n.
143 **your form** 'the form which custom
prescribes for you'
143–5 **It ... people** The inflammatoriness

of this remark is reduced if one assumes that it is spoken only to Menenius, not publicly (though it is not an
aside, since the Tribunes hear it). Coriolanus always has an imperfect grasp
of the distinction between public and
private utterance.
143–4 **part ... acting** The acting metaphor now becomes a major image to
the end of Act 3.
144 **blush** Cf. 1.10.70; to blush is an
immature social reaction that Coriolanus fears and despises; he prefers his
face to be red with blood.
145 **that?** F's admonitory punctuation is
acceptable but not as stageworthy as
Rowe's emendation
149 **breath** Note the persistent equation
between 'breath' and 'voice' (e.g.
2.1.52, 3.3.121, 4.5.116, 5.2.46).

230

We recommend to you, tribunes of the people,   150
Our purpose to them; and to our noble consul
Wish we all joy and honour.

SENATORS

To Coriolanus come all joy and honour!
A flourish of cornetts. Then exeunt all but Sicinius and
Brutus

BRUTUS

You see how he intends to use the people.

SICINIUS

May they perceive's intent! He will require them   155
As if he did contemn what he requested
Should be in them to give.

BRUTUS   Come, we'll inform them
Of our proceedings here. On th' market-place
I know they do attend us.   *Exeunt*

2.3   *Enter seven or eight Citizens*

FIRST CITIZEN Once, if he do require our voices we ought
    not to deny him.

SECOND CITIZEN We may, sir, if we will.

THIRD CITIZEN We have power in ourselves to do it, but it

---

151 purpose to them; and to] CAMBRIDGE; ~~them, ~~ F; purpose and to them: to
HANMER; purpose:—to them and to COLLIER *(conj.* Mason)   153 SENATORS] F *(Senat.),*
DYCE; *Sic.* ROWE 1714   153.1–2 *A flourish* ... *Brutus*] OXFORD; *Flourish Cornets.* | *Then*
Exeunt. Manet Sicinius and Brutus. F   158 here. On] THEOBALD *(subs.);* heere‸ on F
159 *Exeunt*] ROWE; *not in* F
    2.3.1 Once,] THEOBALD; ~‸ F

Bad breath is thought of as contamin-
ating physically as the plebeians' votes
do politically.
stand upon't insist upon it, be obstinate about it; cf. 4.6.90. Menenius
says this to Coriolanus *sotto voce*, as a
semi-aside, then hurriedly brings the
proceedings to a conclusion.

151 **purpose to them** proposal to them
    (i.e. the people)
154 ff. **You see** ... The Tribunes' usual
    end-of-scene commentary also serves
    to cover the clearing of the Senate
    cushions.
155 **require them** i.e. request their votes
156 **what** that what

157 **we'll** ... **them** Kemball-Cook notes
    that in 2.3 the plebeians show no sign
    of being lobbied in this way, though
    at 2.3.172 Brutus claims they were:
    Shakespeare, as so often, is superim-
    posing two time schemes. This allows
    him to contrast the plebeians' high-
    spirited behaviour on their own in the
    first part of 2.3 with their malignity
    under the Tribunes' influence at its end.
2.3.0.1   *Enter* ... *Citizens* For the per-
    missive direction 'seven or eight', see
    Introduction, p. 144.
    1 FIRST Shakespeare numbers the Citizens
    here quite independently of the num-
    bering in 1.1: see Introduction, p. 94.
    Once 'Once and for all'; the effect is

is a power that we have no power to do. For if he show   5
us his wounds and tell us his deeds, we are to put our
tongues into those wounds and speak for them; so if he
tell us his noble deeds we must also tell him our noble
acceptance of them. Ingratitude is monstrous, and for
the multitude to be ingrateful were to make a monster   10
of the multitude, of the which we, being members,
should bring ourselves to be monstrous members.

FIRST CITIZEN   And to make us no better thought of, a little
help will serve; for once we stood up about the corn, he
himself stuck not to call us the many-headed multitude.   15

THIRD CITIZEN   We have been called so of many, not that
our heads are some brown, some black, some abram,
some bald, but that our wits are so diversely coloured;
and truly I think if all our wits were to issue out of
one skull, they would fly east, west, north, south, and   20
their consent of one direct way should be at once to all
the points o'th' compass.

SECOND CITIZEN   Think you so? Which way do you judge
my wit would fly?

---

14 once] F; once when ROWE

---

again of entering a discussion *in medias res*.

1 **voices** See 2.2.139 n. Of the 48 uses of this word in the play, 34 occur in Act 2, of which 30 are in this one scene. It is interestingly close to 'Volsces' in sound, since the two represent Martius' parallel enemies.

4–5 **power . . . no power** Such word-plays and chop-logic are typical of Shakespeare's crowds, but Third Citizen is making an important distinction here between *legal* prerogative and *moral* right. See 228–9 and 2.2.27–30.

7 **tongues . . . wounds** A characteristic Shakespearian image: cf. *Caesar* 3.1.263–4, 3.2.223–4, *Richard III* 1.2.55–6, *1 Henry IV* 1.3.96; but one that is particularly pertinent to this play's emphasis on links between language, the state and the body. Cf. Introduction, pp. 80 ff.

9 **Ingratitude is monstrous** This has a proverbial effect typical of the plebeians though it is not in the proverb anthologies: cf. *Troilus* 3.3.141–2, *Lear* 1.5.39.

13–14 **And . . . serve** 'i.e. the patricians will need little prompting to think us no better than monsters' (Brockbank)

14 **once** Rowe supplies the missing relative, 'once when' (see Abbott §244)
we . . . corn Cf. 1.1.186–7, 3.1.45–7, 63, 122–32.

15 **stuck not** did not hesitate
many-headed multitude A proverbial expression (Tilley M1308) of classical origin to describe the instability of people *en masse*: cf. 3.1.95 (Hydra), 4.1.1–2.

17 **abram** A colloquial version of 'auburn', then meaning 'blond' (*OED*).

21–2 **their . . . compass** 'their agreement about a single goal would be to fly off at once in each direction' (a joke in the vein of 'he galloped off in all directions')

THIRD CITIZEN Nay, your wit will not so soon out as an-   25
other man's will, 'tis strongly wedged up in a blockhead. But if it were at liberty, 'twould sure southward.

SECOND CITIZEN Why that way?

THIRD CITIZEN To lose itself in a fog where, being three
parts melted away with rotten dews, the fourth would   30
return for conscience' sake, to help to get thee a wife.

SECOND CITIZEN You are never without your tricks. You
may, you may.

THIRD CITIZEN Are you all resolved to give your voices?
But that's no matter, the greater part carries it. I say,   35
if he would incline to the people there was never a
worthier man.

Enter Coriolanus in a gown of humility ⌈and a hat⌉,
with Menenius

Here he comes, and in the gown of humility. Mark his
behaviour. We are not to stay all together, but to come
by him where he stands by ones, by twos, and by   40
threes. He's to make his requests by particulars, wherein
every one of us has a single honour in giving him our
own voices with our own tongues. Therefore follow
me, and I'll direct you how you shall go by him.

35–6 it. I say, if] THEOBALD; ~, ~~. If F   37.1 *and a hat*] *not in* F   39 all together]
F3; altogether F1

27–30 **southward ... dews** Cf. 1.5.1 n.
30 **rotten** unwholesome, corrupting:
cf. 3.3.122
31 **for ... wife** An unclear joke, which
Second Citizen justifiably fails to understand: Wilson's 'presumably to look
after the poor creature' suits the
epithet 'blockhead' (l. 26) better than
Brower's 'because of the bastards he
has fathered'.
32–3 **You ... may** Have your little joke!
35 **that's ... it** there need not be unanimity, a majority vote is sufficient. This
was unusual in the early 17th century: see Introduction, p. 43.
   it. I say, Theobald's emendation makes
better sense, though F's punctuation is
grammatically possible.
37.1 *gown of humility* Cf. 2.1.230 n.,
2.2.136 n., 2.3.110 n.
   and a hat Cf. 2.3.94–6, 163.

39–44 **We ... him** Third Citizen's mar-
shalling of the others prepares the
audience for what is to follow; but at
this stage he seems to act on Martius'
behalf, not against him, as the
Tribunes will claim the Citizens were
instructed; cf. 2.2.157 n.
41 **by particulars** (a) 'one by one' but (b)
perhaps also misapplying the familiar
legal term 'bill of particulars', by
which one party in a suit could request
the other to clarify items of his decla-
ration. (This latter might suggest that
the Tribunes had indeed issued instructions, as they claim, but that the
plebeians had not understood their
legal jargon.)
42 **single honour** an individual right (not
only to vote but to do so in person to
the candidate)

ALL THE CITIZENS Content, content.   *Exeunt Citizens*   45
MENENIUS
　O sir, you are not right. Have you not known
　The worthiest men have done't?
CORIOLANUS   What must I say?
　'I pray, sir'? Plague upon't, I cannot bring
　My tongue to such a pace. 'Look, sir, my wounds.
　I got them in my country's service, when   50
　Some certain of your brethren roared and ran
　From th' noise of our own drums'?
MENENIUS   O me, the gods!
　You must not speak of that, you must desire them
　To think upon you.
CORIOLANUS   Think upon me? Hang 'em!
　I would they would forget me like the virtues   55
　Which our divines lose by 'em.
MENENIUS   You'll mar all.
　I'll leave you. Pray you, speak to 'em, I pray you,
　In wholesome manner.
CORIOLANUS   Bid them wash their faces
　And keep their teeth clean.   *Exit Menenius*
　　Enter three of the Citizens
　　　　　　　　So, here comes a brace.

45, 132, 161 ALL THE CITIZENS] F (*All.*), OXFORD   45 *Exeunt Citizens*] CAPELL; *not in* F   47 say?] THEOBALD; ~, F   48 I pray, sir?] F4; ~~_∧ ~? FI; ~~, ~,—THEOBALD
59 *Exit Menenius*] F (*Exit after* manner. *l. 58*) *Enter ... Citizens*] F (*after* manner. *Exit l.*

46 **you ... right** you are making a mistake (in behaviour, not in understanding)
47–9 **What ... wounds** Coriolanus partly mimics his instructions here. Charles Pemberton describes three distinct emotional states that Macready found in the lines: 'What ... say?' was 'tinged with a wish to yield to his friend's advice'; 'Plague ... pace' by 'dashing them out of his mouth impatiently, as if too nauseous for endurance', and 'Look ... wounds' 'now qualified by angry scorn at the baseness involved' (*The Literary Remains of Charles Reese Pemberton*, ed. John Fowles (1843), 242–7).
49 **to ... pace** A metaphor from the trained, measured gate of a horse.
50–2 **I ... drums** Typically, Martius re-

members only the plebeians' cowardice, not their rescue of him or his enthusiastic support by Cominius' men; cf. Aufidius' anger at the soldiers who save him in 1.9.
54 **think upon you** be solicitous for. Hibbard comments, 'This phrase—badly chosen by the normally diplomatic Menenius—was part of the Elizabethan beggar's patter and, as such, it rankles with Coriolanus'.
55–6 **like ...'em** 'as they forget the virtuous instructions which our priests waste on them'
58 **wholesome** Menenius means 'decent, proper', but Martius sardonically quibbles on the meaning 'cleanly'.
59 *three ... brace* See Introduction, p. 94.

You know the cause, sir, of my standing here.   60
THIRD CITIZEN
We do, sir. Tell us what hath brought you to't.
CORIOLANUS Mine own desert.
SECOND CITIZEN Your own desert?
CORIOLANUS Ay, but not mine own desire.
THIRD CITIZEN How not your own desire?   65
CORIOLANUS No, sir, 'twas never my desire yet to trouble
  the poor with begging.
THIRD CITIZEN You must think if we give you anything
  we hope to gain by you.
CORIOLANUS Well then, I pray, your price o'th' consulship?   70
FIRST CITIZEN The price is to ask it kindly.
CORIOLANUS Kindly, sir, I pray let me ha't. I have wounds
  to show you which shall be yours in private. (*To Second
  Citizen*) Your good voice, sir. What say you?
SECOND CITIZEN You shall ha't, worthy sir.   75
CORIOLANUS A match, sir. There's in all two worthy
  voices begged. I have your alms. Adieu.

---

58); Re-enter two of the Citizens (*after* clean. *l.* 59)... Re-enter a third Citizen. (*after*
brace. *l.* 59) CAMBRIDGE *three*] F; *two* ROWE (*adjusting speech-prefixes*); *Second and Third*
WILSON (*adjusting speech-prefixes*) 63 desert?] ROWE; ~. F 64 but not] CAMBRIDGE; but
F1; not F3 72 Kindly, sir,] F4; ~‿ ~, F1; ~, ~? JOHNSON

The contradiction probably stems from
the permissive entry to the scene,
'seven or eight Citizens': see 2.3.0.1 n.
brace 'a hunting term for a pair of shot
birds tied together for ease of carrying'
(Gurr); Menenius uses the same disparaging term at 3.1.244.

63 **desert?** Expressing eagerness, as Brockbank suggests, but also surely a certain surprise at the candidate's
immodest abruptness. Coriolanus'
prose shows that he is trying to talk
on the plebeians' level: for his soliloquy
at 109 ff. he reverts to blank verse.

64 **but not mine** The Third Citizen's reply
in the next line makes it clear that F's
'but mine' has dropped a 'not'.

70 **price** Martius uses mercantile phrasing
contemptuously throughout this scene;
cf. 3.3.91–2, 4.1.14–15

71 **kindly** (a) pleasantly, genially, but also
(b) recognizing common 'kind' with
the Citizens both as members of Rome

and fellow human beings, cf. 1.10.83,
3.1.85 n. (see *OED* 2b, and *kind, sb.*
11, 12, 13)

72 **Kindly** When it heads a request like
this, 'Kindly' has a sarcastic edge, with
the implication of 'do what (by nature
or custom) you *should* do, but don't
wish to' (not in *OED*). Not to add the
comma (as Gomme suggests) is to lose
the witty edge of Martius' reply.

73 **which ... private** In Kemble's productions, the chief comedian 'used to peer
about for Kemble's wounds like a
flimsy connoisseur examining a statue
of some mighty Roman' (*London Magazine*, Apr. 1823); similarly, in RSC
1977 First Citizen tried to look under
Coriolanus' 'gown of humility', but
without the farcical shading of Kemble's
actor: cf. 162–9 n.

76 **A match** 'Agreed, a bargain!' In
Kemble's and subsequent 19th-cen-
tury productions (including Macready's), when Coriolanus put out a

THIRD CITIZEN (*to the other Citizens*) But this is something
    odd.

SECOND CITIZEN An 'twere to give again—but 'tis no matter.   80
                                                    Exeunt Citizens

        Enter two other Citizens

CORIOLANUS Pray you now, if it may stand with the tune
    of your voices that I may be consul, I have here the
    customary gown.

⌈FOURTH⌉ CITIZEN You have deserved nobly of your
    country, and you have not deserved nobly.   85

CORIOLANUS Your enigma?

⌈FOURTH⌉ CITIZEN You have been a scourge to her
    enemies, you have been a rod to her friends. You have
    not, indeed, loved the common people.

CORIOLANUS You should account me the more virtuous   90
    that I have not been common in my love. I will, sir,
    flatter my sworn brother the people to earn a dearer
    estimation of them. 'Tis a condition they account
    gentle. And since the wisdom of their choice is rather
    to have my hat than my heart, I will practise the in-   95
    sinuating nod and be off to them most counterfeitly;

80.1 *Exeunt Citizens*] F (*Exeunt.*)   82 voices‸] CAMBRIDGE; ~, F   84, 87, 102 FOURTH]
CAMBRIDGE (4.); 1. F; 3 *Cit.* MALONE   86 enigma?] ROWE; Ænigma. F

hand here to dismiss the voters, one of
them comically tried to shake it to seal
the bargain, resulting in Kemble's
'snatching away his hand from their
friendly familiarity–and bidding them
adieu with withering *sang froid*' (*The
News*, 24 Nov. 1816). See Introduction, pp. 102–3.

80 **An 'twere** if it were

80.1 *Exeunt Citizens* Perhaps one of the
three Citizens merely moves apart to
watch subsequent proceedings; cf. Introduction, p. 94.

81–3 **if... gown** From the abrupt arrogance of 'my own desert' (l. 62), Coriolanus switches to contemptuous
frivolity: 'Let me be consul, I'm wearing the right suit.'

81 **stand** agree

87–9 **You ... people** This is the only comment by a Citizen that might conscious-

ly reflect the Tribunes' 'lessoning' (l.
173), but cf. 2.3.41 n.

87–8 **scourge ... rod** Brockbank cites
Psalm 89:32 (1585), 'I will visit their
offences with the rod, and their sin
with scourges'

91 **common** facile and vulgar (playing on
'common people,' l. 89, as did
earlier on 'kindly')

92 **sworn brother** Martius' intention is
doubly sarcastic, both in the brotherly
relation suggested and in its association with flattery

92–3 **dearer ... of** higher valuation from
(with a pun on 'dearer'; cf. 'price', l. 70)

93 **condition** form of behaviour

94 **gentle** aristocratic

95–6 **I ... them** Cues for Martius to bow
and doff his hat, cf. l. 163.

96–7 **counterfeitly ... counterfeit** 'hypocritically ... imitate': Martius is again
playing on words

that is, sir, I will counterfeit the bewitchment of some
popular man, and give it bountiful to the desirers.
Therefore, beseech you I may be consul.

⌈ FIFTH ⌉ CITIZEN We hope to find you our friend, and   100
therefore give you our voices heartily.

⌈ FOURTH ⌉ CITIZEN You have received many wounds for
your country.

CORIOLANUS I will not seal your knowledge with showing them. I will make much of your voices, and so   105
trouble you no farther.

BOTH CITIZENS The gods give you joy, sir, heartily.

CORIOLANUS Most sweet voices.   *Exeunt Citizens*
Better it is to die, better to starve,
Than crave the hire which first we do deserve.   110
Why in this wolvish toge should I stand here
To beg of Hob and Dick that does appear
Their needless vouches? Custom calls me to't.

---

100 fifth] CAMBRIDGE (5.); 2. F; *Fourth* REED   107 BOTH CITIZENS] F (*Both.*)   108
Exeunt Citizens] *After* ROWE; *not in* F   110 hire] F2; higher F1   111 wolvish] F
(Wooluish); woolen *or* foolish MASON *conj.*; woolless COLLIER 1858; woolyish WILSON
conj.; womanish OXFORD   toge] MALONE (*conj.* Stevens); tongue F1; gowne F2   112
does] F1; do F4

97 **bewitchment** (a) bewitching manner,
(b) delusion?

98 **popular man** (a) one who curries
popular favour, a demagogue, (b) one
misled by his own popularity?
bountiful bountifully (see Abbott §1 on
use of adjectives as adverbs)

104 **seal** (a) authenticate, confirm, from
(b) the Elizabethan use of seals to complete legal documents: cf. 3.1.144 and,
literally, 'counter-sealed', 5.3.206

109 ff. **Better it is ...** Coriolanus' suppressed bitterness breaks out not only
in verse but in rhyming couplets,
marking an extreme metrical revulsion
from the vulgar prose he has been
forcing himself to speak. This makes
the speech seem a recitation of reas-
suring principles: see Introduction,
p. 71.

109 **starve** die of hunger and cold (an
ironic foreshadowing of 4.5.5, 25,
76–7); for the rhyme with 'deserve,'
see Kökeritz, p. 250. Coriolanus also
imagines starving to death rather than

asking the plebeians for food at 3.3.90–
2: see Introduction, pp. 79–80.

110 **hire ... deserve**   reward   already
merited

111 **wolvish toge** Another crux: 'toge'
certainly means 'toga', the 'gown of
humility' he is wearing (F's 'tongue'
is an easy misreading, especially if the
manuscript used the abbreviation
'toge'—cf. *Othello* 1.1.24 where Q has
'toged', F 'tongued'); 'wolvish' probably means 'which makes me look like
a wolf in sheep's clothing', continuing
Martius' painful awareness of hypocrisy and also, possibly, his sense that
the archaic custom belongs to the time
of Rome's founding: cf. 115 n.

112 **Hob and Dick** An Elizabethan equivalent of the modern 'every Tom, Dick,
and Harry', i.e. every common no-
body: 'Hob' was a vulgar diminutive
of 'Robert'.

113 **needless vouches** confirmations that
he considers unnecessary (because the
Senate has appointed him already)

What custom wills, in all things should we do't,
The dust on antique time would lie unswept,   115
And mountainous error be too highly heaped
For truth to o'erpeer. Rather than fool it so,
Let the high office and the honour go
To one that would do thus. I am half through.
The one part suffered, the other will I do.   120
      Enter three Citizens more
Here come more voices.—
Your voices! For your voices I have fought,
Watched for your voices, for your voices bear
Of wounds two dozen odd; battles thrice six
I have seen and heard of; for your voices   125
Have done many things, some less, some more.
Your voices! Indeed I would be consul.
⌈SIXTH⌉ CITIZEN He has done nobly, and cannot go with-
      out any honest man's voice.
⌈SEVENTH⌉ CITIZEN Therefore let him be consul. The gods   130
      give him joy and make him good friend to the people!
ALL THE CITIZENS Amen, amen. God save thee, noble consul!
CORIOLANUS Worthy voices.   *Exeunt Citizens*
      Enter Menenius with Brutus and Sicinius
MENENIUS
You have stood your limitation, and the tribunes
Endue you with the people's voice. Remains   135
That in th'official marks invested, you
Anon do meet the Senate.

---

114 wills, ... things∧] POPE; ~∧ ... ~, F do't,] THEOBALD; ~? F   121 more] F (moe)
122, 127 voices!] F (Voyces?)   125 of; ... voices,] F (~: ~,); ~∧ ~, OXFORD   128 SIXTH]
CAMBRIDGE (6.); I. F; 5 REED   130 SEVENTH] CAMBRIDGE (7.); 2. F; 6 REED   133 *Exeunt*
Citizens] ROWE; *not in* F

---

115 **antique time** Literally 'the prevailing
conditions [*OED' time*, 5] in antiquity',
hence 'out-of-date institutions', 'aged
custom', cf. 2.3.164.
117 **o'erpeer** see over
122-7 **voices** The mockery obvious in
the heavy repetition of this word has
been variously highlighted by actors:
Martius is parodying a market
huckster.
123 **Watched** done guard duty

124 **thrice six** Cf. 2.2.98 n.
125-6 **seen and heard ... some less, some**
more Martius' teasing vagueness is
deliberate
134 **limitation** (a) required duration,
(b) 'as much as you can stand'?
135 **Endue** endow
Remains it only remains (for the common omission of 'it', see Abbott §404)
136 **marks** insignia of office: see
3.1.0.1-2 n.

CORIOLANUS   Is this done?

SICINIUS

The custom of request you have discharged.
The people do admit you, and are summoned
To meet anon upon your approbation.   140

CORIOLANUS

Where, at the Senate-house?

SICINIUS   There, Coriolanus.

CORIOLANUS

May I change these garments?

SICINIUS   You may, sir.

CORIOLANUS

That I'll straight do, and, knowing myself again,
Repair to th' Senate-house.

MENENIUS

I'll keep you company. (*To the Tribunes*) Will you
along?   145

BRUTUS

We stay here for the people.

SICINIUS   Fare you well.
                    Exeunt Coriolanus and Menenius

He has it now, and by his looks methinks
'Tis warm at's heart.

BRUTUS   With a proud heart he wore
His humble weeds. Will you dismiss the people?
          Enter the Plebeians

SICINIUS

How now, my masters, have you chose this man?   150

FIRST CITIZEN   He has our voices, sir.

BRUTUS

We pray the gods he may deserve your loves.

145 (*To the Tribunes*)] OXFORD; *not in* F

138–40 **The custom . . . approbation** Sici-
    nius' vocabulary here is stiff with legal
    terminology: 'custom of request . . .
    discharged . . . admit . . . summoned . . .
    approbation'.
140 **upon your approbation** to ratify their
    approval of you; cf. l. 205, 'He's not
    confirmed, we may deny him yet'
147 ff. **He has . . .** Gurr suggests that the

blank verse in which the Tribunes plot
adds an ominous intensity
148 **'Tis . . . heart** (a) 'the consulship
    is dear to him' (Gomme), (b) or poss-
    ibly a malicious reference to the
    discomfort he has paid for it, play-
    ing on heartburn; cf. *1 Henry IV*
    3.3.49–50: 'So should I be sure to be
    heartburnt.'

SECOND CITIZEN
Amen, sir. To my poor unworthy notice
He mocked us when he begged our voices.

THIRD CITIZEN
Certainly. He flouted us downright.   155

FIRST CITIZEN
No, 'tis his kind of speech. He did not mock us.

SECOND CITIZEN
Not one amongst us save yourself but says
He used us scornfully. He should have showed us
His marks of merit, wounds received for's country.

SICINIUS Why, so he did, I am sure.   160

ALL THE CITIZENS No, no; no man saw 'em.

THIRD CITIZEN
He said he had wounds which he could show in private,
And with his hat, thus waving it in scorn,
'I would be consul,' says he. 'Agèd custom
But by your voices will not so permit me;   165
Your voices therefore.' When we granted that,
Here was 'I thank you for your voices, thank you.
Your most sweet voices. Now you have left your voices
I have no further with you.' Was not this mockery?

SICINIUS
Why, either were you ignorant to see't,   170
Or, seeing it, of such childish friendliness
To yield your voices?

BRUTUS   Could you not have told him
As you were lessoned: when he had no power
But was a petty servant to the state,
He was your enemy, ever spake against   175

---

170 Why,] F4; ~ͺ FI   see't,] COLLIER; ~? F   173 lessoned:] F; ~? HANMER

---

161 **No ... 'em** If 'No, no' were a general
response overlapping with the 'No' of
'No man saw 'em', ll. 160 and 161
could combine as a single blank verse.

162–9 **He ... you** The speech is full of cues
for the speaker to mimic Coriolanus'
speech and actions; thus 'Little Sim-
mons' in Kemble's production, having
'caught the peculiarities of the great
tragedian, and transferred them to his

own small person, ... waved his hand
in imitation of the would-be consul,
and exclaimed, "Your voices! your
most sweet voices!" ' (*London Mag.*,
Apr. 1823).

169 **no ... you** no further use for you

170 **ignorant to see't** too simple-minded
to see it

173 **lessoned** instructed; cf. 2.2.157 n.

175–7 **ever ... weal** Cf. the plebeians'

Your liberties and the charters that you bear
I'th' body of the weal; and now arriving
A place of potency and sway o'th' state,
If he should still malignantly remain
Fast foe to th' plebeii, your voices might   180
Be curses to yourselves? You should have said
That as his worthy deeds did claim no less
Than what he stood for, so his gracious nature
Would think upon you for your voices and
Translate his malice towards you into love,   185
Standing your friendly lord.

SICINIUS   Thus to have said
As you were fore-advised had touched his spirit
And tried his inclination, from him plucked
Either his gracious promise which you might,
As cause had called you up, have held him to,   190
Or else it would have galled his surly nature,
Which easily endures not article
Tying him to aught. So putting him to rage,
You should have ta'en th'advantage of his choler
And passed him unelected.

BRUTUS   Did you perceive   195
He did solicit you in free contempt
When he did need your loves, and do you think
That his contempt shall not be bruising to you
When he hath power to crush? Why, had your bodies
No heart among you? Or had you tongues to cry   200

---

180 plebeii] F; plebeians ROWE   181 yourselves?] REED; your selues. F   193 aught.]
THEOBALD 1740 (~;); ought, F   196 contempt‸] F1 (~,); ~. F2   199 Why,] F1; ~‸ F4

emphasis on their traditional privileges, 2.2.140 n.

177 **weal** commonwealth, state
     arriving arriving at, reaching (preposi-
     tions were frequently omitted with
     verbs of motion, Abbott §198)
178 **sway o'** authority in; cf. 2.1.200 n.
180 **plebeii** plebeians
184 **think upon** Cf. the phrasing of
     Menenius' advice to Martius, 2.3.54 n.
185 **Translate** transform, change
186 **Standing ... lord** 'sticking up' for

you, as your patron: a stock phrase,
cf. *2 Henry IV* 4.2.80
187 **touched** (a) tested, (b) inflamed by
     challenging, cf. 2.1.251 n.?
190 **As ... up** as occasion had demanded;
     cf. 1.7.84
192 **article** any condition or stipulation,
     cf. 1.10.77 n.
196 **free** undisguised, frank
200 **heart** (a) courage, (b) possibly 'wis-
     dom', cf. 1.1.113 n. Another use of
     the body-politic image.
200-1 **cry | Against** rebel against

241

Against the rectorship of judgement?

SICINIUS   Have you
~~Ere now denied the asker,~~ and now again,
Of him that did not ask but mock, bestow
Your sued-for tongues?

THIRD CITIZEN

He's not confirmed, we may deny him yet.   205

SECOND CITIZEN And will deny him.
I'll have five hundred voices of that sound.

FIRST CITIZEN

I twice five hundred, and their friends to piece 'em.

BRUTUS

Get you hence instantly, and tell those friends
They have chose a consul that will from them take   210
Their liberties, make them of no more voice
Than dogs that are as often beat for barking,
As therefor kept to do so.

SICINIUS   Let them assemble,
And on a safer judgement all revoke
Your ignorant election. Enforce his pride   215
And his old hate unto you. Besides, forget not
With what contempt he wore the humble weed,
How in his suit he scorned you; but your loves,
Thinking upon his services, took from you
Th'apprehension of his present portance,   220

203 Of] F; On THEOBALD   208 I‸ twice] F1; I, twice F4; Ay, twice ROWE
213 therefor] F (therefore), OXFORD

201 **rectorship of judgement** the rule of
reason; 'rectorship' is another lawyer-
like image, not used elsewhere in
Shakespeare
201-4 **Have ... tongues?** 'Have you on
previous occasions refused to vote for
one who asked and now are prepared
to grant your votes to one who
mocked instead of asking?'
203 **Of** on ('bestow of' was acceptable
idiom, Abbott §178)
205 **He's ... yet** Cf. 140 n. The previous
half-line creates a pause which gives
this comment emphasis. It is a new
idea, not yet a decision (or the scene
will end too early); and it is interesting
that one of the Citizens says this,

not one of the Tribunes, who seem
nonplussed.
208 **piece** eke out, supplement
213 **therefor** Spelled thus because it
means 'for that purpose' (i.e. to bark).
214 **safer** sounder
215 **Enforce** emphasize
216 **forget not** i.e. 'do not fail to mention'
217 **weed** apparel, garment
218 **suit** (a) appeal, (b) punning on
'apparel'?
220 **apprehension** (a) understanding,
(b) dread? (*OED*'s first reference is
1648)
portance bearing and demeanour,
cf. *Othello* 1.3.138

Which most gibingly, ungravely he did fashion
After the inveterate hate he bears you.
BRUTUS   Lay
A fault on us your tribunes, that we laboured
No impediment between, but that you must
Cast your election on him.
SICINIUS   Say you chose him   225
More after our commandment than as guided
By your own true affections, and that your minds,
Preoccupied with what you rather must do
Than what you should, made you against the grain
To voice him consul. Lay the fault on us.   230
BRUTUS
Ay, spare us not. Say we read lectures to you,
How youngly he began to serve his country,
How long continued, and what stock he springs of,
The noble house o'th' Martians, from whence came
That Ancus Martius, Numa's daughter's son,   235
Who after great Hostilius here was king;
Of the same house Publius and Quintus were,
That our best water brought by conduits hither;

---

221 most gibingly] F; gibingly POPE; gibing most HUDSON (*conj.* Lettsom)

221 **most** This word is extra-metrical, but there is no ground for supposing it a compositor's addition; in fact, it improves the rhythm and also distinguishes between 'gibingly' (which is Coriolanus' point of view) and 'ungravely' (which is the plebeians').

223–4 **laboured ... between** urged that nothing should stand in your way. Wilson sets off 'No impediment between' as a conditional clause meaning 'provided that no hitch occurred in the interim', but in context there is no reason for Sicinius to make such a reservation; it weakens his instructions to no purpose.

227 **affections** inclinations

228 **must** had been obliged by us

229 **against the grain** This predates the first citation of the metaphor in *OED* (1650).

231 **read ... you** cf. 'lessoned' (173), lectured: another Inns of Court phrasing

234–41 **The noble ... ancestor** Brock-bank notes the irony by which the genealogical opening of Plutarch's 'Life' is here put into the mouth of Martius' enemy, allowing us 'to recognize the element of patrician propaganda' behind such standard appeals to inherited nobility. See Introduction, p. 27.

235–6 **Ancus Martius ... Numa ... Hostilius** Traditionally, Numa Pompilius was the second king of Rome (715–673 BC), Tullus Hostilius was third (673–642 BC), and Ancus Martius was fourth (642–617 BC); Coriolanus' own dates are circa 525–493 BC. This descent from a line of kings is extra fuel to the plebeians' fear of Martius, cf. 4.6.33–4.

237 **Publius** This character in Plutarch has not been identified.
Quintus Quintus Martius Rex did not begin the building of the *Aqua Martia* till 144 BC, so an anachronism.

And Censorinus that was so surnamed,
And nobly named so, twice being censor,   240
~~Was his great ancestor.~~
SICINIUS   One thus descended,
That hath beside well in his person wrought
To be set high in place, we did commend
To your remembrances, but you have found,
Scaling his present bearing with his past,   245
That he's your fixed enemy, and revoke
Your sudden approbation.
BRUTUS   Say you ne'er had done't—
Harp on that still—but by our putting on;
And presently when you have drawn your number,
Repair to th' Capitol.
⌈A CITIZEN⌉   We will so.
⌈ANOTHER CITIZEN⌉   Almost all   250
Repent in their election.   *Exeunt Plebeians*
BRUTUS   Let them go on.
This mutiny were better put in hazard
Than stay, past doubt, for greater.
If, as his nature is, he fall in rage
With their refusal, both observe and answer   255

239–41 *And Censorinus ... ancestor.*] DELIUS; And Nobly nam'd, so twice being Censor, | Was his great Ancestor. F; And Censorinus, named so by the people, | And nobly named so, twice being Censor, | Was ... ancestor. LEO; And Censorinus, darling of the people | (And nobly nam'd so for twice being Censor) | Was ... ancestor. POPE; And Censorinus, nobly named so, | Twice being by the people chosen censor, | Was ... ancestor. GLOBE; And Censorinus, nobly named so, | Twice being censor, was ... ancestor. SISSON   249–50 A CITIZEN We ... ANOTHER CITIZEN Almost ...] OXFORD; *All.* We ... almost ... F

239 **Censorinus** Another anachronism: Caius Martius Rutilus received the title Censorinus in 265 BC, when he was made 'censor' for the second time; the position was not instituted till *circa* 443 BC. The hiatus in F was almost certainly caused by the compositor omitting a line, probably because of eye-skip between two lines which both began with 'And'. The name Censorinus must certainly have been part of the missing line, and 'that was so surnamed' follows this in North.
245 **Scaling** weighing (in the scales)
247 **sudden** hasty, rash

248 **putting on** incitement, putting you up to it
249 **presently** immediately, at once
    drawn ... number gathered your crowd of supporters
252 **put in hazard** ventured, risked
253 **Than ... greater** (a) 'than wait for a greater one that undoubtedly would come later'; less probably (b) 'than wait for a greater one whose result would be more certain'
255–6 **observe ... anger** look out for and take advantage of the opportunities afforded by his anger

The vantage of his anger.

SICINIUS   To th' Capitol, come.
We will be there before the stream o'th' people,
And this shall seem, as partly 'tis, their own,
Which we have goaded onward.   *Exeunt*

3.1   *Cornetts. Enter Coriolanus, Menenius, all the*
       gentry; Cominius, Titus Lartius, and other
       Senators

CORIOLANUS
Tullus Aufidius then had made new head?

LARTIUS
He had, my lord, and that it was which caused
Our swifter composition.

CORIOLANUS
So then the Volsces stand but as at first,
Ready when time shall prompt them to make road   5
Upon's again.

COMINIUS   They are worn, lord consul, so
That we shall hardly in our ages see
Their banners wave again.

CORIOLANUS (*to Lartius*)   Saw you Aufidius?

LARTIUS
On safeguard he came to me, and did curse
Against the Volsces for they had so vilely   10

3.1] F (*Actus Tertius.*)   0.2 *Lartius*] F (*Latius*). *Similarly in speech-prefixes* at ll. 2, 9,
12, 13, 19.   1 head?] ROWE; ~. F   5 road] F; raid OXFORD; inroad POPE   10 vilely]
F (vildly)

3.1.0.1–3 *Cornetts . . . Senators*   The
    previous scene gives this complacent,
    confidently formal entry (cf. ll. 22–5)
    an irony that Plutarch lacks. This is
    sharpened visually because Coriolanus
    has now made another costume
    change, into the regalia of 'lord con-
    sul' (l. 6), in which he will soon be
    banished.
0.2 **gentry** An English, rather than
    Roman, class-division, representing
    those patricians who are not also Sen-
    ators, with perhaps a special sense
    here of the *young nobility*, who, ac-

cording to Plutarch, championed Martius during the confrontation with the
Tribunes that follows.
1 **made new head** raised a fresh army
    (cf. 2.2.86)
3 **swifter composition** coming to terms
    more quickly than expected (presum-
    ably the terms for restoring Corioles,
    which Lartius was instructed to ar-
    range; 1.10.75–8, 2.2.35–6)
5 **road** inroad, incursion
6 **worn** worn out, exhausted
7 **ages** lifetimes
9 **On safeguard** under safe-conduct

Yielded the town. He is retired to Antium.

CORIOLANUS
~~Spoke he of me?~~

LARTIUS   He did, my lord.

CORIOLANUS   How? What?

LARTIUS
How often he had met you sword to sword;
That of all things upon the earth he hated
Your person most; that he would pawn his fortunes   15
To hopeless restitution, so he might
Be called your vanquisher.

CORIOLANUS At Antium lives he?

LARTIUS At Antium.

CORIOLANUS
I wish I had a cause to seek him there,   20
To oppose his hatred fully. Welcome home.

⌈*Exit Lartius*⌉

Enter Sicinius and Brutus

Behold, these are the tribunes of the people,
The tongues o'th' common mouth. I do despise them,
For they do prank them in authority
Against all noble sufferance.   25

SICINIUS Pass no further.

CORIOLANUS Ha, what is that?

BRUTUS
It will be dangerous to go on. No further.

CORIOLANUS What makes this change?

MENENIUS The matter?   30

COMINIUS
Hath he not passed the noble and the common?

---

21 *Exit Lartius*] This edition; *not in* F   31 noble ... common] F1; Noble ...
Commons F2; nobles ... commons ROWE

16 **To hopeless restitution** beyond hope of
recovery
so provided that
20–1 **I ... fully** Ironically foreshadowing
their actual meeting in 4.5.
21 *Exit Lartius* See 1.10.75–6 n. for a
discussion of Lartius' movements in
the play.
24 **prank them** dress themselves up,
flaunt themselves

25 **Against ... sufferance** beyond what
the nobility can endure. Brockbank
notes that 'noble' has reverted to a
class designation (as also at l. 31) from
which events will shake it loose again
at 273, 329, 332.
31 **passed** been approved by
noble ... common the nobility and the
common people

BRUTUS
  Cominius, no.
CORIOLANUS   Have I had children's voices?
FIRST SENATOR
  Tribunes, give way. He shall to th' market-place.
BRUTUS
  The people are incensed against him.
SICINIUS   Stop,
  Or all will fall in broil!
CORIOLANUS   Are these your herd?   35
  Must these have voices, that can yield them now
  And straight disclaim their tongues? What are your
      offices?
  You being their mouths, why rule you not their teeth?
  Have you not set them on?
MENENIUS   Be calm, be calm.
CORIOLANUS
  It is a purposed thing, and grows by plot   40
  To curb the will of the nobility.
  Suffer't, and live with such as cannot rule
  Nor ever will be ruled.
BRUTUS   Call't not a plot.
  The people cry you mocked them, and of late
  When corn was given them gratis, you repined,   45

33, 66, 78 FIRST SENATOR] F (*Senat.*), CAPELL

32 **children's voices** For Martius' readiness to see the plebeians as children,
  see Introduction, p. 61.
35 **herd** F's 'Heard' also makes sense in
  the context of 'voices', 'tongues', and
  'mouths' which follow, but the
  emendation agrees better with Martius'
  habitual animal comparisons. Shakespeare probably intended a word-play
  on 'herd/ heard'; cf. 2.1.92 n.
37 **straight** immediately
38–9 **You . . . on?** The body-politic metaphor merges into a bear-baiting image
  of setting dogs on to bite.
38 **rule** control
40 **purposed** premeditated
42 **Suffer't, and** i.e. 'if you suffer it, be
  prepared to'
42–3 **such . . . ruled**   Wilson   compares

More's comment in Hand D of *More*
(ll. 62–3): 'Then what a rough and
riotous charge have you | To lead
those that the Devil cannot rule.'
44 ff **of late . . .** In Plutarch Coriolanus'
  opposition to the corn dole occurs between his rejection for the consulship
  and his arraignment and exile. By
  changing this to a recapitulation of
  arguments that must have been made
  before the rejection Shakespeare obscures the temporal sequence to re-
  emphasize famine as a chief cause of
  plebeian unrest and to suggest that
  Martius may use his new authority to
  reopen issues he has already been out-
  voted on, as indeed he proceeds to do
  about the granting of tribunes.
45 **gratis** At 1.1.185 ff. Martius objected

Scandalled the suppliants for the people, called them
Time-pleasers, flatterers, foes to nobleness.

CORIOLANUS
Why, this was known before.

BRUTUS   Not to them all.

CORIOLANUS
Have you informed them sithence?

BRUTUS   How! I inform them?

⌈CORIOLANUS⌉
You are like to do such business.

BRUTUS   Not unlike,   50
Each way to better yours.

CORIOLANUS
Why then should I be consul? By yon clouds,
Let me deserve so ill as you, and make me
Your fellow tribune.

SICINIUS   You show too much of that
For which the people stir. If you will pass   55
To where you are bound, you must enquire your way,
Which you are out of, with a gentler spirit,
Or never be so noble as a consul,
Nor yoke with him for tribune.

MENENIUS   Let's be calm.

---

46 suppliants‸] F4; ~: F1   49 How! ... them?] This edition; ~? ... ~? F; ~! ...
~! POPE; ~? ... ~! HIBBARD; ~, ... ~? OXFORD   50 CORIOLANUS] THEOBALD; *Com.* F

to them seeking corn 'at their own
rates'; in Plutarch, corn was not dis-
tributed free until later.
repined expressed regret, complained

46 **Scandalled** slandered
47 **Time-pleasers** time-servers, oppor-
tunists
49 **sithence** since then
50 CORIOLANUS F's ascription to Cominius
is quite possible (cf. ll. 60–4) and adds
variety to the interchange; on the
other hand, Coriolanus' 'Why then . . .
tribune' (52–4) clearly assumes that
Brutus' preceding speech, in answer to
50, was addressed to him. Abbreviations of the two names could easily be
confused by the compositor, cf. 237.

50–1 **Not . . . yours** Brutus seems to mean
that Coriolanus can alienate the people
quite adequately without help from
him, but his use of the familiar double
negative allows Coriolanus to assume
that he is claiming to do better than
Coriolanus in any 'business'; hence
Coriolanus' reply.
54 **that** that characteristic
56 **To . . . bound** (a) literally, the market-
place, (b) figuratively, the consulship
57 **are out of** have strayed from
57–8 **gentler . . . noble** Cf. 3.1.25 n.; Sicinius is playing off the spiritual
meaning of these terms against their
purely social significance.
59 **yoke with him** be paired with Brutus

COMINIUS
The people are abused, set on. This palt'ring   60
Becomes not Rome, nor has Coriolanus
Deserved this so dishonoured rub, laid falsely
I'th' plain way of his merit.
CORIOLANUS   Tell me of corn!
This was my speech, and I will speak't again—
MENENIUS Not now, not now.   65
FIRST SENATOR Not in this heat, sir, now.
CORIOLANUS Now as I live,
I will. My nobler friends, I crave their pardons.
For the mutable, rank-scented meinie,
Let them regard me, as I do not flatter,   70
And therein behold themselves. I say again,
In soothing them we nourish 'gainst our Senate
The cockle of rebellion, insolence, sedition,
Which we ourselves have ploughed for, sowed, and
    scattered
By mingling them with us, the honoured number   75
Who lack not virtue, no, nor power, but that
Which they have given to beggars.
MENENIUS   Well, no more.
⌜FIRST⌝ SENATOR
No more words, we beseech you.
CORIOLANUS   How, no more?

---

60 abused, set on.] ROWE (on;); abus'd: set on, F; abus'd.—Set on;—THEOBALD; abused.
Set on! CHAMBERS   64 again—] ROWE; ~. F   69 meinie] F1 (Maynie); many F4,
CAMBRIDGE   78 How, no more?] F (How?); ~!—~~! ROWE

60 **abused** deceived, misled
  set on incited, cf. 3.1.38–9 n.
  palt'ring trickery, playing fast-and-loose
62 **dishonoured** dishonourable (Abbot §74)
62–3 **rub . . . laid falsely . . . plain way** Three terms from lawn bowling, which mean 'impediment or obstruction', 'treacherously placed', and 'level path'; cf. 5.2.21–2 n.
69 **For** as for
  meinie multitude, crowd
70–1 **regard . . . themselves** heed me, because I am no flatterer and thus pro-

vide a true reflection of themselves (playing on 'regard')
72 **soothing** flattering, mollifying
73 **cockle** tares, darnel. 'Shakespeare found this word in North . . . and it suggested to him the parable of the wheat and the tares in the Bible (Matthew 13.24–30) which he uses in lines [74–5]' (Hibbard).
75 **By . . . us** i.e. by allowing the Tribunes to share with us in the government
  honoured honourable (cf. l. 62 n.), i.e. the aristocratic
76 **virtue** Cf. 'valour is the chiefest virtue', 2.2.81–3 n.

As for my country I have shed my blood,
Not fearing outward force, so shall my lungs   80
~~Coin words till their~~ decay against those measles
Which we disdain should tetter us, yet sought
The very way to catch them.

BRUTUS

You speak o'th' people as if you were a god
To punish, not a man of their infirmity.   85

SICINIUS

'Twere well we let the people know't.

MENENIUS   What, what? His choler?

CORIOLANUS

Choler! Were I as patient as the midnight sleep,
By Jove, 'twould be my mind.

SICINIUS   It is a mind
That shall remain a poison where it is,
Not poison any further.

CORIOLANUS   'Shall remain'?   90
Hear you this Triton of the minnows? Mark you
His absolute 'shall'?

COMINIUS   'Twas from the canon.

CORIOLANUS   'Shall'?

---

92 canon] ROWE; Cannon F

81 **Coin words ... against** (a) speak against, (b) recite spells against (leprosy)? **till their decay** till death **measles** scabs (cf. 1.1.163), with perhaps an overtone of Old French *mesel*, 'leper'; referring both to the disease and to its carriers. This is the first of a series of body-politic images in the scene.

82 **tetter** infect with skin irruptions; cf. *Hamlet* 1.5.71–3, where the connection with leprosy also applies

85 **man ... infirmity** Editors have cited Hebrews, 4: 15, Acts, 14: 15, and Romans, 6: 19 as analogues; cf. 'kindly', 2.3.71 n.

86–7 **His choler? ... Choler!** These extra syllables at the end of l. 86 and beginning of 87 together form another half-line, which might be rendered thus: 'MENENIUS What, what? | His choler? CORIOLANUS Choler! | Where I as patient ...'—emphasizing choler as an explanation: see Introduction, p. 54.

87 **patient** calm

88 **be my mind** be my opinion; rather than Wilson's 'fill my mind'

90–108 **shall** Cf. similar angry repetitions of 'Corn' (3.1.63), 'must', 'will', and 'mildly' in 3.2, and 'traitor' and 'boy' in 5.6.

91 **Triton ... minnows** Triton was a minor seagod who was merely trumpeter to Neptune, as the Tribunes are to the 'small fry' of the people; the juxtaposition of Triton and Hydra (l. 95) may have arisen because the Greek root of 'hydra' means 'flood'? (G. K. Hunter, *NQ*, 198 (1953), 100–1).

92 **from the canon** out of order, unconstitutional. The Tribunes were supposed to express the wish of the people, not make decisions; they had the right of veto, but no authority to promulgate laws—as Martius will proceed to emphasize.

O good but most unwise patricians, why,
You grave but reckless senators, have you thus
Given Hydra here to choose an officer   95
That, with his peremptory 'shall', being but
The horn and noise o'th' monster's, wants not spirit
To say he'll turn your current in a ditch
And make your channel his? If he have power,
Then vail your impotence; if none, awake   100
Your dangerous lenity. If you are learned,
Be not as common fools; if you are not,
Let them have cushions by you. You are plebeians
If they be senators, and they are no less
When, both your voices blended, the great'st taste   105

---

93 good,] THEOBALD; God! F   94 reckless] F (wreaklesse)   95 here] F; leave COLLIER
1858   97 monster's] F (monsters), DELIUS   99 he] F; they HANMER. *See next note.*
100, 103] F; HANMER *exchanges* F's Then vail your Ignorance *with* Let them have
cushions by you, *also changing* he *to* they *in l.* 99.   100 impotence] COLLIER 1858
(īpotance); Ignorance F

93 ff. **O good . . .** The shrewd political
analysis which follows justifies Plutarch's insistence that, besides a 'great
heart', Martius was also possessed of
considerable 'natural wit' (as North's
sidenote emphasizes). Thomas Jefferson
was sufficiently impressed to copy it
into his commonplace book, apparently from memory, during his student
days in the early 1760s (Esther C.
Dunn, *Shakespeare in America*, 1939,
pp. 97–8).

93 **O good** Though F's 'God' makes sense,
it provides neither an antithesis to 'but
most unwise' nor a parallel to 'grave
but reckless' in the next line, nor is
'God' used like this elsewhere in the
play.

95 **Given** allowed
   Hydra The many-headed monster
   of Greek myth, killed by Hercules;
   cf. ll. 133, 158, and 2.3.15 n.

97 **horn and noise** A hendiadys for 'noisy
   horn', recalling Triton's role as trumpeter; cf. l. 91 n.
   o'th' monster's Double genitives are
   not infrequent in Shakespeare.
   wants lacks

98–9 **turn . . . his** i.e. divert (*OED, turn,*
   v. 13) your water supply into his own
   ditch, use your authority for his own

ends. See Introduction, pp. 5–6.

99–100 **If . . . impotence** 'if this man has
   power, then let it be your weakness to
   submit to him'

100 **vail** bow in submission; cf. *Shrew*
   5.2.181
   impotence F's 'Ignorance' does not fit
   the context and was probably the compositor's misreading of the manuscript
   abbreviation 'īpotance' under the influence of 'learned' and 'fools' which
   follow: the word conveys a criticism of
   lack of virility as well as powerlessness.
   awake rouse from

101 **learned** wise

103 **them** i.e. the 'common fools' of l.
   102, the Tribunes
   cushions by you seats with you (or,
   possibly, instead of you) in the Senate;
   cf. 2.2.0.1 n.; 'to set beside the
   cushion' can mean 'to put one in place
   of another' (J. M. Purcell, *Explicator*,
   15 (1957), 36).

105 **When . . . blended** 'when the voices
   of plebeians are blended with those of
   you Senators'

105–6 **the . . . theirs** Either (a) the dominant flavour will suit them best, or
   (b) the dominant flavour will taste
   more strongly of them

Most palates theirs. They choose their magistrate,
And such a one as he, who puts his 'shall',
His popular 'shall', against a graver bench
Than ever frowned in Greece. By Jove himself,
It makes the consuls base, and my soul aches   110
To know, when two authorities are up,
Neither supreme, how soon confusion
May enter 'twixt the gap of both and take
The one by th'other.

COMINIUS   Well, on to th' market-place.

CORIOLANUS

Whoever gave that counsel to give forth   115
The corn o'th' storehouse gratis, as 'twas used
Sometime in Greece—

MENENIUS   Well, well, no more of that.

CORIOLANUS

Though there the people had more absolute power—
I say they nourished disobedience, fed
The ruin of the state.

BRUTUS   Why shall the people give   120
One that speaks thus their voice?

CORIOLANUS   I'll give my reasons,
More worthier than their voices. They know the corn
Was not our recompense, resting well assured

---

117 Greece—] F3; ~. F1   118 power] – OXFORD; powre‿ F   120 Why‿] F; ~, CAPELL

---

108 **popular** belonging to the people, expressing the people's wish
bench governing body (cf. l. 168 n. and 2.1.79–80 n.); originally the highest English court, King's Bench

109 **Than ... Greece** Cf. note to 116–18 below.

111–14 **when ... other** This is the political heart of the play, with Martius generalizing beyond his individual situation to argue against any division of authority in government because this leaves a state vulnerable to disruption.

111 **up** exerting themselves

112 **confusion** chaos

113–14 **take ... other** use one to destroy the other

114 **market-place** See Introduction, p. 95.

116–18 **as ... power** Cf. l. 109. The whole passage is very close to North, but in the play we never learn whose idea it was to distribute corn, nor where it came from. Plutarch makes it clear that the corn was specially imported to relieve the famine, but here it might refer to corn that had been hoarded, 129 n.

119 **they** i.e. 'Whoever gave that counsel ...', l. 115

122 **more worthier** Shakespeare often uses double comparatives and superlatives for extra emphasis, cf. 4.7.8, 'more proudlier'

123 **recompense** reward to them for services rendered

They ne'er did service for't. Being pressed to th' war,
Even when the navel of the state was touched,   125
They would not thread the gates. This kind of service
Did not deserve corn gratis. Being i'th' war,
Their mutinies and revolts, wherein they showed
Most valour, spoke not for them. Th'accusation
Which they have often made against the Senate,   130
All cause unborn, could never be the native
Of our so frank donation. Well, what then?
How shall this bosom multiplied digest
The Senate's courtesy? Let deeds express
What's like to be their words: 'We did request it,   135
We are the greater poll, and in true fear
They gave us our demands.' Thus we debase
The nature of our seats, and make the rabble
Call our cares fears, which will in time
Break ope the locks o'th' Senate and bring in   140
The crows to peck the eagles.

MENENIUS   Come, enough.

BRUTUS

Enough with over-measure.

CORIOLANUS   No, take more.

---

131 native] F; motive ARDEN (*conj.* Johnson)   133 bosom multiplied] F; bisson
multitude DYCE (*conj.* Collier 1858); bissom multitude SINGER; beesom multitude
KITTREDGE

124 **pressed** conscripted
125 **navel** the vital centre (an interesting-
    ly precise use of the body-politic image,
    akin to Volumnia's later use of 'bo-
    wels' and 'womb' of 'our dear nurse')
    touched threatened
126 **thread** pass through one by one;
    cf. the echo of Matthew 19: 24 in *Ri-
    chard II* 5.5.16–17: 'It is as hard to
    come as for a camel | To thread the
    postern of a small needle's eye.' Al-
    though Martius is ostensibly referring
    to the gates of Rome, his phrasing
    inevitably conjures up the soldiers' re-
    fusal to follow his own entry into Cori-
    oles.
129 **accusation** i.e. that the Senators are
    hoarding corn, cf. 1.1.15–20, etc.
131 **All . . . unborn** without any cause
    native origin? Cf. *OED a.* 3b, 'original,
    parent', though there is no recorded

use to mean 'origin'. Johnson's conjectural emendation to 'motive' is
possible but lacks the metaphoric link
to 'unborn', reflecting a 'natal' thread
that runs throughout the speech.
132 **frank donation** generous gift
133 **bosom multiplied** monster of many
    stomachs
    digest assimilate, understand
134 **deeds** i.e. their actions
136 **greater poll** majority
    true very
137 **They** i.e. the patricians
139 **cares** concern, solicitude
141 **crows** punning on (a) carrion birds;
    cf. 4.5.42 n., (b) crowbars (to 'Break
    ope the locks o'th' Senate')
    eagles (a) the primate of birds, whom
    it is unnatural for inferior 'crows' to
    subjugate, (b) the emblems of Roman
    power (particularly the army)

What may be sworn by, both divine and human,
Seal what I end withal! This double worship,
Where one part does disdain with cause, the other   145
Insult without all reason, where gentry, title, wisdom
Cannot conclude but by the yea and no
Of general ignorance, it must omit
Real necessities, and give way the while
To unstable slightness. Purpose so barred, it follows   150
Nothing is done to purpose. Therefore beseech you—
You that will be less fearful than discreet,
That love the fundamental part of state
More than you doubt the change on't, that prefer
A noble life before a long, and wish   155
To jump a body with a dangerous physic
That's sure of death without it—at once pluck out
The multitudinous tongue; let them not lick
The sweet which is their poison. Your dishonour
Mangles true judgement, and bereaves the state   160

---

145 Where one] ROWE; Whereon F

144 **Seal** confirm
144–51 **This double ... purpose** Cf. Montaigne, 'Of Glory': 'And the judgement
   of our inclinations and actions, (the
   weightiest and hardest matter that is)
   we refer it to the idle breath of the
   vain voice of the common sort and
   base rascality ...' (*Essays*, trans. John
   Florio, Everyman edn., ii. 347).
144 **double worship** divided authority;
   cf. l. 111
146 **Insult** make insulting accusations,
   cf. ll. 129–31
   without all (a) without any, (b) beyond
   all?
147 **conclude** make decisions
148 **general** popular, common
   it i.e. 'This double worship' (l. 144)
   omit neglect, leave disregarded
150 **slightness** trifling, inessentials
   Purpose so barred planning thus
   thwarted
151 **to purpose** effectively, as planned
   you i.e. you nobles
152 **less ... discreet** less cowardly than
   discerning
154 **More ... doubt** (a) 'even more than

you dread,' or (b) 'rather than dread'?
Johnson's paraphrase gets the drift:
'you who do not so much fear the
danger of violent measures, as wish
the good to which they are necessary,
the preservation of the original con-
stitution of our government'. For
Coriolanus this means the authority of
the patricians, of course; his phrasing
here echoes his appeal for volunteers
on the battlefield at 1.7.70–3: it is an
appeal for public service.
156 **To ... physic** 'to risk using a dangerous medicine on a body'
158 **multitudinous tongue** those who
   speak for the many, i.e. the Tribunes
   (yet another body-politic reference)
159 **sweet** taste of power or, possibly, of
   flattery (Caroline Spurgeon emphasizes
   Shakespeare's recurrent association
   of flattery with dogs licking sweet-
   meats: *Shakespeare's Imagery*, 1936,
   pp. 194–9)
   Your dishonour i.e. the dishonour
   done to you
160 **judgement** justice

Of that integrity which should become't,
Not having the power to do the good it would
For th'ill which doth control't.

BRUTUS   He's said enough.

SICINIUS

He's spoken like a traitor, and shall answer
As traitors do.

CORIOLANUS   Thou wretch, despite o'erwhelm thee!   165
What should the people do with these bald tribunes,
On whom depending, their obedience fails
To th' greater bench? In a rebellion,
When what's not meet but what must be was law,
Then were they chosen. In a better hour   170
Let what is meet be said it must be meet,
And throw their power i'th' dust.

BRUTUS

Manifest treason.

SICINIUS   This a consul? No.

BRUTUS

The aediles, ho!

    Enter an Aedile

        Let him be apprehended.

SICINIUS

Go call the people,   ⌈*Exit Aedile*⌉
(*To Coriolanus*)   in whose name myself   175
Attach thee as a traitorous innovator,

---

163 He's] F (Has)   164 He's] F (Ha's)   168 bench? In a rebellion,] POPE; ~, ~~~: F
174 The] F; Ye HINMAN *conj.* (*in 'Textual Companion'*)   *Enter an Aedile*] CAMBRIDGE;
after l. 172 in F   175 *Exit Aedile*] COLLIER; *not in* F; *Exit Brutus.* CAPELL

---

161 **integrity** (a) sense of wholeness,
(b) moral probity?
163 **control** overpower, master
164 **answer** pay the penalty
165 **despite** contempt
166 **bald** 'meanly endowed', both literally
with hair and metaphorically with intelligence
168 **greater bench** i.e. the Senate, cf. 108 n.
169 **When . . . be** when what is not right
but could not be avoided
was law (a) controlled events, (b) was
made law?

171 **Let . . . be meet** 'let it be said that the
right thing to do shall be done'
174 **The** Hinman's conjectured 'Ye' is
possible but unnecessary
aediles The *Aediles Plebeii* were two
plebeians appointed to assist the
tribunes and implement their decisions; at one place North calls them
'sergeants' (i.e. police officers) as the
closest Elizabethan equivalent.
176 **Attach** arrest
innovator revolutionary (the only use
of this noun in Shakespeare, though

A foe to th' public weal. Obey, I charge thee,
And follow to thine answer.
⌈*He tries to seize Coriolanus*⌉
CORIOLANUS   Hence, old goat!
ALL ⌈THE PATRICIANS⌉
  We'll surety him.
COMINIUS (*to Sicinius*) Agèd sir, hands off.
CORIOLANUS (*to Sicinius*)
  Hence, rotten thing, or I shall shake thy bones   180
  Out of thy garments.
SICINIUS   Help, ye citizens!
    Enter a rabble of Plebeians, with the Aediles
MENENIUS On both sides more respect.
SICINIUS
  Here's he that would take from you all your power.
BRUTUS Seize him, aediles!
ALL ⌈THE CITIZENS⌉ Down with him!—down with him!—   185
SECOND SENATOR Weapons!—weapons!—weapons!—
    They all bustle about Coriolanus
ALL Tribunes!—Patricians!—Citizens!—What ho!

178 *He tries . . . Coriolanus*] This edition; *not in* F; *Laying hold on Coriolanus* ROWE (*after
myself, l. 175*)   179 ALL THE PATRICIANS] MALONE (*subs.*); *All.* F   Agèd] ROWE; Ag'd
F   181 Help, ye] MALONE; ~∧ ~ F1; ~∧ me F3; ~~, SCHMIDT   185, 194, 200, 203,
229 ALL THE CITIZENS] F (*All.*)   186 SECOND SENATOR] F (2 Sen.), BROCKBANK (*subs.*);
Senators, etc. CAMBRIDGE; *Two Senators* ROSSITER conj. (*in* Brockbank); *Senators* CHAMBERS;
A Senator SISSON   186.1 *They . . . Coriolanus*] F; *They . . . Coriolanus, crying* CAMBRIDGE
187 ALL] CAMBRIDGE; *not in* F; CITIZENS *and* PATRICIANS *in dispersed cries* OXFORD

'innovation' occurs disapprovingly
elsewhere); cf. 2.2.140 n.

178 **answer** (a) interrogation, trial,
(b) punishment?
   old goat Furness suggests that this
insult refers to Sicinius' beard (cf.
2.1.84–6), Arden to the bad breath of
which the plebeians are constantly accused (cf. 'rotten thing', l. 180)
179 **surety** go bail for
180 **Hence** The text here is full of cues for
action: see Introduction, p. 105.
180–1 **rotten . . . garments** Steevens compares *K. John* 2.1.456–8, 'Here's a stay
| That shakes the rotten carcass of old
Death | Out of his rags.'
182 **respect** consideration, thought
186 SECOND SENATOR There is clearly a

distinction between this speaker and
the person who tries to be a peacemaker at ll. 66, 78, 199, 233. It
would be logical to give this line to
one (or more) of the 'young nobility'
who Plutarch says sided with Coriolanus.
187 ALL The following three lines must be
divided amongst the various groups on
stage, taking care not to separate them
too clearly into two camps because,
not only are the Senators divided into
those calling for weapons and those
trying to make peace, but Plutarch
says some of the Citizens also favoured
restraint (Spencer, pp. 328, 330–1).
The effect must be of confusion, not
polarization.

Sicinius!—Brutus!—Coriolanus!—Citizens!
Peace!—Peace!—Peace!—Stay!—Hold!—Peace!

MENENIUS

What is about to be?—I am out of breath.—   190
Confusion's near.—I cannot speak.—You tribunes,
To th' people!—Coriolanus, patience!—
Speak, good Sicinius.

SICINIUS   Hear me, people, peace!

ALL ⌈ THE CITIZENS ⌉   .

Let's hear our tribune! Peace! Speak, speak, speak!

SICINIUS

You are at point to lose your liberties.   195
Martius would have all from you, Martius
Whom late you have named for consul.

MENENIUS   Fie, fie, fie!

This is the way to kindle, not to quench.

FIRST SENATOR

To unbuild the city, and to lay all flat.

SICINIUS

What is the city but the people?

ALL ⌈ THE CITIZENS ⌉   True,   200

The people are the city.

BRUTUS   By the consent of all

We were established the people's magistrates.

ALL ⌈ THE CITIZENS ⌉

You so remain.

MENENIUS   And so are like to do.

---

189 Peace] CAMBRIDGE (*no speech-prefix*); *All.* Peace F; SOME CITIZENS *and* PATRICIANS Peace OXFORD; *Patricians* Peace ALEXANDER; *Menenius* Peace HIBBARD; AEDILES Peace '*Textual Companion*' *conj.*   191 cannot∧ speak.] F; ~. ~~~ Speak∧ RANN (*conj.* Mason) You∧ tribunes,] DELIUS; ~, ~∧ F   192 To th' people!] F; Speak to the people DYCE 1866 (*conj.* Tyrwhitt)   people!] F (~:); ~, OXFORD   194 Speak, speak, speak!] F; Speak, speak, speak, speak. KEIGHTLEY   199, 233 FIRST SENATOr] CAPELL; *Sena.* F

---

190 I ... **breath** See Introduction, p. 105.
191 **Confusion** anarchy, cf. l. 112 n.
191–2 **You ... people!** This understands a verb such as 'go' or 'speak'. An alternative punctuation would be: 'I cannot ... Speak you, Tribunes, to the people.' In effect, 'speak' belongs to both clauses.

195 **at ... lose** on the point of losing
196 **Martius ... Martius** Like Aufidius at 5.6.88–90, Sicinius insultingly omits the honorific 'Coriolanus', rubbing the omission in by repetition.
200 **What ... people?** See Introduction, p. 76 n. 2.

CORIOLANUS
    That is the way to lay the city flat,
    To bring the roof to the foundation,   205
    And bury all which yet distinctly ranges
    In heaps and piles of ruin.
SICINIUS   This deserves death.
BRUTUS
    Or let us stand to our authority,
    Or let us lose it. We do here pronounce,
    Upon the part o'th' people in whose power   210
    We were elected theirs, Martius is worthy
    Of present death.
SICINIUS   Therefore lay hold of him,
    Bear him to th' rock Tarpeian; and from thence
    Into destruction cast him.
BRUTUS   Aediles, seize him.
ALL THE CITIZENS
    Yield, Martius, yield.
MENENIUS   Hear me one word.   215
    Beseech you, tribunes, hear me but a word.
AEDILES Peace, peace!
MENENIUS ⌈*to Brutus*⌉
    Be that you seem, truly your country's friend,
    And temp'rately proceed to what you would
    Thus violently redress.
BRUTUS   Sir, those cold ways   220
    That seem like prudent helps are very poisons

204 CORIOLANUS] POPE; *Com.* F   215 ALL THE CITIZENS] F (*All. Ple.*)   216 Beseech] F
('beseech)   221 poisons] OXFORD (*conj.* Johnson); poysonous F

204 CORIOLANUS Sicinius' immediate re-
    sponse 'This deserves death' (l. 207),
    followed by Brutus' 'Martius is worthy
    of present death' (211–12), makes it
    certain that Coriolanus speaks these
    lines, not F's '*Com<inius>*'. The
    phrase 'lay the city flat' may be influenced by
    the contemporary term 'Levellers' for
    17th-century opponents of enclosure.
206 **distinctly ranges** is hierarchically or-
    dered; referring to Rome's architecture
    both literally and as a metaphor for
    social differentiation
208 **Or** either

stand to uphold
212 **present** immediate
213 **rock Tarpeian** A promontory at the
    south end of the Capitoline Hill from
    which traitors were thrown in execu-
    tion.
221 **poisons** Johnson's conjecture is more
    effective than F's 'poysonous', which
    was probably a misreading of manu-
    script 'poysones', cf. ll. 88–90. The
    equation 'poison/disease' is particular-
    ly strong in this play because it is the
    antithesis of the theme of food as nour-
    ishment.

Where the disease is violent. Lay hands upon him,
And bear him to the rock.

Coriolanus draws his sword

CORIOLANUS   No, I'll die here.

There's some among you have beheld me fighting.
Come, try upon yourselves what you have seen me.   225

MENENIUS

Down with that sword! Tribunes, withdraw a while.

BRUTUS

Lay hands upon him.

MENENIUS   Help Martius, help!

You that be noble, help him, young and old.

ALL ⌈THE CITIZENS⌉ Down with him, down with him!

In this mutiny the Tribunes, the Aediles, and the
people are beat in, ⌈and exeunt⌉

MENENIUS (*to Coriolanus*)

Go get you to your house. Be gone, away!   230
All will be naught else.

SECOND SENATOR (*to Coriolanus*) Get you gone.

⌈CORIOLANUS⌉   Stand fast.

We have as many friends as enemies.

MENENIUS

Shall it be put to that?

⌈FIRST⌉ SENATOR   The gods forbid!

(*To Coriolanus*) I prithee, noble friend, home to thy house.
Leave us to cure this cause.

MENENIUS   For 'tis a sore   235

---

223 *Coriolanus … Sword*] F (*Corio.*)   225 seen me] F; seen me do KEIGHTLEY; seen
HINMAN *conj.* (*in 'Textual Companion'*)   229.2 *and exeunt*] *at end of l.* 229 *in* F (*Exeunt.*)
230 your] ROWE; our F   231 CORIOLANUS] WARBURTON; *Com.* F, SISSON

229.2 **beat … exeunt** i.e. beaten off stage
    into the tiring house, but not followed
    by their pursuers; cf. 1.9.13.3 n.
230 **your** Rowe's emendation is plausible;
    there is no suggestion elsewhere that
    Menenius and Coriolanus share a
    house, and confusion of 'our' and
    'your' occurs commonly in F
231 **naught** ruined, brought to naught
    CORIOLANUS Warburton's emendation is
    surely correct. To follow F by giving
    the speech to Cominius sits ill with his
    'Come, sir, along with us' (l. 237) and

is explicitly contradicted by his comment at 246–8. Cominius has been
placatory throughout the scene, and,
pace Sisson, I do not see him as a
natural soldier: see Introduction,
p. 24.
235 **cause** disease, illness (*OED sb.* 12)
235–6 **sore … us** i.e. a danger to all the
    patricians, not just Coriolanus. Line
    236 is regular if one allows a beat after
    'us' for the 'that' which is grammatic-
    ally understood.

Upon us you cannot tent yourself.
Be gone, beseech you.

⌈COMINIUS⌉   Come, sir, along with us.

⌈CORIOLANUS⌉

I would they were barbarians, as they are,
Though in Rome littered; not Romans, as they are not,
Though calved i'th' porch o'th' Capitol.

⌈MENENIUS⌉   Be gone.   240
Put not your worthy rage into your tongue.
One time will owe another.

CORIOLANUS   On fair ground
I could beat forty of them.

MENENIUS   I could myself
Take up a brace o'th' best of them—
Yea, the two tribunes!   245

COMINIUS

But now 'tis odds beyond arithmetic,
And manhood is called foolery when it stands
Against a falling fabric.

(*To Coriolanus*)   Will you hence
Before the tag return, whose rage doth rend
Like interrupted waters, and o'erbear   250

---

237 beseech] F ('beseech) COMINIUS] F2; *Corio.* F1   238 CORIOLANUS] STEEVENS (*conj.* Tyrwhitt); *Mene.* F   240 MENENIUS] STEEVENS (*conj.* Tyrwhitt); *not in* F

236 **tent** treat, cure; cf. 1.10.31 n.

237, 238, 240 COMINIUS ... CORIOLANUS ... MENENIUS All editors agree on this re-allocation of speeches. The errors in F probably arose from the marginal addition of two speeches interrupting a single speech of Menenius, which were not understood by the compositor.

239–40 **littered ... calved** Two more examples of the animal imagery that Martius habitually applies to the plebeians. The implication of his speech is that, if they *were* barbarians, he could attack them without compunction, but Menenius breaks in before the sense is completed.

241 **worthy rage** 'anger that does you credit' (Wilson)

242 **One ... another** 'there will be another ... occasion to compensate for this one'. Brockbank compares *Twelfth*

Night 5.1.373, 'the whirligig of time brings in his revenges'.

244 **Take up** take on. Menenius is joking to defuse Coriolanus' rage (though cf. 3.2.32–5, 4.1.56–8, and 1.1.239 n.).

246 **arithmetic** calculation; i.e. 'they infinitely outnumber us'

247 **manhood** courage; the Roman 'virtue' whose essence is 'valour', cf. 2.2.81–3 n.
   foolery foolhardiness, folly

247–8 **stands ... fabric** tries to withstand a falling building. Cf. this caution to Cominius' comment on retreat at 1.7.1 ff.

249 **tag** rabble, rag-tag (cf. *Caesar* 1.2.258, 'the tag-rag people')—an image continued in 'patched | With cloth of any colour' (ll. 253–4)

250–1 **o'erbear ... bear** overwhelm what usually contains them. This image of

What they are used to bear?

MENENIUS (*to Coriolanus*)   Pray you, be gone.

I'll try whether my old wit be in request

With those that have but little. This must be patched

With cloth of any colour.

COMINIUS Nay, come away.   255

Exeunt Coriolanus and Cominius

A PATRICIAN This man has marred his fortune.

MENENIUS

His nature is too noble for the world.

He would not flatter Neptune for his trident

Or Jove for's power to thunder. His heart's his mouth.

What his breast forges, that his tongue must vent,   260

And, being angry, does forget that ever

He heard the name of death.

A noise within

Here's goodly work!

A PATRICIAN   I would they were abed!

MENENIUS

I would they were in Tiber! What the vengeance,

Could he not speak 'em fair?

Enter Brutus and Sicinius, with the rabble again

SICINIUS   Where is this viper   265

255.1 *Exeunt ... Cominius*] F; *Exeunt ... Cominius and Others*. CAPELL   256 A
PATRICIAN] F (*Patri*.); I. P. CAPELL   263 A PATRICIAN] F (*Patri*.); I. P. CAPELL; 2 *Pat*.
MALONE

floodwater overflowing river banks is a
favourite with Shakespeare.

252 **whether** Contracted colloquially to
'wh'er' (Abbott §466).

256 **This ... fortune** Patrician impatience
with Martius' intransigence now emerges clearly; even Menenius laments
'Could he not speak 'em fair?' (l. 265).
The patrician speaker here could well
be the First Senator who tried to make
peace earlier.

257 **too ... world** Menenius' phrase combines exasperation and admiration,
but his colloquialism will prove tragic-
ally exact

259 **Jove ... thunder** Another reference
to the sheer power of Coriolanus'

voice, cf. its 'thunder-like percussion',
1.5.32.

His ... mouth 'what he feels he immediately utters'. Brockbank cites Eccle-
siastes, 21: 26, 'The heart of fools is
in their mouth; but the mouth of the
wise is in his heart', but this was also
a trope for sincerity: cf. Tilley, 'What
the heart thinks, the tongue speaks'.
See Introduction, p. 83.

264 **What the vengeance** A phrase used
to strengthen interrogations (*OED*,
vengeance, 3), approximating modern
'Why the hell'; cf. 2.2.5.

265 **viper** Traditionally an emblem of
treachery, cf. l. 289; they were
thought to eat their way out through
their mother's womb, cf. 5.3.124–5.

That would depopulate the city and
Be every man himself?

MENENIUS   You worthy tribunes—

SICINIUS

He shall be thrown down the Tarpeian rock
With rigorous hands. He hath resisted law,
And therefore law shall scorn him further trial   270
Than the severity of the public power,
Which he so sets at naught.

FIRST CITIZEN   He shall well know
The noble tribunes are the people's mouths,
And we their hands.

ALL ⌈ THE CITIZENS ⌉   He shall, sure on't.

MENENIUS   Sir, sir.

SICINIUS   Peace!

MENENIUS

Do not cry havoc where you should but hunt   275
With modest warrant.

SICINIUS   Sir, how comes't that you
Have holp to make this rescue?

MENENIUS   Hear me speak.
As I do know the consul's worthiness,
So can I name his faults.

---

267 tribunes –] ROWE; ~. F   274, 283 ALL THE CITIZENS] CAPELL; *All.* F   274 shall,
sure on't] FI (~ ∧ ~ ont); ~ ∧ ~ out F2, CAPELL; shall∧ be ~~ POPE; shall, be ~~ THEOBALD
276 comes't] F (com'st), CAPELL

266–7 **depopulate . . . himself** An interesting comment on Coriolanus' insistence
  on aloneness and inability to accept
  the plebeians as his 'kind'.
273 **noble tribunes** Brockbank notes
  how this reverses the earlier class-
  appropriation of 'noble' (l. 25). The
  process is completed when First Senator
  picks the phrase up at 329 and Sicinius then calls Menenius 'Noble' because he is to be 'the people's officer',
  332.
274 **sure on't** 'be sure of it'
275 **cry havoc** The leader's signal to allow
  slaughter and plunder; cf. *Caesar*
  3.1.276, 'Cry "havoc!" and let slip the
  dogs of war': Shakespeare habitually
  combines it with an association of war

and hunting, as here; cf. *K. John*
  2.1.357, *Hamlet* 5.2.318. Hibbard
  notes this ironic inversion of 1.1,
  where Coriolanus thought of himself
  as the hunter and the plebeians as his
  'quarry'.
276 **modest warrant** restricted licence (to
  kill)
277 **holp** helped (from 'holpen': Abbott
  §343)
  rescue Sicinius is using one of his legal
  terms: 'the forcible taking of a person
  or goods out of legal custody' (*OED*),
  a serious crime in English law. Suddenly the threat is turned against
  Menenius himself, and he shows real
  courage in facing it, as he did in facing
  the mob in 1.1.

SICINIUS Consul? What consul?   280
MENENIUS The consul Coriolanus.
BRUTUS He consul?
ALL ⌈ THE CITIZENS ⌉ No, no, no, no, no!
MENENIUS
  If, by the tribunes' leave and yours, good people,
  I may be heard, I would crave a word or two,   285
  The which shall turn you to no further harm
  Than so much loss of time.
SICINIUS   Speak briefly then,
  For we are peremptory to dispatch
  This viperous traitor. To eject him hence
  Were but our danger, and to keep him here   290
  Our certain death. Therefore it is decreed
  He dies tonight.
MENENIUS   Now the good gods forbid
  That our renownèd Rome, whose gratitude
  Towards her deservèd children is enrolled
  In Jove's own book, like an unnatural dam   295
  Should now eat up her own!
SICINIUS
  He's a disease that must be cut away.
MENENIUS
  O, he's a limb that has but a disease;
  Mortal to cut it off, to cure it easy.

---

290 our] THEOBALD; one F; moe CAMBRIDGE *conj.*   298 disease;] ROWE; ~ₐ F

286 **turn you to** bring about for you
  (*OED, turn, v.* 43b)
288 **peremptory** A term in Roman law
  meaning 'finally decided' (*OED* 1);
  cf. 'it is decreed', l. 291.
289–91 **To ... death** i.e. 'to banish him
  would only create danger for us (i.e.
  of his return), while to keep him would
  mean our certain death'; cf. 3.3.84–5
  n., Introduction, p. 31.
290 **our** F's 'one' is possible, but Theobald's emendation provides a persuasive parallelism between 'our danger'
  and 'our death'. Orthographically, it is
  very easy to confuse the two words.
294 **deservèd** deserving, meritorious
295 **Jove's own book** 'probably means the

rolls and registers of the Capitol, which
was Jove's temple. Cf. ˙ *Caesar*, III.
2.[37–8]: "The question of his death
is enrolled in the Capitol".' (Gordon)
295–6 **unnatural ... own** A key image,
  cf. 5.3.185–90; in Roman mythology
  the founders of the city were suckled
  by a she-wolf.
297 **He's ... away** The Tribunes turn
  Menenius' own body-politic and disease imagery against Martius; cf. ll.
  308–10, 221–2, 312–13. Menenius'
  plea that Martius is not himself a
  disease but only a limb that has the
  disease was foreshadowed by his criticism at 235–6.
299 **Mortal** fatal

What has he done to Rome that's worthy death?   300
Killing our enemies, the blood he hath lost—
Which I dare vouch is more than that he hath
By many an ounce—he dropped it for his country;
And what is left, to lose it by his country
Were to us all that do't and suffer it   305
A brand to th'end o'th' world.
SICINIUS   This is clean cam.
BRUTUS
Merely awry. When he did love his country
It honoured him.
SICINIUS   The service of the foot,
Being once gangrened, is not then respected
For what before it was.
BRUTUS   We'll hear no more.   310
(*To the Citizens*) Pursue him to his house and pluck him
        thence,
Lest his infection, being of catching nature,
Spread further.
MENENIUS   One word more, one word!
This tiger-footed rage, when it shall find
The harm of unscanned swiftness, will too late   315
Tie leaden pounds to's heels. Proceed by process,
Lest parties—as he is beloved—break out

---

301 enemies,] F; ~? HANMER   308 SICINIUS] HANMER (*conj.* Warburton); *Menen.* F;
omitted LETTSOM *conj.*   310 BRUTUS] F; *Sicinius* LETTSOM *conj.*

306 **brand** mark of infamy
  clean cam totally off the point,
  completely twisted; 'cam' is an Elizabethan borrowing from Welsh, used
  here for its abrupt, contemptuous
  colloquialism
307 **Merely** completely
308 SICINIUS Warburton's emendation of
  F's *Menen.* is persuasive because, as
  Wilson points out, the speech not only
  supports what Brutus has just said but
  also contradicts Menenius' previous
  argument, since the only cure for gan-
  grene is amputation of the diseased
  limb.
314 **tiger-footed rage** Not a particularly

Roman epithet, one might think, but
Arden cites Holland's translation of
Pliny, viii. 18, 'This beast (the Tiger)
is most dreadful for incomparable
swiftness' and 'for very anger . . .
rageth on the shore and the sands'.
315 **unscanned swiftness** unconsidered
  haste. Arden compares *Dream* I.I.237,
  'unheedy haste'.
316 **to's** to its; cf. *Winter's Tale* 4.4.680,
  'with his clog at his heels'
  by process i.e. by process of law;
  cf. 'lawful form' (l. 328). Menenius is
  cleverly using the Tribunes' own legal-
  ism as they have done his body-politic
  argument.

And sack great Rome with Romans.

BRUTUS If it were so?

SICINIUS (*to Menenius*) What do ye talk?   320
  Have we not had a taste of his obedience:
  Our aediles smote, ourselves resisted? Come.

MENENIUS
  Consider this: he has been bred i'th' wars
  Since a could draw a sword, and is ill-schooled
  In bolted language. Meal and bran together   325
  He throws without distinction. Give me leave,
  I'll go to him and undertake to bring him
  Where he shall answer by a lawful form—
  In peace—to his utmost peril.

FIRST SENATOR   Noble tribunes,
  It is the humane way. The other course   330
  Will prove too bloody, and the end of it
  Unknown to the beginning.

SICINIUS   Noble Menenius,
  Be you then as the people's officer.
  (*To the Citizens*) Masters, lay down your weapons.

BRUTUS   Go not home.

SICINIUS
  Meet on the market-place. (*To Menenius*) We'll attend
    you there,   335
  Where if you bring not Martius, we'll proceed
  In our first way.

MENENIUS   I'll bring him to you.

---

319 SO?] F1; ~—F3 ~! BROCKBANK   327 bring him] POPE; bring him in peace F,
KEIGHTLEY; bring him in GOMME   328–9 form— | In peace—] F (forme (In peace));
KEIGHTLEY *omits* F's *second* In peace

---

317 **parties** factions
320 **What** why (*OED* 19)
325 **bolted** refined, sifted. The image, continued in 'Meal and bran', relates
  to the general 'corn' imagery of the
  play.
327 **bring him** F's 'bring him in peace' is
  usually explained as a compositorial
  anticipation of 3.1.329, but a survival
  of a false start in Shakespeare's papers
  is equally likely. Proudfoot conjectures

retaining "in peace" but omitting "go"'
  (Oxford *Textual Companion*, p. 597).
328–9 **answer . . . peril** 'stand his trial
  peacefully even though his life be at
  stake' (Hibbard)
330 **humane** properly human (cf. 1.1.17,
  'humanely'). The two words were not
  distinguished in Shakespeare's time.
  Cf. the plebeians' earlier appeal for
  Martius to act 'kindly', 2.3.71 n.
335 **attend** await

(*To the Senators*) Let me desire your company. He must
      come,
Or what is ~~worst will follow.~~
⌈FIRST⌉ SENATOR   Pray you, let's to him.
            Exeunt ⌈*Tribunes and Citizens at one door, Patricians*
                                        at another door⌉

3.2   *Enter Coriolanus with Nobles*
CORIOLANUS
      Let them pull all about mine ears, present me
      Death on the wheel or at wild horses' heels,
      Or pile ten hills on the Tarpeian rock,
      That the precipitation might down stretch
      Below the beam of sight, yet will I still   5
      Be thus to them.
              Enter Volumnia
A PATRICIAN
      You do the nobler.
CORIOLANUS   I muse my mother
      Does not approve me further, who was wont
      To call them woollen vassals, things created
      To buy and sell with groats, to show bare heads   10

---

339 FIRST SENATOR] ROWE; *Sena.* F   339.1–2 *Exeunt ... another door*] OXFORD; *Exeunt Omnes.* F
  3.2.6.1 *Enter ... Volumnia*] F; *after war, l. 13 in* DYCE   7 A PATRICIAN] CAPELL (*subs.*); *Noble.* F; *One Pat.* MALONE

3.2 This scene is wholly Shakespeare's invention and is obviously meant to parallel but also contrast with 5.3: see Introduction, pp. 32, 53.

0.1 *Nobles* These should probably be the 'young nobility' who Plutarch says approved of Coriolanus' intransigence (cf. 4.1.0.2), as distinct from the older Senators who enter with Menenius at 24.1 to advise conciliation.

2 **Death ... heels** Elizabethan, not Roman, forms of execution, as Malone notes; death on the wheel involved having all one's bones systematically broken by the executioner. Cf. Menenius' unpleasant threats at 5.2.64–5.

4 **precipitation** drop, precipice

5 **Below ... sight** farther than sight can reach

beam of sight 'Vision was then conceived as a ray proceeding from the eye to the object perceived' (Kemball-Cook).

6.1 *Enter Volumnia* The scene is presumably at Coriolanus' house (cf. 3.1.230), which Plutarch tells us belonged to his mother. See Introduction, p. 22.

7 **muse** wonder, am puzzled

9 **woollen vassals** slaves wearing coarse woollen clothes

10 **groats** English four-penny pieces; the implication is that they are merely petty traders
   show bare heads i.e. as a mark of respect and subservience, cf. 1.10.40. 2–3 n.

In congregations, to yawn, be still, and wonder,
When one but of my ordinance stood up
To speak of peace or war. (*To Volumnia*) I talk of you.
Why did you wish me milder? Would you have me
False to my nature? Rather say I play   15
The man I am.

VOLUMNIA   O, sir, sir, sir,
I would have had you put your power well on
Before you had worn it out.

CORIOLANUS   Let 't go.

VOLUMNIA
You might have been enough the man you are
With striving less to be so. Lesser had been   20
The tryings of your dispositions if
You had not showed them how ye were disposed
Ere they lacked power to cross you.

CORIOLANUS   Let them hang.

VOLUMNIA Ay, and burn too.

      Enter Menenius, with the Senators

MENENIUS (*to Coriolanus*)
Come, come, you have been too rough, something too
      rough.   25

---

18 Let 't] This edition (*conj.* Wilson); Let F; Let's F4; Let it THEOBALD   21 tryings]
This edition; things F; thwartings THEOBALD; taxings SISSON; crossings HIBBARD

---

12 **ordinance** rank
15–16 **play ... am** An acting image which is revealingly ambiguous; see Introduction, pp. 84–5.
18 **Let 't go** (a) never mind! Cf. *K. John* 3.3.33, 'I had a thing to say—but let it go'; (b) F's 'Let go' would mean 'Have done', which is less pertinent to Volumnia's preceding speech.
19–20 **You ... so** Cf. Lady Macbeth in *Macbeth* 1.7.49–51.
21 **tryings** testings, trials; 'ry' could easily be mistaken for 'hi' in secretary hand, resulting in F's nonsensical 'things'. Of other alternatives that have been suggested, Sisson's 'taxings' seems most orthographically plausible.
23 **Ere ... you** i.e. before they had lost the

power to deny you confirmation as consul
Let ... hang A favourite Coriolanus phrase. At 1980 Ashland he held up his cheek for Volumnia to kiss as she replied 'Ay, and burn too', suggesting a familiar routine between them; ironically, her retort foreshadows Coriolanus' eventual threat to burn all Rome.
25 **Come, come** In rehearsal for 1984 NT Peter Hall drew attention to the tempo contrast between Menenius' urgency and Volumnia's more calculated rhythms of cajolery. Uncharacteristically she repeats 'pray' (l. 28) and 'prithee' (74, 91, 100, 109) clauses until she finally loses her temper at 125.

You must return and mend it.

FIRST SENATOR   There's no remedy
~~Unless, by not so doing, our good city~~
Cleave in the midst and perish.

VOLUMNIA (*to Coriolanus*)   Pray be counselled.
I have a heart as little apt as yours,
But yet a brain that leads my use of anger   30
To better vantage.

MENENIUS   Well said, noble woman.
Before he should thus stoop to th' herd, but that
The violent fit o'th' time craves it as physic
For the whole state, I would put mine armour on,
Which I can scarcely bear.   35

CORIOLANUS What must I do?

MENENIUS Return to th' tribunes.

CORIOLANUS Well, what then, what then?

MENENIUS Repent what you have spoke.

CORIOLANUS
For them? I cannot do it to the gods,   40
Must I then do't to them?

VOLUMNIA   You are too absolute,
Though therein you can never be too noble,
But when extremities speak. I have heard you say,
Honour and policy, like unsevered friends,
I'th' war do grow together. Grant that, and tell me   45
In peace what each of them by th'other lose

---

26 FIRST SENATOR] CAPELL; *Sen.* F   29 as little apt] F; as little soft SINGER *conj.*; of mettle
apt STAUNTON *conj.*   32 herd] THEOBALD; heart F   40 them?] F3; ~. FI   42–3 noble,
... speak.] F; ~. ... ~, HIBBARD

29 **apt** compliant, yielding
30–1 **leads ... vantage** 'teaches me to
    make better use of my anger' (Wilson)
32 **herd** F's 'heart' is probably a misread-
    ing of manuscript 'heard' (as at
    3.1.35), influenced by 'heart' in 29;
    the epithet is a favourite with Martius
33 **fit** (a) fever, cf. *Caesar* 1.2.121–3; less
    probably (b) frenzy, cf. *Titus* 4.1.17
40 For Gomme's suggestion of 'Fore' is an
    attractive possibility
41–3 **You ... speak** The obscurity of this
    sentence arises from the logical contra-

diction Volumnia has landed herself
in: she wishes to confirm her teaching
that it is noble of Coriolanus to be
uncompromising but to insist that this
is not so in the present circumstances.
43 **extremities speak** absolute necessity
    demands. Hibbard tries to lessen the
    contradiction by attaching 'But when
    extremities speak' to the following
    rather than the preceding lines.
44 **policy** stratagems
    unsevered inseparable

That they combine not there.

CORIOLANUS   Tush, tush!

MENENIUS   A good demand.

VOLUMNIA

If it be honour in your wars to seem
The same you are not, which for your best ends
You adopt your policy, how is it less or worse   50
That it shall hold companionship in peace
With honour, as in war, since that to both
It stands in like request?

CORIOLANUS   Why force you this?

VOLUMNIA

Because that now it lies you on to speak
To th' people; not by your own instruction,   55
Nor by th' matter which your heart prompts you,
But with such words that are but roted in
Your tongue, though but bastards and syllables
Of no allowance to your bosom's truth.
Now this no more dishonours you at all   60
Than to take in a town with gentle words,
Which else would put you to your fortune and
The hazard of much blood.

---

54 you on] F; on you POPE   57 roted] MALONE *after* F (roated); rooted JOHNSON

---

47 **there** i.e. 'in peace'. Menenius' completion of Volumnia's verse line completely ignores Martius' interruption.

48–53 **If . . . request** i.e. 'if it is honourable in war to make use of deceit to encompass your aims, how is it less honourable in peacetime, since in peace and war alike it is equally necessary?' (Gomme).

53 **force** (a) enforce, urge (on me); (b) argue so illogically?

54–9 **Because . . . truth** F has two metrically irregular lines—'that are but roted in your tongue, | Though but bastards and syllables'—and none of the suggested relinings is wholly satisfactory. Perhaps Shakespeare intended this roughness to reflect the rapid improvisations and pauses of Volumnia's argument, whose explanations are opportunistic, not logical. Volumnia's

disingenuousness here should make us look closely at her later arguments in 5.3.

54 **lies you on** is incumbent on you
55 **instruction** inclination, emotional prompting
57 **roted** learned by rote
58 **bastards** i.e. no genuine issue of your mind
59 **Of . . . to** with no claim for acknowledgement by
61 **take in** capture
62 **your fortune** reliance on your luck
63 **The . . . blood** Oxford's *Textual Companion* suggests that this part-line may be the result of the compositor deliberately wasting space to fill up the end of a page, but it surely marks an emphatic pause before Volumnia moves from abstract argument to personal example.

I would dissemble with my nature where
My fortunes and my friends at stake required   65
I should do so in honour. I am in this
Your wife, your son, these senators, the nobles;
And you will rather show our general louts
How you can frown than spend a fawn upon 'em
For the inheritance of their loves and safeguard   70
Of what that want might ruin.

MENENIUS   Noble lady!
(*To Coriolanus*) Come, go with us, speak fair. You may
    salve so,
Not what is dangerous present, but the loss
Of what is past.

VOLUMNIA   I prithee now, my son,
    ⌈*She takes his bonnet*⌉
Go to them with this bonnet in thy hand,   75
And thus far having stretched it—here be with them—
Thy knee bussing the stones—for in such business

67–8 son, these ... nobles; ... you,] THEOBALD (*conj.* Warburton); ~: These ... ~,
... ~, F   71 lady!] ROWE; ~, F   74.1 *She ... bonnet*] OXFORD; *not in* F   76 —here
... them—] F ((here ... them))

64–6 I...honour 'I would pretend to be
other than I am, if, because my fortunes and my friends were at risk,
honour so required it' (Brockbank).
Cf. ll. 14–16: for Martius honour is
dependent on integrity of personality,
for Volumnia on loyalty to self-interest
and one's social group.

66 I am in this in this I speak for, represent. By putting a comma after 'this'
and stressing 'I', Johnson invited the
interpretation 'I am involved in this,
(and so is your wife ... etc.)', but such
a reading is strained, besides involving
alteration to F. Moreover, the original
recalls the undercurrents of 1.3.2, 'If
my son were my husband ...'

68 our general louts 'the vulgar clowns of
our community' (Arden)

70 inheritance obtaining (again a patrician property metaphor)

71 that want i.e. failure to 'spend a fawn
upon 'em'

73 Not ... but not only ... but also
present in the present (i.e. his life)

74 what is past i.e. the consulship

74.1 bonnet cap or hat. Cf. 2.3.37.1 n.
and the description of Bolingbroke's
wooing of the crowd in *Richard II*
1.4.30.

75–88 Go ... person The syntax and
grammar of this long, parenthetically
interrupted speech are confusing for
the same reason 54 ff. were so rough:
they represent rapid shifts of thought
as Volumnia energetically improvises
and rehearses the way Coriolanus
must appeal to the crowd. She clearly
mimes the first part of her instructions,
with acting cues at 'thus' in ll. 76, 80.
See Introduction, p. 105.

76 stretched it stretched it out to them;
cf. 2.3.163
be with them do what they wish, give
them what they expect (and all they
deserve), cf. 2.3.94–8

77 bussing kissing. She demonstrates a
curtsey, with a play on 'business' at
the end of the line (King).

Action is eloquence, and the eyes of th'ignorant
More learned than the ears—waving thy head,
Which offer thus, correcting thy stout heart,   80
Now humble as the ripest mulberry
That will not hold the handling; or say to them
Thou art their soldier and, being bred in broils,
Hast not the soft way which, thou dost confess,
Were fit for thee to use as they to claim,   85
In asking their good loves; but thou wilt frame
Thyself, forsooth, hereafter theirs so far
As thou hast power and person.
MENENIUS (*to Coriolanus*)   This but done
Even as she speaks, why, their hearts were yours;
For they have pardons, being asked, as free   90

---

80 Which] F; With (W^th) RANN (*conj.* Johnson); While STAUNTON *conj.*; And CAPELL offer thus,] *'Textual Companion' conj.*; often thus‸ F; often, thus, CAMBRIDGE   81 Now] F; Now's COLLIER 1858 (MS); Bow HUDSON (*conj.* Mason)   82 or] F; *omitted* HANMER; so KINNEAR *conj.* (*in* Cambridge)

78–9 **Action . . . ears** To illustrate this emphasis on gesture in classical (and Renaissance) oratory, Arden cites Bacon's essay 'Of Boldness': 'Question was asked of Demosthenes, What was the chief part of an orator? He answered, "Action; what next? Action. What next again? Action. . . . the reason is plain. There is in human nature, generally, more of the fool than of the wise" ' (*Essays*, 1625, no. 12).

79 **waving** Brockbank compares *Hamlet* 2.1.94, 'And thrice his head thus waving up and down', but notes that Volumnia may also be bowing in all directions

80 **Which offer** F's With often' has been one of the major stumbling blocks for interpretation. Because the manuscript abbreviation 'W^ch' can easily be misread as 'W^th', the usual emendation since Johnson has been to replace 'Which' with 'With', reading the phrase as 'With often thus correcting thy stout heart'. Oxford's idea of changing 'often' to 'offer' (another easy graphical error) makes the phrase into a demonstrative double parenthesis more typical of the syntax of the whole speech, with 'offer' continuing

the implications of 'stretched it', 'be with them', and the image of a mulberry asking to be picked.
stout proud, cf. *Twelfth Night* 2.5.165
81 **humble** humble yourself (*OED v.*¹ 3b)
82 **that . . . handling** 'that drops off as soon as it is touched'. In the circumstances the image is faintly comic and betrays Volumnia's contempt for the softness she is urging. For the mulberry as an emblem of readiness to yield, Arden cites Erasmus' *Adages* under Proclivitas, 'Maturior Moro'. Interestingly, it was an image applied by Aeschylus to Hector.
or 'or again'; to indicate an ancillary, not an alternative idea: Volumnia goes on to suggest apologies and promises that can supplement submissive gestures.
83–6 **Thou . . . loves** This is an argument we have just heard from Menenius at 3.1.323–6; the close repetition diminishes our sense of its honesty.
87 **theirs** according to their wishes
90–1 **For . . . purpose** 'if they are asked, they will grant a pardon as readily as they will argue pointlessly'; 'free' also has a nuance of 'with generosity'

As words to little purpose.

VOLUMNIA   Prithee now,
Go, and be ruled, although I know thou hadst rather
Follow thine enemy in a fiery gulf
Than flatter him in a bower.

     Enter Cominius

                 Here is Cominius.

COMINIUS

I have been i'th' market-place; and, sir, 'tis fit   95
You make strong party, or defend yourself
By calmness or by absence. All's in anger.

MENENIUS

Only fair speech.

COMINIUS   I think 'twill serve, if he
Can thereto frame his spirit.

VOLUMNIA   He must, and will.
Prithee now, say you will, and go about it.   100

CORIOLANUS

Must I go show them my unbarbèd sconce?
Must I with my base tongue give to my noble heart
A lie that it must bear? Well, I will do't.
Yet were there but this single plot to lose,

---

101 unbarbèd] ROWE; vnbarb'd F   102 Must I] F; *omitted* WILSON   103 bear? Well,]
POPE; ~∧ ~? F   104 plot to lose,] THEOBALD; Plot, to loose∧ F

91–2 **Prithee . . . ruled** The contradiction
of plea and command between Volum-
nia's 'Prithee' and 'Go, and be ruled'
is comically reversed at ll. 99–100.

93 **fiery gulf** Mainly a contrast to 'bower',
but also possibly reminiscent of the
Roman legend of Marcus Curtius.
Within the play it recalls Martius's solo
entrance into the gates of Corioles
and foreshadows his later intention to
burn Rome.

94 *Enter Cominius* The order of
suppliants here (Volumnia, Menenius,
Cominius) is the reverse of that in
Act 5.

101 **unbarbèd sconce** uncovered head (as
a sign of respect, cf. 10 n.). Coriolanus'
wording is deliberately contemptuous.

102 **Must I** This repetition creates an
alexandrine, and it is possible that the

compositor accidentally duplicated the
beginning of l. 101, a common
enough error: Wilson therefore omits
the second 'Must I', while Pope and
others regularize by omitting 'I with'.
The repetition may be intentional,
however, to show rising scorn: cf.
Richard II 4.1.218.
noble patrician

103 **Well . . . do't** The oscillation in Martius between obedience and rebelliousness was pointed in 1984 NT by giving
him a Hamlet-like series of false starts
at ll. 103, 106, 112, 122, 132–4,
136, 143 before he finally got off the
stage at 148, the anxious Senators
reflecting each swing of his indecision.

104 **plot** piece of earth (i.e. his body; the
ultimate 'property')

This mould of Martius, they to dust should grind it   105
And throw't against the wind. To th' market-place.
You have put me now to such a part which never
I shall discharge to th' life.
COMINIUS   Come, come, we'll prompt you.
VOLUMNIA
I prithee now, sweet son, as thou hast said
My praises made thee first a soldier, so,   110
To have my praise for this, perform a part
Thou hast not done before.
CORIOLANUS   Well, I must do't.
Away, my disposition; and possess me
Some harlot's spirit! My throat of war be turned,
Which choired with my drum, into a pipe   115
Small as an eunuch or the virgin voice
That babies lull asleep! The smiles of knaves
Tent in my cheeks, and schoolboys' tears take up
The glasses of my sight! A beggar's tongue

---

115 choired] F (quier'd); quired CAMBRIDGE   drum, ... pipe‸] POPE; ~‸ ... ~, F; ~,
... ~, ROWE   116 eunuch] F; eunuch's HANMER   117 lull] F; lulls ROWE

105 **mould** (a) 'earth regarded as the material of the human body' (*OED sb.*[1] 4), linking to 'plot' and 'dust', (b) 'form', cf. 5.3.22–3

113 ff. **Away** ... The element of exaggeration in Martius' imagery has been reflected in parodic action by many recent Coriolanuses. Olivier in particular guyed the lines, while in 1984 NT Ian McKellen's parody included a mimicry of one of Volumnia's own gestures at 'possess me | some harlot's spirit' (ll. 113–14), which made her turn angrily away, to the Senators' embarrassment.

114 **harlot** (a) beggar, (b) prostitute, (c) actor (cf. 'harlotry players', *1 Henry IV*, 2.5.399–400)?
throat of war yet another reference to the power of Coriolanus' voice
turned Oxford's suggestion of 'tuned' is possible and certainly suits the context, but F's reading makes perfectly good sense.

115 **choired with** sang in tune with

116 **small** small in volume and high in pitch, cf. *Twelfth Night* 1.4.32–3, 'thy

small pipe | Is as the maiden's organ, shrill and sound'
eunuch (a) a 'eunuque' was a musical instrument, flute-like in shape with taut parchment at one end (David Z. Crookes, *Music and Letters*, 67 (1986), 159–61); (b) possibly also an adjective bridging to 'virgin': the image is of a reverse voice-change from maturity back to adolescence.

117 **lull** Grammatically this should be in the singular, but Shakespeare often lets a preceding plural object—in this case 'babies'—determine the number of the verb.

118 **Tent ... take up** Two military metaphors: 'encamp' and 'occupy, capture'; cf. 'armed knees ... stirrup' of ll. 120–1 and 'the word' of 144.
schoolboys' tears This anticipates Aufidius' gibe at 5.6.103.

119 **glasses ... sight** eyeballs. Throat, cheeks, eyeballs, tongue, lips, knees, (and possibly, according to Brockbank, alms = arms) constitute another list of *disjecta membra*, separated bodily parts: see Introduction, p. 81.

Make motion through my lips, and my armed knees,   120
Who bowed but in my stirrup, bend like his
That hath received an alms!—I will not do't,
Lest I surcease to honour mine own truth,
And by my body's action teach my mind
A most inherent baseness.

VOLUMNIA   At thy choice, then!   125
To beg of thee it is my more dishonour
Than thou of them. Come all to ruin. Let
Thy mother rather feel thy pride than fear
Thy dangerous stoutness, for I mock at death
With as big heart as thou. Do as thou list.   130
Thy valiantness was mine, thou suck'st it from me,
But owe thy pride thyself.

CORIOLANUS   Pray be content.
Mother, I am going to the market-place.
Chide me no more. I'll mountebank their loves,
Cog their hearts from them, and come home beloved   135
Of all the trades in Rome. Look, I am going.
Commend me to my wife. I'll return consul,
Or never trust to what my tongue can do
I'th' way of flattery further.

VOLUMNIA   Do your will.   *Exit*

---

131 suck'st] F; sucked'st ROWE 1714

122 **I...do't** Because of the element of parody earlier in the speech, the suddenness of this volte-face provokes laughter unless it is preceded by a longish pause.

123 **surcease** cease

125 **inherent** that will become 'permanently indwelling' (*OED* 2); this is Shakespeare's only use of the word. There is a complex tension here between 'teach' and 'inherent' as well as between 'body's action' and 'mind'; the train of thought resembles that of Sonnets 110 and 111. See Introduction, p. 85.

129 **stoutness** (a) obstinacy, (b) pride: i.e. 'let me be a victim of your pride rather than be afraid to confront its dangerous obstinacy'. The implication that Martius may kill her anticipates her

more serious threat of suicide in 5.3.

132 **owe** (a) own, (b) be indebted for. Both meanings apply because Volumnia is trying to claim Coriolanus' heroism as *her* 'property' (l. 131).

134 **mountebank** cheat by means of a performance. A mountebank was a quack who sold his wares by mounting a platform (or 'bank') and attracting customers with story-telling and comic patter.

135 **Cog** swindle (originally with false dice)

137 **Commend ... wife** A curious comment in the circumstances, with perhaps a hint of provocation: Volumnia does sometimes act as though she were a privileged intermediary between her son and his wife, cf. 2.1.171 n.

139 **Do your will** Volumnia's curt dismissiveness can be explained in the imme-

COMINIUS

    Away! The tribunes do attend you. Arm yourself   140
    To answer mildly, for they are prepared
    With accusations, as I hear, more strong
    Than are upon you yet.

CORIOLANUS

    The word is 'mildly'. Pray you let us go.
    Let them accuse me by invention, I   145
    Will answer in mine honour.

MENENIUS Ay, but mildly.

CORIOLANUS Well, mildly be it, then—mildly!   *Exeunt*

3.3 *Enter Sicinius and Brutus*

BRUTUS

    In this point charge him home: that he affects
    Tyrannical power. If he evade us there,
    Enforce him with his envy to the people,
    And that the spoil got on the Antiates
    Was ne'er distributed.

        Enter an Aedile

                What, will he come?   5

AEDILE

    He's coming.

BRUTUS   How accompanied?

3.3.5 *Enter an Aedile*] CAPELL; *at end of line in* F

---

diate context by the way that Coriolanus, even in his acceptance, has
ridiculed her advice, with terms like
'mountebank', 'cog', and 'flattery',
which force her to face an hypocrisy
she does not wish to acknowledge; but
when we see her use a similar tactic
in 5.3, where there is no question of
provocation or hypocrisy, it becomes
clear that this is also an ingrained
family pattern.

144 **word** password; an ironic use of a
military term

145 **by invention** by bogus accusations

148 **mildly!** See Introduction, p. 39. Actors have pointed this in various ways:
Irving (1901) delivered the word with

concentrated contempt; Burton (1954
OV) bellowed it furiously; in 1938 OV
Olivier gave the word a flinty, upward-
rising snap; but more interestingly, in
1959 SMT he merely mouthed it and
'at the moment of shaping it with lips
and facial muscles, he convulsively
retched' with the 'psychological overtones of a child's rejection of food
forced on him' (Kitchin, p. 146).

3.3.1 **charge him home** press home your
accusations against him

1–2 **affects | Tyrannical power** aims to
become king; cf. ll. 64–5

3 **Enforce him** attack him
envy malice, hatred

4 **spoil . . . Antiates** See Introduction,
p. 26.

AEDILE

With old Menenius, and those senators
That always favoured him.

SICINIUS   Have you a catalogue
Of all the voices that we have procured,
Set down by th' poll?

AEDILE   I have, 'tis ready.   10

SICINIUS

Have you collected them by tribes?

AEDILE   I have.

SICINIUS

Assemble presently the people hither,
And when they hear me say 'It shall be so
I'th' right and strength o'th' commons', be it either
For death, for fine, or banishment, then let them,   15
If I say 'Fine', cry 'Fine!', if 'Death', cry 'Death!',
Insisting on the old prerogative
And power i'th' truth o'th' cause.

AEDILE   I shall inform them.

BRUTUS

And when such time they have begun to cry,
Let them not cease, but with a din confused   20
Enforce the present execution
Of what we chance to sentence.

AEDILE   Very well.

9–11 **voices . . . tribes** Plutarch describes how the Tribunes craftily arranged for a meeting of the people in an 'Assembly of Tribes', where each tribe had one vote determined by a simple majority within that tribe, instead of in an 'Assembly of Centuries', where voting power was weighted according to income and the wealthy patricians consequently had an absolute majority (98 of the 193 centuries, against 95 for all the other Roman classes put together). This was misleadingly glossed by Amyot 'a cause que les voix se contoyent par teste', which North then elaborated to 'for by this means the multitude of poor needy people . . . came to be of greater force, because their voices were numbered by the poll', which is clearly how Shakespeare understood the situation, cf. 3.1.136.

9 **voices . . . procured** most probably, (a) 'votes we have already made certain of'; but possibly also (b) 'the claque that we have paid', cf. ll. 13–16

12 **presently** immediately

13–22 **And . . . sentence** The shrewdly independent plebeians of 1.1 are now to be completely manipulated.

17–18 **old prerogative | And power** See Introduction, pp. 40–1.

18 **i' . . . cause** in the justice of the case. Hibbard remarks very appositely, 'For an audience in 1608 or thereabouts these words would probably have had a distinctly Puritan ring'. The Puritans were among James's most vociferous opponents in the House of Commons.

21 **present execution** immediate carrying into effect

SICINIUS

Make them be strong, and ready for this hint
When we shall hap to give't them.

BRUTUS   Go about it.

Exit Aedile

(*To Sicinius*) Put him to choler straight. He hath been used   25
Ever to conquer and to have his worth
Of contradiction. Being once chafed, he cannot
Be reined again to temperance. Then he speaks
What's in his heart, and that is there which looks
With us to break his neck.

SICINIUS   Well, here he comes.   30

Enter Coriolanus, Menenius, and Cominius, with other
⌈ *Senators and Patricians* ⌉

MENENIUS (*to Coriolanus*) Calmly, I do beseech you.

CORIOLANUS (*to Menenius*)

Ay, as an hostler that for th' poorest piece
Will bear the knave by th' volume.—(*Aloud*) Th'hon-
   oured gods
Keep Rome in safety and the chairs of justice
Supplied with worthy men, plant love among's,   35
Throng our large temples with the shows of peace,

---

24 Go‸] F; ~, CAPELL   24.1 *Exit Aedile*] POPE; *not in* F   30.1–2 *Enter ... Patricians*]
DYCE; *after* neck. *in* F   *other Senators and Patricians*] OXFORD; *others* F   32 for th'] F2;
fourth F1   33 (*Aloud*)] This edition; *not in* F   35 among's] DYCE; amongs F1;
amongst you F2; amongst us STEEVENS–REED   36 Throng] THEOBALD; Through F

26–7 **to have ... contradiction** probably
(a) to be as contradictory as he pleases;
less probably, (b) to acquire fame or
win glory through conflict, to flourish
in opposition (Schmidt), in support of
which Wilson quotes North that Martius thought 'that to overcome always,
and to have the upper hand in all
matters, was a token of magnanimity'.
29 **looks** looks likely, promises
30 **With us** with help from us
   break his neck as a result of precipitation from the Tarpeian rock. However,
cf. 4.7.24–5, where Aufidius uses the
same image, thus paralleling the two
conspiracy scenes. Menenius also uses
the phrase to describe Martius'

revenge on the Romans (5.4.33),
echoing the latter's favourite ejaculation 'Hang 'em.' Cf. also Volumnia's
'tread upon his neck' (1.3.48).
30.1–2 **Enter ... Patricians** The scene
that follows is, in effect, an informal
trial of Coriolanus and the language
on both sides is thick with legal terminology. Modern stagings have
often conveyed this by having the
Tribunes sit behind a table and wield
a gavel or ostentatiously flourish
documents.
32 **piece** (of money)
33 **Will ... volume** will put up with being
called knave to any extent
36 **shows** ceremonies

And not our streets with war!

FIRST SENATOR   Amen, amen.

MENENIUS   A noble wish.

Enter the Aedile with the Citizens

SICINIUS

Draw near, ye people.

AEDILE   List to your tribunes. Audience!

Peace, I say.

CORIOLANUS   First, hear me speak.

SICINIUS *and* BRUTUS   Well, say.—Peace ho!

CORIOLANUS

Shall I be charged no further than this present?   40

Must all determine here?

SICINIUS   I do demand

If you submit you to the people's voices,

Allow their officers, and are content

To suffer lawful censure for such faults

As shall be proved upon you.

CORIOLANUS   I am content.   45

MENENIUS

Lo, citizens, he says he is content.

The warlike service he has done, consider. Think

Upon the wounds his body bears, which show

Like graves i'th' holy churchyard.

CORIOLANUS   Scratches with briers,

Scars to move laughter only.

MENENIUS   Consider further   50

37.1 *Citizens*] OXFORD; *Plebeians* F   39 SICINIUS *and* BRUTUS] OXFORD; *Both Tri.* F

37 **And . . . wish** The eager (and metric-
  ally equivalent) responses by First
  Senator and Menenius would be sim-
  ultaneous, making the line regular.
38 **Audience!** Attention!
40 **this present** A legal phrase usually
  signifying the precise document in a
  case: i.e. 'no further than the present
  accusation'.
41 **determine** be determined, settled
  demand demand to know
43 **Allow** acknowledge
45 **I am content** It is usual for the actor
  playing Coriolanus to make a long

pause before this response, indicating
his reluctance and the extreme effort
he has to make for self-control. The
1977 RSC prompt-book, for example,
indicates a pause of twenty seconds.
49 **graves . . . churchyard** The precise significance of this anachronistic comparison is not clear: 'We are left at
  liberty to think of the size, or the number of the wounds, or of the sanctity
  of the hero's person, in the comparison' (Arden); cf. 2.1.151–2, 'Every
  gash was an enemy's grave', where
  Menenius is also the speaker.

That when he speaks not like a citizen,
You find him like a soldier. Do not take
His rougher accents for malicious sounds,
But, as I say, such as become a soldier
Rather than envy you.   55

COMINIUS Well, well, no more.

CORIOLANUS What is the matter
  That, being passed for consul with full voice,
  I am so dishonoured that the very hour
  You take it off again?   60

SICINIUS Answer to us.

CORIOLANUS Say then!—'Tis true, I ought so.

SICINIUS
  We charge you that you have contrived to take
  From Rome all seasoned office, and to wind
  Yourself into a power tyrannical,   65
  For which you are a traitor to the people.

CORIOLANUS
  How, traitor!

MENENIUS   Nay, temperately—your promise.

CORIOLANUS
  The fires i'th' lowest hell fold in the people!
  Call me their traitor, thou injurious tribune!
  Within thine eyes sat twenty thousand deaths,   70

---

53 accents] THEOBALD; Actions F   62 then!—'Tis] This edition; ~: 'tis F   68 hell∧
fold] POPE; ~. Fould F1; ~, Fould F2   70–2 deaths, ... clutched∧ ... millions, ...
tongue∧ ... numbers,] ROWE; ~∧ ... ~: ... ~∧ ... ~, ... ~. F

---

53 **accents** F's error may have arisen from
the compositor misreading 'accents' as
'accons', a manuscript abbreviation
for 'actions' (Sisson)

55 **envy you** show ill-will towards you

56 **Well ... more** Cominius, perhaps remembering Coriolanus' abrupt exit
from the Senate in 2.3, tries to cut
Menenius short, but the damage has
already been done.

60–1 **You ... us** This should probably be
one line. Its shortness would reflect a
charged pause between Coriolanus' aggressive 'Say then!' and ' 'Tis true, I
ought so', which is how Olivier delivered it.

63 **contrived** plotted

64 **seasoned** (a) 'established and settled by

time' (Johnson), (b) 'qualified, tempered' (Schmidt, Arden), as distinct
from 'power tyrannical', l. 65?
wind insinuate

65 **tyrannical** Both in the general sense
and in the specific sense of aiming to
be king.

66 **traitor** Cf. 3.1.164; this accusation,
which so particularly incenses Coriolanus, does not occur in Plutarch.

68 **fold in** enfold. This is the first time
Coriolanus entertains the idea of Rome
going up in flames, an image that will
recur with increasing frequency.

69 **their traitor** traitor to them
injurious insulting, calumniating

70 **Within** i.e. 'if within'

70, 71 **sat ... clutched** Both verbs are in

In thy hands clutched as many millions, in
Thy lying tongue both numbers, I would say
'Thou liest' unto thee with a voice as free
    As I do pray the gods.
SICINIUS Mark you this, people?   75
ALL ⌈ THE CITIZENS ⌉ To th' rock, to th' rock with him!
SICINIUS Peace!
    We need not put new matter to his charge.
    What you have seen him do and heard him speak,
    Beating your officers, cursing yourselves,   80
    Opposing laws with strokes, and here defying
    Those whose great power must try him—even this,
    So criminal and in such capital kind,
    Deserves th'extremest death.
BRUTUS   But since he hath
    Served well for Rome—
CORIOLANUS   What do you prate of service?   85
BRUTUS
    I talk of that that know it.
CORIOLANUS   You?
MENENIUS
    Is this the promise that you made your mother?
COMINIUS
    Know, I pray you—
CORIOLANUS   I'll know no further.
    Let them pronounce the steep Tarpeian death,
    Vagabond exile, flaying, pent to linger   90
    But with a grain a day, I would not buy
    Their mercy at the price of one fair word,

---

75 this,] F4; ~ₐ F1   76, 107, 120, 138, 143 ALL THE CITIZENS] F (*All.*)   85 Rome—]
F3; ~. F1   88 you—] ROWE; ~. F   90 flaying, pent] F (Fleaing); fleaing. Pent JOHNSON

the subjunctive. Brockbank notes that
'clutched' was a comparatively new
verb in English at this time.

73 **free** candid
81 **Opposing ... strokes** 'taking arms
against legal authority' (Gomme)
83 **capital** punishable by death
84–5 For the actual reason for this

change of sentences (l. 102), see Introduction, p. 31.
85–6 **What ... You?** Cf. Aufidius' comment at 4.7.31, 'The tribunes are no
soldiers': Coriolanus can only understand 'service' in a military sense,
whereas Brutus is laying claim to civic
responsibility.
90 **pent** let me be imprisoned

Nor check my courage for what they can give
To have't with saying 'Good morrow'.
SICINIUS   For that he has,
As much as in him lies, from time to time   95
Envied against the people, seeking means
To pluck away their power, as now at last
Given hostile strokes, and that not in the presence
Of dreaded justice, but on the ministers
That doth distribute it, in the name o'th' people,   100
And in the power of us the tribunes, we
E'en from this instant banish him our city
In peril of precipitation
From off the rock Tarpeian, never more
To enter our Rome gates. I'th' people's name   105
I say it shall be so.
ALL ⌈THE CITIZENS⌉
It shall be so, it shall be so! Let him away!
He's banished, and it shall be so!
COMINIUS
Hear me, my masters and my common friends.
SICINIUS
He's sentenced. No more hearing.
COMINIUS   Let me speak.   110
I have been consul, and can show for Rome
Her enemies' marks upon me. I do love

96 Envied] F; Inveigh'd HUDSON (*conj*. Becket), OXFORD   97 as] F; has HANMER; and HUDSON *conj*.   100 doth] F1; doe F2   109 friends.] F; ~—ROWE   111 for] THEOBALD; from F

93 **courage** spirit, mettle (Dyce), cf. *3 Henry VI* 2.2.57
94 **for that** inasmuch as. The legalistic phrasing of Sicinius' indictment makes it sound like a prearranged document.
96 **Envied** shown malice. Oxford makes a case for 'inveighed', based on orthography and lack of precedent for the combination 'envied *against*', but 'envy' (meaning malice) is a key word in this play, and the combination with 'against' is quite clear and is no more strained than a dozen other linguistic innovations in the text.

97 **as** See Abbott § 113, 114.
98 **not** not only; cf. 3.2.73
100 **doth** Brockbank notes that the singular verb may have been influenced by 'it'
102 **banish ... city** In Chap. 29 of Book 1 of his *Discorsi* Machiavelli has the Tribunes *save* Martius from the wrath of the Plebeians by banishing him (see Dacres's 1636 translation, p. 125): cf. 84–5 n.
103 **precipitation** being thrown
105 **Rome gates** Shakespeare often uses proper names as adjectives (Abbott § 22)

My country's good with a respect more tender,
More holy and profound, than mine own life,
My dear wife's estimate, her womb's increase,   115
And treasure of my loins. Then if I would
Speak that—
SICINIUS   We know your drift. Speak what?
BRUTUS
There's no more to be said, but he is banished
As enemy to the people and his country.
It shall be so!
ALL ⌈THE CITIZENS⌉ It shall be so, it shall be so!   120
CORIOLANUS
You common cry of curs, whose breath I hate
As reek o'th' rotten fens, whose loves I prize
As the dead carcasses of unburied men
That do corrupt my air: I banish you!
And here remain with your uncertainty: 125
Let every feeble rumour shake your hearts;
Your enemies, with nodding of their plumes,
Fan you into despair! Have the power still

117 that—] ROWE; ~. F

115 **estimate** public reputation
115–16 **womb's ... loins** i.e. children;
showing that Volumnia's sentiments
in 1.3 were typical of the patrician
code, not peculiar to her alone
121 **cry** howling pack, cf. *Dream* 4.1.123
121–2 **breath ... fens** Cf. 1.1.57 n. about
citizens' stinking breath.
122 **reek** stinking vapour
rotten fens Brockbank compares *Tempest* 2.1.51–2, ' As if it had lungs, and
rotten ones ... Or as 'twere perfumed
by a fen'; cf. 4.1.31 n.
124 **I banish you** A famous theatrical
'point' which actors have emphasized
in many ways. Kemble and Phelps delivered it with a 'sublimity of disdain'
(Henry Morley, *The Journal of a London
Playgoer from 1851 to 1866* (1891),
p. 217); Kean, on the contrary, 'with
all the virulence of execration and rage
of impotent despair' (W. Hazlitt, *Complete Works*, ed. P. P. Howe, 1933,
xviii. 290); Olivier with quiet contempt—an effect underlined by Denis
Arndt at 1980 Ashland with a long

preliminary stare of disgust; and Ian
Richardson at 1967 RSC in a chilling,
deadly whisper. Kemble gave a stately
sweep of the arm in dismissal; Irving
contrived a curious gesture with his
cloak—'saying this, he, with consum-
mate art, gathering the folds of his
toga in both hands, and sweeping it
hither and thither, seemed as though
with the wind which it caused, to clear
away the mob like dust in the swirl'
(*News of the World*, 21 Apr. 1901);
while both Edwin Forrest and Alan
Howard threatened physical violence.
125–34 **And here ... blows!** Hibbard suggests that 'Here, perhaps, are to be
seen the first glimmerings, as yet in-
completely formulated, of the hero's
decision to turn against Rome'.
125 **remain** may you remain
128 **Fan ... despair** Wilson compares
Macbeth 1.2.49–50, 'the Norwegian
banners flout the sky | And fan our
people cold'. Cf. also the contemptuous
'Fluttered' in 5.6.116.
128–34 **Have ... blows!** The difficulty of

To banish your defenders, till at length
Your ignorance—which finds not till it feels—   130
Making but reservation of yourselves—
Still your own foes—deliver you
As most abated captives to some nation
That won you without blows! Despising
For you the city, thus I turn my back.   135
There is a world elsewhere.

> *Exeunt Coriolanus, Cominius, and Menenius*
> *with the rest of the Patricians*
> *The Citizens all shout, and throw up their caps*

AEDILE

The people's enemy is gone, is gone.

ALL THE CITIZENS

Our enemy is banished, he is gone. Hoo-hoo!

SICINIUS

Go see him out at gates, and follow him

130–2 ignorance— . . . foes—] F (ignorance . . . foes))   130–1 feels— . . . yourselves—]
OXFORD; ~, . . . ~, F   131 but] F; not CAPELL   134–5 blows! Despising . . . city, thus]
CAPELL (*conj.* Pope); ~, despising . . . ~. Thus F   136.1–2 *and* . . . *Patricians.*] OXFORD
(*conj.* Capell); *with Cumalijs.* F   136.3 *The* . . . *caps.*] F; *after* Hoo-hoo! CAMBRIDGE
136.2 *The Citizens*] OXFORD; *They* F

---

this sentence reflects Coriolanus' passion, but its sense can be untangled if
'which finds not till it feels' and 'Still
your own foes' are recognized as
parenthetical elaborations to the main
sentence. The lines foreshadow the action from 4.6 to 5.4.

130 **finds . . . feels** foresees nothing until
it experiences it; cf. *Lear* 4.1.62–3
131 **Making . . . yourselves** leaving no
one in the city except yourselves
132–3 **Still . . . nation**   F's lineation
(which editors often change) conveys
the slow, biting stresses on 'Still',
'own', and 'foes' which express Coriolanus' concentrated rage
132 **Still . . . foes** as always, your own
worst enemies
133 **abated** abject, humbled
134–5 **Despising . . . city** Gomme points
out that, having tried to exclude the
plebeians from his ideal of Rome, Coriolanus now goes to the opposite extreme of despising Rome because the
plebeians are part of it, an attitude

that will soon allow him to contem-
plate the destruction of his fellow patricians and even his own family.
135 **thus . . . back** A clear cue for action.
There . . . elsewhere Another famous
'point' that actors have developed in
many ways. Burton delivered the line
with an effective pause before 'elsewhere'; Howard in 1977 RSC pointed
it by stripping off his consul's robe,
throwing it on the ground at 'There is
a *world*', with a single pause before a
massive, escalating 'ELSE-*WHERE*!',
followed by a triple pause before his exit
and First Citizen's comment in an incredulous small voice, 'The people's
enemy is gone'; while in 1984 NT it was
actually delivered from off stage with
Coriolanus' disembodied voice booming
through the theatre's loudspeakers.
136.2 **with . . . Patricians** The manuscript obviously had the Latin direction for 'with others', *cum aliis*, which
F's compositor mistook for a proper
name and rendered nonsensically as
'*with Cumalijs*.' See Folio Text, p. 139.

As he hath followed you, with all despite.   140
Give him deserved vexation. Let a guard
Attend us through the city.

ALL THE CITIZENS

Come, come, let's see him out at gates. Come.
The gods preserve our noble tribunes! Come.   *Exeunt*

4.1   *Enter Coriolanus, Volumnia, Virgilia, Menenius,*
       Cominius, with the young nobility of Rome

CORIOLANUS

Come, leave your tears. A brief farewell. The beast
With many heads butts me away. Nay, mother,
Where is your ancient courage? You were used
To say extremities was the trier of spirits,
That common chances common men could bear,   5
That when the sea was calm all boats alike
Showed mastership in floating; fortune's blows

---

140 despite.] CAPELL (~, F3); ~ˏ F1   143 gates] F1; the gates F2   gates. Come.] F
(~, come,); ~; come, come. KEIGHTLEY (*conj.* Capell)
   4.1] F (*Actus Quartus.*)   4 extremities was] F1; Extreamity was F2; extremities were
MALONE   5 chancesˏ] F2 (*subs.*); ~. F1

---

141 **vexation** mortification, insult
143–4 **Come,   come . . . Come . . . Come**
   These reiterated cues combine eagerness and hesitation, as the Citizens
   finally leave together like a 'pack of
   hounds harrying its prey' (Ripley). See
   Introduction, p. 106.
144 **noble tribunes** Brockbank draws attention to this now-confirmed redefini-
   tion of 'noble'
   Exeunt The act division here is very prob-
   lematic: see Introduction, pp. 27–8, 137.
4.1 Shakespeare develops this scene from
   a few lines in North, relating how
   Coriolanus took 'his leave of his
   mother and wife, finding them weeping, and shrieking out for sorrow, and
   had also comforted them to be content
   with his chance'. Hibbard notes that
   the same group who welcomed him to
   Rome in 2.1 now sends him into exile.
0.2 *young nobility of Rome* These personal followers are like the Conspirators who support Aufidius in 5.6 and
   rescue him in 1.9.
1 ff. **Come, . . .** In both 1977 RSC and
   1984 NT Coriolanus gave the impres-

sion that, at this point, he was actually eager to leave, looking forward
to release from the strain of trying to
be heroic in a non-ideal Rome. In Plutarch, however, he was master of the
situation because he had already
decided on revenge (Spencer, p. 333).
1–2 **beast . . . heads** Cf. Horace, *Epistles*
   1.1.76, 'Bellua multorum es capitum'
   (you are a monster of many heads),
   and Introduction, p. 79.
3–9 **You . . . cunning** Cf. *Troilus* 1.3.16–53
   for an analogous argument.
3 **You were used** See Abbott § 295 for
   the construction.
4 **extremities was** great crises were
5 **common chances . . . bear** 'even common men can cope with everyday
   happenstance'
6–7 **when . . . floating** Cf. *Troilus*, 1.3.33–6,
   'The sea being smooth, | How many
   shallow bauble-boats dare sail | Upon
   her patient breast, making their way
   | With those of nobler bulk!'
7–9 **fortune's . . . cunning** i.e. 'when fate
   strikes her hardest blows, it requires
   upper-class training to take one's

When most struck home, being gentle wounded craves
A noble cunning. You were used to load me
With precepts that would make invincible   10
The heart that conned them.
VIRGILIA O heavens, O heavens!
CORIOLANUS Nay, I prithee, woman—
VOLUMNIA
Now the red pestilence strike all trades in Rome,
And occupations perish!
CORIOLANUS   What, what, what?   15
I shall be loved when I am lacked. Nay, mother,
Resume that spirit when you were wont to say,
If you had been the wife of Hercules
Six of his labours you'd have done, and saved
Your husband so much sweat. Cominius,   20
Droop not; adieu. Farewell, my wife, my mother;
I'll do well yet. Thou old and true Menenius,
Thy tears are salter than a younger man's
And venomous to thine eyes. My sometime general,
I have seen thee stern, and thou hast oft beheld   25
Heart-hard'ning spectacles. Tell these sad women
'Tis fond to wail inevitable strokes

25 thee] F (the), F3

wounds calmly' (or, possibly, 'like a gentleman,' though this would render 'gentle' and 'noble' tautologous). Possibly, 'cunning' also puns on 'conning' (steering), as an extension of the preceding 'sea . . . boats' imagery; cf. 'conned', l. 11?

11 **conned** studied, learned by heart
14 **red pestilence** typhus (which causes red skin eruptions). Another of the play's disease images; but one that may tap a faint memory of the blood-covered Martius of Act 1.
15 **occupations** handicrafts, trades
   What . . . what? Come, come, come!
16 **I . . . lacked** Cf. *Antony* 1.4.43–4, 'And the ebbed man, ne'er loved till ne'er worth love, | Comes deared by being lacked', and *Much Ado* 4.1.219–24.
18–20 **If . . . sweat** In 1959 SMT Olivier invariably got a laugh on this. Hercules is the demigod of Greek mythology

who to prove his deity had to perform twelve tasks or 'labours'. However, it ceases to be funny in retrospect when Martius' attack on Rome is compared to one of those labours at 4.6.104. Note also that Volumnia always imagines herself as the hero's *wife*, not mother: see Introduction, p. 48.

21 **Droop not** A cue for the actor playing Cominius.
23–4 **tears . . . eyes** The idea that tears' saltiness inflames and damages the eyes occurs also in *Hamlet* 1.2.154–5, 4.5.155–6 and *Troilus* 5.3.57, but the only (slight) analogue to the idea of their growing more salty with age is in *Lear* 4.6.40–1. In 1984 NT Coriolanus tasted Menenius' tears on his fingertip to point the line.
27 **'Tis . . . strokes** A commonplace: cf. Tilley C921, C923, F83.
   fond foolish

As 'tis to laugh at 'em. My mother, you wot well
My hazards still have been your solace, and—
Believe't not lightly—though I go alone,   30
Like to a lonely dragon that his fen
Makes feared and talked of more than seen, your son
Will or exceed the common or be caught
With cautelous baits and practice.
VOLUMNIA   My first son,
Whither wilt thou go? Take good Cominius   35
With thee a while. Determine on some course
More than a wild exposure to each chance
That starts i'th' way before thee.
⌈VIRGILIA⌉   O the gods!

28 My] F; *omitted* POPE, WILSON   35 Whither wilt thou] CAPELL; Whether will thou
FI; Whither will you F2   37 exposure] F (exposture), ROWE   38 VIRGILIA] KEIGHTLEY;
Cor. F

28–9 **My ... solace**   An interestingly
sardonic comment; cf. l. 28 n. and
1.3.5–25, 1.10.13–15, 2.1.165–6.
See Introduction, p. 65.
28 **My** Wilson (following Pope) omits
on the grounds that it is extra-metrical
(it is not; the line is an alexandrine)
and 'lets the style down also': this
latter is, of course, the whole point—
Martius is beginning to distance himself from Volumnia: it conveys a
remonstrative nuance of 'you, who are
my mother'.
  wot know
29 **still** always
30 **Believe't not lightly** be very sure of this
31 **Like ... fen** The 'monstrous beasty
bred in filthy fen' of Spenser's *Faerie
Queene*, 1.7.26, is compared to the
Hydra of the Lernaean marsh. Though
Coriolanus is using the image to evoke
the pathos of isolation (cf. Job, 30: 29
in the Geneva Bible, and Isaiah,
34: 11–13 and 13: 20–2), its deeper
significance is that he is now applying
to himself epithets of menace that formerly he used about the plebeians: for
'fen' cf. 3.3.121–2, and for 'Hydra'
and other monster images, 3.1.95 n.
The implicit menace in the dragon
comparison emerges clearly at 4.7.23
and 5.4.12–13, and is related to references to Coriolanus as a 'serpent'
(1.9.3) and 'viper' (3.1.265, 289).

lonely *OED*'s first example of the word
33–4 **Will ... practice** The irony is that
both of these alternatives will prove
true.
33 **or ... or** either ... or
  exceed the common surpass the
achievements of ordinary men, do
something exceptional
34 **cautelous** crafty, deceitful
  practice stratagems, trickery
  first best, most noble; cf. 4.5.114 n.
Volumnia seems to have only the one
child (cf. 1.3.6, 5.3.163) but likes to
imagine herself as the Roman mother
of many sons (1.3.20–3). A similar
uncertainty about children who may
have died crops up with Lady Macbeth,
who has 'given suck' though Macbeth
'has no children'.
36–8 **some ... thee** Wilson (after Maxwell)
compares *Winter's Tale* 4.4.539–41 for
a similar idea in similar phrasing
37 **exposure** Wilson suggests plausibly
that F's 'exposture' was a compositor's
misassimilation to 'posture' of a word
that was then quite new. *OED* gives
no other example of 'exposture' and
cites Shakespeare also for the first
example of 'exposure', so possibly he
had not himself at this stage decided
on the exact form of the neologism.
38 **starts** starts up; cf. 'thrust forth', l. 41
  VIRGILIA F's ascription to *Corio.* is
possible, but the distress of the ejacula-

286

COMINIUS

   I'll follow thee a month, devise with thee
   Where thou shalt rest, that thou mayst hear of us   40
   And we of thee. So, if the time thrust forth
   A cause for thy repeal, we shall not send
   O'er the vast world to seek a single man,
   And lose advantage, which doth ever cool
   I'th' absence of the needer.

CORIOLANUS   Fare ye well.   45

   Thou hast years upon thee, and thou art too full
   Of the wars' surfeits to go rove with one
   That's yet unbruised. Bring me but out at gate.
   Come, my sweet wife, my dearest mother, and
   My friends of noble touch. When I am forth,   50
   Bid me farewell, and smile. I pray you, come.
   While I remain above the ground you shall
   Hear from me still, and never of me aught
   But what is like me formerly.

MENENIUS   That's worthily

   As any ear can hear. Come, let's not weep.   55
   If I could shake off but one seven years
   From these old arms and legs, by the good gods,
   I'd with thee every foot.

CORIOLANUS   Give me thy hand. Come.

                             Exeunt

---

47 wars'] F (warres), STEEVENS; war's ROWE

tion sits ill with his toughness in the rest of the scene, whereas it is precisely analogous to Virgilia's earlier 'O heavens, O heavens', l. 12. If the manuscript speech heading were *vir.* (with a minuscule initial), this would be easy to misread as *cor.* in secretary hand.

42 **A ... repeal** an occasion for recalling you
44 **advantage** the opportune moment
48 **at gate** For the omission of the article, see Abbott § 143.
50 **noble touch** proved nobility (a metaphor from the touchstone used to test

gold, cf. 2.3.187 n.). Clearly, the nobles have not yet let him be hooted; cf. 4.5.76–9.
52–3 **you ... still** Yet at 4.6.20–1 Menenius says they have received no messages from him.
53–4 **never ... formerly** A line of considerable irony in both its inexactitude and, at a deeper level, its correctness.
56–8 **If ... foot** Cf. 2.1.111–2, where Menenius says a letter from Martius has given him seven years' health, and 1.1.239 n., 3.2.32–5.
58.1 *Exeunt* Presumably the off-stage hooting of the plebeians would begin at this juncture.

4.2   *Enter the two tribunes, Sicinius and Brutus, with the Aedile*

SICINIUS *(to the Aedile)*

Bid them all home. He's gone, and we'll no further.
The nobility are vexed, whom we see have sided
In his behalf.

BRUTUS   Now we have shown our power,
Let us seem humbler after it is done
Than when it was a-doing.

SICINIUS *(to the Aedile)*   Bid them home.   5
Say their great enemy is gone, and they
Stand in their ancient strength.

BRUTUS   Dismiss them home.
                                    ⌈*Exit Aedile*⌉

Here comes his mother.

        Enter Volumnia, Virgilia, ⌈*weeping,*⌉ *and Menenius*

SICINIUS Let's not meet her.

BRUTUS Why?   10

SICINIUS They say she's mad.

BRUTUS

They have ta'en note of us. Keep on your way.

VOLUMNIA

O, you're well met! Th'hoarded plague o'th' gods
Requite your love!

MENENIUS   Peace, peace, be not so loud.

4.2.7.1 *Exit Aedile*] CAPELL; *not in* F   8.1 *Enter . . . Menenius*] F; *before* Here . . .
mother. DELIUS; *after l. 12 in* DYCE   *weeping*] This edition; *not in* F   14 Requite] F
(requit), F3

4.2 See Introduction, p. 28.

1 **Bid . . . home** The double repetition of
this command at ll. 5 and 7 suggests
the Tribunes' nervousness about their
own power to control the mob they
have aroused; cf. 4.6.2–4, 29–31.

2–3 **The nobility . . . behalf** Sicinius' description of the nobles here agrees with
their behaviour in 3.3 but not with
the description of them by Coriolanus
at 4.6.129–9 nor Menenius' account at
4.6.129–31, 130–1.

2 **whom** For the confusion of 'who/
whom', see Abbott §410.

8 **Here . . . mother**   Brutus'   warning

draws audience attention to the entrance of Volumnia and company in
anticipation of a quarrel to follow,
with the next four lines allowing
opportunity for the two groups to
come into confrontation despite the
Tribunes' attempts at evasion.

11 **mad** (a) 'furious' (cf. *1 Henry IV*
1.3.52), (b) 'mentally unbalanced',
cf. 18 n., 47

13 **hoarded** i.e. 'kept in store for punishment', cf. *Lear* 2.2.335: an ironic use
of the word, considering the plebeians'
earlier accusations of grain hoarding

VOLUMNIA
> If that I could for weeping, you should hear—   15
> Nay, and you shall hear some. ⌜*To Sicinius*⌝ Will you
>   be gone?

VIRGILIA ⌜*to Brutus*⌝
> You shall stay too! I would I had the power
> To say so to my husband.

SICINIUS (*to Volumnia*)   Are you mankind?

VOLUMNIA
> Ay, fool. Is that a shame? Note but this, fool:
> Was not a man my father? Hadst thou foxship   20
> To banish him that struck more blows for Rome
> Than thou hast spoken words?

SICINIUS   O blessèd heavens!

VOLUMNIA
> More noble blows than ever thou wise words,
> And for Rome's good. I'll tell thee what—yet go!
> Nay, but thou shalt stay too. I would my son   25

16 *To Sicinius*] This edition; *not in* F; *to Brutus* JOHNSON; *to the tribunes* OXFORD
17 VIRGILIA You . . . too! I] F; You . . . too! *Vir.* I WARBURTON *to Brutus*] This edition; *not in* F; *to Sicinius* JOHNSON; *to the tribunes* OXFORD   18 *to Volumnia*] OXFORD; *not in* F
19 this,] STAUNTON; ~ ∧ F   23–4 words, . . . good.] ROWE (*subs.*); ~ . . . . ~, F

17–18 VIRGILIA There seems no reason to suppose Virgilia incapable of the spirit expressed in 'You shall stay too!', as Warburton's reallocation supposes; on the other hand, it is more likely that she arrests Brutus' exit after Volumnia has blocked Sicinius' (rather than the other way round, as in Johnson), since the latter's objection at l. 18 is clearly addressed to Volumnia (though grammatically it can refer to both women).
18 **mankind** Though Volumnia chooses to understand it in its normal sense of 'belonging to the human race', Sicinius intends the word to mean either (a) 'masculine, virago-like' (*OED a.*¹, B. 3) or (b) 'furious, mad' (*OED a.*²), cf. ll. 11, 46–7; or possibly both: cf. *Winter's Tale* 2.3.68, 'a mankind witch'.
19 **this** F's 'this' would make 'this fool' the object of 'Note', the clause being then a separate sentence addressed to Menenius and Virgilia; however, since the rest of the speech is addressed to Sicinius, it is more plausible to see

'fool' as a vocative.
20 **foxship** (a) 'ingratitude' (Verity), cf. *Lear* 3.7.27, (b) 'low cunning': both qualities traditionally ascribed to the fox; Volumnia is also retorting to the 'mankind' slur
22 **O . . . heavens!** This seems an unusual exclamation for Sicinius and may indicate that on her last words Volumnia seizes (or offers to strike) him, as Martius did earlier. A more likely speaker is Virgilia (cf. 4.1.12, 38).
23 **More** F's spelling 'moe' was a usage indicating 'more in number', whereas 'more' was usually (though not invariably, cf. l. 21) reserved for 'more in quantity', a distinction no longer meaningful. Brockbank notes that 'more in quantity' would have made the phrase ambiguous (i.e. it could mean that Coriolanus' blows have been nobler than Sicinius' words have been wise), whereas 'moe' avoids this ambiguity.
25 **too** 'after all'; she is still addressing Sicinius

Were in Arabia, and thy tribe before him,
His good sword in his hand.

SICINIUS   What then?

VIRGILIA   What then?
He'd make an end of thy posterity.

VOLUMNIA Bastards and all.
Good man, the wounds that he does bear for Rome!   30

MENENIUS Come, come, peace.

SICINIUS
I would he had continued to his country
As he began, and not unknit himself
The noble knot he made.

BRUTUS   I would he had.

VOLUMNIA
'I would he had'! 'Twas you incensed the rabble: 35
Cats, that can judge as fitly of his worth
As I can of those mysteries which heaven
Will not have earth to know.

BRUTUS (*to Sicinius*) Pray, let's go.

VOLUMNIA Now pray, sir, get you gone.   40
You have done a brave deed. Ere you go, hear this:
As far as doth the Capitol exceed
The meanest house in Rome, so far my son—

27–30 VIRGILIA What . . . posterity. VOLUMNIA Bastards . . . Rome!] F; *Vol.* What . . .
Rome! HANMER; *Vol.* What . . . all. *Vir.* Good . . . Rome! MURRY (*in* Brockbank); *Vir.*
What then! *Vol.* He'd . . . Rome! BROCKBANK, HINMAN *conj.* (*in* '*Textual Companion*')
43–4 son— . . . this, . . . see?—] F (Sonne⌄ . . . this (do you see))

26 **in Arabia** i.e. in the desert, where
he would be free to slaughter without interference; cf. 1.1.194–7 and
5.6.128–30 n.; also *Cymbeline* 1.1.
168–70, *Richard II* 4.1.65, *Macbeth*
3.4.103.
  tribe Perhaps a reference to the vote-
rigging at 3.3.9–11; see note.
27 **What . . . posterity** Again there seems
no good reason for reallocating F's division of speeches: Virgilia's resistance
at 5.3.126–8 harps on the same topic,
which obviously the deprivation of her
husband would make central for her;
while l. 30 shows the same obsession
with 'wounds . . . for Rome' that Volumnia touted in 1.3 and 2.1.
33 **unknit** untied

34 **noble knot** 'the close bond, of service
on his part and gratitude on the part
of Rome, which held them together'
(Hibbard)
36 **Cats** A term of contempt (like Coriolanus' 'curs'); cf. *Dream* 3.2.261,
Merchant 4.1.47, *All's Well* 4.3.243.
37–8 **mysteries . . . know**   Cf. *Lear*
5.3.16–17: another example of the
patrician mythologizing of Coriolanus
as a demigod.
39 **Pray . . . go** Brutus may be addressing
Volumnia, but more probably he says
this to Sicinius.
42–3 **As . . . Rome** Another example of
the characteristic patrician equation of
hierarchy and buildings, cf. 3.1.204–
7, 4.6.89, 104.

This lady's husband here, this, do you see?—
Whom you have banished does exceed you all.   45
BRUTUS
Well, well, we'll leave you.
SICINIUS   Why stay we to be baited
With one that wants her wits?   *Exeunt Tribunes*
VOLUMNIA   Take my prayers with you!
I would the gods had nothing else to do
But to confirm my curses. Could I meet 'em
But once a day, it would unclog my heart   50
Of what lies heavy to't.
MENENIUS   You have told them home,
And, by my troth, you have cause. You'll sup with me?
VOLUMNIA
Anger's my meat: I sup upon myself
And so shall starve with feeding. (*To Virgilia*) Come,
    let's go.
Leave this faint puling and lament as I do,   55
In anger, Juno-like. Come, come, come.
                        Exeunt Volumnia and Virgilia
MENENIUS   Fie, fie, fie.
                                        Exit

47 *Exeunt*] F (*Exit*)   55 faint puling] ROWE; faint-puling F   56 *Exeunt ... Virgilia*] F (*Exeunt*)

46–7 **baited | With** 'harrassed by'; cf. 9 ff. n.
50 **unclog** Brockbank notes that the metaphor is from the practice of fettering animals or men with blocks of wood called 'clogs'
51 **told them home** 'rebuked them thoroughly', cf. 1.5.9, 3.3.1
54 **starve with feeding** i.e. kill myself by indulging my anger; cf. 3.1.295–6. The image is a perversion of such traditional emblems of maternal self-sacrifice as the pelican who nourishes her young with her own blood, and at the same time an absurd extreme of Volumnia's contempt for nourishment and assertions of self-sufficiency (see Introduction, p. 79). Eating of one's own heart was used as an emblem both of sorrow (e.g. Thomas Combe, *The Theatre of Fine Devices*, 1614, p. 8) and of envy, 'Invidia' (cf. G. Whitney, *A Choice of Emblems*, 1586, p. 4; Andreas Alciati, *The Latin Emblems*, ed. Peter M. Daly *et al.* (1985), no. 71).
55 **faint puling** feeble whimpering; cf. *Two Gentlemen* 2.1.24, *Romeo* 3.5.183–5: a cue for Virgilia
In ... Juno-like In the *Aeneid* it was the wrath of Juno which caused the destruction of the Trojans, who through Aeneas became the ancestors of Rome. Thus there is an irony in the phrase that Volumnia, who is thinking merely of a queen-like image, does not intend. Cf. 2.1.98, 5.3.46 n.

4.3   *Enter Nicanor, a Roman, and Adrian, a Volsce*

NICANOR I know you well, sir, and you know me. Your
name, I think, is Adrian.

ADRIAN It is so, sir. Truly, I have forgot you.

NICANOR I am a Roman, and my services are, as you are,
against 'em. Know you me yet?   5

ADRIAN Nicanor, no?

NICANOR The same, sir.

ADRIAN You had more beard when I last saw you, but
your favour is well approved by your tongue. What's
the news in Rome? I have a note from the Volscian   10
state to find you out there. You have well saved me a
day's journey.

NICANOR There hath been in Rome strange insurrections,
the people against the senators, patricians, and nobles.

ADRIAN Hath been?—is it ended then? Our state thinks   15
not so. They are in a most warlike preparation, and
hope to come upon them in the heat of their division.

NICANOR The main blaze of it is past, but a small thing

4.3.0.1 *Nicanor, . . . Adrian,*] OXFORD; *not in* F   1 NICANOR] OXFORD; *Rom.* F; *so*
throughout the scene   3 ADRIAN] OXFORD; *Volce.* F; *so throughout the scene*   9 approved]
STEEVENS; appear'd F; affear'd HANMER

4.3 For a discussion of the relevance of
this Shakespeare addition to Plutarch,
see Introduction, p. 29. The scene
offers some welcome comic relief before
the final tragedy, with the play's tone
modulating back into seriousness via
the comedy of Coriolanus' encounters
with Aufidius' servants and their commentary at the end of 5.4.

0.1 *Nicanor . . . Volsce* For the origin of
these names see Introduction, p. 20.
In 1977 RSC Nicanor was recogniz-
ably a Roman Senator who had been
seen on stage before, and his lowering
of his hood at 'Know you me yet?' (l.
5) foreshadowed the same gesture by
Coriolanus at 4.5.64 with the almost
identical line, 'Know'st thou me
yet?' (though, interestingly, Coriolanus speaks in the less polite second-
person singular; cf. 4.5.55 n.).

5 'em i.e. the Romans

8–9 favour . . . tongue facial appearance
is confirmed by your way of speaking

9 approved confirmed; cf. *Hamlet* 1.1.27.
F's 'appear'd' is sometimes retained by
editors and interpreted transitively as
'made manifest', but no other example
of such a usage is to be found in
Shakespeare nor is the sense as plausible in context.

10 note i.e. note of instruction; cf.
Measure 4.2.105

13–16 There . . . not so This suggestion of
continuing strife within Rome agrees
with Plutarch but is contradicted by
the beginning of Shakespeare's 4.6, a
scene he has invented.

16–17 They . . . them i.e. the Volscians . . .
the Romans

16 preparation A reference to the already
conscripted army of ll. 40–2; cf. 1.2.15

18–24 blaze . . . flame . . . glowing . . .
breaking out The idea of civil war as
a glowing fire easily fanned to flame is
a commonplace, but in this play it
also contributes to a major thread of
imagery.

would make it flame again, for the nobles receive so to
heart the banishment of that worthy Coriolanus that   20
they are in a ripe aptness to take all power from the
people, and to pluck from them their tribunes for ever.
This lies glowing, I can tell you, and is almost mature
for the violent breaking out.

ADRIAN Coriolanus banished?   25

NICANOR Banished, sir.

ADRIAN You will be welcome with this intelligence,
Nicanor.

NICANOR The day serves well for them now. I have heard
it said the fittest time to corrupt a man's wife is when   30
she's fallen out with her husband. Your noble Tullus
Aufidius will appear well in these wars, his great op-
poser Coriolanus being now in no request of his country.

ADRIAN He cannot choose. I am most fortunate thus accidentally to encounter you. You have ended my busi-   35
ness, and I will merrily accompany you home.

NICANOR I shall between this and supper tell you most
strange things from Rome, all tending to the good of
their adversaries. Have you an army ready, say you?

ADRIAN A most royal one: the centurions and their   40
charges distinctly billeted already in th'entertainment,
and to be on foot at an hour's warning.

NICANOR I am joyful to hear of their readiness, and am
the man, I think, that shall set them in present action.
So, sir, heartily well met, and most glad of your company.   45

32 will] F2; well F1

21–2 **ripe . . . pluck** 'An example of image-
drift. The fruit image in *ripe aptness*,
first used of the nobles, is transferred
to the tribunes in *pluck*' (King).
29 **them** i.e. the Volscians
30–1 **the   fittest . . . husband** Another
sexual-marital metaphor applied to
warfare; cf. 4.5.228–33.
34 **He cannot choose** he is bound to
40 **royal** This is an unexpected and possibly
significant adjective, considering the
Tribunes' fears of Coriolanus' ambition.

centurions A centurion was the officer
in command of a 'century', cf. 1.8.3
n.
40–1 **their charges** i.e. the troops in their
charge, under their command
41 **distinctly billeted** individually written
down on the enrolment lists
in th'entertainment (a) in the mobil-
ization, (b) 'receiving pay' (Hibbard),
cf. 5.6.79, 'The charges of the action'.
44 **present** immediate

ADRIAN You take my part from me, sir. I have the most
　　cause to be glad of yours.
NICANOR Well, let us go together.   *Exeunt*

4.4   *Enter Coriolanus in mean apparel, disguised and*
　　　muffled
CORIOLANUS
　A goodly city is this Antium. City,
　'Tis I that made thy widows. Many an heir
　Of these fair edifices fore my wars
　Have I heard groan and drop. Then know me not,
　Lest that thy wives with spits and boys with stones   5
　In puny battle slay me.
　　　　Enter a Citizen
　　　　　　　　　Save you, sir.
CITIZEN
　And you.
CORIOLANUS Direct me, if it be your will,
　Where great Aufidius lies. Is he in Antium?
CITIZEN
　He is, and feasts the nobles of the state
　At his house this night.
CORIOLANUS   Which is his house, beseech you?   10
CITIZEN
　This here before you.
CORIOLANUS   Thank you, sir. Farewell.
　　　　　　　　　　　　　　Exit Citizen

4.4.6 *Enter a Citizen*] DYCE; *at end of line in* F

4.4.0.1–2 *mean . . . muffled* In Plutarch
'the disguise is assumed, while Shakespeare leaves us to imagine a state of
destitution' (Wilson); cf. 4.5.62–3.
　disguised and muffled Probably like the
conspirators in *Caesar* 2.1.73–4, 'their
hats . . . plucked about their ears | And
half their faces buried in their cloaks'.
1 A . . . **Antium** Coriolanus would presumably indicate the façade of the tiring house here. One of the side doors
would then be identified as Aufidius'
house at l. 11, through which Coriolanus would leave at the end of the

scene, to reappear through the other
side door at 4.5.4.1, as though entering the interior of the house.
2–5 **widows . . . heir . . . wives** This emphasis on the damage he has done to
women and families is characteristic of
Coriolanus. See Introduction, pp. 54, 80.
3 **fore my wars** in the face of my assaults
(*OED, war, sb.*[1] 4b)
5 **wives** Possibly just 'women', but more
probably 'married women', cf. 2–5 n.
6 **Save you** i.e. 'The gods save you', a
greeting
8 **lies** dwells

O world, thy slippery turns! Friends now fast sworn,
Whose double bosoms seem to wear one heart,
Whose hours, whose bed, whose meal and exercise
Are still together, who twin as 'twere in love   15
Unseparable, shall within this hour,
On a dissension of a doit, break out
To bitterest enmity. So fellest foes,
Whose passions and whose plots have broke their sleep
To take the one the other, by some chance,   20
Some trick not worth an egg, shall grow dear friends
And interjoin their issues. So with me.
My birthplace hate I, and my love's upon
This enemy town. I'll enter. If he slay me,
He does fair justice; if he give me way,   25
I'll do his country service.   *Exit*

---

13 seem ... one] F4; seemes ... one F1; seene ... on F2   23 hate] CAPELL; haue F;
leaue PROUDFOOT *conj.* (*in* '*Textual Companion*')

12–26 **O world ... service** Brockbank
notes that this soliloquy serves the
same purpose as North's explanation
of Coriolanus' turmoil of mind as he
ruminated for several days at his
country house, where 'In the end,
seeing he could revolve no way to take
a profitable or honourable course, but
only was pricked forward still to be
revenged of the Romans, he thought
to raise up some great wars against
them, by their nearest neighbours.
Whereupon he thought it his best way
first to stir up the Volsces against
them' (Spencer, p. 334). Shakespeare's understanding goes much
deeper, however: the sentiments Martius expresses in this, his closest
approach to soliloquy, are less
about vengeance than about the
shocking loss of certainty he thinks
he has discovered in human
relationships—Rossiter (*Angel with
Horns*, p. 250) parallels it to Henry
IV's midnight meditation on the
frailty of political alliances (*2 Henry IV*
3.1.44 ff.).
12 **slippery turns** unreliable changes;
cf. *Troilus* 3.3.78–81
13 **double** (a) 'separate', but also playing
on (b) 'deceitful'. The commonplace of

two bodies with a single heart can also
be found in *Dream* 3.2.204–15 (especially 213) and *As You Like It* 1.3.
72–5.
15 **still** always
17 **dissension of a doit** dispute over a trifle
(cf. 1.6.6 n., 5.4.57). Cf. 'controversy
of threepence' (2.1.69), where the
legal overtone of a suit for a trivial
amount is clearer.
18 **fellest** most deadly
19–20 **Whose ... other** 'whose enmity
has disturbed their sleep, with plot-
ting how to defeat (literally, 'capture')
one another': an interesting anticipation of Aufidius' similar confession at
4.5.124–7. See also 3.1.113–14 n.
21 **trick ... egg** worthless trifle, cf. Q2 of
Hamlet, Add. Pass. J44 and Introduction, p. 80. This phrase and 'dissension of a doit' show how little
Coriolanus seems to understand the
reason for what has happened to him.
22 **interjoin ... issues** (a) throw in their
lot together, (b) 'let their children in-
termarry' (Clarendon)
23 **hate** In secretary hand a 't' can resemble a 'v', hence F's 'haue'.
25 **give me way** (a) grant my desire,
(b) give me my free course; cf. 5.6.
31–2

4·5 *Music plays. Enter a Servingman*

FIRST SERVINGMAN Wine, wine, wine! What service is here? I think our fellows are asleep. ⌈*Exit*⌉

Enter Second Servingman

SECOND SERVINGMAN Where's Cotus? My master calls for him. Cotus! *Exit*

Enter Coriolanus, as before

CORIOLANUS

A goodly house. The feast smells well, but I 5
Appear not like a guest.

Enter the First Servingman

FIRST SERVINGMAN What would you have, friend? Whence are you? Here's no place for you. Pray go to the door.

Exit

CORIOLANUS

I have deserved no better entertainment
In being Coriolanus. 10

Enter Second Servingman

SECOND SERVINGMAN Whence are you, sir? Has the porter his eyes in his head, that he gives entrance to such companions? Pray get you out.

CORIOLANUS Away!

SECOND SERVINGMAN Away? Get you away. 15

CORIOLANUS Now thou'rt troublesome.

SECOND SERVINGMAN Are you so brave? I'll have you talked with anon.

Enter Third Servingman. The First meets him

4.5.1 FIRST SERVINGMAN] F (*1 Ser.;* then 1); *similarly 2 Ser., 3 Ser.; then 2, 3* 2 *Exit*] ROWE; *not in* F 2.1 *Second*] F (*another*) 3 master] F (M.), F4 3.1 *as before*] OXFORD; *not in* F 10.1 *Servingman*] F (*Servant.*) 18.1 *Third . . . First*] F (3 . . . 1)

4.5.0.1 *Music plays* This direction, with First Servingman's call for 'wine' and 'service' and the three servants' entrances and exits, immediately establishes the context of Aufidius' feast. See Introduction, p. 90: the music would be played in the gallery, as in actual dining halls.

2 **fellows** i.e. fellow-servants

Exit F's stage directions for the servants are very inadequate. Clearly, if First Servingman is to re-enter at l. 6.1, as F directs, he has to exit after

his first speech; cf. notes to the stage directions at 18.1 and 22.

3 **Cotus** See Introduction, p. 20.

6 **Appear . . . guest** Alluding to the description of him as 'in mean apparel, disguised and muffled' (4.4.0.1; cf. 'as before', 4.5.4.1).

8 **go . . . door** leave, get out

9 **entertainment** reception

13 **companions** fellows, rascals

17 **brave** insolent

18.1 *The First meets him* As F instructed First Servingman to exit at l. 8, this

THIRD SERVINGMAN What fellow's this?

FIRST SERVINGMAN A strange one as ever I looked on. I 20
cannot get him out o'th' house. Prithee, call my master to him.　　　　　　　　　　　　　⌈*He retires*⌉

THIRD SERVINGMAN What have you to do here, fellow?
Pray you, avoid the house.

CORIOLANUS

Let me but stand. I will not hurt your hearth. 25

THIRD SERVINGMAN What are you?

CORIOLANUS A gentleman.

THIRD SERVINGMAN A marvellous poor one.

CORIOLANUS True, so I am.

THIRD SERVINGMAN Pray you, poor gentleman, take up 30
some other station. Here's no place for you. Pray you,
avoid. Come.

CORIOLANUS

Follow your function. Go and batten on cold bits.

　　He pushes him away from him

THIRD SERVINGMAN What, you will not?—Prithee tell my
master what a strange guest he has here. 35

SECOND SERVINGMAN And I shall.　　　　　　　*Exit*

---

22 *He retires*] CAMBRIDGE; *not in* F　　33.1 *He*] OXFORD; *not in* F

---

direction presumably means that he
now enters from a different door; Third
Servingman probably enters by the
same door as Coriolanus used, as
though from outside.

22 *He retires* Cf. stage direction at l. 53.
Although F has the direction '*Enter
two of the Servingmen.*' at 148.2, First
and Second Servingman talk of the
'strange alteration' they have witnessed (149) and know that the
stranger is Coriolanus, and F has indicated no exit for either. It seems consistent, therefore, to have them merely
'Retire' at 23 and 53 respectively, so
they may overhear what passes between Coriolanus and their master,
then 'come forward' to discuss it at
148.2.

24 **avoid** leave, quit

25 **hearth** North says, 'he got him up
straight to the chimney hearth'. Like
his shabbiness and apparent hunger,
this suggests the harsh experience of
cold to which raw nature has sub-
jected Coriolanus; cf. 4.4.0.1 n.

31 **station** (a) place to stand in, (b) punning on 'status', or 'place' (Brockbank). Cf. 2.1.211.

33 **Follow your function** attend to your
proper (servile) duties; cf. *Othello* 4.2.29
batten gorge, grow fat, cf. *Hamlet*
3.4.66
cold bits left-over scraps of meat,
orts

33.1 *He . . . him* Cf. 50.1, 'He beats him
away'. These physical encounters are
usually played for sardonic comedy,
because, as First Servingman remembers at ll. 153–4, Coriolanus' physical
superiority is so contemptuously absolute. In 1984 NT, however, Peter Hall
suggested that Coriolanus intends no
humour but manhandles the servants
to make sure Aufidius will be sent for.

THIRD SERVINGMAN Where dwell'st thou?

CORIOLANUS Under the canopy.

THIRD SERVINGMAN Under the canopy?

CORIOLANUS Ay.   40

THIRD SERVINGMAN Where's that?

CORIOLANUS I'th' city of kites and crows.

THIRD SERVINGMAN I'th' city of kites and crows? What
an ass it is! Then thou dwell'st with daws too?

CORIOLANUS No, I serve not thy master.   45

THIRD SERVINGMAN How, sir! Do you meddle with my
master?

CORIOLANUS Ay, 'tis an honester service than to meddle
with thy mistress. Thou prat'st and prat'st. Serve with
thy trencher. Hence!   50

> *He beats him away.* ⌈ *Exit Third Servingman.* ⌉
> *Enter Aufidius with the Second Servingman*

AUFIDIUS Where is this fellow?

SECOND SERVINGMAN Here, sir. I'd have beaten him like a
dog but for disturbing the lords within.   ⌈ *He retires* ⌉

AUFIDIUS

Whence com'st thou? What wouldst thou? Thy name?
Why speak'st not? Speak, man. What's thy name?

CORIOLANUS ⌈ *unmuffling* ⌉   If, Tullus,   55

50.1 *He*] OXFORD; *not in* F   *Exit Third Servingman*] CAMBRIDGE; *not in* F   50.2 *Second*]
CAMBRIDGE; *not in* F   53 *He retires*] CAMBRIDGE; *not in* F; *The Servingmen stand aside*
OXFORD; *Servants retire.* BROCKBANK (*after l. 58*)   55 *unmuffling*] CAPELL; *not in* F

---

38 **Under the canopy** beneath the sky.
Cf. *Hamlet* 2.2.301, with perhaps a
suggestion of the 'heavens' of the
canopy over the stage.

42 **city of kites and crows** Again an enigmatic phrase evoking raw, predatory
nature, since kites and crows are
scavengers, carrion eaters living, like
the servants, on 'cold bits'.

44 **daws** i.e. jackdaws, proverbially stupid
birds

46–9 **meddle with ... meddle with** The
Servingman means merely 'interfere
with' but Coriolanus puns on the
meaning 'have illicit sexual relations
with', then gets impatient with the
whole exchange.

50 **trencher** serving platter

50.2 *Enter Aufidius* See Introduction,

p. 98 for conventions of representing
such an entrance.

53 *He retires* See l. 23 n.

54 **name** The importance of 'name' is reiterated in the lines that follow, cf. 55,
58, 59, 60, 64, 65, 66, 69, 74. The
metre allows for pauses after the first,
second and fourth questions and also
after 'Speak, man'; while 55 is leng-
thened by Coriolanus' silence before he
speaks, then by pauses after 'If' and
'Tullus'.

55 **Tullus** This use of his praenomen by
an apparent stranger might be expected to elicit some response from
Aufidius. Cf. his own use of the more
polite family name 'Martius' at ll. 102
(see note), 107, 127, and 148. He
only uses Coriolanus' praenomen,

Not yet thou know'st me, and seeing me dost not
Think me for the man I am, necessity
Commands me name myself.

AUFIDIUS   What is thy name?

CORIOLANUS

A name unmusical to the Volscians' ears
And harsh in sound to thine.

AUFIDIUS   Say, what's thy name?   60
Thou hast a grim appearance, and thy face
Bears a command in't. Though thy tackle's torn,
Thou show'st a noble vessel. What's thy name?

CORIOLANUS

Prepare thy brow to frown. Know'st thou me yet?

AUFIDIUS

I know thee not. Thy name?   65

CORIOLANUS

My name is Caius Martius, who hath done
To thee particularly, and to all the Volsces,
Great hurt and mischief. Thereto witness may
My surname Coriolanus. The painful service,
The extreme dangers, and the drops of blood   70
Shed for my thankless country, are requited
But with that surname—a good memory

'Caius', when he plots his downfall at
4.7.56 and 5.6.90.

59–64 Coriolanus' warnings here are
like Macbeth's to Young Siward at
5.7.5–12

62 **tackle** rigging of a ship (referring to
Coriolanus' dress)

63 **vessel** Playing on (a) ship, (b) 'the
body as receptacle of the soul' (Wilson), cf. *All's Well* 2.3.206, *Cymbeline*
4.2.321.

65 **I . . . name?** Granville-Barker's suggestion (p. 182) that Aufidius' refusal
to recognize Martius was partly 'wine-
flushed stubbornness' was followed in
1959 SMT; this also helped explain the
rash generosity to which he immediately swung.

66 ff. **My name . . .** This speech is very
close to 'Coriolanus' oration to Tullus
Aufidius' in North's Plutarch (see

Spencer, p. 337), but it is skilfully
recadenced to give a clipped, ironic
effect that conveys the enormous self-
control Coriolanus is exerting, contrasting with the effusive energy and
length of Aufidius' reply, which is
Shakespeare's own invention.

66–9 **who . . . Coriolanus** Coriolanus
seems, almost perversely, to challenge
Aufidius' response: cf. 4.3.0.1 n.,
4.5.55 n.: cf. Introduction, p. 67.

69 **painful** arduous

70 **extreme** Accented on the first syllable.

71–2 **requited . . . surname** Martius' concern with names reflects his damaged
sense of self: cf. 5.1.11–15, 5.6.90–2,
and Introduction, p. 83; cf. also
5.3.171.

72 **memory** (a) memorial, cf. North, 'a
good memory and witness', (b) reminder, cf. 74, 'Only that name remains'

And witness of the malice and displeasure
Which thou shouldst bear me. Only that name remains,
The cruelty and envy of the people,   75
Permitted by our dastard nobles, who
Have all forsook me, hath devoured the rest,
And suffered me by th' voice of slaves to be
Whooped out of Rome. Now this extremity
Hath brought me to thy hearth. Not out of hope—   80
Mistake me not—to save my life, for if
I had feared death, of all the men i'th' world
I would have 'voided thee, but in mere spite
To be full quit of those my banishers
Stand I before thee here. Then if thou hast   85
A heart of wreak in thee, that wilt revenge
Thine own particular wrongs and stop those maims
Of shame seen through thy country, speed thee straight,
And make my misery serve thy turn. So use it
That my revengeful services may prove   90
As benefits to thee; for I will fight
Against my cankered country with the spleen
Of all the under-fiends. But if so be

---

79 Whooped] F (Hoop'd), HANMER   83 'voided] F (voided), STEEVENS 1778; avoided
POPE   86 that wilt] F; that will HANMER; and wilt CAPELL *conj.*

73–5 **malice ... envy** Key terms in
the psychology of this play, both
meaning 'hatred by the underdog', cf.
83 n.
76 **dastard** cowardly; a remarkable
change from 'friends of noble touch',
4.1.50
78–9 **And ... Rome** Cf. 4.2.2–3 n.,
4.6.129–31, 139–40. Although he follows North closely in this speech,
Shakespeare adds the detail of the
crowd's jeering at Coriolanus here
and at 3.3.138–41: 'Whooped', appropriately, is a hunting term (cf.
3.1.275–6), and continues the play's
identification of the plebeians with
their 'voices'.
82–3 **of ... thee** Macbeth uses almost the
identical words to Macduff, 5.10.4
83 **'voided** avoided
in mere spite out of pure spite; 'spite'
comes directly from North but has

something of the same negative, petty
implications as the 'malice' and 'envy'
of 73–5 (see note)
84 **full quit** of (a) 'to get my own back
on'; but also (b) 'to be finally rid of
(by dying)' (Arden)
86 **of wreak** disposed to vengeance;
cf. North, 'if thou hast any heart to be
wrecked of the injuries thy enemies
have done thee' (Spencer, p. 337)
87–8 **maims | Of shame** shameful in-
juries or mutilations (another body-
politic metaphor, which is not in
North)
88 **through** throughout
92 **cankered** corrupted; literally 'gangren-
ous or ulcerated', another body-politic
image that is not in North
spleen ferocity, cf. *Richard III* 5.6.80,
'Inspire us with the spleen of fiery
dragons', and *1 Henry IV* 5.2.19
93 **under-fiends** devils from hell below

Thou dar'st not this, and that to prove more fortunes
Thou'rt tired, then, in a word, I also am   95
Longer to live most weary, and present
My throat to thee and to thy ancient malice,
Which not to cut would show thee but a fool,
Since I have ever followed thee with hate,
Drawn tuns of blood out of thy country's breast,   100
And cannot live but to thy shame unless
It be to do thee service.

AUFIDIUS   O Martius, Martius!

Each word thou hast spoke hath weeded from my heart
A root of ancient envy. If Jupiter
Should from yon cloud speak divine things   105
And say ' 'Tis true', I'd not believe them more
Than thee, all-noble Martius. Let me twine
Mine arms about that body where-against
My grainèd ash an hundred times hath broke,
And scarred the moon with splinters.

He embraces Coriolanus

                                        Here I clip   110

---

105 yon] F (yond)   110 scarred] F; scar'd ROWE   *He . . . Coriolanus*] OXFORD; *not in* F
clip] F (cleep)

---

94 **prove** try, cf. *Cymbeline* 1.5.38; cf. North, 'prove fortune any more', i.e. 'take more chances'

96–8 **present . . . fool** A cue for Coriolanus to expose his throat. Cf. *Richard III* 1.2.165 ff., and Cassius in *Caesar* 4.2.155–7.

100 **tuns** casks, barrels-worth

101–2 **And . . . service** Brockbank notes that Shakespeare introduces this provocative idea that Aufidius will be shamed if he lets Coriolanus live but does not make use of him. North, to the contrary, says 'And it were no wisdom in thee to save the life of him who hath been heretofore thy mortal enemy and whose service now can nothing help nor pleasure thee' (Spencer, p. 337).

102 **O . . . Martius!** This foreshadows Martius' own climactic 'O mother, mother!' (5.3.183), and should probably be prefaced by a similar long pause: it conveys the same impression of emotions too strong and contradict-

ory for words (see next note).

102, 107 **Martius** Aufidius' whole speech has a slightly forced effusiveness; cf. Introduction, p. 84

104 **ancient** (a) former, (b) long established

104–6 **If Jupiter . . . true** This refers to 'The classical conception of thunder as an omen of assent from Jupiter, "the thunderer" (*Tonans* or *Tonitrualis*)' (Verity). Kemball-Cook notes the shortness of l. 105 but suggests that 'cloud' and 'speak' are both stressed, 'giving an effective pause after "cloud" when the actor may point at the sky'.

106–7 **I . . . Martius** Dramatic irony; cf. 1.9.2 n.

108 **where-against** against which

109 **grainèd ash** (a) lance made of straight-grained ash (less easily broken than a cross-grained shaft); less probably (b) lance with a pronged head (*OED ppl. a.*³).

110 **scarred** This reading is now generally preferred, though Brockbank notes

The anvil of my sword, and do contest
As hotly and as nobly with thy love
As ever in ambitious strength I did
Contend against thy valour. Know thou first,
I loved the maid I married; never man   115
Sighed truer breath. But that I see thee here,
Thou noble thing, more dances my rapt heart
Than when I first my wedded mistress saw
Bestride my threshold. Why, thou Mars, I tell thee
We have a power on foot, and I had purpose   120
Once more to hew thy target from thy brawn,
Or lose mine arm for't. Thou hast beat me out
Twelve several times, and I have nightly since
Dreamt of encounters 'twixt thyself and me—
We have been down together in my sleep,   125
Unbuckling helms, fisting each other's throat—
And waked half dead with nothing. Worthy Martius,
Had we no other quarrel else to Rome but that
Thou art thence banished, we would muster all
From twelve to seventy, and, pouring war   130

that Folio spellings of 'scarr'd' for 'scared' (*Winter's Tale* 3.3.64) and 'scarre' for 'scare' (*Troilus* 5.11.21) make Rowe's emendation equally plausible, as does *Richard III* 5.6.71, 'Amaze the welkin with your broken staves' (Malone).
   clip embrace (OE *clyppan*), cf. 1.7.29

111 **anvil ... sword** i.e. Coriolanus, whose armour has been struck by Aufidius' sword as an anvil is hit by a hammer; cf. *Hamlet*, 2.2.491–4
   contest rival, compete
114 **first** Probably (a) 'in the first place'; less probably (b) 'noblest of men', cf. 'My first son', 4.1.34 n.
117 **noble thing** An oxymoron which recalls the dehumanizing use of 'thing' at 2.2.107, 4.6.94, 5.4.18.
117–19 **more ... threshold** For this confusion of the marital and the martial, cf. 1.7.30–2 n.
117 **dances** (a) sets dancing (*OED v.* 6, but with no example this early); (b) 'dances', with 'my rapt heart' as subject and 'that' (l. 116) meaning 'because' (Brockbank)

rapt enraptured
119 **Bestride** step across. Poole (p. 83) suggests that Aufidius has here transferred to his wife a verb more appropriate to Martius, cf. 2.2.90.
   thou Mars A play on 'Martius' and the name of the Roman god of war (cf. 197 and 1.4.10), that is ironically remembered at 5.6.102–3.
120 **power** army
121 **target** shield or buckler worn on the arm
   brawn brawny, muscular arm
122 **out** outright
123 **Twelve** Yet at 1.11.7–8 he says 'Five times'. 'Either Aufidius or our poet has a very treacherous memory' (Theobald).
   several separate
125 **down together** i.e. wrestling hand-to-hand on the ground; Arden compares *Henry V* 4.7.152. This dream provides cues for their single combat in 1.9.
128 **other** Some editors omit this word as redundant and extrametrical, but it is unlikely to be a compositor's error; the repetition of 'other ... else' may indicate Aufidius' emphaticness.

Into the bowels of ungrateful Rome,
Like a bold flood o'erbear't. O, come, go in,
And take our friendly senators by th' hands
Who now are here taking their leaves of me,
Who am prepared against your territories,   135
Though not for Rome itself.

CORIOLANUS   You bless me, gods.

AUFIDIUS

Therefore, most absolute sir, if thou wilt have
The leading of thine own revenges, take
Th'one half of my commission and set down—
As best thou art experienced, since thou know'st   140
Thy country's strength and weakness—thine own ways:
Whether to knock against the gates of Rome,
Or rudely visit them in parts remote
To fright them ere destroy. But come in.
Let me commend thee first to those that shall   145
Say yea to thy desires. A thousand welcomes!
And more a friend than ere an enemy;
Yet, Martius, that was much. Your hand. Most welcome!

                    Exeunt Coriolanus and Aufidius

⌈*The two Servingmen come forward*⌉

FIRST SERVINGMAN Here's a strange alteration!

SECOND SERVINGMAN By my hand, I had thought to have   150

---

132 o'erbear't] WHITE (*conj.* Jackson); o're-beate F; o'er-bear ROWE   139–41 down—
... weakness—] CAMBRIDGE; downeˏ ... weaknesse, F   148.1 *Coriolanus and Aufi*dius]
CAPELL; *not in* F   148.2 The ... *forward*] CAMBRIDGE; *Enter two of the Seruingmen.* F
149 alteration!] F (~?)

---

131 **bowels** Another body-politic metaphor, cf. 5.3.103–4.
132 **o'erbear't** Shakespeare always uses
'o'erbear' transitively elsewhere, so
White's emendation is preferable to
Malone's 'o'erbear' besides being closer
to F's 'o're-beate', cf. 3.1.250–1 n.
137 **absolute** incomparable, perfect
139 **my commission** those under my command because of the commission (in
the sense both of authority and task)
that the state has given me
set down Probably (a) 'determine' (*OED,
set, v.* 143g) with 'thine own ways' as
predicate, cf. *Cymbeline* 1.4.162; improbably (b) 'encamp' (*OED* 143a), cf.

5.3.2, since this makes the syntax of
the rest of the sentence obscure.
146 **A thousand welcomes** Ironically
recalling Menenius' similar hyperbole
at 2.1.179, 'A hundred thousand
welcomes!'
148 **Martius** Aufidins' third use of the
name; cf. 102 n.
Your hand Cf. 200–1 n. See Introduction, pp. 102–3.
148.2 **The ... forward** See l. 23 n.
150 **By my hand** An oath (cf. *All's Well*
3.6.72), but also, comically, a dative
('By my hand I had thought to have
strucken him with a cudgel') that
stands in antithesis to 'my mind'.

strucken him with a cudgel, and yet my mind gave me
his clothes made a false report of him.

FIRST SERVINGMAN What an arm he has! He turned me
about with his finger and his thumb as one would set
up a top.   155

SECOND SERVINGMAN Nay, I knew by his face that there
was something in him. He had, sir, a kind of face,
methought—I cannot tell how to term it.

FIRST SERVINGMAN He had so, looking, as it were—
would I were hanged but I thought there was more in   160
him than I could think.

SECOND SERVINGMAN So did I, I'll be sworn. He is simply
the rarest man i'th' world.

FIRST SERVINGMAN I think he is; but a greater soldier
than he, you wot one.   165

SECOND SERVINGMAN Who? My master?

FIRST SERVINGMAN Nay, it's no matter for that.

SECOND SERVINGMAN Worth six on him.

FIRST SERVINGMAN Nay, not so, neither; but I take him to
be the greater soldier.   170

---

158 methought—] ROWE; ~, FI; ~. F2   159 were—] ROWE; ~, F   164-5 is; but . . .
he, . . . one.] F; ~: ~ . . . ~_∧ . . . on. DYCE; ~: ~ . . . he, . . . on. BROCKBANK ; ~_∧ yet . . . ~_∧
. . . on. OXFORD

---

151 **gave me** misgave me, warned me,
cf. *Henry VIII* (*All is True*) 5.2.143
154-5 **set . . . top** start a child's top spin-
ning
158 **I . . . it** Cf. 'as it . . . think' (159-61);
like all the other commentators on
Coriolanus' character, the servants are
baffled: cf. 1.1.36 n.
164-74 **but . . . too** The editors' confusion
about which leader either Servingman
prefers is an effect that Shakespeare
may have created deliberately by
keeping the third-person pronouns of
this passage unclear. Such 'riddling
obliquity' (Brockbank) suits the comedy of the Servingmen's politic wariness
(cf. ll. 185-6) and the uncertainty of
a shift in Volscian allegiances at so
early a stage in the new alliance, whilst
indicating clearly the breach to come
(cf. 4.7.1) and providing a further

instance of the play's concern for
betrayal, double-talk, and fascination
with surrogate power: see 168-9 n.
164-5 **but . . . one** All the readings proposed for this clause are about equally
plausible; see previous note. Oxford's
'yet a greater soldier than he you wot
on' is attractively straightforward.
167 **it's . . . for** never mind about
168-9 **him . . . him** The first 'him' probably refers to Aufidius, the second
to Coriolanus, with First Servingman
agreeing about Coriolanus' superiority
(cf. ll. 190-2) but moderating the
invidiousness of Second Servingman's
praise. It is First Servingman who chal-
lenges Third Servingman's disrespect-
ful reference to Aufidius (184), whereas
Second Servingman calls for them to
trust each other and be less guarded in
their remarks (187-9): see 164-74 n.

SECOND SERVINGMAN Faith, look you, one cannot tell how to say that. For the defence of a town our general is excellent.

FIRST SERVINGMAN Ay, and for an assault too.

Enter the Third Servingman

THIRD SERVINGMAN O, slaves, I can tell you news—news, you rascals!   175

FIRST *and* SECOND SERVINGMEN What, what, what? Let's partake.

THIRD SERVINGMAN I would not be a Roman of all nations. I had as lief be a condemned man.   180

FIRST *and* SECOND SERVINGMEN Wherefore? Wherefore?

THIRD SERVINGMAN Why, here's he that was wont to thwack our general, Caius Martius.

FIRST SERVINGMAN Why do you say 'thwack our general'?

THIRD SERVINGMAN I do not say 'thwack our general';   185
but he was always good enough for him.

SECOND SERVINGMAN Come, we are fellows and friends. He was ever too hard for him. I have heard him say so himself.

FIRST SERVINGMAN He was too hard for him directly. To   190
say the truth on't, before Corioles he scotched him and notched him like a carbonado.

SECOND SERVINGMAN An he had been cannibally given, he might have broiled and eaten him too.

177, 181, 240 FIRST *and* SECOND] F (*Both.*)   180 lief] F4 (lieve); liue F1   190–1 him‿ directly. To . . . on't, before] OXFORD; ~‿ ~, to . . . on't‿ before F; ~‿ ~, . . . ~: before POPE; ~, ~‿ . . . ~. Before HIBBARD (*conj.* Smith)   194 broiled] POPE; boyld F

---

180 **lief** gladly, willingly

188–9 **He . . . him . . . him . . . himself** The first pronoun refers to Coriolanus, the others to Aufidius.

190 **directly** (a) 'without being evasive about it'; cf. *1 Henry IV* 2.4.84, *Cymbeline* 1.4.155, *Othello* 2.1.220; less probably (b) 'in direct encounter, face to face', cf. 1.7.59

190–1 **To . . . on't** Oxford points out that F's punctuation relates this phrase to the preceding, rather than the succeeding clause. Either arrangement makes sense, and choice depends on how one interprets 'directly': if the latter means 'face to face', Oxford's arrangement is preferable.

191 **scotched** gashed, slashed

192 **carbonado** meat scored across and broiled over hot coals (Latin *carbo*, coal)

193 **An** if

194 **broiled** grilled. Pope's emendation agrees better with 'carbonado', though Sisson, after arguing against the need for consistency, claims that 'pork is in fact often "scotched" before boiling, in the Midlands at least'.

FIRST SERVINGMAN But more of thy news.   195
THIRD SERVINGMAN Why, he is so made on here within
    as if he were son and heir to Mars; set at upper end
    o'th' table, no question asked him by any of the sena-
    tors but they stand bald before him. Our general him-
    self makes a mistress of him, sanctifies himself with's   200
    hand, and turns up the white o'th' eye to his dis-
    course. But the bottom of the news is, our general is
    cut i'th' middle, and but one half of what he was yes-
    terday, for the other has half by the entreaty and grant
    of the whole table. He'll go, he says, and sowl the por-   205
    ter of Rome gates by th'ears. He will mow all down
    before him, and leave his passage polled.
SECOND SERVINGMAN And he's as like to do't as any man
    I can imagine.
THIRD SERVINGMAN Do't? He will do't; for look you, sir,   210
    he has as many friends as enemies; which friends, sir,
    as it were durst not—look you, sir—show themselves,
    as we term it, his friends whilst he's in dejectitude.
FIRST SERVINGMAN 'Dejectitude'? What's that?

---

205 sowl] F (sole), ROWE (*subs.*)   207 polled] F (poul'd), ROWE (*subs.*)   213, 214
dejectitude] COLLIER 1858 (deictitude); Directitude F; discreditude MALONE *conj.*

---

196 **so made on** made so much of
197–8 **at . . . table** i.e. in the place of hon-
    our
199 **but** unless
    bald i.e. bareheaded as a mark of re-
    spect, cf. 1.10.40.2–3 n. Elizabethans
    customarily wore hats indoors as well
    as out, including at table.
200 **makes . . . him** Cf. 117–19 n.
200–1 **sanctifies . . . hand** 'touches his
    hand as though it were a sacred relic'
    (Hibbard), cf. 148 n. and *Romeo*
    1.5.92–3, *As You Like It* 3.4.12
201 **turns . . . eye** (in pious admiration)
202 **bottom** essential part, essence,
    cf. *1 Henry IV* 4.1.50
203 **cut . . . middle** i.e. his power is
    divided in half: another, slightly dis-
    placed body-politic image; King glosses
    it 'like a joint of meat'
204 **the other** (Coriolanus)
205 **sowl** A dialect word meaning 'seize
    by the ears': Steevens comments, 'Per-

haps Shakespeare's allusion is to Hercules dragging out Cerberus'.
206–7 **mow . . . him** Another mower
image, cf. 1.3.36–7.
207 **polled** shorn, despoiled
211 **he has . . . enemies** Cf. 3.1.232. This
agrees with Plutarch's version, in
which Martius' intention is not to destroy all Rome but rather to make an
alliance between the Volscians and the
Roman patricians in order to wrest
power back from the plebeians: cf.
4.3.13–16 n.
213 **dejectitude** (a) First Servingman's
question suggests that this may be a
neologism, and Second Servingman's
reply indirectly conveys that what he
intended by it was the opposite of
'his crest up again and the man in
blood': in secretary hand 'deiectitude'
could easily be misread as 'directitude';
(b) alternatively, F's reading may be
the correct transliteration of a comic

THIRD SERVINGMAN But when they shall see, sir, his crest   215
up again and the man in blood, they will out of their
burrows like conies after rain, and revel all with him.

FIRST SERVINGMAN But when goes this forward?

THIRD SERVINGMAN Tomorrow, today, presently. You
shall have the drum struck up this afternoon. 'Tis as it   220
were a parcel of their feast, and to be executed ere they
wipe their lips.

SECOND SERVINGMAN Why, then we shall have a stirring
world again. This peace is nothing but to rust iron,
increase tailors, and breed ballad-makers.   225

FIRST SERVINGMAN Let me have war, say I. It exceeds
peace as far as day does night. It's sprightly walking,
audible and full of vent. Peace is a very apoplexy,
lethargy; mulled, deaf, sleepy, insensible; a getter of
more bastard children than war's a destroyer of men.   230

SECOND SERVINGMAN 'Tis so, and as war in some sort

217 burrows] F (Burroughs)   224 is nothing] F1; is worth nothing F4   227 sprightly walking] F; ~, waking POPE   229 sleepy] F3 (*subs.*); sleepe F1   230 war's] ROWE 1714; warres F   231 war] ROWE 1714; warres F

malapropism for 'discreditude': this fits
the meaning of Second Servingman's
reply but not his imagery. Neither the
Servingmen nor the plebeians are
given malaprop humour elsewhere,
whereas the comedy of neologisms is
several times exploited in the play.

215–16 **his crest up** An image from hunting and cock-fighting, cf. *1 Henry IV*
1.1.97–8, *K. John* 4.3.150, *Caesar*
4.2.26.

216 **in blood** 'in full vigour and ready
for action'; another hunting term
(cf. 1.1.156 n.), that also reminds us
of the long period Coriolanus was literally covered in blood in Act 1
will out i.e. 'will come out'. The
omission of a verb of motion in an
expression of purpose or desire was
common (Abbott §405); cf. 1.1.66.

217 **conies** rabbits

219 **presently** immediately now

221 **parcel** part, portion. War is frequently associated with feasting imagery in
this play; cf. 1.10.10–11 n.

225 **increase tailors** Because men, having
no use for armour, will go in for elaborate dress; cf. 1.10.45.

227 **sprightly walking** See Introduction,
pp. 107–8.

228 **full of vent** Sisson notes that the
imagery is of war as a hunting dog
(cf. 'the dogs of war' of *Caesar*
3.1.276), in which 'vent' is 'The scent
given off by a hunted animal' (*OED*
sb.[2] 13a).
apoplexy, lethargy Cf. *2 Henry IV*,
1.2.113–14, 'This apoplexy is, as I
take it, a kind of lethargy . . . a kind of
sleeping in the blood'.

229 **mulled** (a) stupefied (*OED, mull, v.*[2]);
or (b) 'softened, rendered mild' (*OED
v.*[1]). The latter is the less probable,
considering the adjectives with which
it is linked.

230 **bastard children** Cf. 3.2.58–9, where
Volumnia disparages mollifying words
as 'bastards'.

231 **war** F's 'warres' was probably a
result of contamination from 'warres'
(i.e. war's) in the previous line (Oxford)

may be said to be a ravisher, so it cannot be denied but
peace is a great maker of cuckolds.

FIRST SERVINGMAN ~~Ay, and it makes~~ men hate one
another.   235

THIRD SERVINGMAN Reason: because they then less need
one another. The wars for my money! I hope to see
Romans as cheap as Volscians.

⌈*A sound within*⌉

They are rising, they are rising.

FIRST *and* SECOND SERVINGMEN In, in, in, in.   *Exeunt*   240

4.6   *Enter the two tribunes, Sicinius and Brutus*

SICINIUS

We hear not of him, neither need we fear him.
His remedies are tame, the present peace
And quietness of the people, which before
Were in wild hurry. Here do we make his friends
Blush that the world goes well, who rather had,   5
Though they themselves did suffer by't, behold
Dissentious numbers pest'ring streets than see
Our tradesmen singing in their shops and going
About their functions friendly.

BRUTUS

We stood to't in good time.

Enter Menenius

Is this Menenius?   10

238.1 *A sound within*] OXFORD; *not in* F   240 FIRST *and* SECOND SERVINGMEN] F (*Both.*)
4.6.2 tame, the] F; tame i'th' THEOBALD; tame—the SISSON; ta'en the JOHNSON *conj.*;
~. The WHITE   4 hurry. Here_∧] F; ~_∧ here, HUDSON; ~, ~_∧ WHITE   10 *Enter Menenius*]
CAMBRIDGE; *after* friendly. F

240 **They ... rising** i.e. the Volscian lords
are rising from table. Repetition of this
phrase and 'In, in, in, in' ends the
scene on an accelerated, urgent tempo
that contrast comically with the complacent leisure of the next scene.

4.6 The harmonious condition of Rome
with which this scene opens is Shakespeare's invention; its use of singing in
the shops as a symptom of civic content is reminiscent of Dekker's *The
Shoemaker's Holiday* (1599). Most modern directors have emphasized a holi-

day mood at the beginning of the
scene to contrast sharply with both
the servants' praise of war in 4.5 and
the milling confusion with which 4.6
ends. The situation is ironic, of course,
because we already know what is
about to happen.

7 **pest'ring** obstructing, crowding
9 **functions** proper occupations, cf.
4.5.33

10 **stood to't** made a stand, stood firm
about it. Kemball-Cook notes that, of
the two Tribunes, Brutus is the more

SICINIUS

  'Tis he, 'tis he. O, he is grown most kind of late.

  (To Menenius) Hail, sir.

MENENIUS Hail to you both.

SICINIUS

  Your Coriolanus is not now much missed

  But with his friends. The commonwealth doth stand   15

  And so would do were he more angry at it.

MENENIUS

  All's well, and might have been much better if

  He could have temporized.

SICINIUS Where is he, hear you?

MENENIUS Nay, I hear nothing.   20

  His mother and his wife hear nothing from him.

    Enter three or four Citizens

ALL THE CITIZENS *(to the Tribunes)*

  The gods preserve you both.

SICINIUS   Good e'en, our neighbours.

BRUTUS

  Good e'en to you all, good e'en to you all.

FIRST CITIZEN

  Ourselves, our wives and children, on our knees

  Are bound to pray for you both.

SICINIUS   Live and thrive.   25

BRUTUS Farewell, kind neighbours.

  We wished Coriolanus had loved you as we did.

---

12 Hail, sir.] F; *Both Tri.* Hail, sir. GLOBE; Hail, sir! *Bru.* Hail, Sir! CAPELL
14 Coriolanus] F; Coriolanus, sir, CAPELL   not now] HINMAN *conj. (in 'Textual Companion');* not F   22, 28 ALL THE CITIZENS] F (*All.*)   22, 23 Good e'en] F (Gooden); Good den COLLIER   24 FIRST CITIZEN] F (1)

complacent and patronizing: e.g. ll. 23, 26–7, 31–4, 38–9; cf. 3.3.84–5.

14 **not** Hinman's conjecture would fit the sense and regularize the metre; if the manuscript had two words following each other as graphically similar as 'not now', it would be quite easy for one of them to be omitted.

20–1 **Nay . . . him** Cf. Coriolanus' promise at 4.1.52–4.

22 **Good e'en** Cf. 2.1.90 n.

27 **wished** Hilda Hulme (*Explorations in Shakespeare's Language*, 1977, p. 267) notes that 'In some Midland dialects of the present time the perfect form of *wished* does not always refer to past time, but often is temporally the same as the present, only it implies that the wish cannot be fulfilled'.

ALL THE CITIZENS
  Now the gods keep you!
SICINIUS *and* BRUTUS   Farewell, farewell.

                                        Exeunt Citizens

SICINIUS
  This is a happier and more comely time
  Than when these fellows ran about the streets   30
  Crying confusion.
BRUTUS   Caius Martius was
  A worthy officer i'th' war, but insolent,
  O'ercome with pride, ambitious past all thinking,
  Self-loving—
SICINIUS   And affecting one sole throne
  Without assistance.
MENENIUS   I think not so.   35
SICINIUS
  We should by this, to all our lamentation,
  If he had gone forth consul found it so.
BRUTUS
  The gods have well prevented it, and Rome
  Sits safe and still without him.
         Enter an Aedile

AEDILE   Worthy tribunes,
  There is a slave whom we have put in prison   40
  Reports the Volsces, with two several powers,
  Are entered in the Roman territories,
  And with the deepest malice of the war
  Destroy what lies before 'em.
MENENIUS   'Tis Aufidius,

---

28 SICINIUS *and* BRUTUS] F (*Both Tri.*), OXFORD   33 ambitious͜ ... thinking,] F4; ~, ...
͜ FI   34 Self-loving—] CAPELL (*subs.*); ~. F   35 assistance] F (assistãce), ROWE; assis-
tants HANMER   36 lamentation] F2; Lamention FI   37 found] F; find HANMER; have
found MALONE *conj.*

---

35 **assistance** partners or associates   43 **deepest malice ... war** Though this
37 **found** i.e. have found   may mean merely 'the deepest malice
39 **Enter an Aedile** See Introduction, p.   *possible* in war', it also suggests a
   107: this Aedile is the first of four   greater savagery than has been used
   messengers whose rapid succession   before in the conflict with the
   breaks down the Tribunes' confidence;   Volscians, a vindictive 'scorched earth'
   Shakespeare uses the same device fre-   policy: cf. *Richard II* 1.1.155, 'Deep
   quently, most notably towards the end   malice makes too deep incision'.
   of *Richard III* and in 5.5 of *Troilus*.

Who, hearing of our Martius' banishment, 45
Thrusts forth his horns again into the world,
Which were inshelled when Martius stood for Rome,
And durst not once peep out.

SICINIUS   Come, what talk you of Martius?

BRUTUS (*to the Aedile*)

Go see this rumourer whipped. It cannot be
The Volsces dare break with us.

MENENIUS   Cannot be? 50

We have record that very well it can,
And three examples of the like hath been
Within my age. But reason with the fellow,
Before you punish him, where he heard this,
Lest you shall chance to whip your information 55
And beat the messenger who bids beware
Of what is to be dreaded.

SICINIUS   Tell not me.

I know this cannot be.

BRUTUS   Not possible.

    Enter a Messenger

MESSENGER

The nobles in great earnestness are going
All to the Senate-house. Some news is coming 60

---

52 hath] F1; haue F4   60 coming] F; come ROWE; come in MALONE

46–8 **Thrusts ... peep out** Arden compares Nashe's *Pasquil's Apologie* (ed. McKerrow, i. 131), 'I wonder how these silly snails ... dare thrust out their feeble horns against so tough and mighty adversaries'; to which Brockbank adds the anonymous interlude *Thersites* (1537) whose hero does battle with a snail till it draws in its horns (*Dodsley's Old Plays*, ed. Hazlitt, i. 413).

47 **inshelled** drawn into the shell

48 **what** why, for what

49 **rumourer whipped** Shakespeare always uses this situation ironically; cf. *Richard III* 4.4.438.1, *Antony* 2.5.61

50 **break** i.e. break the recent peace terms
MENENIUS Kemball-Cook notices the complex tone secured by having the news announced to the Tribunes and Menenius together so that their reactions play off each other: 'Menenius passes through astonishment and anxiety to sardonic resignation. At least the Tribunes have not had the last word.'

51 **record** Accented on the second syllable.

52 **hath** 'An example of the surviving plurals in -*th*, very common in the words *hath* and *doth* especially' (Arden).

53 **reason with** talk with, question

55 **information** i.e. source of information

60 **coming** (a) Sisson suggests that this means the process is continuing, i.e. 'Some has arrived, and more is to come'; (b) assuming contamination by 'going' at the end of the previous line, Oxford accepts Rowe's emendation to 'come'.

That turns their countenances.

SICINIUS 'Tis this slave—

(*To the Aedile*) Go whip him fore the people's eyes!—his raising,

Nothing but his report.

MESSENGER Yes, worthy sir,

The slave's report is seconded, and more,

More fearful, is delivered.

SICINIUS What more fearful? 65

MESSENGER

It is spoke freely out of many mouths—

How probable I do not know—that Martius,

Joined with Aufidius, leads a power 'gainst Rome,

And vows revenge as spacious as between

The young'st and oldest thing.

SICINIUS This is most likely! 70

BRUTUS

Raised only that the weaker sort may wish

Good Martius home again.

SICINIUS The very trick on't.

MENENIUS This is unlikely.

He and Aufidius can no more atone 75

Than violent'st contrariety.

Enter a Second Messenger

SECOND MESSENGER

You are sent for to the Senate.

A fearful army, led by Caius Martius

---

61 slave—] BROWER; ~: F; ~. OXFORD   76 contrariety] F; contrarieties HANMER; contraries CAPELL   76:1 *Enter a Second*] CAMBRIDGE; *Enter* F; *Enter another* OXFORD

---

61 **turns** alters; possibly 'turns pale', or 'curdles' (like milk)

62 **raising** incitement, rumour-raising

63 **report** Oxford's direction '*Exit Aedile*' is unnecessary; the Messenger interrupts before the Aedile has time to leave.

64 **seconded** supported by a second report

69 **as ... between** big enough to encompass, wide enough to include

72 **Good** A word that betrays Brutus' weakness in the face of opposition.

74 **This is unlikely** Gomme suggests a stress on 'is': Menenius could easily believe the news of Aufidius' renewed aggression but not this treachery by Martius (though the reason he gives for his disbelief is negative, not positive).

75 **atone** be reconciled, be made one

76 **violent'st contrariety** opposite extremes. Strictly the construction requires a plural, and the singular 'contrariety' does not occur elsewhere in Shakespeare but does in Averell.

Associated with Aufidius, rages
Upon our territories, and have already   80
O'erborne their way, consumed with fire and took
What lay before them.
    Enter Cominius
COMINIUS (*to the Tribunes*) O, you have made good work!
MENENIUS What news, what news?
COMINIUS
You have holp to ravish your own daughters and   85
To melt the city leads upon your pates,
To see your wives dishonoured to your noses—
MENENIUS What's the news? What's the news?
COMINIUS
Your temples burned in their cement, and
Your franchises, whereon you stood, confined   90
Into an auger's bore.
MENENIUS   Pray now, your news?
    (*To the Tribunes*)
You have made fair work, I fear me. (*To Cominius*)
    Pray, your news.
If Martius should be joined wi'th' Volscians—
COMINIUS
If? He is their god. He leads them like a thing
Made by some other deity than nature,   95
That shapes man better, and they follow him
Against us brats with no less confidence
Than boys pursuing summer butterflies,

---

87 noses –] CAPELL; ~. F   91 auger's bore] F (Augors boare), ROWE   93 wi'th']
ALEXANDER; with F

81 **O'erborne their way** overcome everything in their way; cf. 4.5.132 n.
84, 88, 91 MENENIUS Menenius' agitated
attempts to interrupt Cominius' flow
of commination build the scene's mo-
mentum.
85 **holp** helped; cf. 3.1.277 n.
86 **leads** lead-covered roofs, cf. 2.1.207
89 **in ... cement** down to their foundations, into their mortar. The accent is
on the first syllable of 'cement'.
90 **franchises** (a) freedoms, (b) votes?
whereon you stood (a) about which
you were adamant, cf. ll. 10, 100–1;

(b) on which you based your authority
91 **auger's bore** the small hole made by
an auger (a boring tool)
97 **brats** Johnson defines 'brat' as 'A
child, so called in contempt' because
of its insignificance, and Coriolanus
will later lose his temper at being
called 'boy', cf. 5.6.103, 105, 113.
98 **Than ... butterflies** This recalls Young
Martius mammocking a butterfly at
1.3.62–8; yet cf. also 5.4.11–14.
Cf. *Lear* 4.1.37, 'As flies to wanton
boys are we to th' gods'.

Or butchers killing flies.

MENENIUS (*to the Tribunes*) You have made good work,
   You and your apron-men, you that stood so much   100
   Upon the voice of occupation and
   The breath of garlic-eaters!

COMINIUS
   He'll shake your Rome about your ears.

MENENIUS
   As Hercules did shake down mellow fruit.
   You have made fair work!   105

BRUTUS But is this true, sir?

COMINIUS Ay, and you'll look pale
   Before you find it other. All the regions
   Do smilingly revolt, and who resists
   Are mocked for valiant ignorance,   110
   And perish constant fools. Who is't can blame him?
   Your enemies and his find something in him.

MENENIUS We are all undone unless
   The noble man have mercy.

COMINIUS   Who shall ask it?
   The tribunes cannot do't for shame; the people   115
   Deserve such pity of him as the wolf
   Does of the shepherds. For his best friends, if they
   Should say 'Be good to Rome', they charged him even

---

109 resists] F; resist HANMER

99 **flies** Comparisons to butchers killing flies are not infrequent in Elizabethan literature: cf. *Othello* 4.2.68, 'as summer flies are in the shambles'.

100 **apron-men** mechanics and tradesmen, who wear aprons; cf. *Caesar* 1.1.7 and *Antony* 5.2.205–6 for similar sneers

101 **voice of occupation** workmen's votes (and clamour)

102 **breath** A similar play on 'vote' and literal 'breath' (cf. next note).
   garlic-eaters i.e. 'the lower-classes, whose breath stinks of the garlic they eat'. Garlic seems to have been popular with Elizabethan workmen both as flavouring and as a medicament; cf. *Measure* 3.1.442, *Dream* 4.2.38.

103 **your Rome** See Introduction, p. 45.

104 **As . . . fruit** The penultimate 'labour' of Hercules (cf. 4.1.18–20 n.) was to gather golden fruit from the Islands of the Blessed, to get which he had to defeat just such a dragon as Coriolanus now identifies himself with; cf. 4.1.31 n. and *Pericles* 1.70.
   mellow fruit i.e. fruit so ripe it is ready to fall of its own accord, cf. 3.2.81–2, and *Hamlet* 3.2.182

109 **who resists** whoever resist (Abbott §251)

111 **constant** (a) loyal, (b) persistent

112 **something** i.e. something to admire (even though *you* didn't think so). The comment is sarcastic.

117 **For** as for

118–20 **charged . . . And therein showed**

As those should do that had deserved his hate,
And therein showed like enemies.

MENENIUS   'Tis true.   120
If he were putting to my house the brand
That should consume it, I have not the face
To say 'Beseech you, cease'. (*To the Tribunes*) You have
    made fair hands,
You and your crafts! You have crafted fair!

COMINIUS   You have brought
A trembling upon Rome such as was never   125
S'incapable of help.

SICINIUS *and* BRUTUS Say not we brought it.

MENENIUS How? Was't we?
We loved him, but like beasts and cowardly nobles
Gave way unto your clusters, who did hoot   130
Him out o'th' city.

COMINIUS   But I fear
They'll roar him in again. Tullus Aufidius,
The second name of men, obeys his points
As if he were his officer. Desperation
Is all the policy, strength, and defence   135
That Rome can make against them.

        Enter a troop of Citizens

MENENIUS   Here come the clusters.
(*To the Citizens*) And is Aufidius with him? You are they
That made the air unwholesome when you cast

---

127 SICINIUS *and* BRUTUS] OXFORD; *Tri.* F; *Both Trib.* DYCE

i.e. 'they would charge [entreat]...
And therein show' (Malone): a subjective construction (Abbott §361)

119 **those** (the Tribunes and plebeians)
123 **made...hands** Cf. Tilley H99, 'Used
ironically; to make a mess of a thing';
with a play on 'handicrafts' (see next
note); cf. *Henry VIII* (*All is True*)
5.3.69. See 'in hand', 1.1.52 n.
124 **crafted** (a) worked skilfully (playing
on 'crafts'), (b) acted craftily, intri-
gued: a pun rather than a neologism
126 **S'incapable of help** so incapable of
being helped

129–31 **like...city** Cf. 4.1.58.1 n.
130, 136 **clusters** See Introduction, pp. 89,
94 for a comment on possible staging.
132 **roar** i.e. roar for mercy; cf. 2.3.51,
5.6.100, and *1 Henry IV* 2.5.263
133 **second...men** i.e. second (to Coriolanus) in renown
obeys his points (a) 'obeys him in every
point' (Onions), or (b) 'obeys his commands' (Clarendon). Brockbank notes
that 'a point of war' was a drum or
trumpet signal, so the implication is
that Aufidius obeys promptly like a
well-trained officer.
138–9 **cast...caps** Cf. 3.3.136.2–3.

Your stinking greasy caps in hooting at
Coriolanus' exile. Now he's coming,   140
And not a hair upon a soldier's head
Which will not prove a whip. As many coxcombs
As you threw caps up will he tumble down,
And pay you for your voices. 'Tis no matter.
If he could burn us all into one coal,   145
We have deserved it.

ALL THE CITIZENS Faith, we hear fearful news.

FIRST CITIZEN For mine own part,
When I said 'banish him' I said 'twas pity.

SECOND CITIZEN And so did I.   150

THIRD CITIZEN And so did I, and to say the truth so did
very many of us. That we did, we did for the best, and
though we willingly consented to his banishment, yet
it was against our will.

COMINIUS
You're goodly things, you voices.

MENENIUS   You have made good work,   155
You and your cry! Shall's to the Capitol?

COMINIUS O, ay, what else?

                          Exeunt Menenius and Cominius

---

147 ALL THE CITIZENS] F (*Omnes.*)   155 made] F1; made you F2, CAPELL   157.1
Menenius and Cominius] CAPELL (*subs.*); *both.* F

142 **coxcombs** fools' heads (by association
with the headdress of professional
jesters); cf. *Shrew* 2.1.223

145 **coal** cinder, piece of charcoal
(*OED sb.* 2). Another of the many
'fire' images used by or applied to
Coriolanus, an end-of-the-world trope.

148 **For ... part** The only reason for this
short line seems to be metrical: it
makes a regular decasyllable with
'Faith, we hear fearful news' (l. 147).
The Citizens go on to speak prose.

153–4 **willingly ... will** This contradiction also appears in George Chapman's
1608 translation of the *Iliad*, iv. 43,
where Zeus reluctantly grants Hera's
determination to destroy Troy: see
Introduction, p. 4.

156 **cry** (a) 'pack of hounds' (cf. 3.3.121
n.), if this is addressed to the Tribunes;
(b) 'hooting', if it is addressed to the

Citizens, cf. 'voices' (l. 155)
Shall's shall we ('go' understood); see
Abbott §215

157 **O ... else** Cominius' half-line leaves
an ominous pause. Kemball-Cook suggests that 'A producer will be fully
justified in giving [the people] a me-
nacing   movement   towards   the
Tribunes, presaging the attack on Brutus reported in 5.4.[36–9].' The
crowd's reluctance to leave, signalled
by the repetition of 'Go' (ll. 158, 160)
and 'Come' (162, 165), might support
this; but it could equally well reflect
their uncertainty and lack of decision.
Sir Frank Benson added business in
which 'the two tribunes were most
realistically strangled and battered to
pieces by the ungrateful mob' (*The Globe*,
20 Apr. 1910): see Introduction,
p. 122.

SICINIUS

Go, masters, get you home. Be not dismayed;
These are a side that would be glad to have
This true which they so seem to fear. Go home,   160
And show no sign of fear.

FIRST CITIZEN The gods be good to us! Come, masters,
let's home. I ever said we were i'th' wrong when we
banished him.

SECOND CITIZEN So did we all. But come, let's home.   165

Exeunt Citizens

BRUTUS I do not like this news.

SICINIUS Nor I.

BRUTUS

Let's to the Capitol. Would half my wealth
Would buy this for a lie.

SICINIUS   Pray let's go.   *Exeunt*

4.7 *Enter Aufidius with his Lieutenant*

AUFIDIUS Do they still fly to th' Roman?

LIEUTENANT

I do not know what witchcraft's in him, but
Your soldiers use him as the grace fore meat,
Their talk at table, and their thanks at end,
And you are darkened in this action, sir,   5
Even by your own.

AUFIDIUS   I cannot help it now,

165.1 *Exeunt Citizens*] F (*Exit Cit.*)   169 *Exeunt*] F (*Exeunt Tribunes.*)

159 **side** faction

168-9 **Would . . . lie** This is an important
clue to the social (not to speak of
moral) status of Brutus. Shakespeare
sees him as one of the new middle
class of London, the rich bourgeois and
professionals who supported Parliament's struggle against James.

4.7 Hibbard notes that this scene fulfils
two purposes: 'to explain the reasons
for Aufidius' turning against Coriolanus, and so to prepare us for the
catastrophe', and 'to sum up his hero's
character . . . and give a number of
possible interpretations of his earlier
behaviour'—though, like all the play's

commentators on Coriolanus, Aufidius
finds he can come to no conclusion, a
bafflement reflected in his choked, con-
torted syntax. Our prior awareness of
Aufidius' intention lends irony to Volumnia's success in 5.3.

3-4 **grace . . . table** See Introduction,
p. 78.

5 **darkened** eclipsed, put in the shade;
cf. 2.1.255
action campaign, military action

6 **your own** Most probably, following the
lines preceding, (a) 'your own men';
less probably (b) 'your own action' (in
making Coriolanus co-commander).

Unless by using means I lame the foot
Of our design. He bears himself more proudlier,
Even to my person, than I thought he would
When first I did embrace him. Yet his nature   10
In that's no changeling, and I must excuse
What cannot be amended.

LIEUTENANT   Yet I wish, sir—
I mean for your particular—you had not
Joined in commission with him, but either
Have borne the action of yourself or else   15
To him had left it solely.

AUFIDIUS
I understand thee well, and be thou sure,
When he shall come to his account, he knows not
What I can urge against him. Although it seems—
And so he thinks, and is no less apparent
To th'vulgar eye—that he bears all things fairly   20
And shows good husbandry for the Volscian state,
Fights dragon-like, and does achieve as soon
As draw his sword, yet he hath left undone
That which shall break his neck or hazard mine   25
Whene'er we come to our account.

LIEUTENANT
Sir, I beseech you, think you he'll carry Rome?

AUFIDIUS
All places yields to him ere he sits down,

4.7.8 proudlier] F1; proudly F2   15 Have] F (haue); had POPE   19 him. Although]
CAPELL; ~, although F; ~; though POPE

7 **Unless** in case
using means taking steps (against
Coriolanus)
8 **more proudlier** An intensified comparative; cf. 3.1.122, 'More worthier':
see Abbott §11.
11 **changeling** (a) fickle thing, (b) reneg-
ade? (Brockbank); cf. *1 Henry IV*
5.1.76
13 **for . . . particular** as far as you personally are concerned; cf. *Troilus* 2.2.9
14 **Joined in commission** A phrase from
North, meaning 'shared the position of
general'.
15 **Have** could have

borne . . . yourself taken responsibility
for the campaign by yourself
19 **What . . . him** Cf. 'he hath left undone
| That which shall break his neck',
ll. 24–5, and 5.6.64, 'faults he made
before the last': see Introduction, p. 26.
22 **husbandry for** management on behalf
of, concern for the welfare of (with
perhaps an ironical reminder for the
audience of the actual wife's distress?)
23 **dragon-like** Cf. 4.1.31 n.
28 ff. **All places . . .** See Introduction,
p. 26. See Eugene Waith, *The Hercu-
lean Hero* (1962), pp. 132–4, for a
close analysis of the speech.

And the nobility of Rome are his;
The senators and patricians love him too.   30
The tribunes are no soldiers, and their people
Will be as rash in the repeal as hasty
To expel him thence. I think he'll be to Rome
As is the osprey to the fish, who takes it
By sovereignty of nature. First he was   35
A noble servant to them, but he could not
Carry his honours even. Whether 'twas pride,
Which out of daily fortune ever taints
The happy man; whether defect of judgement,
To fail in the disposing of those chances   40
Which he was lord of; or whether nature,
Not to be other than one thing, not moving
From th' casque to th' cushion, but commanding peace
Even with the same austerity and garb
As he controlled the war; but one of these—   45
As he hath spices of them all—not all,
For I dare so far free him—made him feared,

---

37 'twas] F3; 'was FI   39 defect] F2; detect FI   43 casque] F (Caske), STEEVENS–
REED 1793   45 war; but] THEOBALD; warre. But F   45–6 —As . . . all—] F ((As . . .
all))   47 him—] CAMBRIDGE; ~, F

29–30 **nobility . . . senators and patricians**
 Shakespeare seems to be distinguishing
 between the 'young nobility' of
 4.1.0.2 (and probably 3.2.0.1), who
 Plutarch says always remained loyal
 to Coriolanus, and the older, less committed 'senators and patricians', the
 one title deriving from 'senex' (old
 man), the other from 'pater' (father)—
 though, strictly, there was no distinction between 'nobility' and 'patricians'.
 Gordon suggests that Shakespeare was
 misled by finding the appositional phrase
 'the Nobility and Patricians' in North,
 who adopted it from Amyot; naturally,
 it is not to be found in Plutarch.

34–5 **As . . . nature** The osprey is a fish-
 hawk, to whose kingly status fish were
 popularly thought to surrender by
 turning belly-up.

37 **even** with a proper balance, equably;
 cf. 2.1.220 n.

38 **out . . . fortune** as a result of an 'inter-

rupted train of success' (Johnson)

39 **happy** fortunate, lucky

40 **the disposing** making best use

41 **whether nature** whether it was his
 nature

43 **casque** helmet (representing his military career)
 cushion i.e. seat in the Senate, cf.
 2.2.0.1 n., 3.1.103 (representing civil
 and political life)

44 **austerity and garb** A hendiadys for
 'austere demeanour' (*OED, garb, sb.*² 2).

45–7 **but one . . . him** Kemball-Cook notes
 the complexity of Aufidius' indecision
 here: he 'seems to hover between
 saying "Only one of these faults was
 responsible for Coriolanus' downfall—I
 can venture to acquit him of suffering
 from all three"; and "He has elements
 of each fault in his make-up, but none
 in its entirety".'

46 **spices** touches, traces

47 **free** absolve

So hated, and so banished. But he has a merit
To choke it in the utt'rance. So our virtues
Lie in th'interpretation of the time,   50
And power, unto itself most commendable,
Hath not a tomb so evident as a chair
T'extol what it hath done.
One fire drives out one fire, one nail one nail;
Rights by rights falter, strengths by strengths do fail.   55
Come, let's away. When, Caius, Rome is thine,
Thou art poor'st of all; then shortly art thou mine.

Exeunt

5.1   *Enter Menenius, Cominius, Sicinius, and Brutus, the*
two tribunes, with others

MENENIUS
No, I'll not go! You hear what he hath said

---

49 virtues,] F2 (*subs.*); Vertue, F1   52 tomb] F; tongue KEIGHTLEY   evident] F;
eloquent WHITE   a chair] F; a cheer COLLIER 1858 (MS); a tear HUDSON *conj.*; a choir
BULLOCH *conj.* (*in* Cambridge); the chair KINNEAR *conj.* (*in* Cambridge)   55 Rights ...
falter] DYCE; Rights ... fouler F; Rights ... founder MALONE (*conj.* Johnson); Rights ...
fuller HIBBARD (*conj.* Perring); Right's ... fouler POPE (by right), SISSON   57 Thou art]
F; Thou'rt POPE, SISSON
   5.1] F (*Actus Quintus.*)   0.1 Sicinius, and] F (*Sicinius,*)

---

48 **merit** (his valour)
49 **To ... utt'rance** (a) choke back any
    talk of whichever fault was respons-
    ible; (b) but stifles it (ie. merit) by
    being so self-opinionated. The first
    reading relates to what precedes it and
    is the more grammatically straightfor-
    ward; the second relates to what suc-
    ceeds it (cf. ll. 51–3) and is closer to
    the source passage in Plutarch.
49–55 **So ... fail** Cf. Ulysses' speech about
    the effect of time on reputation in
    Troilus 3.3.139 ff.
50 **Lie ... time** (a) are at the mercy of
    each age's interpretation, (b) are at
    the mercy of contemporary opinion;
    cf. *1 Henry IV* 5.1.139, 'Detraction
    will not suffer it'
52–3 **Hath ... done** A notorious crux:
    'and power, which thinks itself praise-
    worthy, has no more certain way to
    destroy itself than by proclaiming its
    successes publicly'. The next lines
    explain why this is so: power inevit-

ably stirs up an opposition that will
replace it.
52 **evident** inevitable, certain
    chair rostrum for an oration, cf. *Caesar*
    3.2.64, 'the public chair'
54 **One ... nail** Proverbial: Tilley F277,
    N77
55 **falter** This seems a better emendation
    of F's 'fouler'—which probably mis-
    represented manuscript 'faulter' or
    'foulter' (Wilson)—than Hibbard's
    adjectival 'fuller', though the latter is
    possible. This part of the proverbial
    couplet has not been traced to à source.
    strengths by ... fail Hibbard finds an
    analogue in Erasmus, *Adagia* (949c),
    'Fortis in alium fortiorem incidit' (the
    strong man meets a stronger)
56 **Caius** Ironically, this is the one time in
    the play that the hero's most personal,
    intimate name is used alone (though
    Volumnia separates it out at 2.1.168,
    after having first used 'Martius').
5.1 In Plutarch there are actually three

Which was sometime his general, who loved him
In a most dear particular. He called me father,
But what o' that? (*To the Tribunes*) Go, you that ban-
        ished him;
A mile before his tent fall down, and knee   5
The way into his mercy.—Nay, if he coyed
To hear Cominius speak, I'll keep at home.

COMINIUS

He would not seem to know me.

MENENIUS (*to the Tribunes*)   Do you hear?

COMINIUS

Yet one time he did call me by my name.
I urged our old acquaintance and the drops   10
That we have bled together. 'Coriolanus'
He would not answer to, forbade all names;
He was a kind of nothing, titleless,
Till he had forged himself a name o'th' fire
Of burning Rome.

MENENIUS (*to the Tribunes*) Why, so: you have made good
        work!   15
A pair of tribunes that have wracked fair Rome

4–5 him; . . . tent‸] CAMBRIDGE (*subs.*); ~‸ . . . ~, F   5 knee] F1; kneele F2   14 o'] F
(a'); i' JOHNSON   16 wracked] F; rack'd JOHNSON; reck'd WARBURTON (*conj.* Theobald);
wreck'd MASON; sack'd HANMER; fair] HANMER; for F

embassies before that of Coriolanus'
family; Shakespeare reduces these to
two and also personalizes them: see
Introduction, p. 24.

0.2 *others* 1984 NT included a small group
of Citizens among these 'others', to
demonstrate that the impending attack
had united all sections of Rome, as
Plutarch explains (see Spencer, p. 348).

1–2 **he . . . general** i.e. Cominius

3 **In . . . particular** 'with the closest personal affection' (*OED, particular,* 6d)

5–6 **knee | The way** make your way on
your knees (like penitents approaching
a shrine); cf. *More* II. D. 122–3 (Oxford, p. 892).

6 **coyed** 'condescended unwillingly' (Steevens), 'showed reluctance' (Arden),
rather than 'disdained' (*OED v.*[1] 4b)

8 **would not seem** i.e. affected not to
(another acting reference)

11–15 **'Coriolanus' . . . Rome** See Introduction, p. 84. There may be a reminiscence here of Herostratus who
sought to perpetuate his name by
burning down the temple of Diana at
Ephesus.

14 **forged** This verb has a telling ambiguity: (a) shaped by melting first in
fire, (b) counterfeited (*OED v.*[1] 5).
o'th' fire F's 'a th' fire' is more usually
rendered 'of the fire' (which makes
satisfactory sense in context), rather
than 'in the fire' (Johnson), although
the latter is more precise with 'forge'.

15 **burning Rome** The idea of burning
Rome, not in Plutarch, probably comes
in by analogy with Troy.

16–17 **wracked . . . cheap** i.e. 'have
brought down the price of coal by
offering the ruins of fair Rome as fuel'
(Dyce 1866)

16 **wracked** Menenius, with characteristic

To make coals cheap—a noble memory!

COMINIUS
I minded him how royal 'twas to pardon
When it was less expected. He replied
It was a bare petition of a state   20
To one whom they had punished.

MENENIUS   Very well.
Could he say less?

COMINIUS
I offered to awaken his regard
For's private friends. His answer to me was
He could not stay to pick them in a pile   25
Of noisome, musty chaff. He said 'twas folly,
For one poor grain or two, to leave unburnt
And still to nose th'offence.

MENENIUS   For one poor grain or two!
I am one of those; his mother, wife, his child,
And this brave fellow too: we are the grains.   30
(*To the Tribunes*) You are the musty chaff, and you are
    smelt
Above the moon. We must be burnt for you.

---

19 less] F; least POPE   20 bare] F; base MASON (*conj.*); rare DYCE (*conj.* Williams);
mere STEEVENS–REED 1793   27 leave] F; leave't HUDSON (*conj.* Daniel)   27–8 unburnt‸
...nose‸] F; ~, ... ~, CAMBRIDGE   28 two!] F (~?)

---

word-play, combines (a) 'wrack' as a
variant of 'wreck', meaning 'ruin', as
in 'rack and ruin' (cf. North, 'all
went still to wrack at Rome': Spencer,
p. 345), and (b) 'rack' meaning 'impose
a great effort, strain'. There may even
be a nuance of 'wreaked', meaning
'revenged in spite', cf. 4.5.86 n.
  fair F's 'for' agrees with the subordinate sense (b) above, while Hanmer's
'fair' suits sense (a) better

17 coals charcoal, cf. 4.6.145 n.
  a...memory posthumous repute; i.e.
  'What a fine memorial to leave behind
  you!' (sarcastically), cf. 4.5.72, 5.6.154
18 royal A revealing adjective, considering the Tribunes' fears (cf. 3.3.65 n.);
  to which Coriolanus' use of 'state' (l.
  20) may be a bitter response.

19 When...less the less it was
20 bare (a) barefaced (Chambers),
  (b) threadbare, beggarly (Brockbank)
21 Very well well said, very just
23 offered ventured, tried
25–8 a pile...offence Shakespeare combines the play's themes of corn-harvest
  and stinking proletariat with Matthew
  3: 12's metaphor of winnowing the
  saved from the damned and Genesis
  18: 24–33's account of the destruction
  of Sodom when even a few virtuous
  citizens could not be found.
28 nose th'offence smell the offensive
  matter (the 'noisome, musty chaff')
32 Above the moon Cf. *Hamlet* 3.3.36,
  Much Ado 2.1.232–4; the point being
  that in the Ptolemaic cosmos creation
  above the moon's sphere was supposed
  to be free from corruption.

SICINIUS

Nay, pray be patient. If you refuse your aid
In this so-never-needed help, yet do not
Upbraid's with our distress. But sure, if you   35
Would be your country's pleader, your good tongue,
More than the instant army we can make,
Might stop our countryman.

MENENIUS   No, I'll not meddle.

SICINIUS

Pray you go to him.

MENENIUS   What should I do?

BRUTUS

Only make trial what your love can do   40
For Rome towards Martius.

MENENIUS

Well, and say that Martius return me,
As Cominius is returned, unheard—what then?
But as a discontented friend, grief-shot
With his unkindness? Say't be so?

SICINIUS   Yet your good will   45
Must have that thanks from Rome after the measure
As you intended well.

MENENIUS   I'll undertake't.

I think he'll hear me. Yet to bite his lip
And hum at good Cominius much unhearts me.
He was not taken well, he had not dined.   50

---

45 unkindness?] CAPELL; ~. F   49 hum] F (humme); 'hmh' OXFORD

---

34 **In . . . help** at this time when help was never so badly needed

37 **instant army . . . make** the sort of army we can mobilize immediately

44 **But as** merely as
discontented who has not been granted satisfaction
grief-shot grief-stricken (not in *OED*)

46–7 **after . . . well** in proportion to your good intentions

48–9 **bite . . . at** conventional signs of anger (consequently, performance cues for Coriolanus?); cf. *Richard III* 4.2.28, *Shrew* 2.1.243

49 **hum** A hum was a sound of disapproval, cf. 5.4.21. In *Henry V* 1.2.202 it is associated with a surly judge delivering prisoners to execution (see E. A. Armstrong, *Shakespeare's Imagination*, 1963, p. 141).
unhearts discourages

50 **taken well** tackled at a propitious moment, cf. *Dream* 3.2.16, *Hamlet* 3.3.80
dined Dinner was served between 11.00 a.m. and noon in Elizabethan times (*Shakespeare's England*, ii. 134); cf. 5.2.34.

The veins unfilled, our blood is cold, and then
We pout upon the morning, are unapt
To give or to forgive; but when we have stuffed
These pipes and these conveyances of our blood
With wine and feeding, we have suppler souls   55
Than in our priest-like fasts. Therefore I'll watch him
Till he be dieted to my request,
And then I'll set upon him.

BRUTUS

You know the very road into his kindness,
And cannot lose your way.

MENENIUS   Good faith, I'll prove him.   60
Speed how it will, I shall ere long have knowledge
Of my success.   *Exit*

COMINIUS   He'll never hear him.

SICINIUS   Not?

COMINIUS

I tell you he does sit in gold, his eye
Red as 'twould burn Rome, and his injury
The jailer to his pity. I kneeled before him;   65
'Twas very faintly he said 'Rise', dismissed me

60–1 him.... will,] DYCE 1866 (*conj.* Heath); ~, ... ~. F   61 I] F; Ye THEOBALD *conj.*;
You HANMER   62 Not?] F3; ~. F1; No? CAPELL   63 in gold] F; engall'd BLACKSTONE
conj. (*in* Cambridge)

51–7 **The veins . . . request** These lines
not only reflect ironically on Menenius' body-politic fable in 1.1, they also
expose his reductively manipulative
attitude to others, even one loved like
Coriolanus.
52 **pout** look sullen, cf. *Romeo*, 3.3.143
54 **These pipes** i.e. the digestive tract
conveyances channels (*OED* 8); the
'veins' of l. 51
55 **suppler** more amenable, cf. *Troilus*,
2.3.218
57 **dieted to** conditioned, by feeding, to
accept
60 **prove** test, try
61 **Speed . . . will** however things turn
out, no matter what happens
62 **my success** the results, good or bad, of
my attempt
62–74 **He'll . . . them on** Kemball-Cook
notes that the remaining lines of the

scene supply 'dramatic time' during
which 'Menenius may be supposed to
find his way to Coriolanus' camp, so
that the scenes are continuous'. Uncharacteristically for Cominius, they
are also packed with quasi-legal phrasing: hear, sit, injury, jailer, dismissed,
bound, oath, hold (or F's 'yield'), conditions, solicit, entreaties.
63 **sit in gold** See Introduction, p. 98 for
a comment on this as a possible staging cue; cf. 5.2.57.1 n.
63–4 **his eye | Red ... Rome** Cf. *Hamlet*
2.2.466, *First Part of the Contention*
3.1.154, *K. John* 4.2.163, 'With eyes
as red as new-enkindled fire'; though,
as Brockbank notes, 'Here the metaphor is more formidable, as the symbolic fire is proleptically actual'.
64 **his injury** his sense of the wrong done
to him

Thus, with his speechless hand. What he would do,
He sent in writing after me, what he would not:
Bound with an oath to hold to his conditions.
So that all hope is vain—   70
Unless his noble mother and his wife,
Who, as I hear, mean to solicit him
For mercy to his country—therefore let's hence,
And with our fair entreaties haste them on.   *Exeunt*

5.2   *Enter Menenius to the Watch or guard*
FIRST WATCHMAN Stay. Whence are you?
SECOND WATCHMAN Stand, and go back.

---

68 He ... me, ... not:] This edition; He ... me; ... not, F; He ... me, ... not, SISSON;
What he would not, he sent in writing after me. JERVIS *conj.* (*in* Cambridge)   69 to
hold to his] OXFORD (*conj.* Solly, *in* Cambridge); to yeeld to his F; to yield no new JOHNSON
(*conj.*); to yield to no SINGER   70 vain—] This edition; ~, F   71 Unless] F; Unless in
KITTREDGE (*conj.* Steevens-Reed 1793); Unless from CAPELL   wife,] F; ~, – THEOBALD;
~; MALONE   73 country—] This edition; ~: F
   5.2.1, 2 FIRST WATCHMAN, SECOND WATCHMAN] F (1. *Wat.*, 2. *Wat.*; *then* 1, 2)

67 **Thus** A cue for Cominius to ape Coriolanus' gesture.
67–9 **What ... oath** These lines have
caused trouble because F's syntax
and punctuation obscure the obvious
meaning, which is that Coriolanus
'sent in writing after' Cominius both
'what he would do' and 'what he
would not', and 'bound' both of these
things 'with an oath'. Probably 'what
he would not' was a marginal addition
wrongly inserted by the compositor at
the end instead of the beginning of
l. 68, and the manuscript intention
was: 'What he would do, | What he
would not, he sent in writing after me:
| Bound with an oath ...' There is no
need to suppose a missing clause.
69 **hold** F's 'yield' makes sense if glossed
as 'comply' (Brockbank), but *OED v.*
17, which he cites, means 'eventual
compliance with a position at first opposed', which does not suit the context. Since Coriolanus has offered
conditions (cf. 5.3.14), the emendation 'yield to no conditions' is also
ruled out. Solly's conjecture 'hold' is
plausible both semantically and orthographically, since that word in secretary hand could easily be misread as
'yeld' (Wilson, Oxford).

conditions Cf. 5.3.14 and Introduction, p. 26.
70 **So ... vain—** The shortness of this line
is appropriate: Cominius dribbles off
despondently, then has an invigorating new idea: see next note.
71–3 **Unless ... country—** I follow Sisson's suggestion that this is 'a broken
construction, significant of Cominius'
perturbation', and, I would add, his
rebound from dejection into fresh
energy as the new half-formulated idea
occurs to him. Alternatively, one can
accept Wilson's gloss of 'Unless' as 'if
it were not for' (cf. *All's Well* 4.1.5);
or, less probably, Brockbank's suggestion that we understand 'Unless' to
mean 'Unless we put hope in'.
5.2 Coriolanus is supposed to have
pitched camp at the Fossa Cluilia, at
the fourth milestone on the *via Latina*
south from Rome (see 5.3.207–8 n.).
This scene depicts the second of three
stages of pressure put on Coriolanus,
and with its emphasis on 'father' and
'son' (ll. 62, 69, 80, and 5.3.10) prepares for the climactic family appeal of
5.3; at the same time, its emphatic
irony and pathos contrast with the
tragic tone of the later scene.
0.1 *Watch or guard* Two names for

325

MENENIUS
> You guard like men; 'tis well. But by your leave,
> I am an officer of state, and come
> To speak with Coriolanus.

FIRST WATCHMAN   From whence?   5

MENENIUS
>   From Rome.

FIRST WATCHMAN You may not pass, you must return.
> Our general will no more hear from thence.

SECOND WATCHMAN
> You'll see your Rome embraced with fire before
> You'll speak with Coriolanus.

MENENIUS   Good my friends,
> If you have heard your general talk of Rome   10
> And of his friends there, it is lots to blanks
> My name hath touched your ears. It is Menenius.

FIRST WATCHMAN
> Be it so; go back. The virtue of your name
> Is not here passable.

MENENIUS   I tell thee, fellow,
> Thy general is my lover. I have been   15
> The book of his good acts, whence men have read
> His fame unparalleled, haply amplified;
> For I have ever varnishèd my friends,

---

17 haply] HANMER; happely F1; happily F3   18 varnishèd] WILSON (*conj.* Edwards); verified F; magnified HANMER; notified SINGER; rarefied STAUNTON *conj.*; amplified HUDSON (*conj.* Lettsom); vivified BULLOCH *conj.* (*in* Cambridge)

sentries; though possibly 'or' is a mis-reading of 'on' (Brower).

11 **lots to blanks** 'a certainty'; perhaps 'a thousand to one' (*OED*, *lot*, *sb.* 5), according to whether 'lots' is understood as the winning tickets in a lottery (as opposed to 'blanks', which are the losing tickets) or as all the tickets in a lottery.

12–13 **touched . . . virtue** King suggests that First Watchman is punning on the healing 'virtue' of the royal 'touch', as in *Macbeth* 4.3.144, though this would not suit a Roman context.

14 **passable** A quibble on (a) current, valid, and (b) 'able to pass', cf. *Cymbeline* 1.2.8.

14–23 **I tell . . . leasing** Menenius' astonish-ing self-betrayal discredits him in drama-tic preparation for Martius' rejection of him, and also exposes blatantly the patricians' tactic of elevating Coriolanus for their own advantage.

15 **lover** dear friend; cf. ll. 87, 91

16 **book** recorder; cf. *Lucrece* 615–16

18–28 **For . . . back** Productions which present Menenius sympathetically have tended to cut this naive boast of lying on Coriolanus' behalf, and also the threat to have the guard tortured to death (ll. 64–5): see Introduction, p. 124.

18–20 **For . . . suffer** i.e. 'I have always praised my friends, of whom he's the chief one, with all the embellishment that truth would allow'

18 **varnishèd** F's reading, 'verified', is

Of whom he's chief, with all the size that verity
Would without lapsing suffer. Nay, sometimes,   20
Like to a bowl upon a subtle ground,
I have tumbled past the throw, and in his praise
Have almost stamped the leasing. Therefore, fellow,
I must have leave to pass.

FIRST WATCHMAN Faith, sir, if you had told as many lies   25
in his behalf as you have uttered words in your own,
you should not pass here, no, though it were as virtuous to lie as to live chastely. Therefore go back.

MENENIUS Prithee, fellow, remember my name is Menen-
ius, always factionary on the party of your general.   30

SECOND WATCHMAN Howsoever you have been his liar,
as you say you have, I am one that, telling true under
him, must say you cannot pass. Therefore go back.

MENENIUS Has he dined, canst thou tell? For I would not
speak with him till after dinner.   35

FIRST WATCHMAN You are a Roman, are you?

MENENIUS I am as thy general is.

FIRST WATCHMAN Then you should hate Rome as he
does. Can you, when you have pushed out your gates
the very defender of them, and in a violent popular   40

---

23 almost] F ((almost))   37 am‸] F1; ~, F4

glossed by *OED* (*verify*, 1c) as 'to support or back up by testimony' but only
the present instance is cited as example.
The emendation Wilson adopts from
Edwards is close to *Hamlet* 4.7.105–6:
'And set a double varnish on the fame
| The Frenchman gave you'; and is
plausible orthographically since manuscript 'vernished' could easily be misread under the influence of 'amplified'
at the end of the preceding line and
'verity' at the end of the following line.

19 **size** punning on (a) stature, (b) a substance used to stiffen and fix colours in
cloth, or the sticky wash used by artists
as a base for paint; cf. *Hamlet* 2.2.465

20 **lapsing** slipping into exaggeration

21–2 **Like ... throw** Metaphors from
bowling, which Caroline Spurgeon
(*Shakespeare's Imagery*, 1935, p. 110)
identifies as Shakespeare's favourite

game; cf. 3.1.62–3.

21 **subtle** tricky, deceiving

22 **tumbled ... throw** overshot the mark,
gone beyond what was intended
('throw' is the distance to be thrown)

23 **stamped the leasing** 'given currency
to falsehood' (Anglo-Saxon *leasung*, cf.
Twelfth Night 1.5.93): a legal metaphor ('set the seal on'), or possibly one
from coining

30 **factionary ... of** active in support of,
a partisan for

31 **Howsoever** notwithstanding
liar Spelled 'lier' in F

34–5 **dined ... after dinner** Cf. 5.1.50 n.

36 **You ... you?** (a) Menenius' reply suggests that First Watchman asks this
sceptically, since Menenius' epicurean-
ism is so unlike Coriolanus; (b) alternatively, it may reflect the Watchman's
belief that Rome is totally decadent, as
the following lines suggest.

ignorance given your enemy your shield, think to
front his revenges with the easy groans of old women,
the virginal palms of your daughters, or with the palsied intercession of such a decayed dotant as you seem
to be? Can you think to blow out the intended fire your   45
city is ready to flame in with such weak breath as this?
No, you are deceived; therefore back to Rome, and prepare for your execution. You are condemned, our
general has sworn you out of reprieve and pardon.

MENENIUS Sirrah, if thy captain knew I were here, he   50
would use me with estimation.

FIRST WATCHMAN Come, my captain knows you not.

MENENIUS I mean thy general.

FIRST WATCHMAN My general cares not for you. Back, I
say, go, lest I let forth your half-pint of blood. Back!   55
That's the utmost of your having. Back!

MENENIUS Nay, but fellow, fellow—

Enter Coriolanus with Aufidius

CORIOLANUS What's the matter?

MENENIUS (*to First Watchman*) Now, you companion, I'll
say an errand for you. You shall know now that I am   60
in estimation. You shall perceive that a jack guardant
cannot office me from my son Coriolanus. Guess but by

---

44 dotant] F1; dotard F4   57 fellow—] THEOBALD; ~. F   60 errand] F (arrant), POPE
62–5 Coriolanus.... him, ... suffering.] HANMER (*subs.*); ~, ...~: ...~, F   62 but
by] MALONE; but F; by HANMER

---

42 **front** confront, oppose
43 **virginal...daughters** i.e. 'the sup-
   plicating hands (palms up) of your
   virginal daughters'
   palsied Brockbank notes that this
   metaphor is used by North for the
   paralysis of the whole city, 'as those
   which through the palsy have lost all
   their sense and feeling'
44 **dotant** An alternative spelling (and
   possible error) for 'dotard', for which
   OED cites only this passage.
51 **estimation** respect
54–6 **Back...Back!...Back!** A cue for
   Menenius to make three sallies: cf. Introduction, p. 107. This is comic but
   also emphasizes his determination and
   thus the pathos of his defeat.
56 **That's...having** (a) all you'll get

(referring to 'estimation', ll. 51, 61),
(b) as far as you can go, (c) possibly
emphasizing 'your half pint of blood'
(Warburton)
57.1 **Enter Coriolanus** Many productions
   indicate Coriolanus' change of sides by
   having him appear in Volscian uniform, though cf. 5.1.63 n. and Introduction, p. 98.
59 **companion** 'fellow', used contemptuously, cf. 4.5.13
60 **say...you** 'deliver a report for you',
   i.e. circumvent your version of what
   has happened
61 **jack guardant** knavish watchman.
   Brockbank notes that 'guardant' is an
   heraldic phrase.
62 **office** 'use his petty authority' (with
   'to gainsay' understood), cf. Hamlet's

my entertainment with him if thou stand'st not i'th'
state of hanging, or of some death more long in specta-
torship and crueller in suffering. Behold now presently,   65
and swoon for what's to come upon thee.

(To Coriolanus) The glorious gods sit in hourly synod
about thy particular prosperity, and love thee no
worse than thy old father Menenius does! O, my son,
my son, thou art preparing fire for us. Look thee,   70
here's water to quench it. I was hardly moved to come
to thee, but being assured none but myself could move
thee, I have been blown out of our gates with sighs,
and conjure thee to pardon Rome and thy petitionary
countrymen. The good gods assuage thy wrath and   75
turn the dregs of it upon this varlet here, this, who like
a block hath denied my access to thee!

CORIOLANUS Away!

MENENIUS How? Away?

CORIOLANUS

Wife, mother, child, I know not. My affairs   80

66, 99 swoon] F (swoond)   73 our] F4; your F1 ; yon KEIGHTLEY *conj.*

'insolence of office' (3.1.75); 'jack in
office' was a common phrase for petty
officialdom.

62-3 **Guess . . . if** Malone's emendation is
preferable to F: it makes better sense
for Menenius to ask the guards to
judge from his reception how they will
be punished than for them merely to
guess what that reception will be; and
it is more probable that 'by' was
omitted (because of the proximity of
'my') than that it was confounded
with 'but'.

65 **presently** immediately

67 ff. **The glorious gods . . .** Gurr notes
how artificially 'ornate and studied'
Menenius' plea is, and Gomme that its
prose 'is strongly rhythmical and contains a number of phrases which could
be scanned as verse'; however, it is
significant that Menenius does not at-
tain the dignity of verse, though Coriolanus answers him in it.

67 **sit** i.e. may they sit

71 **here's water** Oxford adds the direction

'*Weeping*', but Menenius is merely
using tears rhetorically as a contrast
to 'fire' at this stage. It makes a sharp
contrast to give him real tears after his
rejection which he does not even mention (though Coriolanus recognizes his
'cracked heart', 5.3.9).

hardly moved with difficulty persuaded

73 **our** F's 'your' has been defended on
the ground that Menenius still wishes
to regard Coriolanus as a Roman; but
'your' suggests that the gates are not
Menenius's too, and uses a second
person plural whereas the rest of the
speech uses second person singular;
'our' expresses more accurately
Menenius' emphasis on their common
bond.

74 **petitionary** suppliant; another Menenius coinage

77 **block** (a) blockage, (b) blockhead

80 **Wife . . . not** Menenius has only mentioned his own relation to Coriolanus,
but this reply shows where the latter's
thoughts are and what he dreads;
cf. 5.3.20-1.

Are servanted to others. Though I owe
My revenge properly, my remission lies
In Volscian breasts. That we have been familiar,
Ingrate forgetfulness shall poison rather
Than pity note how much. Therefore be gone.   85
Mine ears against your suits are stronger than
Your gates against my force. Yet, for I loved thee,
    He gives him a letter
Take this along. I writ it for thy sake,
And would have sent it. Another word, Menenius,
I will not hear thee speak.—This man, Aufidius,   90
Was my beloved in Rome; yet thou behold'st.
AUFIDIUS You keep a constant temper.
                 Exeunt Coriolanus and Aufidius
    The Guard and Menenius remain
FIRST WATCHMAN Now, sir, is your name Menenius?
SECOND WATCHMAN 'Tis a spell, you see, of much power.
  You know the way home again.   95
FIRST WATCHMAN Do you hear how we are shent for
  keeping your greatness back?
SECOND WATCHMAN What cause do you think I have to
  swoon?
MENENIUS I neither care for th' world nor your general.   100
  For such things as you, I can scarce think there's any,

---

85 pity᛬ note . . . much.] THEOBALD (*conj.* Thirlby); ~: Note . . . ~, F   87.1 *He . . . letter*]
POPE (*after* sent it); *not in* F   92.1 *Coriolanus and Au*fidius] CAPELL; *not in* F

81 **servanted to** subordinated to the service of (the Volscians)

81–2 **I owe . . . properly** my revenge belongs to me personally (cf. 3.2.132)

82 **remission** power to pardon or release from. The grammar also allows an ironic, unintentional counter-meaning, however: 'power to *be* pardoned or released from'.

83–5 **That . . . much** 'Our friendship shall be poisoned by your ungrateful forgetfulness rather than pity shall remind me of how great that friendship used to be.'

84 **poison** F's reading makes sense, but Theobald's emendation, 'prison', agrees better with Cominius' phrasing at 5.1.65.

87 **for** because

87, 88, 90 **thee . . . thy . . . thee** As Martius tries to soften his rejection, he switches into the second person singular.

90–1 **This . . . behold'st** Coriolanus reveals his sense of acting a part before the Volscian audience (and Aufidius' reply is sardonically ambiguous).

96 **shent** rebuked, chided

99 **swoon** Though actually it was First Watchman who was thus threatened? Brockbank suggests that F's 'swound' here and at l. 66 is more properly a dialect form than an archaic spelling: this might agree with Menenius' other familiar and eccentric usages; cf. 2.1.102 n.

you're so slight. He that hath a will to die by himself
fears it not from another. Let your general do his
worst. For you, be that you are long, and your misery
increase with your age. I say to you as I was said to,   105
'Away!'   *Exit*

FIRST WATCHMAN A noble fellow, I warrant him.

SECOND WATCHMAN The worthy fellow is our general.
He's the rock, the oak, not to be wind-shaken. *Exeunt*

5.3 *Enter Coriolanus and Aufidius with Volscian soldiers.*
⌈*Coriolanus sits in a chair of state*⌉

CORIOLANUS
We will before the walls of Rome tomorrow
Set down our host. My partner in this action,
You must report to th' Volscian lords how plainly
I have borne this business.

AUFIDIUS   Only their ends

109.1 *Exeunt*] F (*Exit Watch.*)
   5.3.0.1–2 *with Volscian soldiers*] OXFORD; *not in* F; *with Others.* CAPELL   0.2 *Coriolanus sits in a chair of state*] WILSON (subs.); *not in* F; *Coriolanus and Aufidius sit* OXFORD

102 **slight** insignificant
104 **long** for a long time
105–6 **I ... 'Away!'** Menenius is often
   played as heart-broken, but there is as
   much acerbity as sorrow in his reaction here, which parallels Martius' 'I
   banish you' of 3.3.124. This acerbity
   becomes blatant in 5.4, where his
   credibility is undercut both by his
   malicious exaggerations of an encounter whose more human reality we
   have witnessed and by his certainty that
   Volumnia must fail like himself when
   we already know she has succeeded.
108–9 **The ... wind-shaken** 'a   most
   powerful piece of unconscious irony'
   (Hibbard)
5.3.0.1–2 **Enter ... state** This scene is
   the climax of the play. For its probable
   setting, see North: 'Now was Martius
   set then in his chair of state, with all
   the honours of a general, and when
   he had spied the women coming afar
   off, he marvelled what the matter
   meant: but afterwards knowing his
   wife which came foremost, he determined at the first to persist in his

obstinate   and   inflexible   rancour'
(Spencer, p. 352). Since Aufidius is
co-commander, some editors and directors give him a chair of state also,
but there is no mention of this in the
play (or in Plutarch: see the next
note), and to have only one chair emphasizes the pre-emption of command
that Aufidius had complained of in 4.7
and will repeat in 5.6.37–40. Ripley
suggests that the entrance may well
have been blocked to provide an inversion of Martius' triumph in 2.1: see
Introduction, p. 115.
2 **My ... action** In Plutarch only Coriolanus was with the invading army;
   Aufidius 'thought it best for [Corio-
   lanus] to have the leading of those that
   should make the wars abroad: and
   himself would keep home, to provide
   for the safety of the cities and of his
   country, and to furnish the camp also
   of all necessary provision abroad'
   (Spencer, p. 344).
3 **plainly** straightforwardly, openly
4 **Only their ends** i.e. the purposes of the
   Volscian lords exclusively

You have respected, stopped your ears against   5
The general suit of Rome, never admitted
A private whisper, no, not with such friends
That thought them sure of you.

CORIOLANUS   This last old man,
Whom with a cracked heart I have sent to Rome,
Loved me above the measure of a father,   10
Nay, godded me indeed. Their latest refuge
Was to send him, for whose old love I have—
Though I showed sourly to him—once more offered
The first conditions, which they did refuse
And cannot now accept, to grace him only   15
That thought he could do more. A very little
I have yielded to. Fresh embassies and suits,
Nor from the state nor private friends, hereafter
Will I lend ear to.

           Shout within

                    Ha, what shout is this?
Shall I be tempted to infringe my vow   20
In the same time 'tis made? I will not.

15–16 accept, . . . more.] F (*subs.*); ~; . . . more, SINGER 1856 (*conj.* Heath); ~, . . . ~,
JOHNSON   17 to] F (too)   19 *Shout within*] CAMBRIDGE; *after* this? F   21.2 *attendants*]
F; *attendants, all in mourning.* THEOBALD

6–7 **general . . . private** i.e. both official and personal appeals

8–19 **This . . . to** Gurr remarks that the wordiness of Coriolanus' explanation betrays discomfort.

9 **with . . . heart** This refers to Menenius, but its syntactical ambiguity also allows it to convey a sense of Martius' own sadness; Granville-Barker (p. 261) assumed it referred to Martius himself.

11 **godded** made a god of, idolized
   latest refuge last resort (though cf. 5.2.80 n. and 5.3.22–33)

14 **first conditions** See 4.7.19 n.

15–16 **accept . . . more.** 'The sense varies according to interpretation of F's colon after *more*. If this is treated as a full stop, Coriolanus appears to have conceded to Menenius only a renewal of the terms first offered to Cominius; if it is treated as a comma, he appears to have made some extra concession.

There is no evidence elsewhere in the play of an extra concession, and . . . it is often necessary to treat the colon as a full stop' (Brockbank). The 'grace' to Menenius would be the extension of the time limit of the original offer, consequent on its renewal.

16–17 **A . . . to.** I did not yield much!

19 **Shout within** Poole (p. 100) remarks on the fact that this deputation has no trouble passing the guards who stopped Menenius (despite Martius' comment at ll. 18–19), so their appearance has a quality of inexorable fatality, mirroring Martius' own dread.

20–1 **Shall . . . not** These lines may belong to the self-communing semi-soliloquy that begins with l. 22, but they can also be seen as an extension of 17–19.

21.1–2 **Enter . . . attendants** The shabby appearance of the suppliants which is

Enter Virgilia, Volumnia, Valeria, Young Martius,
    with attendants
My wife comes foremost; then the honoured mould
Wherein this trunk was framed, and in her hand
The grandchild to her blood. But out, affection!
All bond and privilege of nature break;   25
Let it be virtuous to be obstinate.
    ⌈*Virgilia curtsies*⌉
What is that curtsy worth? Or those doves' eyes
Which can make gods forsworn? I melt, and am not
Of stronger earth than others.
    Volumnia bows
                        My mother bows,
As if Olympus to a molehill should   30
In supplication nod; and my young boy
Hath an aspect of intercession which
Great nature cries 'Deny not'. Let the Volsces
Plough Rome and harrow Italy! I'll never
Be such a gosling to obey instinct, but stand   35
As if a man were author of himself

---

24 out,] THEOBALD; ~_∧ F1; our_∧ F3   25 nature_∧] F; ~, CAPELL   26.1 *Virgilia curt-sies*] OXFORD; *not in* F   27 doves'] STEEVENS–REED 1793; doves F; dove's ROWE
29 *Volumnia bows*] OXFORD; *not in* F

---

referred to at ll. 39, 95–7 parallels Martius' own 'mean apparel' in 4.4: see Introduction, p. 97.

22–33 **My . . . not** These intimate descriptions are almost certainly a semi-soliloquy: see Introduction, p. 71.

22 **My . . . foremost** This agrees with Plutarch, but Shakespeare exploits it for much greater effect: see Introduction, p. 23. In North, it is Coriolanus who takes the initiative and his mother whom he greets and kisses first.
mould matrix. Cf. *Winter's Tale* 2.3.103, and Nashe (ed. McKerrow, ii. 74) where a mother tells her child she is 'The Mould wherein thou wert cast' (Wilson).

24 **out** begone
affection (a) love, (b) emotion (the opposite of reason)

25 **bond . . . nature** the natural ties of duty and affection; cf. *Lear* 2.2.351

26 **obstinate** obdurate, inflexible (cf. North, 'obstinate and inflexible rancour')

27 **doves' eyes** i.e. his wife's: a reminiscence of the Song of Solomon, 1: 15, 4: 1, 5: 12. Doves were also emblems of peace, of course: cf. 5.6.115.

30 **Olympus** The mountain which was the home of the gods in Greek mythology.

32 **aspect of intercession** pleading look ('aspect' is accented on the second syllable)

35 **gosling** Cf. Volumnia's 'poor hen' image, ll. 163–4, and Martius' earlier reference to the plebeians' 'souls of geese', 1.5.5.
stand stand firm, resist; cf. l. 74. This may indicate that Martius has not yet seated himself but is literally standing (cf. 0.1–2 n.).

36 **author of himself** self-begotten, like a god (*OED, author*, 2a); the phrase derives from Plutarch's '*Life of Theseus*'. The impossibility of this is admitted,

And knew no other kin.

VIRGILIA   My lord and husband.

CORIOLANUS

~~These eyes are not the same I wore in Rome.~~

VIRGILIA

The sorrow that delivers us thus changed

Makes you think so.

CORIOLANUS   Like a dull actor now   40

I have forgot my part, and I am out

Even to a full disgrace. ⌜*Rising*⌝ Best of my flesh,

Forgive my tyranny, but do not say

For that 'Forgive our Romans'.

 ⌜*Virgilia kisses him*⌝

         O, a kiss

Long as my exile, sweet as my revenge!   45

Now, by the jealous queen of heaven, that kiss

I carried from thee, dear, and my true lip

Hath virgined it e'er since. You gods, I prate,

---

42 *Rising*] OXFORD; *not in* F; *before* Like a dull actor WILSON 44 *Virgilia kisses him*] OXFORD; *not in* F 48 prate] POPE 1728; pray F

---

however, by Martius' conditional 'As if' phrasing, so different from Richard of Gloucester's assertive 'I am myself alone' (*3 Henry VI* 5.6.84).

38 **These ... Rome** Cf. 2.1.174 for another use of 'wear' with eyes.

39 **delivers** presents; i.e. they seem different to him, not because his feelings are changed, but because their appearance has been altered by grief

40–2 **Like ... disgrace** Cf. Sonnet 23.1–2, 'As an unperfect actor on the stage | Who with his fear is put besides his part': see Introduction, pp. 55, 85. There is no need to assume that the comment is an aside (Wilson), but presumably there should be a pause before it.

41 **out** A theatre term for forgetting one's lines; cf. *L.L.L.* 5.2.151, 164, 172.

42 **Best ... flesh** Cf. Matthew 14: 5 on marriage: 'they twain shall be one flesh'.

43 **tyranny** cruelty; cf. *Lear* 3.4.2, *Merchant* 4.1.12

44 **For that** i.e. in return for his asking

her to forgive him (cf. Matthew 5: 12)
Virgilia ... him Wilson's '*goes to her*' (l. 42 after 'disgrace') makes Martius the initiator of this embrace, as in Plutarch (see 22 n.); but the way Shakespeare has changed his source to show Coriolanus paying more attention to Virgilia than to Volumnia and the note of surprise in his 'O, a kiss ...', make it more appropriate for Virgilia to take the initiative. Late 18th- and 19th-century productions all offset Coriolanus' harshness by emphasizing his domestic affection in this scene.

45 **Long ... revenge!** A reversal of the martial–marital comparisons of 1.7.29–31, 4.5.114–19

46 **jealous ... heaven** Jove's consort, Juno, who was the guardian and patroness of marriage. Volumnia's earlier self-comparison to Juno may add an extra nuance here to 'jealous'.

48 **virgined it** remained chaste (another of the play's many coinages)
prate Though Hibbard defends F's 'pray', his explanation involves an

And the most noble mother of the world
Leave unsaluted! Sink, my knee, i'th' earth;   50
> *He kneels*

Of thy deep duty more impression show
Than that of common sons.

VOLUMNIA   O, stand up blest,
Whilst with no softer cushion than the flint
I kneel before thee, and unproperly
Show duty as mistaken all this while   55
Between the child and parent.
> ⌈ *She kneels* ⌉

CORIOLANUS   What's this?
Your knees to me? To your corrected son?
> ⌈ *He rises* ⌉

Then let the pebbles on the hungry beach
Fillip the stars; then let the mutinous winds
Strike the proud cedars 'gainst the fiery sun,   60
Murd'ring impossibility to make

50.1 *He kneels*] F (*Kneeles*)   56 *She kneels*] ROWE; *not in* F; *preventing her* CAPELL
57.1 *He rises*] This edition; *not in* F; *Coriolanus rises* OXFORD *at 52.1*

awkward sentence inversion and the
unlikelihood that Coriolanus interprets
what he has just said as a prayer. It
is more likely that F's compositor was
misled by its juxtaposition to 'gods'.
Cf. 5.3.60 n.

50.1 **He kneels** Cf. 2.1.167 n. Plutarch
mentions the whole family kneeling
after the completion of Volumnia's
long plea (cf. 173 and Spencer, p.
357), but this initial exchange of
kneeling between Coriolanus and Volumnia is Shakespeare's addition, and
carries the same complex implications
as the kneeling in *King Lear*: see Introduction, pp. 103–5.

51 **thy** i.e. 'my knee', used vocatively
in l. 50
deep . . . impression 'profound . . .
mark', playing on both the literal and
figurative sense

52 **blest** fortunate. Volumnia means
sarcastically that he is 'lucky', not that
she has given him her parental blessing.

54 **unproperly** unfittingly, against propriety

55 **mistaken** having been mistaken

56 **Between . . . parent** i.e. as owed by the
child to the parent (not vice versa)

57 **corrected** chastised (by her sarcasm)

57.1 **He rises** See Introduction, p. 105.

58 **hungry** By transferring an adjective generally used about the sea
(cf. *Pericles*, scene 12.55–7, *Tempest*
3.3.55) to 'the beach', Coriolanus conveys a sense of disorder that combines
sterility (*OED*, *hungry*, 6) with threat.

59 **Fillip** Knock against (often used contemptuously). 'The point of Coriolanus' hyperbole is that it is the normal
fate of pebbles to be dragged into the
hungry sea and not lifted to the stars'
(Brockbank). Poole (pp. 103–4) remarks that Martius' 'almost hysterical
rhetoric of apocalypse' here is 'close to
the idiom of Lear in the storm, of
Macbeth in the night; here the storm
and the night are all inside Martius,
in his imagination'.

61 **Murd'ring impossibility** destroying the
law by which some things are impossible

What cannot be slight work.
⌜ *He raises her* ⌝

VOLUMNIA   Thou art my warrior,
~~I holp to frame thee. Do you know this lady?~~

CORIOLANUS

The noble sister of Publicola,
The moon of Rome, chaste as the icicle   65
That's candied by the frost from purest snow
And hangs on Dian's temple—dear Valeria!

VOLUMNIA (*showing Young Martius*)

This is a poor epitome of yours
Which by th'interpretation of full time
May show like all yourself.

CORIOLANUS (*to Young Martius*) The god of soldiers,   70

---

62 *He raises her*] This edition; *not in* F; *at* 57.1 OXFORD   63 holp] POPE; hope F
66 candied] OXFORD (*conj*. Daniel); curdied F; curdled ROWE 1714; curded STEEVENS–
REED 1793   68 *showing Young Martius*] POPE; *not in* F   70 *to Young Martius*] OXFORD;
not in F   soldiers,] F3; ~: F1

62 **slight work** an easy task
   He raises her See Introduction, p. 105.
63 **holp** F's spelling 'hope' probably indicates the contemporary pronunciation
64 **Publicola** One of the first Roman
   consuls, *circa* 509 BC, commemorated
   by one of Plutarch's *Lives*.
65–7 **The moon . . . temple** This outburst
   is surprising and, combined with Coriolanus' final 'dear Valeria', led Glynne
   Wickham (*Later Shakespeare*, ed. J. R.
   Brown and B. Harris, 1966, p. 75) to
   suggest that Valeria be interpreted as
   a woman who attracted Coriolanus before Volumnia arranged his marriage
   to Virgilia. There is no evidence for
   this, though it would certainly provide
   an interesting 'subtext' for 1.3 and
   could motivate Valeria's inclusion at
   this point. She is no longer the organ-
   izer of the embassy, as she was in
   Plutarch; and the latter's comment that
   she 'did so modestly and wisely behave
   her self, that she did not shame nor
   dishonour the house she came of' hardly
   explains Coriolanus' sudden lyricism:
   see Introduction, p. 23. Shakespeare
   may have thought of her as a vestal
   virgin (see 1.3.48.1 n.), but Wilson
   Knight's explanation for her dramatic
   function at this point remains the most
   plausible: 'Love is victorious here:

womanhood in its three forms—
mother, wife, maiden—saves Rome'
(*The Imperial Theme*, 1931, p. 18).

65 **moon** Cf. 1.1.255 n. for the connection of chastity with the moon.
66 **candied** Cf. *Timon* 4.3.227, 'Candied with
   ice'. F's anomalous 'curdied' would be
   an easy misreading of this, and Oxford
   notes that neither 'curded' nor 'curdled'
   can properly be applied to an icicle.
66–7 **snow . . . temple** A frequent Shakespeare image; cf. *Othello* 5.2.4–5, *Cymbeline* 2.5.13, *Tempest* 4.1.55, and
   especially *Timon* 4.3.388–9, 'Whose
   blush doth thaw the consecrated snow
   | That lies on Dian's lap'. Diana was
   moon goddess of chastity.
68–70 **a poor . . . yourself** i.e. 'an abridge-
   ment of yourself that time, like an
   orator expounding from notes, may
   develop into a full copy'; cf. to Aufidius' pessimistic sense of 'th'interpretation of the time' at 4.7.50. See
   Introduction, p. 53.
70–5 **The god . . . thee** Considering Martius' own transgressions, this prayer is
   highly ironic; it is obviously how
   Martius still wishes to see himself,
   though covert self-criticism creeps in
   with 'shame'.
70 **god of soldiers** Another reference to
   Mars; cf. 4.5.119, 5.6.102–3.

336

With the consent of supreme Jove, inform
Thy thoughts with nobleness, that thou mayst prove
To shame unvulnerable, and stick i'th' wars
Like a great sea-mark, standing every flaw
And saving those that eye thee!   75

VOLUMNIA Your knee, sirrah.

⌈*Young Martius kneels*⌉

CORIOLANUS That's my brave boy.

VOLUMNIA

Even he, your wife, this lady, and myself
Are suitors to you.

CORIOLANUS   I beseech you, peace!
Or if you'd ask, remember this before: 80
The things I have forsworn to grant may never
Be held by you denials. Do not bid me
Dismiss my soldiers, or capitulate

---

73 stick] F1; strike F2   76.1 *Young Martius kneels*] OXFORD; *not in* F   81–2 things . . .
you denials] CAPELL; thing . . . you denials F1; thing . . . your denials F3; thing . . . you
denial F4

---

71 **inform** imbue, instil

73 **To . . . unvulnerable** both 'incapable of dishonour' and 'incapable of being dishonoured'
stick 'stand firm' and also 'stand out'

74 **sea-mark** a beacon or other stable and conspicuous object by which sailors take their bearings and navigate; cf. *Othello* 5.2.275, and Sonnet 116.5–6, 'an ever fixèd mark | That looks on tempests and is never shaken'. Kemball-Cook remarks that 'by the use of monosyllables, Shakespeare brings several stresses together in the middle of the line, suiting rhythm to sense'.
standing withstanding
flaw (a) a sudden blast of wind, (b) moral weakness?

75 **those . . . thee** i.e. those who look to you for guidance

76.1 **Young Martius kneels** Phelps's prompt-book directs, 'Young Martius about to kneel Coriolanus catches him up. Kisses him', and after 'That's my brave boy' hands him safely to Virgilia. In 1984 NT, on the other hand, Coriolanus stood Young Martius on his shoulders and the child extended his arm in the clenched-fist salute that

Coriolanus had himself used in 1.7; Ian McKellen thought this moment was crucial in Coriolanus' weakening purpose: 'I think it is the sight of his son, the sight of that child, that ultimately sways him' (interview with Kristina Bedford, 21 Aug. 1985; p. 144). 1979 Yerevan gave the episode yet another shading: Coriolanus tried a mock boxing match with his son, to which the boy refused to respond.

81 **things** Though F's singular can be justified, a plural form agreeing with 'denials' makes the meaning much clearer.
forsworn to already sworn not to

82 **Be . . . denials** be taken by you as a refusal to deny *your* requests (a pathetic bit of casuistry on Coriolanus' part)

83 **Dismiss my soldiers** This was one of the demands made by the earlier Roman embassies in Plutarch as a condition for negotiation.
capitulate (a) 'arrange or propose terms, to treat, bargain, parley' (*OED* 2); cf. *1 Henry IV* 3.2.120; (b) surrender (*OED* 4)?

Again with Rome's mechanics. Tell me not
Wherein I seem unnatural. Desire not   85
T'allay my rages and revenges with
Your colder reasons.

VOLUMNIA   O, no more, no more!
You have said you will not grant us anything—
For we have nothing else to ask but that
Which you deny already. Yet we will ask,   90
That, if you fail in our request, the blame
May hang upon your hardness. Therefore hear us.

CORIOLANUS
Aufidius and you Volsces, mark, for we'll
Hear naught from Rome in private.
    ⌈*Sitting*⌉ Your request?

VOLUMNIA
Should we be silent and not speak, our raiment   95
And state of bodies would bewray what life
We have led since thy exile. Think with thyself
How more unfortunate than all living women
Are we come hither, since that thy sight, which should
Make our eyes flow with joy, hearts dance with comforts,   100
Constrains them weep and shake with fear and sorrow,
Making the mother, wife, and child to see
The son, the husband, and the father tearing
His country's bowels out; and to poor we
Thine enmity's most capital. Thou barr'st us   105

---

91 you] F; we ROWE 1714   94 *Sitting*] WILSON; *not in* F

---

84 **mechanics** vulgar workmen (*OED* 26)
86 **allay** abate
91 **fail in** fail to grant
93–4 **Aufidius ... private** This comment emphasizes Coriolanus' awareness of performing before a Volscian audience.
95–7 **our raiment ... exile** This has been interpreted as (a) reflecting their sorrow in dishevelled mourning clothes and haggard faces, or (b) reflecting their actual want, now that Coriolanus' protection has been withdrawn, by rags and emaciation: Plutarch's phrase is 'the wretchedness of our

garbs and aspect'.
96 **bewray** reveal, expose
97 **exile** Accented on the second syllable. **Think with thyself** reflect
103–4 **tearing ... out** This body-politic metaphor is Shakespeare's addition, cf. ll. 124–6.
104 **to poor we** Though this solecism is sometimes excused on the grounds of Volumnia's stress, in fact 'we' is used for 'us' by Shakespeare elsewhere; cf. *Hamlet* 1.4.35, *Caesar* 3.1.95 (Clarendon).
105 **capital** fatal, deadly

Our prayers to the gods, which is a comfort
That all but we enjoy. For how can we,
Alas, how can we for our country pray,
Whereto we are bound, together with thy victory,
Whereto we are bound? Alack, or we must lose   110
The country, our dear nurse, or else thy person,
Our comfort in the country. We must find
An evident calamity, though we had
Our wish which side should win. For either thou
Must as a foreign recreant be led   115
With manacles thorough our streets, or else
Triumphantly tread on thy country's ruin,
And bear the palm for having bravely shed
Thy wife and children's blood. For myself, son,
I purpose not to wait on fortune till   120
These wars determine. If I cannot persuade thee
Rather to show a noble grace to both parts
Than seek the end of one, thou shalt no sooner
March to assault thy country than to tread—
Trust to't, thou shalt not—on thy mother's womb   125
That brought thee to this world.
VIRGILIA   Ay, and mine,

---

107 we,] ROWE 1714; ~? F   108–10 pray, ... bound?] F4; ~? ... ~, FI   116 thor-ough] JOHNSON; through F

109 **Whereto ... victory** The metre here requires the slurring of 'we'are' and 'vict'ry'. The repetition of 'Whereto we are bound' is not an error but is an example of epizeuxis to convey emotion, like the repetition of 'how can we'.

110–11 **or ... or** either ... or

111 **dear nurse** Volumnia is equating Rome with herself as 'mother country'; cf. ll. 123–6, 5.6.99, 3.2.131

113 **evident** certain

115 **foreign recreant** treacherous deserter to a foreign power

118 **bear the palm** (a) be crowned victor, (b) be the most outstanding example?

120–6 **I purpose ... world** In 19th-century productions influenced by Thomson and Sheridan, this threat of suicide was actualized by having Volumnia flourish a dagger, of which Coriolanus

had to disarm her when he took her hand at 183, thus changing the meaning of that crucial gesture. One of Macready's improvements was to jettison this melodramatic piece of business.

120 **purpose** intend

121 **determine** (a) come to an end, (b) make my decision for me?

122 **grace** mercy

124 **to tread** For the use of 'to' for connecting purposes, see Abbott §350 and 416.

125 **Trust ... not** i.e. be sure you shall not march without treading

126–9 **Ay ... fight** This challenging of Martius by Virgilia and his son, added by Shakespeare, is particularly interesting as further proof that Virgilia is no mere weakling.

That brought you forth this boy to keep your name
Living to time.

YOUNG MARTIUS   A shall not tread on me.
I'll run away till I am bigger, but then I'll fight.

CORIOLANUS

Not of a woman's tenderness to be   130
Requires nor child nor woman's face to see.
I have sat too long.
     ⌈*He rises*⌉

VOLUMNIA   Nay, go not from us thus.
If it were so that our request did tend
To save the Romans, thereby to destroy
The Volsces whom you serve, you might condemn us   135
As poisonous of your honour. No, our suit
Is that you reconcile them: while the Volsces
May say 'This mercy we have showed', the Romans
'This we received', and each in either side
Give the all-hail to thee and cry 'Be blest   140
For making up this peace!'—Thou know'st, great son,
The end of war's uncertain; but this certain,
That if thou conquer Rome, the benefit
Which thou shalt thereby reap is such a name

---

128 YOUNG MARTIUS] OXFORD; *Boy.* F   132 *He rises*] CAPELL (*subs.*); *not in* F
142 war's] F (Warres)

130–1 **Not . . . see** i.e. 'if I am not to be
effeminately tender, I must avoid the
sight of children and women'. Wilson
notes that this is probably, though not
necessarily, an aside; and the couplet
rhyme gives it a mechanically gnomic
impression.

132 **Nay . . . thus** This reaction to Coriolanus' move to leave is not in Plutarch;
it serves the dramatic purpose of narrowing attention from the previous
group plea to the more personal plea
into which Volumnia now launches,
and is also a gestural cue for the actor
playing Coriolanus.

136–41 **No, . . . peace!'** This new suggestion (which later he will try to implement) elicited the first move of interest
from Coriolanus in 1980 Ashland; in
the 1963 Nottingham prompt-book it

is Aufidius who 'turns sharply', then
moves closer behind Coriolanus' chair
to watch his rival's reaction; and in
1984 NT Irene Worth's Volumnia actually bowed to Aufidius while making
the suggestion, exchanging a calculating glance with him.

137 **while** so that at the same time

140 **all-hail** general acclamation (by the
Romans and the Volscians alike);
cf. *Macbeth* 1.5.54

142 **The end . . . uncertain** A commonplace that can be found in such Elizabethan schoolbooks as the *Sententiae
Pueriles* (in T. W. Baldwin, *Shakespeare's Small Latine & Lesse Greeke*,
1942, i. 234).
   but this only this is

144–5 **such . . . Whose** i.e. such . . . that
its; cf. Abbott § 278

Whose repetition will be dogged with curses,   145
Whose chronicle thus writ: 'The man was noble,
But with his last attempt he wiped it out,
Destroyed his country, and his name remains
To th'ensuing age abhorred.'—Speak to me, son!
Thou hast affected the fine strains of honour,   150
To imitate the graces of the gods,
To tear with thunder the wide cheeks o'th' air,
And yet to charge thy sulphur with a bolt
That should but rive an oak.—Why dost not speak?
Think'st thou it honourable for a noble man   155
Still to remember wrongs? Daughter, speak you,
He cares not for your weeping. Speak thou, boy,
Perhaps thy childishness will move him more
Than can our reasons. There's no man in the world
More bound to's mother, yet here he lets me prate   160
Like one i'th' stocks. Thou hast never in thy life

---

150 fine] JOHNSON; fiue F; first ROWE 1714   153 charge] THEOBALD; change F
155 noble man] F2; Nobleman F1

---

146 **thus writ** will be thus written
147 **it** i.e. his nobility and his reputation for nobility, here equated
149 **Speak . . . son** Cf. ll. 141, 154, 159, 169, 174, 178, and 181, and Introduction, pp. 102, 107. Salvini and Richard Burton were both particularly praised for the way their absolute stillness conveyed a succession of conflicting emotions. Refusal to respond is one of Volumnia's own tricks, of course: cf. 3.2.139 n. and 5.3.169 n., 178.1 n.
150–4 **Thou hast . . . oak** 'These lines are a statement of what Volumnia wishes her son to say: namely, that he has given the impression of pursuing revenge out of over-refined sentiments of personal honour, in order that in the end he may behave like Jove, who terrifies men with his thunder, but, in his mercy, only directs his lightning at an oak' (Hibbard).
150 **affected** (a) assumed, (b) aspired to?
    fine strains 'The niceties, the refinements' (Johnson)
151 **graces** i.e. both terror and mercy
152 **wide . . . air** Cf. *Richard II* 3.3.56, *Tempest* 1.2.4. Old maps frequently de-

pict the prevailing wind as issuing from the puffed-up checks of Aeolus, god of the winds, or of one of his cherubic followers.
153 **charge** load
    sulphur lightning
    bolt thunderbolt
154 **rive** split (as in 'riven')
156 **Still** always
157 **your weeping** Cf. her similar criticism at 4.2.55; yet Volumnia too sheds tears during this speech (cf. 5.6.95, 99), perhaps during the self-pity of 161–5, 'Thou hast never . . .' or perhaps when he gives in. It is her tears as much as Coriolanus' that Aufidius mocks in 5.6.
160 **More bound to's mother** A two-edged phrase: (a) more indebted to his mother, (b) more emotionally dependent on his mother.
    prate Volumnia picks up Martius' own word at l. 48; cf. also 4.5.49
161 **Like . . . stocks** 'like a vagabond to whose pleas and curses no one pays heed' (after Clarendon)
161–2 **Thou hast . . . courtesy** Kemball-Cook notes that Shakespeare here

---

341

Showed thy dear mother any courtesy,
When she, poor hen, fond of no second brood,
Has clucked thee to the wars and safely home,
Loaden with honour. Say my request's unjust,   165
And spurn me back. But if it be not so,
Thou art not honest, and the gods will plague thee
That thou restrain'st from me the duty which
To a mother's part belongs.—He turns away!
Down, ladies; let us shame him with our knees.   170
To his surname 'Coriolanus' 'longs more pride
Than pity to our prayers. Down: an end!
This is the last.
   ⌈*The ladies and Young Martius kneel*⌉
     So, we will home to Rome
And die among our neighbours.—Nay, behold's.
This boy, that cannot tell what he would have,   175
But kneels and holds up hands for fellowship,
Does reason our petition with more strength
Than thou hast to deny't.—Come, let us go.

---

164 clucked] F2; clock'd F1 170 him with] F2; him with him with F1 171 'longs]
F4; longs F1 173 *The ladies . . . kneel*] OXFORD; *not in* F; *The four all kneel* WILSON (*after*
an end!) 178.1 *They rise*] WILSON; *not in* F; *The Ladies and Young Martius rise* OXFORD
after l. 190

exploits a clumsy mention of 'hitherto'
in North's translation (Spencer, p. 357)
so as to introduce this unjust complaint by Volumnia.

163-4 The comic bathos of this image is
perhaps Volumnia's deliberate attempt
to soften Coriolanus' reaction to her
preceding complaint: wheedling following blame?

163 **fond of** desirous of, wishing for:
cf. Introduction, p. 22.

167 **honest** truthful

168 **restrain'st from** withholdest from,
deniest

169 **To a** (elided into 'T'a' for the metre)
He turns away A cue for action: this
may be less to deny Volumnia than
for Coriolanus to conceal his growing
distress.

171 **surname 'Coriolanus'** See 4.5.71–2 n.
'longs belongs

172 **an end** let's end this

173 *The ladies . . . kneel* Volumnia is

assaying the same trick she recom-
mended to Coriolanus in 3.2
So F has a following comma that is
unnecessary grammatically but probably indicates a significant pause.

173 **home to Rome** Ironically, 'home'
occurs more often in *Coriolanus* than
in any other Shakespeare play; the
unloveliness of the internal rhyme
helps to devalue it here.

174 **Nay, behold's** Wilson is uncharacteristically swept away into claiming '*She
tugs at his tunic*.' What is certain is
that Volumnia is as unable to re-
nounce this mother–son relationship
as Coriolanus himself. Her inability to
leave this scene is like his at the end
of 3.2.

177 **reason** argue for

178.1 *They rise* Following Plutarch,
Oxford keeps the petitioners kneeling
until Coriolanus has taken his
mother's hand (see 185 n.). Most editors place the rise at l. 178, however,

⌈*They rise*⌉
This fellow had a Volscian to his mother;
His wife is in Corioles, and his child   180
Like him by chance.—Yet give us our dispatch.
I am hushed until our city be afire,
And then I'll speak a little.
    He holds her by the hand, silent
CORIOLANUS (*weeping*)   O mother, mother!
What have you done? Behold, the heavens do ope,
The gods look down, and this unnatural scene   185

---

180 his child] F; this child THEOBALD   183 *He . . . silent*] F; *after* O mother, mother!
HONIGMANN *conj.* (*in 'Textual Companion'*)   *He*] OXFORD; *not in* F   183 *weeping*] This
edition; *not in* F

following 'Come, let us go' (which has
less impact if spoken kneeling). This
allows a greater variety of effect: in
both 1977 RSC and 1984 NT, for
example, Volumnia went close to Coriolanus to disown him to his face, then,
as she made her final threat turning
to walk away, he clutched her by the
hand to stay her. In 1984 NT Volumnia's averted face showed triumph; they
turned to each other again; and only
then did Coriolanus speak. Cf. 185 n.

179 **to** for
181 **dispatch** dismissal: with a bitter play
on *coup de grâce*?
182 **hushed** silent (an adjectival form in
Shakespeare's time)
183 **speak a little** 'What she will utter, I
imagine, is a mother's dying curse'
(A. C. Bradley). It is also, of course, the
old parental threat of wrath to come.
He holds . . . silent This is an ambivalent gesture, of loving reconciliation
and acceptance on the one hand but
of surrender and emotional dependence on the other: see Introduction,
p. 102. Ernst Honigmann (*Myriad-
minded Shakespeare*, 1989, pp. 172–3)
suggests that the direction should come
after 'O mother, mother! what have
you done?' (183–4), which is closer to
Plutarch and certainly possible biblio-
graphically; however, this is less interesting theatrically than the F
reading, which actors have given a
wide range of emotional colouring.
weeping Cf. l. 197 and 5.6.100, 103.

North says that even before Volumnia
spoke, 'nature so wrought with him,
that the tears fell from his eyes'.
183–4 **O mother . . . done?** See Introduction, pp. 30, 62.
184–6 **Behold . . . at** D. W. Harding (*SQ*,
20, 1959, p. 253) suggests that this
implies that the sun has suddenly
come out; and when he was at Oxford
Peter Brook drew sketches of how he
would like to direct the play, including
one of Coriolanus walking off here into
brilliantly obliterating sunshine—an
ironic effect used later in his film of
King Lear (see Ralph Berry, *On Directing Shakespeare*, 1989, p. 135).
185–6 **The gods . . . at** The idea of the
gods looking down to mock human
confusion can be found in the *Iliad* and
throughout classical literature; its
chief Renaissance statement was Erasmus' *Praise of Folly*, where human behaviour is specifically seen as ironic
theatre: 'there is no show like it.
Good God, what a theatre!' (trans.
H. H. Hudson, 1941, p. 69).
185 **unnatural scene** Brockbank notes
that Shakespeare uses 'scene' some
forty times in his plays 'invariably in a
theatrical sense'; it combines here with
the long silent handclasp and the
masque-like 'Behold, the heavens do
ope' to create a sense of tableau. According to Dionysus of Halicarnassus, the Volscians were so shocked to
see a mother kneeling to her son that
they 'could not bear the unusual sight
but turned away their eyes' (Bullough,

They laugh at. O my mother, mother, O!
You have won a happy victory to Rome;
But for your son, believe it, O believe it,
Most dangerously you have with him prevailed,
If not most mortal to him. But let it come.—   190
Aufidius, though I cannot make true wars,
I'll frame convenient peace. Now, good Aufidius,
Were you in my stead would you have heard
A mother less, or granted less, Aufidius?

AUFIDIUS
I was moved withal.

CORIOLANUS   I dare be sworn you were.   195
And, sir, it is no little thing to make
Mine eyes to sweat compassion. But, good sir,
What peace you'll make, advise me. For my part,
I'll not to Rome; I'll back with you, and pray you
Stand to me in this cause.—O mother! Wife!   200
      ⌈*He speaks to them apart*⌉

AUFIDIUS (*aside*)
I am glad thou hast set thy mercy and thy honour
At difference in thee. Out of that I'll work
Myself a former fortune.

193 stead] F1 (steed), F4   200.1 *He . . . apart*] WILSON; *not in* F   201 *aside*] ROWE;
not in F   203 *to Volumnia and Virgilia*] ROWE (*subs.*); *not in* F; *The Ladies make signs to
Coriolanus.* JOHNSON

p. 471). If this were the only interpretation of 'unnatural', Volumnia must
still be kneeling at this point (cf. 178
n.); but 'the whole situation is unnatural: a Roman making war on Rome;
a mother pleading with her son for
mercy; a conqueror melted by a
woman' (Chambers)—to which one
might add 'and a mother betraying her
son unwittingly to death', which is the
comment Coriolanus immediately goes
on to make. 'Unnatural' cuts too many
ways to be focused solely on Volumnia's kneeling.

186 **my mother** Cf. 4.1.28 n.; Martius then
also speaks of himself in the third person
as 'your son' with a distancing effect.

190 **mortal** fatally
   But . . . come This phrase of tragic
   acceptance is Shakespeare's addition to

the source and must be borne in mind
when Coriolanus' behaviour in 5.6 is
interpreted: see Introduction, p. 67.

191, 192, 194 **Aufidius** See Introduction,
p. 84, and cf. 4.5.102, 107 n.

191 **true** true to my promise

192 **convenient** i.e. not merely 'expedi-
ent', but 'appropriate' to both parties

195 **withal** by it

200 **Stand to** support

200.1 **He . . . apart** Cf. North: 'he spake a
little apart with his mother and wife,
and then let them return again to
Rome; for so they did request him'
(Spencer, pp. 357–8).

203 **former fortune** fortune like my
former one
   Ay . . . by Coriolanus is presumably
   replying to their urging his return to
   Rome; see l. 200.1 n.

CORIOLANUS (*to Volumnia and Virgilia*) Ay, by and by.
But we will drink together, and you shall bear
A better witness back than words, which we   205
On like conditions will have counter-sealed.
Come, enter with us. Ladies, you deserve
To have a temple built you. All the swords
In Italy, and her confederate arms,
Could not have made this peace.   *Exeunt*   210

5.4   *Enter Menenius and Sicinius*

MENENIUS See you yon quoin o'th' Capitol, yon cornerstone?

SICINIUS Why, what of that?

MENENIUS If it be possible for you to displace it with your
little finger, there is some hope the ladies of Rome, es-   5
pecially his mother, may prevail with him. But I say
there is no hope in't, our throats are sentenced and
stay upon execution.

SICINIUS Is't possible that so short a time can alter the
condition of a man?   10

5.4.1 yon ... yon] F (yon'd ... yon'd)   quoin] CAPELL (coign); coin F

204 **drink together** A traditional way of
   compounding quarrels. However, it is
   a solution more appropriate to Menenius than to the earlier Martius.
205 **better witness** formal treaty; recognizing the legal superiority of a written
   document over verbal communication
   which (the treaty)
206 **On ... counter-sealed** Coriolanus is
   promising to have this renewal of the
   treaty ratified by the Roman Senate (cf.
   5.6.81–4): the Elizabethans used wax
   seals to complete legal documents (cf.
   2.3.104 n.).
207 **Come ... us** Presumably addressed to
   Valeria and Young Martius, but also
   possibly to Aufidius.
207–8 **Ladies ... you** Plutarch notes that
   the grateful Senate 'ordained that
   the magistrates, to gratify and honour
   these ladies, should grant them all that
   they would require. And they only requested that they would build a
   Temple of Fortune of the Women'

(Spencer, p. 359); this was built at the
place Coriolanus had pitched camp,
four miles south of Rome (cf. 5.2 head-
note).
5.4.0.1 **Enter ... Sicinius** This scene
   gives time for the ladies to get back to
   Rome and frames their return ironically because we know that the mercy
   of which Menenius despairs has already been granted: see Introduction,
   p. 29. Within this broad irony is the
   smaller irony that the two speakers
   seem to have exchanged roles: it is
   Menenius now who is bitter about
   Coriolanus, Sicinius who is placatory
   (as in Plutarch it was the plebeians
   who now wanted Martius' return and
   the patricians who opposed it). To emphasize this, 1984 NT had them passing a flask as they entered, with the
   puritanical Sicinius' speech beginning
   to slur.
1 **quoin** cornerstone
10 **condition** disposition, character

MENENIUS There is difference between a grub and a butterfly, yet your butterfly was a grub. This Martius is grown from man to dragon. He has wings, he's more than a creeping thing.

SICINIUS He loved his mother dearly. 15

MENENIUS So did he me, and he no more remembers his mother now than an eight-year-old horse. The tartness of his face sours ripe grapes. When he walks, he moves like an engine, and the ground shrinks before his treading. He is able to pierce a corslet with his eye, 20 talks like a knell, and his hum is a battery. He sits in his state as a thing made for Alexander. What he bids be done is finished with his bidding. He wants nothing of a god but eternity and a heaven to throne in.

SICINIUS Yes: mercy, if you report him truly. 25

MENENIUS I paint him in the character. Mark what mercy his mother shall bring from him. There is no more mercy in him than there is milk in a male tiger. That shall our poor city find; and all this is 'long of you.

---

11 difference] F1; difference F2   21 hum] F; 'hmh!' OXFORD   29 'long] CAPELL; long F

11 **difference** dissimilarity. This is *OED*'s first record of the word.

12 **butterfly** Cf. 1.3.62–3 n.
your (the impersonal usage again)

12, 41 **Martius** It is not just Aufidius who refuses to use the honorific 'Coriolanus' (5.6.88–90); the Romans too drop it in this earlier scene, as does the playwright, very interestingly, in some of his stage directions, e.g. 5.6.131.1, 154.1.

13 **dragon** Cf. 4.1.31 n.
creeping thing In 1977 RSC Menenius rubbed his knees, recalling how, after Coriolanus' 'Away!' (5.2.78), he had followed him some way on his knees in that production.

17 **than . . . horse** i.e. remembers his dam: a final debasement of Act 1's chivalric horse references

17–26 **The tartness . . . character** Menenius is maliciously elaborating a satirical description in the mode of a 17th-century 'character' writer; cf. 26, and 2.1.62 n.

19 **engine** i.e. of war; cf. 2.1.154–7,

2.2.105–8, where the image was used approvingly

20 **corslet** body-armour, covering the torso

21 **hum** 'an interjection expressing dissent or dissatisfaction' (*OED*), cf. 5.1.62–3 n.
battery (of cannon); cf. *K. John* 2.1.463, 'He speaks plain cannon': an anachronism here, however
state chair of state; cf. Introduction, p. 98.

22 **thing . . . Alexander** like a statue of Alexander the Great; cf. 4.6.94–6

23 **wants** lacks

23–5 **nothing . . . mercy** Richmond Noble, *Shakespeare's Biblical Knowledge* (1935), points out the non-classical sources for these attributes of the deity: 'eternity', Isaiah 58: 15; 'heaven' as 'throne', Isaiah 66: 1; 'mercy', the Prayer Book's Communion Service.

26 **in the character** to the life, as he is; but cf. also 17–26 n.

29 **'long of you** your fault, on account of you

SICINIUS The gods be good unto us!   30
MENENIUS No, in such a case the gods will not be good
   unto us. When we banished him we respected not
   them, and, he returning to break our necks, they re-
   spect not us.
      Enter a Messenger
MESSENGER (*to Sicinius*)
   Sir, if you'd save your life, fly to your house.   35
   The plebeians have got your fellow tribune
   And hale him up and down, all swearing if
   The Roman ladies bring not comfort home
   They'll give him death by inches.
      Enter another Messenger
SICINIUS   What's the news?
SECOND MESSENGER
   Good news, good news. The ladies have prevailed,   40
   The Volscians are dislodged, and Martius gone.
   A merrier day did never yet greet Rome,
   No, not th'expulsion of the Tarquins.
SICINIUS   Friend,
   Art thou certain this is true? Is't most certain?
SECOND MESSENGER
   As certain as I know the sun is fire.   45
   Where have you lurked that you make doubt of it?
   Ne'er through an arch so hurried the blown tide

30 The] F; Ye HINMAN *conj.* (*in 'Textual Companion'*)   40, 45, 59, 61 SECOND MESS-
ENGER] DYCE; '*Mes.*' *or* '*Mess.*' F

30, 31 **The gods** The repetition of the phrase makes Hinman's proposed revision less likely.
33 **break our necks** Emphasizing 'our'; cf. 3.3.30 n.
35–9 **Sir ... inches** In 1984 NT Volumnia's triumph in 5.5 ended with business in which Sicinius wrapped the ragged, battered Brutus in his cloak of office and took him away to be cared for. For Benson's more drastic solution, see 4.6.157 n.
36 **plebeians** Accented here on the first syllable.

37 **hale** drag, haul
39 **death by inches** protracted death by torture, cf. 5.2.64–5
41 **are dislodged** have left their positions (a military term)
45 **sun is fire** Cf. 1.5.10, 5.3.60.
47 **blown** (a) swollen, (b) blown by the wind. Arden suggests that Shakespeare is thinking of the wind-driven tide rushing through the arches of Old London Bridge; cf. *Lucrece* 1667, 'As through an arch the violent roaring tide ...'

As the recomforted through th' gates.

Trumpets, hautboys, drums beat, all together

                  Why, hark you,

The trumpets, sackbuts, psalteries, and fifes,

Tabors and cymbals, and the shouting Romans   50

Make the sun dance.

     A shout within

                Hark you!

MENENIUS   This is good news.

I will go meet the ladies. This Volumnia

Is worth of consuls, senators, patricians,

A city full; of tribunes such as you,

A sea and land full. You have prayed well today.   55

This morning for ten thousand of your throats

I'd not have given a doit.

     Sound still with the shouts

                Hark how they joy!

SICINIUS (*to Second Messenger*)

First, the gods bless you for your tidings; next,

Accept my thankfulness.

SECOND MESSENGER   Sir, we have all

---

48 *Trumpets . . . together*] *at end of line* F   *hautboys*] F (*Hoboyes*)   *all together*] F (*altogether*)   50 cymbals] F (*Symboles*), F4   51 *A shout within*] WILSON; *after* Hark you! F   57 *Sound . . . shouts*] OXFORD (*subs.*); *after* joy! F

48, 50 *Trumpets . . . cymbals* See Introduction, p. 100. This contrasts with Coriolanus' silent 'moment of truth' in 5.3, and is further emphasized by three 'hark' speeches at 48, 51, 57, and the second stage direction at 57.

48 *hautboys* 'hautbois', a woodwind instrument (an ancestor of the oboe) that plays loudly with a piercing note much like that of the 'shawm'

49–50 **trumpets . . . cymbals** Clarendon compares the list of instruments in Daniel, 3: 5, where, interestingly, the people were worshipping a golden image set up by Nebuchadnezzar; cf. 5.1.63 n.

49 **sackbuts** loud brass instruments rather like trombones, reserved for especially ceremonious occasions

     psalteries stringed instruments

50 **Tabors** small drums, often accompanied by pipes

51 **Make . . . dance** Clarendon suggests a reference to the old belief that the sun danced on Easter Day; cf. *Twelfth Night* 2.3.56, 'But shall we make the welkin dance indeed?'

52 **This Volumnia** This is the only time her name is mentioned in the dialogue; like Martius' 'My' (5.3.186 n.), Menenius' 'This' is emotionally distancing.

57 **doit** small coin, used figuratively for any trifling sum; cf. 1.6.6 n, 4.4.17

     Sound . . . shouts More probably an authorial reminder for the noise to continue off-stage (Hibbard) than a prompter's note to the musicians (Cambridge, Wilson, etc.).

59 **Accept my thankfulness** Oxford's direction '*Giving money*' is over-explicit and unnecessary. Second Messenger's reply may be slightly tart.

Great cause to give great thanks.

SICINIUS   They are near the city?   60

SECOND MESSENGER

Almost at point to enter.

SICINIUS   We'll meet them,

And help the joy.   *Exeunt*

5.5   *Enter two Senators with the ladies, Volumnia,*
          Virgilia, and Valeria, passing over the stage,
          with other lords

A SENATOR

Behold our patroness, the life of Rome!
Call all your tribes together, praise the gods,
And make triumphant fires. Strew flowers before them.
Unshout the noise that banished Martius,
Repeal him with the welcome of his mother.   5
Cry 'Welcome, ladies, welcome!'

ALL   Welcome, ladies, welcome!

A flourish with drums and trumpets. Exeunt

5.5.0.1–2 *the ladies, ... Valeria,*] OXFORD; *Ladies,* F   0.3 *lords*] F; *Lords and the people.*
ARDEN (*after* Capell); *and Citizens* OXFORD   1 A SENATOR] F (*Sena.*); *First Sen.* CAPELL
4 Unshout] F (Vnshoot), ROWE   6.1 *Exeunt*] F2; *not in* F1

---

61 **at point** about

62 *Exeunt* Menenius may have left earlier, as Kemball-Cook suggests (cf. l.
52), though the absence of his name
from the opening stage direction to 5.5
makes this unlikely. Sicinius and the
Messenger either follow him off, to re-
enter immediately at the end of Volumnia's triumph, or all three may
meet the procession entering as they
go towards the exit, in an inversion
of 4.2: as at 2.1.157, which it also
mirrors ironically, there may be no
real division between the scenes here.
Alternatively, neither Menenius nor
the Tribunes may be part of the
triumph, which would certainly emphasize its irony (see Introduction,
p. 31).

5.5 This scene confronts a director with
two special cruces: what emotion the

ladies should show, especially Volumnia; (cf. E. A. J. Honigmann, *Shakespeare: Seven Tragedies ...*, 1976, pp.
188–9) and the scale and method with
which the procession should be staged:
see Introduction, pp. 31–2.

2 **tribes** Cf. 3.3.9–11 n.?

3 **triumphant fires** Not in North, the
lighting of bonfires at times of national
rejoicing (e.g. the defeat of the Armada) was a British rather than Roman
tradition; cf. *Cymbeline* 3.1.32. This is
the last of the play's fire references,
transformed now from threat to celebration.

5 **Repeal** recall

6.1 *A flourish ... trumpets* F2 puts
this direction after *Exeunt* so that it
begins 5.6, but it seems to suit 5.5
better

5.6   *Enter Tullus Aufidius with attendants*

AUFIDIUS

Go tell the lords o'th' city I am here.
Deliver them this paper. Having read it,
Bid them repair to th' market-place, where I,
Even in theirs and in the commons' ears,
Will vouch the truth of it. Him I accuse   5
The city ports by this hath entered, and
Intends t'appear before the people, hoping
To purge himself with words. Dispatch.

Exeunt attendants
Enter three or four Conspirators of Aufidius' faction
           Most welcome.

FIRST CONSPIRATOR

How is it with our general?

AUFIDIUS   Even so
As with a man by his own alms impoisoned,   10
And with his charity slain.

SECOND CONSPIRATOR   Most noble sir,
If you do hold the same intent wherein
You wished us parties, we'll deliver you
Of your great danger.

AUFIDIUS   Sir, I cannot tell.
We must proceed as we do find the people.   15

THIRD CONSPIRATOR

The people will remain uncertain whilst
'Twixt you there's difference, but the fall of either
Makes the survivor heir of all.

AUFIDIUS   I know it,

5.6.5 accuse‸] ROWE; ~: F   8 *Exeunt attendants*] MALONE; *not in* F

5.6 See Introduction, pp. 28, 66, and
   l. 73 n.
2 **Deliver . . . paper** A cue for action.
3 **market-place** Thus Martius will die in
   the Volscian market-place, a doubly
   alien place.
4 **theirs** For this use of 'theirs' as a pro-
   nominal adjective before the noun, see
   Abbott §161.
5 **Him** he whom. F's punctuation suggests that the compositor mistook
   'Him' for the object of 'accuse'.

6 **ports** gates; cf. 1.8.1
8.2 *three or four* See Introduction, p. 144.
10 **alms** benevolence (literally, food given
   as charity)
   impoisoned cf. 'My valour, poisoned',
   1.11.17
11 **with** by (Abbott §193)
13 **parties** supporters, sharers
14 **Of** from
15 **We . . . people** Cf. 1.11.31–3 n.
17 **difference** disagreement, rivalry

And my pretext to strike at him admits
A good construction. I raised him, and I pawned   20
Mine honour for his truth; who being so heightened,
He watered his new plants with dews of flattery,
Seducing so my friends; and to this end
He bowed his nature, never known before
But to be rough, unswayable, and free.   25
THIRD CONSPIRATOR   Sir, his stoutness
    When he did stand for consul, which he lost
    By lack of stooping—
AUFIDIUS   That I would have spoke of.
    Being banished for't, he came unto my hearth,
    Presented to my knife his throat. I took him,   30
    Made him joint-servant with me, gave him way
    In all his own desires; nay, let him choose
    Out of my files, his projects to accomplish,
    My best and freshest men; served his designments
    In mine own person, holp to reap the fame   35
    Which he did end all his, and took some pride
    To do myself this wrong, till at the last
    I seemed his follower, not partner, and
    He waged me with his countenance as if
    I had been mercenary.
FIRST CONSPIRATOR   So he did, my lord;   40

---

28 stooping—] ROWE; ~. F   31 joint-servant] F; joint servant SISSON   33–4 projects
∧ . . . accomplish, . . . men;]F3; ~, . . . ~∧ . . . ~, F1

---

19 **pretext** Accented on the second syllable.
19–20 **admits . . . construction** is capable
    of an honourable interpretation
21 **truth** integrity, loyalty
    heightened raised to a position of
    eminence
22–5 **He . . . free**   See   Introduction,
    pp. 68–9.
22 **plants** (a) 'used figuratively for posi-
    tion and dignity' (Hibbard); (b) Brock-
    bank's suggestion, 'those on whom he
    conferred honour' (cf. *Macbeth* 1.4.28–
    9), fits what follows but not what
    precedes the metaphor.
25 **free** unrestrainable
26 **stoutness** obstinacy, unyieldingness;
    cf. 3.2.129
28 **That . . . of** I was coming to that

31 **joint-servant** i.e. equal partner in
    serving the state
    gave him way (a) made opportunity for
    him (*OED*, *give*, *v.* 49d), (b) gave way
    to him (*OED* 49f)?
33 **files** ranks
34 **designments** designs, enterprises
36 **end** gather in; a harvesting term,
    cf. Milton, *L'Allegro* 109–10: 'His
    shadowy flail had threshed the corn |
    That ten day-labourers could not end'.
39–40 **waged . . . mercenary** i.e. 'patron-
    ized me not only as if I were a hired
    soldier but also one who could be paid
    merely by his condescension'. Cf.
    North on Aufidius' envy: 'This fell out
    the more because every man honoured
    Martius, and thought he only could do

The army marvelled at it; and in the last,
When he had carried Rome and that we looked
For no less spoil than glory—

AUFIDIUS   There was it,
For which my sinews shall be stretched upon him.
At a few drops of women's rheum, which are   45
As cheap as lies, he sold the blood and labour
Of our great action; therefore shall he die,
And I'll renew me in his fall.

> *Drums and trumpets sound, with great shouts of the*
> *people*

                              But hark.

FIRST CONSPIRATOR
Your native town you entered like a post,
And had no welcomes home; but he returns   50
Splitting the air with noise.

SECOND CONSPIRATOR   And patient fools,
Whose children he hath slain, their base throats tear
With giving him glory.

THIRD CONSPIRATOR   Therefore, at your vantage,
Ere he express himself or move the people
With what he would say, let him feel your sword,   55
Which we will second. When he lies along,
After your way his tale pronounced shall bury

---

43 glory—] F3; ~. F1   44–6 him. ... lies,] F4 (*subs.*); ~, ... ~; F1   48 *Drums ...
people*] OXFORD; *at end of line in* F (*sounds*)   55–7 sword, ... second. When ... way₍]
THEOBALD (*subs.*); Sword: ... second, when ... way. F

all, and that all other governors and
captains must be content with such
credit and authority as he would
please to countenance with them'
(Spencer, pp. 347–8), whence Shakespeare equates 'countenance' meaning
'grant' with the contemporary evil of
paying soldiers only with 'good looks'
(Johnson). 'It is Coriolanus' natural
and habitual assumption of authority
that galls Aufidius' (Hibbard).

41 **in the last** at the last. Clarendon compares 'in the best', *Hamlet* 1.5.27, and
'in the least', *Lear* 1.1.190.

42 **had carried** (a) 'had conquered'; possibly (b) 'might have conquered' (Abbott

§361)

43 **There was it** that was the thing;
cf. *1 Henry IV* 3.3.12

44 **my ... him** my strength shall be
strained to the uttermost against him

45 **rheum** used contemptuously for
'tears'; cf. *K. John* 2.2.22, 4.3. 108

49 **native town** (Antium)
post messenger (bringing news of
Martius, ll. 2–5)

53 **at your vantage** seizing your opportunity

56 **along** stretched out dead

57 **After ... pronounced** telling his story
as you please. This advice anticipates
(and thus undercuts) Aufidius' volte-
face at ll. 147–51.

His reasons with his body.

AUFIDIUS   Say no more:

Here come the lords.

Enter the Lords of the city

ALL THE LORDS You are most welcome home.   60

AUFIDIUS I have not deserved it.

But, worthy lords, have you with heed perused
What I have written to you?

ALL THE LORDS   We have.

FIRST LORD   And grieve to hear't.

What faults he made before the last, I think
Might have found easy fines. But there to end   65
Where he was to begin, and give away
The benefit of our levies, answering us
With our own charge, making a treaty where
There was a yielding—this admits no excuse.

AUFIDIUS He approaches. You shall hear him.   70

*Enter Coriolanus marching with drum and colours, the
Commoners being with him*

CORIOLANUS

Hail, lords! I am returned your soldier,
No more infected with my country's love
Than when I parted hence, but still subsisting
Under your great command. You are to know
That prosperously I have attempted, and   75
With bloody passage led your wars even to
The gates of Rome. Our spoils we have brought home

59.1 *Enter ... city*] F; *after* body. OXFORD   60, 63 ALL THE LORDS] F (*All Lords.*, *All.*)

58 **reasons** explanations, the reasons he gives for behaving as he did

64 **made** committed. Cf. 4.7.18–19, 24–6 and Introduction, p. 26.

65 **easy fines** light punishment

67 **benefit ... levies** profit from the expense of enrolling an army (see next note)

67–8 **answering ... charge** 'accounting to us with a mere return of expenses' (Arden); cf. ll. 78 n., 94–6

70.1–2 *Enter ... him* See Introduction, pp. 68–9.

the ... him This is Shakespeare's addition—in Plutarch the Volscian commoners are mentioned only for their antagonism to Coriolanus—and the phrasing of the direction suggests a certain disorderliness in their approach.

71 **your soldier** Cf. Volumnia's advice at 3.2.82–3.

73 **hence** i.e. from Antium
subsisting remaining (*OED* 4c)

75 **prosperously ... attempted** my endeavours have been successful

Doth more than counterpoise a full third part
The charges of the action. We have made peace
With no less honour to the Antiates   80
~~Than shame to th' Romans.~~ And we here deliver,
Subscribed by th' consuls and patricians,
Together with the seal o'th' Senate, what
We have compounded on.
            ⌈ *He offers the Lords a scroll* ⌉
AUFIDIUS   Read it not, noble lords,
But tell the traitor in the highest degree   85
He hath abused your powers.
CORIOLANUS Traitor? How now?
AUFIDIUS Ay, traitor, Martius.
CORIOLANUS Martius?
AUFIDIUS

Ay, Martius, Caius Martius. Dost thou think   90
I'll grace thee with that robbery, thy stol'n name
'Coriolanus', in Corioles?

---

78 Doth] F; Do POPE   84 *He ... scroll*] OXFORD (*subs.*); *not in* F   85 traitor‸] F;
~, THEOBALD

78 **more ... part** (a) outweighs by more
than a third, (b) outweighs more than
a third of? F's phrasing is ambiguous,
and North offers no guidance because
this detail does not occur in Plutarch.
If (a) is the correct reading, the complaint at ll. 65–9 is inaccurate (based
presumably on Aufidius' false report; cf.
3.3.4–5 for the Tribunes' similar tactics); if (b) is correct, Coriolanus' return to face the Volsces is even more
foolhardy.
80 **Antiates** inhabitants of Antium,
cf. 1.7.53
82 **and patricians** Kemball-Cook notes
that Shakespeare may have thought
the patricians had some sort of official
position distinct from the Senate,
cf. 4.7.29–30 n.
84 **compounded on** agreed to
85 **in ... degree** of the most extreme kind;
cf. *Richard III* 5.5.150, *Twelfth Night*
1.5.51. The implication is that, having
once betrayed Rome, he has now betrayed the Volscians too.
87 **Traitor?** Cf. the Tribunes' accusation

at 3.1.164–5, 3.3.66–7.
89 **Martius** Cf. 5.4.12, 41 n., and Sicinius' similar omission of the honorific
at 3.1.196, 336: see Introduction,
p. 84.
91–2 **with ... Corioles?** To avoid the apparent contradiction of place, Kemball-
Cook suggests that 'in Corioles' be
considered a transposed participle
going with 'that robbery' (i.e. 'that
robbery in Corioles, thy stolen name
"Coriolanus" '), as in *Timon* 4.2.13, 'A
dedicated beggar to the air'. 'I fluttered
your Volscians in Corioles' (5.6.115–16)
may also suggest that Martius is not
talking to the actual inhabitants of
Corioles. Neither argument is very convincing, however: see Introduction,
p. 95.
92 **Coriolanus** Because of the scansion of
this one line, Peter Hall preserved
the pronunciation 'Cor-eye-olanus'
throughout his 1984 NT production.
However, a *difference* of pronunciation
between cognomen and place-name
here would emphasize Aufidius' point.

You lords and heads o'th' state, perfidiously
He has betrayed your business, and given up,
For certain drops of salt, your city, Rome—   95
I say your city—to his wife and mother,
Breaking his oath and resolution like
A twist of rotten silk, never admitting
Counsel o'th' war. But at his nurse's tears
He whined and roared away your victory,   100
That pages blushed at him, and men of heart
Looked wond'ring each at others.

CORIOLANUS   Hear'st thou, Mars?

AUFIDIUS

Name not the god, thou boy of tears.

CORIOLANUS   Ha?

AUFIDIUS   No more.

CORIOLANUS

Measureless liar, thou hast made my heart
Too great for what contains it. 'Boy'? O slave!—   105
Pardon me, lords, 'tis the first time that ever

95–6 Rome— ... your city—] OXFORD; ~, ... your city, F; ~, ... 'your city',
CAMBRIDGE   102 each at others] F; each at other ROWE; at each other STEEVENS
103 AUFIDIUS No more.] F (*Auf.*); *First Lord.* No more. TYRWHITT *conj.* (*in* Cambridge)

95 **drops of salt** i.e. the tears of Volumnia
and Virgilia; cf. ll. 45, 99
97 **oath and resolution** 'sworn purpose',
a hendiadys
98 **twist** plaited thread; cf. 1.10.45
98–9 **never ... war** never taking the
advice of his fellow officers
99 **nurse's** i.e. Volumnia's; cf. 5.3.111 n.
100 **whined and roared** An exaggeration
of Martius' 'O mother, mother!' and 'O
my mother, mother, O!' (5.3.183,
186) that none the less provides
possible cues as to how they were delivered
101 **heart** courage
102 **each at others** at one another, each
at the others
102–3 **Hear'st ... god**   Cf.   1.4.10,
4.5.119 n.
103 **boy of tears** In 1959 SMT Olivier's
reaction to this insult revealed a
'shock of recognition that showed its
accuracy' (Kitchin, p. 141): cf. Martius' scorn of tears in 3.2. 'Boy' may

also carry overtones of the sexually
passive partner in a homosexual liai-
son (as in *Troilus* 5.1.14–17) and even
of social inferiority, cf. l. 105 n.
103 **Ha?** This interjection is extrametrical.
No more (a) than a 'boy of tears';
(b) possibly a double negative meaning
'any more', concluding 'Name not the
god'? Some editors have given the line
to the Volscian lord who is trying to
make peace; cf. l. 111.
104–5 **thou ... it** Brockbank compares
Antony 1.1.6–8 and 4.15.40–1,
'Heart, once be stronger than thy con-
tinent; | Crack thy frail case'.
105 **'Boy'? O slave!** This suggests that
'boy' could also be a class term, signifying not only youth but also subordination and servitude.
106–7 **'tis ... scold** This almost comically
inaccurate statement means either
that in his new attempt to be 'politic'
Coriolanus is blatantly disingenuous,
or that he is astonishingly ignorant of

I was forced to scold. Your judgements, my grave lords,
Must give this cur the lie, and his own notion—
Who wears my stripes impressed upon him, that
~~Must bear my beating to his grave—shall join~~   110
To thrust the lie unto him.

FIRST LORD   Peace both, and hear me speak.

CORIOLANUS

Cut me to pieces, Volsces. Men and lads,
Stain all your edges on me. 'Boy'! False hound,
If you have writ your annals true, 'tis there
That, like an eagle in a dovecote, I   115
Fluttered your Volscians in Corioles.
Alone I did it, boy!

AUFIDIUS   Why, noble lords,
Will you be put in mind of his blind fortune,
Which was your shame, by this unholy braggart,
Fore your own eyes and ears?

ALL THE CONSPIRATORS   Let him die for't!   120

---

112 Volsces. Men] OXFORD; ~‸ ~ F   113 hound,] F (~:); ~! CAMBRIDGE   116 Fluttered] F3; Flatter'd F1   117 it,] F; ~. ROWE, CAMBRIDGE   boy!] F2 (Boy!), SISSON; Boy. F1; 'Boy!' CAMBRIDGE; Boy? KITTREDGE   119 braggart,] ROWE; ~? F, SISSON   120, 121, 131 ALL THE] F (*All*)

---

his own nature and has learned nothing from his recent experience. Shakespeare leaves the choice open.

108 **cur** Cf. 'You common cry of curs', 3.3.121.
notion sense of the truth
109–10 **Who ... grave** Cf. 'disciplined', 2.1.123 n.
109 **that** who (qualifying 'him', not 'stripes'), i.e. Aufidius
112 **Cut ... pieces** Cf. Martius' baring of his throat to Aufidius at 4.5.96–8, and the crowd's 'Tear him to pieces' (l. 121), the play's culminating reference to the theme of the body and its members.
113 **Stain** (a) discolour with blood, (b) dishonour; cf. 1.11.18
edges sword edges; cf. 1.4.30
114 **'tis there** it is recorded there
115 **eagle** Cf. 3.1.141 n.
dovecote Cf. 5.3.27 n.
115–16 **I | Fluttered** F1's 'Flatter'd' possibly puns on '*flatter*: to float, flutter'

(*OED v.* 2) but, as the latter was used intransitively, it is more likely to be a simple misprint; cf. 'Fan', 3.3.128 for a similar image. In 1959 SMT Olivier delivered this with a long drawn out 'I ...' and sharp, sneering 'Fluttered'. Nineteenth-century actors tried to illustrate it with gesture: whereas John Vandenhofﬁ merely described two or three circles over his head (*Edinburgh Dramatic Review*, 6 Apr. 1824), Samuel Phelps paused before 'fluttered', then 'lifting his arm to its full height above his head, he shook it to and fro, as in the act of startling a flock of doves' (Godfrey Turner, 'The First Nights of My Young Days', *The Theatre*, 1 June 1887).

117 **boy!** This reading means that Coriolanus retaliates in *tu quoque* fashion by calling Aufidius 'boy'. Alternatively, it can be punctuated so that he merely repeats the epithet indignantly, as at l. 105.
118 **blind fortune** sheer good luck

ALL THE PEOPLE Tear him to pieces!—Do it presently!—
He killed my son!—My daughter!—He killed my
cousin Marcus!—He killed my father!

SECOND LORD Peace, ho! No outrage: peace!
The man is noble, and his fame folds in   125
This orb o'th' earth. His last offences to us
Shall have judicious hearing. Stand, Aufidius,
And trouble not the peace.

CORIOLANUS ⌈ *drawing his sword* ⌉ O that I had him,
With six Aufidiuses, or more, his tribe,
To use my lawful sword.

AUFIDIUS   Insolent villain!   130

ALL THE CONSPIRATORS
Kill, kill, kill, kill, kill him!
          Two Conspirators draw and kill Martius, who falls.
          Aufidius stands on him

LORDS   Hold, hold, hold, hold!

---

128 (*drawing his sword*)] OXFORD; *not in* F   131.1 *Two Conspirators draw*] OXFORD; *Draw both the Conspirators* F; *The Conspirators all draw.* ROWE; *The Conspirators draw.* CAMBRIDGE *kill*] F4; *kils* F1   131.2 *Aufidius ... him*] F; *Aufidius stands on his body.* CAMBRIDGE; *Aufidius and Conspirators stand on him* OXFORD

121–3 **Tear ... father!** Though they have no actual share in the killing (a fact some productions have ignored: see Introduction, p. 111), Shakespeare makes the Volscian crowd who were just cheering him as clamorous for Coriolanus' death as the plebeians were in Rome, whereas North comments less tendentiously on 'none of the people once offering to rescue him' (Spencer, p. 362). The shouts are confused and overlapping, and consequently in prose.

121 **presently** immediately

125–6 **folds ... earth** envelops the whole world

127 **judicious hearing** a proper trial by law
Stand stop, hold off (taken with ironic literalness at 131.2)

128–30 **O ... sword** 'His mother's son to the last, Coriolanus almost repeats her words to Sicinius at [4.2.25–7]' (Hibbard).

129 **his tribe** (a) i.e. his 'gens', all those related to him by blood, so that he might extirpate the whole line; (b) but see also 5.5.2 and 3.3.9–11 n.

130 **lawful sword** (a) sword to execute justice, (b) 'the sword of lawful war. Coriolanus wishes himself opposed in the battlefield to Aufidius and his kin' (Brockbank)

131 **Kill ... him** Arden cites Cotgrave: '*A mort, a mort*: Kill, kill; the cry of bloody soldiers pursuing their fearful enemies unto death'; cf. *Lear* 4.5.183, *Venus* 652. This contrasts starkly with Coriolanus' apparent refusal to use his sword for civil strife just previously, 130 n. (b); cf. 3.1.275–6.

131 **Two ... draw** It is not clear whether F's '*both*' assumes that there are only two Conspirators (cf. l. 8 n.) or that only two are positioned to kill Coriolanus, the rest being dispersed to make their opinions sound more representative of the crowd.
kill ... falls See Introduction, pp. 110 ff. for examples of spectacular acting of this death.

131.2 **Aufidius ... him** Cf. 5.3.124–5, 128, 1.3.48; see Introduction, pp. 113–14.

AUFIDIUS
My noble masters, hear me speak.
FIRST LORD   O Tullus!
SECOND LORD
Thou hast done a deed whereat valour will weep.
THIRD LORD
Tread not upon him. Masters all, be quiet!
Put up your swords.   135
AUFIDIUS
My lords, when you shall know—as in this rage
Provoked by him you cannot—the great danger
Which this man's life did owe you, you'll rejoice
That he is thus cut off. Please it your honours
To call me to your Senate, I'll deliver   140
Myself your loyal servant, or endure
Your heaviest censure.
FIRST LORD   Bear from hence his body,
And mourn you for him. Let him be regarded
As the most noble corpse that ever herald
Did follow to his urn.
SECOND LORD   His own impatience   145
Takes from Aufidius a great part of blame.
Let's make the best of it.
AUFIDIUS   My rage is gone,

---

134 him. Masters all,] CAMBRIDGE (Rowe *subs.*); ~ˎ ~, ~ˎ F1; ~, ~, ~ˎ F4; ~, ~;
~ˎ SCHMIDT, CLARENDON, OXFORD (*subs.*)

134–5 **Tread ... swords** The first command seems to be addressed to Aufidius, the second to the crowd in
general, the third to the Conspirators.
The shortness of l. 135 indicates a
pause while the tumult dies down,
which gives psychological time for
Aufidius to begin to change his attitude, first to self-justification, then to
some degree of remorse.
138 **did owe you** held in store for you
140 **deliver** show, prove
143 **mourn you for him** The next sentence
suggests that this should be addressed
to the Volscians at large.
144–5 **herald ... urn** This was an English, rather than Roman, practice:
Arden cites the description of Sir Philip

Sidney's funeral of 1587 in John
Nichols, *Progresses and Public Processions
of Queen Elizabeth* (1823), ii. 483–94.
North reports that many Volscians
condemned Coriolanus' murder and
'men came out of all parts to honour
his body, and did honorably bury him,
setting out his tomb with great store
of armour and spoils, as the tomb of a
worthy person and great captain'
(Spencer, p. 362). See Introduction,
pp. 14–15.
145 **urn** This 'may refer to a precise form
of burial or to entombment generally'
(Brockbank); cf. *Henry V* 1.2.228,
Hamlet 1.4.30.
impatience rage, anger
147 ff. **My rage is gone ...** See Intro-

And I am struck with sorrow. Take him up.
Help three o'th' chiefest soldiers; I'll be one.
Beat thou the drum, that it speak mournfully.   150
Trail your steel pikes. Though in this city he
Hath widowed and unchilded many a one,
Which to this hour bewail the injury,
Yet he shall have a noble memory. Assist.

Exeunt bearing the body of Martius.
A dead march is sounded

154.2 *is sounded*] F (*Sounded*)

duction, p. 114. Cf. l. 57 n. and the
Tribunes' similar change of tactics after
Coriolanus' banishment at 4.2.3–4.

149 **one** i.e. the fourth. Four captains
bore off Hamlet 'like a soldier' in *Hamlet* 5.2.349–50. If the other bearers
here are the three Conspirators, an
extra level of irony is gained: see Introduction, p. 115.

151 **Trail . . . pikes** This involved holding
the pikes at a slope with their butt
ends near the ground, instead of over
the bearers' shoulders. It was the usual
practice at military funerals in this
period (e.g. Sidney's, referred to in
144–5 n.).

152 **widowed and unchilded** Martius'
offence to the human values represented by wives and mothers is thus
one of the final emphases of the
play: 'unchilded' may mean 'killed the
child of' or 'prevented from having

children (because their husbands have
been killed)'. Its moral significance
remains the same: cf. Introduction,
p. 80.

154 **memory** Both posthumous repute
and a tomb to commemorate him (see
the North quotation in 144–5 n.).
Assist Its separation from the rest of
the hexameter gives this command a
curt, extra-metrical effect; as usual
Aufidius cannot act alone.

154.1–2 *Exeunt . . . sounded* See Introduction, pp. 114–15. In 1984 NT four
soldiers carried the body round the stage
to present it as an emblem to all sections of the audience, then left through
the central gates as the Citizens trailed
off to either side, with electronic music
building to ear-shattering pitch then
ceasing abruptly when the gates
boomed shut, as they had boomed
when Martius was trapped alone in
Corioles earlier.

ALTERATIONS TO LINEATION

THIS list records mainly the present text's departures from the lineation of F, with an indication of the provenance for such departures. Relineation by previous editors that has not been adopted is only recorded when it is deemed to have special merit.

1.1.52–3 What . . . you] THEOBALD; hand/ matter/ F
   59–60 Why . . . yourselves] THEOBALD; *as prose* F
   90–2 Well . . . deliver] CAPELL; Well/ think/ tale/ F
  116–17 In . . . then?] CAPELL; they/ speaks/ F
  231–2 Were . . . make] OXFORD; *as prose* F
  243–5 Lead . . . Martius] POPE; *as prose* F
  257–61 Such . . . Cominius] POPE; *as prose* F
  270–1 Of . . . Martius] THEOBALD; Cominius/ F
1.3.75 No . . . doors] POPE; madam/ F
  107–13 Let . . . mirth] POPE; now/ mirth/ would/ lady/ door/ us/ No/ not/ F
1.4.1 Yonder . . . met] POPE; news/ F
   25 With . . . Titus] POPE; shields/ F
1.6.19–20 Than . . . fight] CAPELL; *as one line* (and fight *turned down*) F
1.7.58–60 By . . . Antiates] F; vows/ directly/ POPE; made/ me/ CLARENDON (*conj.*), OXFORD
1.8.5–7 We . . . upon's] F; sir/ POPE; Hence/ WALKER (*conj.* Cambridge)
1.9.6–7 If . . . hare] THEOBALD; *as one line* F
1.10.13–14 Pray . . . blood] POPE; more/ F
  15–17 When . . . country] F; done/ induced/ HANMER, OXFORD
  19–22 You . . . traducement] POPE; deserving/ own/ theft/ F
  44–50 Made . . . forth] F; grows/ made/ say/ bled/ note/ THEOBALD, OXFORD
  50–1 You . . . hyperbolical] CAMBRIDGE (*conj.* Knight); *as one line* F; forth/ THEOBALD, OXFORD
  65–6 Martius . . . ever] JOHNSON; *as one line* F; addition/ OXFORD; Bear/ STEEVENS
  79–81 The . . . is't] HANMER; me/ gifts/ general/ F
2.1.108–9 I . . . me] OXFORD; tonight/ F

154–5 These ... tears] POPE; Martius/ noise/ F; him/ HANMER
160–1 With ... Coriolanus] CAPELL; Caius/ F
164–7 No ... prosperity] POPE; *as prose* F
177–80 I ... Welcome] POPE; turn/ general/ all/ welcomes/ laugh/ F
182–5 That ... warriors] POPE; thee/ on/ have/ home/ relish/ F
186–7 We ... right] POPE; nettle/ folly/ F; and/ folly/ OXFORD;
nettle/ STEEVENS
196–8 And ... thee] MALONE; fancy/ wanting/ Rome/ F
206–7 Clamb'ring ... horsed] POPE; him/ up/ F
212–13 Commit ... spoil] POPE; damask/ F
217–18 On ... consul] POPE; *as one line* F
218–19 Then ... sleep] POPE; *as prose* F
225–6 With ... question] POPE; honours/ F
233–4 It ... him] STEEVENS; word/ carry it/ F
235–7 I wish ... will] POPE; *as prose* F
238–9 It ... destruction] ROWE; *as prose* F
256–9 You ... gloves] F; thought/ seen/ blind/ STEEVENS,
OXFORD; thought/ consul/ and/ DYCE
2.2.35–6 Having ... remains] POPE; Volsces/ F
38–9 To ... you] POPE; hath/ F
52–64 We ... speak] POPE; *as prose* F
68–9 Sir ... not] POPE; *as one line* F
82–3 That ... be] F2; virtue/ F1
117–18 Run ... called] F2; 'twere/ F1
121–2 He ... him] ROWE; *as prose* F
125–6 Than ... content] POPE; deeds/ F
127–8 He's ... for] POPE; *as one line* F
128–9 Let ... Coriolanus] F; *as one line* STEEVENS
131–2 The senate ... consul] ROWE 1714; *as prose* F
132–3 I ... services] ROWE 1714; *as one line* F
133–4 It ... people] ROWE 1714; *as prose* F
137–8 For ... doing] F; you/ CAPELL
138–40 Sir ... ceremony] CAPELL; voices/ F
141–2 Pray ... have] CAPELL; custom/ F
143–5 It ... people] POPE; acting/ F
2.3.47–8 What ... bring] POPE; sir/ F
52–4 O ... you] POPE; that/ F
125–7 I ... consul] F; have/ voices/ POPE, OXFORD
134–7 You ... senate] POPE; limitation/ voice/ invested/ F
148–9 With ... people] POPE; weeds/ F
160–1 Why ... 'em] F; *as one line* CAPELL
162 He ... private] POPE; wounds/ F
184–5 Would ... love] F2; voices/ F1

201–4 Have ... tongues] POPE; asker/ mock/ F
213–16 Let ... not] THEOBALD; judgement/ pride/ F; judgement/
election/ you/ POPE
222–8 Lay ... do] CAPELL; tribunes/ between/ on him/
commandment/ that/ F
250–1 We ... election] HANMER; *as one line* F
3.1.27–30 Ha ... matter] F; to/ STEEVENS; that/ further/ BROCKBANK
34–5 Stop ... broil] POPE; *as one line* F
50–1 Not ... yours] JOHNSON; *as one line* F
63–4 Tell ... again] POPE; speech/ F
67–8 Now ... pardons] OXFORD; will/ F; friends/ CAPELL
69–71 For ... again] F; them/ and/ CAPELL
88–90 It ... further] POPE; poison/ F
92–3 Shall ... why] POPE; *as one line* F
119–20 I ... state] POPE; *as one line* F
182–4 On ... aediles] F; would/ CAPELL; he/ OXFORD
192–3 To ... Sicinius] CAPELL; *as one line* F
197–8 Fie ... quench] POPE; *as prose* F
200–1 True ... city] CAPELL; *as one line* F
201–2 By ... magistrates] POPE; *as prose* F
215–16 Hear ... word] JOHNSON; *as prose* F
226 Down ... while] POPE; *as prose* F
227–8 Help ... old] HANMER; *as prose* F
231–2 Stand ... enemies] CAPELL; *as one line* F
235–7 For ... you] This edition (*conj.* Bowers); us/ F
240–1 Be ... tongue] CAPELL; *as one line* F
242–3 On ... them] CAPELL; *as one line* F
243–5 I could myself ... tribunes] This edition; *as prose* F;
myself/ CAPELL, OXFORD
263–5 Here's ... viper] POPE; work/ bed/ Tiber/ fair/ F; work/
Tiber/ fair OXFORD
266–7 That ... himself] POPE; *as one line* F
272–4 He ... hands] JOHNSON; are/ F
274 He ... Peace] STEEVENS; on't/ Peace/ F; sir/ Peace/
CAMBRIDGE, OXFORD
276–7 Sir ... rescue] POPE; holp/ F
277–9 Hear ... faults] POPE; know/ F
284 If ... people] POPE; leave/ F
307–8 Merely ... him] POPE; awry/ F
332–3 Noble ... officer] POPE; *as one line* F
3.2.6–7 Be ... mother] This edition (*conj.* Bowers); them/ nobler/
F; *as one line* OXFORD
25–6 Come ... it] POPE; *as prose* F

35–9 Which . . . spoke] F; do/ then/ CAMBRIDGE; bear/ Well/
CAPELL

54–63 Because . . . blood] MALONE; that/ people/ matter/ words/
~~tongue/ syllables/ truth/ all/ words/ and/~~ F; people/
matter/ words/ but/ allowance/ more/ in/ you/ OXFORD

98–9 I . . . spirit] ROWE; *as prose* F

101–2 Must I go . . . heart] F; Must I/ With CAPELL; sconce/
Must my POPE (*omitting* I with); sconce/ With my WILSON
(*omitting second* Must I)

3.3.5–6 Was . . . accompanied] F; distributed/ CAPELL

9–10 Of . . . poll] POPE; *as one line* F (poll *turned up*)

30–1 With . . . you] CAMBRIDGE; neck/ comes/ F, OXFORD; neck/
STEEVENS

33 Will . . . gods] POPE; volume/ F

37 And . . . wish] This edition; war/ Amen, amen/ F,
OXFORD; amen/ STEEVENS

39 Peace . . . ho] OXFORD; say/ First . . . speak/ F; say/ First
STEEVENS

49–50 Scratches . . . only] CAPELL; move/ F

82–3 even . . . kind] POPE; *as one line* F; OXFORD

84–5 But . . . Rome] POPE; *as one line* F

107–8 F; so/ Let . . . banished/ OXFORD; so/ It . . . banished/
And so it shall be. STEEVENS

132–3 Still . . . nation] F; most/ CAPELL

4.2.5–7 Bid . . . strength] POPE; gone/ F

7–8 Dismiss . . . mother] POPE; *as one line* F

8–10 Here . . . Why] F; *as one line* STEEVENS

11–12 They say . . . way] F; us/ CAPELL

13–14 O . . . love] CAPELL; met/ F

27–8 What then?/ He'd . . . posterity] HANMER; *as one line* F

4.4.7–10 Direct . . . night] CAPELL; *as prose* F

4.5.5–6 A . . . guest] POPE; house/ F; feast/ OXFORD

9–10 I . . . Coriolanus] CAPELL; *as prose* F

33 Follow . . . bits] F (*as prose*)

55–8 If . . . myself] STEEVENS; *as prose* F

105–7 Should . . . twine] F; say/ thee/ CAPELL

164–5 I . . . one] POPE; he/ F

179–80 I . . . man] F; nations/ Textual Companion *conj.*

4.6.11–13 'Tis . . . both] OXFORD; late/ F; kind/ CAPELL; *as prose*
ROWE; 'tis he/ sir/ BOWERS *conj.*

14–16 Your . . . it] CAPELL (Coriolanus, sir,); *as prose* F;
Coriolanus/ friends/ do/ GLOBE

17–18 All's . . . temporized] CAPELL; *as prose* F

26–8	Farewell ... you] F; Coriolanus/ HANMER
34–5	And ... assistance] THEOBALD; *as one line* F
57–8	Tell ... be] POPE; *as one line* F
94	If ... thing] F; If/ CAPELL
103–5	He'll ... work] F; Hercules/ CAPELL
111–14	And perish ... mercy] F; fools/ his/ unless, WALKER *conj.* (*in* Cambridge)
120–1	'Tis ... brand] POPE; *as one line* F
128–31	How ... city] OXFORD; him/ nobles/ hoot/ F; beasts/ clusters/ POPE
139–40	Your ... coming] POPE; hooting/ F
157–61	O ... fear] F; home/ would/ seem/ SCHMIDT
4.7.14–16	Joined ... solely] MALONE (*subs.*); borne/ F; born/ him/ POPE (*omitting* either)
5.1.21–2	Very ... less] JOHNSON; *as one line* F
70–2	So ... him] JOHNSON; mother/ F, OXFORD
5.2.1–2	Stay ... back] F; *as one line* STEEVENS
3–5	You ... Rome] POPE; leave/ Coriolanus/ F; well/ officer/ Coriolanus/ whence/ OXFORD
6–7	You ... thence] OXFORD; *as prose* F; general/ POPE
50–1	Sirrah ... estimation] POPE; here/ F
94–5	'Tis ... again] POPE; power/ F
108–9	The ... wind-shaken] F4; rock/ F1; general/ CAPELL (He is)
5.3.4–7	Only ... friends] CAPELL; respected/ Rome/ F
36–7	As ... kin] ROWE 1714; *as one line* F
40–2	Like ... flesh] POPE; part/ F
56–7	What's ... son] POPE (What is); me/ F
62–3	Thou ... lady] ROWE; thee/ F
85–7	Wherein ... reasons] POPE; t'allay/ F, OXFORD
126–9	Ay ... fight] POPE (*subs.*); boy/ time/ away/ F
182–3	I ... little] POPE; *as one line* F
203–4	Ay ... bear] HANMER; together/ F
5.4.1	See ... corner-stone] POPE; *as one verse line* (stone *turned up*) F
43–4	Friend ... most certain] POPE (is it not); true/ F
58–9	First ... thankfulness] POPE; tidings/ F
59–60	Sir ... thanks] CAPELL; *as one line* F, OXFORD
61–2	We'll ... joy] CAPELL (We will); *as one line* F, OXFORD
5.6.9–11	Even ... slain] POPE; *as prose* F
11–13	Most ... deliver you] POPE; intent/ F
58–9	Say ... lords] POPE; *as one line* F
121–3	Tear ... father] CAPELL; presently/ cousin/ F, OXFORD; presently/ Marcus/ CAPELL *conj.*

128–30 O ... sword] POPE; more/ F; Aufidiuses/ OXFORD

130–1 Insolent ... him] STEEVENS; villain/ him/ F; *as one line*
OXFORD

~~131–2 Hold ... speak] STEEVENS; hold!/ speak/ F; *as one line*~~
OXFORD

132–3 O ... weep] STEEVENS; Tullus/ whereat/ F; whereat/ OXFORD

134–5 Tread ... swords] F; masters/ OXFORD

136 My ... rage] POPE; lords/ F, OXFORD

154 Yet ... Assist] F; memory/ CAPELL

SOURCES AND ANALOGUES

I PLUTARCH'S 'LIVES OF THE NOBLE GRECIANS AND ROMANS' TRANSLATED BY SIR THOMAS NORTH (1595)

(a) A Summary of the Narrative

Because the patricians have broken their promise to reward plebeian war service against the Sabines by redressing economic grievances, especially usury, the plebeians peacefully secede from Rome and refuse to fight when neighbouring tribes take advantage of the situation to attack the city. Martius recommends that this secession be suppressed violently, but the Senate prefers to send a conciliatory embassy led by Menenius Agrippa, who delivers the parable of the belly and the members. The plebeians agree to return on condition that five tribunes are allowed them, of whom the leaders of the secession, Brutus and Sicinius, are the first to be appointed.

With the plebeians' renewed co-operation, a counter-attack is made on the invading Volscians, and Corioles is captured by Martius, who receives the honorific 'Coriolanus' as recognition of his prowess.

A corn dearth, caused by the neglect of agriculture during the secession and wars, aggravated by Senate proposals to renew the Volscian war and to compel plebeians to colonize captured territory, causes a second plebeian insurrection. Though the plebeians refuse to fight, Coriolanus leads volunteers on a successful foray against the Antiates, which results in rich spoils, but offends the 'home-tarriers and house-doves'.

After Coriolanus has performed the customary humble petitioning of citizens and shown his wounds, the plebeians agree to vote him Consul, but they reverse this decision because he comes to the election in great pomp, backed by all the Senate and nobility, making them fear he will 'take away altogether the liberty from the people'. Coriolanus' indignation at this is fanned by the young nobility who regard him as their leader, and when the Senate imports corn with the intention of relieving the dearth by distributing it free, he argues that famine should rather be used to bring the plebeians to heel and abolish their tribunate. This results in a third plebeian insurrection, with violence erupting when the tribunes try to have Coriolanus arrested. The Senate, in alarm, confirms the corn dole and agrees to let the tribunes confront Coriolanus with their grievances, but Coriolanus' replies are so provocative that another brawl breaks out, with the tribunes demanding his death and the nobles defending him by arms.

A compromise is reached that Coriolanus shall answer the charge of aiming at kingship in a formal trial. The Volscians attack again at this juncture, but peace is rapidly negotiated, and though the Senate is divided on its legality, Coriolanus' trial goes forward. Besides the agreed-on charge, however, he is also accused of opposing corn distribution, trying to abolish tribunes, and unfair division of the spoils of his expedition against Antium; and by changing traditional voting patterns, the tribunes narrowly secure his banishment.

With his natural choler aggravated by companions in exile, Coriolanus decides to join Aufidius at Antium, and the two of them succeed in tricking the reluctant Volscians into breaking truce and renewing the war with Rome. In Rome itself, meanwhile, relations between patricians and plebeians remain strained and turbulent.

Coriolanus is appointed general of the Volscian expedition, while Aufidius chooses to remain at home. He conducts two campaigns, sparing the estates of Roman nobles to foster discord at Rome. The Roman plebeians then vote to repeal his banishment, but it is the Senate which now opposes this. The offended Coriolanus decides to march on Rome itself.

The Senate capitulates to the plebeian plan and sends an embassy composed of Coriolanus' friends with an offer to restore him to full honour and possession. Insisting on his new loyalties, however, Coriolanus demands that the Romans not only restore all territory taken from the Volscians but also award them the freedom of Rome. He gives the defenders thirty days to decide, during which time he withdraws the invading Volscian army (thus giving Aufidius a pretext for complaint later).

After taking seven cities belonging to Roman allies, Coriolanus returns to besiege Rome. Second and third embassies are sent, asking that the Volscians retire again while the Romans try to decide on Coriolanus' terms, but this is refused. Then Valeria, inspired by heaven, persuades Volumnia to lead a fourth embassy, and Volumnia succeeds in persuading Coriolanus to give up the attack. There is much rejoicing in Rome, and a temple to 'Fortuna Muliebris' is erected in the women's honour in which the image of Fortune miraculously speaks in their praise.

Coriolanus returns to Antium, is accused of treason by the jealous Aufidius, offers to give up his command and to stand trial against his accusers, but, when this is convened, is murdered before he can speak in his own defence. Most of the Volscians condemn this killing, and Coriolanus is given an honourable burial and an elaborate tomb, while in Rome his family is authorized to wear black for the maximum period of mourning.

Soon after, the Volscians fall out with their allies and are defeated by the Romans in a battle where Aufidius is slain. The Volscians then have to accept complete subjection to Rome.

(b) *Selected Passages from North's Plutarch*

(i) *Martius canvasses to be consul, is repudiated, and opposes free corn doles and the tribunate* (cf. Spencer, pp. 317–24). Shortly after this, Martius stood for the Consulship; and the common people favoured his suit, thinking it would be a shame to them to deny and refuse the chiefest nobleman of blood and most worthy person of Rome, and specially him that had done so great service and good to the commonwealth. For the custom of Rome was, at that time, that such as did sue for any office should for certain days before be in the market-place, only with a poor gown on their backs and without any coat underneath, to pray the citizens to remember them at the day of election; which was thus devised, either to move the people the more by requesting them in such mean apparel, or else because they might show them their wounds they had gotten in the wars in the service of the commonwealth, as manifest marks and testimony of their valiantness. . . .

Now Martius, following this custom, showed many wounds and cuts upon his body, which he had received in seventeen years' service at the wars and in many sundry battles, being ever the foremost man that did set out feet to fight. So that there was not a man among the people but was ashamed of himself to refuse so valiant a man. And one of them said to another: 'We must needs choose him Consul; there is no remedy.'

But when the day of election was come, and that Martius came to the market-place with great pomp, accompanied with all the Senate and the whole nobility of the city about him, who sought to make him Consul with the greatest instance and entreaty they could or ever attempted for any man or matter, then the love and goodwill of the common people turned straight to an hate and envy toward him, fearing to put this office of sovereign authority into his hands, being a man somewhat partial toward the nobility and of great credit and authority amongst the patricians, and as one they might doubt would take away altogether the liberty from the people. Whereupon, for these considerations, they refused Martius in the end, and made two other that were suitors Consuls.

The Senate, being marvellously offended with the people, did account the shame of this refusal rather to redound to themselves than to Martius. But Martius took it in far worse part than the Senate and was out of all patience[,] . . . being a stout man of nature, that never yielded in any respect, as one thinking that to overcome always and to have the upper hand in all matters was a token of magnanimity and of no base and faint courage, which spitteth out anger from the most weak and passioned part of the heart, much like the matter of an impostume, [so he] went home to his house full freighted with spite and malice against the people, being accompanied with all the lustiest young gentlemen, whose minds were nobly bent as those that came of noble race, and commonly used for to follow and honour him. But then specially they flocked about him and kept him company—to his much harm. For they did but kindle and inflame his choler more and more, being sorry with him for the injury the people offered him, because he was their captain and leader to the wars, that taught them all martial discipline and stirred up in them a noble emulation of honour and valiantness, and yet without envy, praising them that deserved best.

In the mean season there came great plenty of corn to Rome, that had been bought part in Italy and part was sent out of Sicilia, as given by Gelon, the tyrant of Syracusa; so that many stood in great hope that, the dearth of victuals being helped, the civil dissension would also cease. The Senate sat in council upon it immediately. The common people stood also about the palace where the council was kept, gaping what resolution would fall out, persuading themselves that the corn they had bought should be sold good cheap and that which was given should be divided by the poll without paying any penny; and the rather, because certain of the Senators amongst them did so wish and persuade the same.

But Martius, standing upon his feet, did somewhat sharply take up those who went about to gratify the people therein, and called them people-pleasers and traitors to the nobility. Moreover, he said, they nourished against themselves the naughty seed and cockle of insolency and sedition, which had been sowed and scattered abroad amongst the people, whom they should have cut off, if they had been wise, and have prevented their greatness; and not, to their own destruction, to have suffered the people to stablish a magistrate for themselves, of so great power and authority as that man had to whom they had granted it; who was also to be feared because he obtained what he would, and did nothing but what he listed, neither passed for any obedience to the Consuls, but lived in all liberty, acknowledging no superior to command him, saving the only heads and authors of their faction, whom he called magistrates.

'Therefore,' said he, 'they that gave counsel and persuaded that the corn should be given out to the common people *gratis*, as they used to do in the cities of Greece, where the people had more absolute power, did but only nourish their disobedience, which would break out in the end, to the utter ruin and overthrow of the whole state. For they will not think it is done in recompense of their service past, sithence they know well enough they have so oft refused to go to the wars when they were commanded; neither for their mutinies when they went with us, whereby they have rebelled and forsaken their country; neither for their accusations which their flatterers have preferred unto them, and they have received, and made good against the Senate; but they will rather judge we give and grant them this as abasing ourselves, and standing in fear of them, and glad to flatter them every way. By this means their disobedience will still grow worse and worse; and they will never leave to practise new sedition and uproars. Therefore it were a great folly for us, methinks, to do it. Yea, shall I say more? we should, if we were wise, take from them their Tribuneship, which most manifestly is the embasing of the Consulship and the cause of the division of the city; the state whereof, as it standeth, is not now as it was wont to be; but becometh dismembered in two factions, which maintains always civil dissension and discord between us, and will never suffer us again to be united into one body.'

Martius, dilating the matter with many such like reasons, won all the young men and almost all the rich men to his opinion; insomuch they rang it out that he was the only man, and alone in the city who stood out against the people and never flattered them. There were only a few old men that spake against him, fearing lest some mischief might fall out upon it; as indeed there followed no great good afterward.

(ii) *Martius joins Aufidius* (cf. Spencer, pp. 336–8). He disguised himself in such array and attire as he thought no man could ever have known him for the person he was, seeing him in that apparel he had upon his back; and, as Homer said of Ulysses,

> *So did he enter into the enemy's town.*

It was even twilight when he entered the city of Antium; and many people met him in the streets, but no man knew him. So he went directly to Tullus Aufidius' house; and when he came thither, he got him up straight to the chimney hearth, and sat him down, and spake not a word to any man, his face all muffled over. They of the house, spying him, wondered what he should be; and yet they durst not bid him rise. For ill-favouredly muffled and disguised as he was, yet there appeared a certain majesty in his countenance and in his silence. Whereupon they went to Tullus, who was at supper, to tell him of the strange disguising of this man. Tullus rose presently from the board, and, coming towards him, asked him what he was and wherefore he came. Then Martius unmuffled himself, and after he had paused a while, making no answer, he said unto him:

'If thou knowest me not yet, Tullus, and, seeing me, dost not perhaps believe me to be the man I am indeed, I must of necessity betray my self to be that I am. I am Caius Martius, who hath done to thyself particularly, and to all the Volsces generally, great hurt and mischief; which I cannot deny, for my surname of Coriolanus that I bear. For I never had other benefit nor recompense of all the true and painful service I have done, and the extreme dangers I have been in, but this only surname—a good memory and witness of the malice and displeasure thou shouldst bear me. Indeed the name only remaineth with me. For, the rest the envy and cruelty of the people of Rome have taken from me, by the sufferance of the dastardly nobility and magistrates, who have forsaken me and let me be banished by the people. This extremity hath now driven me to come as a poor suitor to take thy chimney hearth, not of any hope I have to save my life thereby—for, if I had feared death, I would not have come hither to have put my life in hazard—but pricked forward with spite and desire I have to be revenged on them that thus have banished me, whom now I begin to be avenged on, putting my person between thy enemies. Wherefore, if thou hast any heart to be wreaked of the injuries thy enemies have done thee, speed thee now, and let my misery serve thy turn; and so use it as my service may be a benefit to the Volsces; promising thee, that I will fight with better good will for all you than ever I did when I was against you, knowing that they fight more valiantly, who know the force of their enemy, than such as have never proved it. And if it be so that thou dare not, and that thou art weary to prove fortunate any more, then am I also weary to live any longer. And it were no wisdom in thee to save the life of him who hath been heretofore thy mortal enemy and whose service now can nothing help nor pleasure thee.'

Tullus, hearing what he said, was a marvellous glad man, and, taking him by the hand, he said unto him:

'Stand up, O Martius, and be of good cheer; for in proffering thyself unto us thou dost us great honour; and by this means thou mayest hope also of greater things at all the Volsces' hands.'

So he feasted him for that time, and entertained him in the honourablest manner he could, talking with him in no other matters at that present. But, within few days after, they fell to consultation together in what sort they should begin their wars.

(iii) *Volumnia's plea* (cf. Spencer, pp. 354–8). 'If we held our peace, my son, and determined not to speak, the state of our poor bodies and present sight of our raiment would easily betray to thee what life we have led at home, since thy exile and abode abroad. But think now with thyself how much more unfortunately than all the women living we are come hither, considering that the sight which should be most pleasant to all other to behold, spiteful fortune hath made most fearful to us; making myself to see my son, and my daughter here her husband, besieging the walls of his native country; so as that which is the only comfort to all other in their adversity and misery, to pray unto the gods and to call to them for aid, is the only thing which plungeth us into most deep perplexity. For we cannot, alas, together pray both for victory for our country and for safety of thy life also. But a world of grievous curses, yea, more than any mortal enemy can heap upon us, are forcibly wrapped up in our prayers. For the bitter sop of most hard choice is offered thy wife and children, to forgo the one of the two: either to lose the person of thyself or the nurse of their native country. For myself, my son, I am determined not to tarry till fortune in my lifetime do make an end of this war. For if I cannot persuade thee, rather to do good unto both parties than to overthrow and destroy the one, preferring love and nature before the malice and calamity of wars—thou shalt see, my son, and trust unto it, thou shalt no sooner march forward to assault thy country but thy foot shall tread upon thy mother's womb, that brought thee first into this world. And I may not defer to see the day either that my son be led prisoner in triumph by his natural countrymen, or that he himself do triumph of them and of his natural country. For if it were so, that my request tended to save thy country in destroying the Volsces, I must confess, thou wouldst hardly and doubtfully resolve on that. For, as to destroy thy natural country, it is altogether unmeet and unlawful; so were it not just, and less honourable to betray those that put their trust in thee. But my only demand consisteth, to make a gaol-delivery of all evils, which delivereth equal benefit and safety both to the one and the other; but most honourable for the Volsces. For it shall appear that, having victory in their hands, they have of special favour granted us singular graces, peace, and amity, albeit themselves have no less part of both than we; of which good, if so it came to pass, thyself is the only author and so hast thou the only honour. But if it fail and fall out contrary, thyself alone deservedly shall carry the shameful reproach and burthen of either party. So, though the end of war be uncertain, yet this notwithstanding is most certain, that, if it be thy chance to conquer, this benefit shalt thou reap of thy goodly conquest: to be chronicled the plague and destroyer of thy country.

And if fortune also overthrow thee, then the world will say that, through desire to revenge thy private injuries, thou hast for ever undone thy good friends, who did most lovingly and courteously receive thee.'

Martius gave good ear unto his mother's words, without interrupting her speech at all; and, after she had said what she would, he held his peace a pretty while and answered not a word. Hereupon she began again to speak unto him, and said:

'My son, why dost thou not answer me? Dost thou think it good altogether to give place unto thy choler and desire of revenge? and thinkest thou it not honesty for thee to grant thy mother's request in so weighty a case? Dost thou take it honourable for a nobleman to remember the wrongs and injuries done him, and dost not in like case think it an honest nobleman's part to be thankful for the goodness that parents do show to their children, acknowledging the duty and reverence they ought to bear unto them? No man living is more bound to show himself thankful in all parts and respects than thyself, who so unnaturally showeth all ingratitude. Moreover, my son, thou hast sorely taken of thy country, exacting grievous payments upon them, in revenge of the injuries offered thee. Besides, thou hast not hitherto showed thy poor mother any courtesy. And therefore it is not only honest, but due unto me, that without compulsion I should obtain my so just and reasonable request of thee. But, since by reason I cannot persuade thee to it, to what purpose do I defer my last hope?'

And with these words herself, his wife, and children fell down upon their knees before him. Martius, seeing that, could refrain no longer, but went straight and lifted her up, crying out:

'O, mother, what have you done to me?'

And holding her hard by the right hand,

'Oh mother,' said he, 'you have won a happy victory for your country, but mortal and unhappy for your son. For I see myself vanquished by you alone.'

These words being spoken openly, he spake a little apart with his mother and wife, and then let them return again to Rome; for so they did request him; and so, remaining in camp that night, the next morning he dislodged and marched homewards into the Volsces' country again; who were not all of one mind, nor all alike contented. For some misliked him and that he had done. Other, being well pleased that peace should be made, said that neither the one nor the other deserved blame nor reproach. Other, though they misliked that was done, did not think him an ill man for that he did, but said he was not to be blamed, though he yielded to such a forcible extremity. Howbeit no man contraried his departure, but all obeyed his commandment, more for respect of his worthiness and valiancy than for fear of his authority.

2. THE MIDLAND UPRISING, 1607–8

(a) *The Diggers of Warwickshire to all Other Diggers*, 1607? (MS. Harl. 787, art. 11, repr. in J. O. Halliwell-Phillipps, ed., *The Marriage of Wit and Wisdom*, Shakespeare Society Publications, vol. 22, 1846, 140–1). Italics are this editor's. For other analogues, see Bullough.

Loving friends and subjects, all under one renowned Prince, for whom we pray long to continue in his most royal estate, to the subverting of all those subjects, of what degree soever that have or would deprive his most true-hearted Commonalty both from life and living. We, as members of the whole, do feel the smart of these encroaching Tyrants, which would grind our flesh upon the whetstone of poverty, and make our loyal hearts to faint with breathing, so that they may dwell by themselves in the midst of their herds of fat wethers [sheep; literally, castrated rams]. *It is not unknown unto yourselves the reason why these merciless men do resist with force against our good intents.* It is not for the good of our most gracious sovereign, whom we pray God that long he may reign amongst us, neither for the benefit of the Commonalty, but only for their own private gain, for *there is none of them but do taste the sweetness of our wants.* They have depopulated and overthrown whole towns, and made thereof sheep pastures, nothing profitable for our Commonwealth, for the common fields being laid open, would yield us much commodity, besides the increase of Corn, on which stands our life. But if it should please God to withdraw his blessing in not prospering the fruits of the Earth but one year (which God forbid) there would a worse, and more fearful dearth happen than did in King Edward the Second's time, when people were forced to eat cats' and dogs' flesh, and women to eat their own children. Much more we could give you to understand, but we are persuaded that you yourselves feel a part of our grievances, and therefore need not open the matter any plainer. But if you happen to show your force and might against us, we for our parts neither respect life nor living; for *better it were in such case we manfully die, than hereafter to be pined [starved] to death* for want of that which these devouring encroachers do serve their fat hogs and sheep withall. For God hath bestowed upon us most bountiful and innumerable blessings, and the chiefest is our most gracious and religious king, who doth and will glory in the flourishing estate of his Commonalty. And so we leave you, commending you to the sure hold and safeguard of the mighty Jehovah, both now and evermore.

From Hampton-field in haste:
we rest as poor delvers and daylabourers,
for the good of the Commonwealth till death.
A.B.C.D. etc.

(*b*) Robert Wilkinson, A SERMON PREACHED at Northampton the *21 of June last past, before the Lord Lieutenant of the* County, *and the rest of the Commissioners there assembled upon occasion of the late Rebellion and Riots in those parts committed.* Prov. 22:2 *The rich and the poor meet together, the Lord is the maker of them all.* Printed at London for John Flasket. 1607 (STC 25662).

Summary. The sermon was delivered soon after a massacre of peasants at Newton, Northamptonshire, on 8 June 1607, and the subsequent hanging and quartering of their leaders. It is dedicated to the nobleman for whom Wilkinson had 'lately' been chaplain, Thomas, Earl of Exeter, Baron of Burleigh, and Lord Lieutenant for the County of Northamptonshire. Taking as his text Matthew 4:4, 'But he answering said: It is written Man shall not live by bread only, but by every word that proceedeth out of the mouth of God', Wilkinson attempts to give a balanced account by pointing out errors on *both* sides. The Bible says men need bread to live, so it is wrong of the gentry to oppress the starving peasantry with enclosures. On the other hand, 'man does not live by bread alone', so it shows want of faith in God's providence for the peasants actively to rebel; and once order has been breached, there is no knowing where such levelling will end. Wilkinson frequently uses body politic imagery to make points on both sides of the argument.

(i) It is time that we are fallen into tempestuous and troublesome times, wherein the excessive covetousness of some hath caused extreme want to other, and that want not well digested hath rioted to the hazard of all; yea and by these stormes we are among the rocks, even two the most dangerous rocks of estate, Oppression of the mighty, and Rebellion of the many, . . . in this we are bold to intreat you, that as you have been means for the due execution of justice upon the rebellious, so likewise (as opportunity shall serve) to promote the cause and complaints of the expelled, half-pined, and distressed poor, that they rebel no more. (Dedication, A3–3 v, A4.)

(ii) God created the earth for men, and not for sheep; therefore if ye will maintain large pastures and stock them with sheep, then remember what God saith by the mouth of *Ezekiel, The Sheep of my pasture are men.* Eze. 34.31. Yea and *we are his people and the sheep of his pasture. Psal.* 100. and the image of God in one man is more worth than all the sheep in the world: and it is time, yea high time to speak of this, the text of it already being written in blood; and no marvel if they which feel it, run mad and wild upon it, since we which but see it are so much amazed at it; . . . whatsoever is done to the wasting of mankind for the benefit of a few in the kind, is against the providence of God . . . (Sermon, C3ᵛ–C4).

(iii) I know ye think it horrible that (as in this late Rebellion) Mechanical men are come to beard Magistrates; and it is horrible indeed, . . . But as it is an ill foot that kicketh at the head and an ill hand that beateth it, so is it an ill head that wisheth the hand cut off, or deviseth a way how to have fewer fingers on the hand. (C4ᵛ).

(iv) The ordinary means of God's providence is, that man must live by bread; a corporal substance to be maintained by corporal sustenance, . . . for the belly saith that bread must be had, and the soul subscribeth that bread must be had too, and though reason may persuade and authority command, and Preachers may exhort with obedience and patience to sustain the want of bread, yet for all that, *Venter non habet aures* [the belly has no ears], in case of extreme hunger men will not be persuaded, but they will have bread. (D2–D2ᵛ–D3).

(v) Therefore consider and see I beseech you, whence arise conspiracies, riots, and damnable rebellions; not [only] from want of bread, but through want of faith, yea want of bread doth come by want of faith; . . . and when a Proclamation came, as good made under a hedge; and that which is horrible to speak: A King of three great kingdoms must capitulate with a Tinker, whether by Proclamation or by Privy Seal he shall manifest his will and pleasure; and yet all this is called Reforming; but . . . these men reformed wickedness but with far greater wickedness . . . Pasture-men indeed destroy a few towns, but mutineers by civil commotion depopulate whole kingdoms, and that partly by making way for foreign enemies, who usually increase their dominions by such advantage . . . (E3–E3ᵛ, F1–F1ᵛ).

INDEX

THIS is a selective guide to points in the Introduction and Commentary of more than routine note. Biblical illustrations are grouped together; so are proverbial parallels. Asterisks identify words which supplement the *Oxford English Dictionary*.

Index

American Literature

British and Irish Literature

Children's Literature

Classics and Ancient Literature

Colonial Literature

Eastern Literature

European Literature

History

Medieval Literature

Oxford English Drama

Poetry

Philosophy

Politics

Religion

The Oxford Shakespeare

A complete list of Oxford Paperbacks, including Oxford World's Classics, OPUS, Past Masters, Oxford Authors, Oxford Shakespeare, Oxford Drama, and Oxford Paperback Reference, is available in the UK from the Academic Division Publicity Department, Oxford University Press, Great Clarendon Street, Oxford OX2 6DP.

In the USA, complete lists are available from the Paperbacks Marketing Manager, Oxford University Press, 198 Madison Avenue, New York, NY 10016.

Oxford Paperbacks are available from all good bookshops. In case of difficulty, customers in the UK can order direct from Oxford University Press Bookshop, Freepost, 116 High Street, Oxford OX1 4BR, enclosing full payment. Please add 10 per cent of published price for postage and packing.